Ecclesiology at the Beginning of the Third Millennium

Theology at the Beginning of the Third Millennium
Series Preface

Theology at the Beginning of the Third Millennium is a new series of theological monographs which seek to examine the *status quaestionis* of various sub-disciplines within the field of theology in this second decade of the third millennium and some half a century after the conclusion of the Second Vatican Council. While the impetus for the series has come from scholars at the University of Notre Dame (Australia), the Catholic Institute of Sydney, and Campion College (Sydney), contributors to the volumes come from a diverse array of theological academies. A feature of the series is the fact that although the majority of the contributors are situated within the Catholic intellectual tradition, scholars from other traditions are also welcome.

The various sub-disciplines which form the subject of each volume are examined from the perspective of scripture scholarship, fundamental, systematic and dogmatic theology, spirituality, historical theology, ecumenical and pastoral theology and the theology of culture. This is consistent with the Balthasarian metaphor that "Truth is Symphonic" and thus created by an harmonious integration of different disciplines or "sections" of the theological orchestra. Consistent with the charism of St. James the contributors share a high degree of respect for the deposit of the faith, a Johannine interest in integrating spirituality and mystical theology with dogmatic and fundamental theology, a Pauline sensitivity to the influence of the Holy Spirit, a Petrine interest in official magisterial teaching and, above all, a Marian disposition of receptivity to the Divine *Logos*.

Ecclesiology at the Beginning of the Third Millennium

EDITED BY
Kevin Wagner,
M. Isabell Naumann,
AND
Peter John McGregor

☙PICKWICK *Publications* · Eugene, Oregon

ECCLESIOLOGY AT THE BEGINNING OF THE THIRD MILLENNIUM

Theology at the Beginning of the Third Millennium 2

Copyright © 2020 Wipf and Stock Publishers. All rights reserved. Except for brief quotations in critical publications or reviews, no part of this book may be reproduced in any manner without prior written permission from the publisher. Write: Permissions, Wipf and Stock Publishers, 199 W. 8th Ave., Suite 3, Eugene, OR 97401.

Pickwick Publications
An Imprint of Wipf and Stock Publishers
199 W. 8th Ave., Suite 3
Eugene, OR 97401

www.wipfandstock.com

PAPERBACK ISBN: 978-1-5326-6533-2
HARDCOVER ISBN: 978-1-5326-6534-9
EBOOK ISBN: 978-1-5326-6535-6

Cataloguing-in-Publication data:

Names: Wagner, Kevin, editor. | Naumann, M. Isabell, editor. | McGregor, Peter John, editor.

Title: Ecclesiology at the beginning of the third millennium / edited by Kevin Wagner, M. Isabell Naumann, and Peter John McGregor.

Description: Eugene, OR: Pickwick Publications, 2020 | Series: Theology at the Beginning of the Third Millennium 2 | Includes bibliographical references and index.

Identifiers: ISBN 978-1-5326-6533-2 (paperback) | ISBN 978-1-5326-6534-9 (hardcover) | ISBN 978-1-5326-6535-6 (ebook)

Subjects: LCSH: Church | Catholic Church—Doctrines | People of God | Vatican Council (2nd : 1962–1965 : Basilica di San Pietro in Vaticano) | Mission of the church

Classification: BX1746.F84 W34 2020 (print) | BX1746.F84 (ebook)

Manufactured in the U.S.A. DECEMBER 5, 2019

Contents

Contributors | vii

Preface—*Nigel Zimmermann* | xiii

1. Ecclesiology at the Beginning of the Third Millennium | 1
   —*Tracey Rowland*

2. Leadership in the Body of Christ | 29
   —*Anthony Randazzo*

3. "Pastoral magisterium"?: The teaching office of the Church in the pontificate of Pope Francis | 40
   —*Mariusz Biliniewicz*

4. Catholic Inc.: On the Mechanized, Managerial Body of Christ | 64
   —*Thomas V Gourlay*

5. The Baptismal Priesthood: Confusion and Potential | 83
   —*James Baxter, OP*

6. Communio After Social Media | 104
   —*Matthew John Paul Tan*

7. The Sacrament of Confirmation and Its role in the Ecclesiology of Communion | 113
   —*Moira Debono, RSM*

8. The Indivisible Totus Christus and the Universal Church | 127
   —*Simon R Wayte, MGL*

9. Ecclesiology and Ecumenism at the Beginning of the
   Third Millennium | 152
   —*Gerard Kelly*

10. Reading *Deus Caritas Est* Missiologically | 169
    —*Peter John McGregor*

11. The Festal Letter in the Life of the Church: A Study of the Festal
    Letters of St Cyril of Alexandria | 191
    —*Kevin Wagner*

12. In the Heart of the Church: The Church, the Catholic University,
    and the State in Australia | 213
    —*Michael Quinlan*

13. Type and Antitype: Aspects of the Mary-Church Relationship
    in Pre-conciliar works | 239
    —*M. Isabell Naumann, ISSM*

Contributors

James Baxter OP is a Dominican friar and the Chaplain to the University of Notre Dame Australia in Sydney. He was ordained to the priesthood in 2016. He completed his formal theological studies in Melbourne through the University of Divinity. His main interests are the grace-nature debate and the theology of the atonement.

Mariusz Biliniewicz completed his Master's degree at the Pontifical Faculty of Theology in Wrocław, Poland, with a thesis written in the area of biblical theology on the primacy of St Peter in the Gospel of Matthew. He completed his PhD at Milltown Institute of Philosophy and Theology (National University of Ireland) in Dublin, Ireland, with a thesis written in the area of systematic theology on the theological background of the liturgical vision of Pope Benedict XVI. He taught briefly at Mater Dei Institute in Dublin, Ireland, and has spoken internationally on a number of theological topics. He is currently working at the School of Philosophy and Theology in Sydney at the University of Notre Dame, Australia, as Senior Lecturer in Theology and Associate Dean of Research and Academic Development.

Moira Debono is a Religious Sister of Mercy of Alma, Michigan, USA and lecturer at the University of Notre Dame-Australia. She studied in Rome at the Athenaeum Sant'Anselmo (STB, STL with a specialty in sacraments) and at the Pope John Paul II Institute for Studies on Marriage and Family at the Lateran University-Rome (STD). Before coming to Australia in 2008, Sister Moira taught at St. John Vianney Seminary in Denver, Colorado and at the University of Portland, Oregon. While in Denver she was also Director of the Office of Liturgy for the Archdiocese. She has given workshops for clergy and conferences and retreats to parish groups and to university students and in various parts of the United States and Canada. Since coming to Australia, she has continued this locally in the Sydney archdiocese, as well as in Brisbane, Albury and Townsville and she is a member of the Archdiocese of Sydney Liturgy Commission.

Thomas V. Gourlay is the manager of Campus Ministry at the University of Notre Dame Australia's Fremantle Campus, and is the president and co-founder of the Christopher Dawson Society for Philosophy and Culture Inc. Currently a Doctoral candidate in the School of Philosophy and Theology at UNDA, Tom also holds bachelors and master's degrees in Education from UNDA, and in 2017 he graduated from The John Paul II Institute for Marriage and Family Studies (Melbourne) with a Master of Theological Studies. Prior to his work in Campus Ministry, Tom worked as a classroom teacher and faculty head of Religious Education in a number of Catholic schools in Western Australia. He has been published in *New Blackfriars*, *The Heythrop Journal*, and *Homiletic and Pastoral Review*, and contributed columns to *Catholic World Report, Crisis Magazine*, and *The Imaginative Conservative*. Tom and his wife Elizabeth have two children and live in Perth, Western Australia.

Gerard Kelly is a priest of the Archdiocese of Sydney and was ordained in 1980. He has taught at the Catholic Institute of Sydney since 1986 and was made President of the Institute in 2004, a position he held until the end of 2017. He is an accomplished research supervisor and is the current editor of the *Australasian Catholic Record*. His research interests in ecumenism have seen him involved in theological dialogue. He is currently the Catholic co-chair of the Australian Lutheran-Roman Catholic Dialogue and chair of the Faith and Unity Commission of the National Council of Churches in Australia.

Peter John McGregor is a lecturer in Theology and Spirituality at the Catholic Institute of Sydney. His research has been published in the *Australasian Catholic Record*, the *Australian eJournal of Theology*, the *Journal of Gospel and Acts Research*, the *Irish Theological Quarterly*, *New Blackfriars*, *Pro Ecclesia*, and *Radical Orthodoxy: Theology, Philosophy, Politics*. He is the author of *Heart to Heart: The Spiritual Christology of Joseph Ratzinger*. His research interests include the theology of Joseph Ratzinger, the relationship between theology and spirituality, and missiology, especially the three-fold office of priest, prophet and king. He is also a member of the Emmanuel Community (*Communauté de l'Emmanuel*), a community of lay people, priests and consecrated people within the Catholic Church who seek to live out the graces of adoration, compassion, and evangelization.

M. Isabell Naumann, ISSM, is the President of the Catholic Institute of Sydney (Ecclesiastical Faculty of Theology) and a Professor of Systematic Theology. She is a Member of the Secular Institute of the Schoenstatt Sisters of Mary (ISSM) and holds the position of province vicar for Australia and the Philippines. For over ten years, she served as the Academic Dean of Studies at the Seminary of the Good Shepherd, Sydney and taught Systematic Theology at the Catholic Institute of Sydney. She is also an Adjunct Professor in Systematic Theology at the University of Notre Dame, Sydney. She serves on various national and international academic boards and councils including the Pontifical Council for Culture, Rome.

Michael Quinlan is Dean of the School of Law, Sydney at The University of Notre Dame Australia. Prior to taking up this role in 2013, he had a distinguished career of over twenty-three years in commercial law. He is the Junior Vice President of the St Thomas More Society, a director of Freedom for Faith and a member of the Wilberforce Foundation. He has a deep interest in the relationship between law and morality and law and religion.

Anthony Randazzo was ordained to the episcopacy in August 2016 and is currently Bishop of Broken Bay. He was ordained priest on November 29, 1991, in Brisbane, Australia. In his early years as a priest he served in parishes and the Regional Tribunal, and was the Director of Vocations for the Archdiocese of Brisbane. In 2004 he was called to Rome where he worked in the Congregation for the Doctrine of the Faith for five years. Upon his return to Australia he served as Rector of the Holy Spirit Seminary of Queensland.

Tracey Rowland holds the St John Paul II Chair of Theology at the University of Notre Dame (Australia). Her civil doctorate (PhD) is from the Divinity School of the University of Cambridge and her pontifical doctorate (STD) is from the Lateran University in Rome. She is a member of the International Theological Commission and her most recent works are: *Catholic Theology* (2017), *The Culture of the Incarnation: Essays in Catholic Theology* (2017) and *Portraits of Spiritual Nobility* (2019).

Matthew Tan is an adjunct Senior Lecturer in Theology at the University of Notre Dame Australia. He completed his PhD in Theology at the Australian Catholic University and his License in Sacred Theology at the Pontifical University of St Thomas Aquinas in Rome. He is the author of two books, his most recent being *Redeeming Flesh: The Way of the Cross with Zombie Jesus*, and is the editor of the theological blog *The Divine Wedgie*, which is part of the Patheos Catholic blogging channel.

Kevin Wagner is the principal convener of the *Theology at the Beginning of the Third Millennium* conference series and co-editor of the eponymous book series. He is a lecturer in Theology at the University of Notre Dame, Australia—Sydney, specializing in Early Church History and Scripture. Kevin was previously the Director of the Emmanuel School of Mission in Rome, a role he shared with his wife. He has a background in Secondary school teaching and has taught Mathematics, Religious Education, and Information Technology at both government and Catholic schools in Sydney, Melbourne and London.

Simon R. Wayte MGL is a priest of the Missionaries of God's Love. He completed a doctorate in Theology at Catholic Theological College of the University of Divinity where he now lectures in Ecclesiology and Mariology. His DTheol, supervised by Rev Prof Gerald O'Collins, AC, SJ, focussed on developing a Christology organized around the concept of presence. Using a holographic analogy, he highlighted the importance of pneumatology in Christology and emphasized the indivisible nature of the continuing presence of the risen Christ in the Church and her liturgy. He has a background in science having previously completed a PhD in astrophysics at Mount Stromlo Observatory, ANU. His current research interests include the areas of Christology, Ecclesiology, Mariology and the dialogue between faith and science.

Nigel Zimmermann is Principal Advisor to the Archbishop of Melbourne. Nigel is an Adjunct Lecturer in Theology with the Institute for Ethics and Society at the University of Notre Dame Australia (UNDA). He received his PhD at the University of Edinburgh, holds a degree in Journalism (QUT) and Master's Degrees in theology (Brisbane College of Theology) and bioethics and medical law (St Mary's University Twickenham). He was a Wingate Scholar in the UK and worked in the Archdiocese of Sydney and the Diocese of Broken Bay, before joining Australian Catholic University (ACU) in 2016 as Associate Director, Church Policy. He writes on contemporary topics facing theology and the Church, and serves on the Executive Committee for the Plenary Council 2020 and the Australian Catholic Life Council. Nigel authored *Levinas and Theology* (2013) and *Facing the Other: John Paul II, Levinas, and the Body* (2015). He edited *The Great Grace:*

Receiving Vatican II Today (2015) and Archbishop Peter A. Comensoli's *In God's Image: Recognising the Profoundly Impaired as Persons* (2018).

Preface

—Nigel Zimmermann

In his great missional exhortation to the Church in the third millennium *Novo Millennio Ineunte*, St John Paul II asked Catholics on every continent to see themselves as missionaries, and to embark on their work with a new sense of urgency:

> Now we must look ahead, we must "put out into the deep," trusting in Christ's words: *Duc in altum!* What we have done this year cannot justify a sense of complacency, and still less should it lead us to relax our commitment. On the contrary, the experiences we have had should *inspire in us new energy*, and impel us to invest in concrete initiatives the enthusiasm which we have felt.[1]

If previous centuries demanded of the Church a definition of its structures and processes, the opening century of the third millennium demanded something else, something *more* even. John Paul II spoke of new energies and of a putting "out into the deep," implying that the evangelical work of the Church will require a depth of faith that is uncompromisingly apostolic, reaching to the Church's biblical and spiritual roots. Such faith is not a retreat into fideism but more a faithful launching out, entering into dialogue with the traditions and currents of thought it encounters in the world. Such a dialogue is motivated by a love for truth, honouring it and learning from it wherever it is discovered, and allowing the truth of the gospel to critically evaluate the conditions of men and women in our own time so that we might enliven faith in their lives and set paths that would enhance their dignity. The Church then is a way of entering into debate and public consciousness not encased by the strictures of past limitations; she is a free communion of people equal in dignity, each tasked differently to serve the same gospel, the

---

1. John Paul II, *Novo Millennio Ineunte*, 15.

same Good News, the same Lord and Master. The ecclesiology evident in this aspirational language relies on the work of the Holy Spirit who moved the apostles to act, and at Pentecost inspired Peter to rush to the roof and proclaim the gospel boldly to all who passed by.

In our time John Paul II has taken his impetus from the Second Vatican Council, an event to which he was a key contributor and ultimately the papal interpreter following its closure. Shaped by influences including Eastern European Catholic devotion, German and French streams of phenomenology, classical Thomism, and the raw experiences of totalitarian oppression (by the Soviets and the Nazis), manual labour in a stone quarry, and the drama of the theater, Karol Wojtyla was a remarkable synthesis of creativity and tradition. He drew from all these threads of experience when he led the Church in its mission into the twenty-first century, raising to the altar more saints than any pope before him, so that the Church could be witnessed in relatable, simple, and concrete ways.

However, in this exciting new context in which the Second Vatican Council laid out a path of promise and productivity in the mission of the Church, there remain scholars and pastors committed to the encrustations of the past, including the fights of yesterday's men. As a student of theology, I learned quickly that there are two battles you will always lose with such lecturers: disagreements over liturgy, and divergent views on ecclesiology. As an undergraduate student you have to work hard if you are to carve out a robust theology of liturgy or the Church in your own developing mind *and* get your essays passed for completion of a course. The classroom in many theological colleges is not the place of great debate and impassioned disagreement that it should be, and in reality every theology graduate has his or her war stories to share, and a few tales of what they had to do just to survive their theology degree with faith and personal integrity intact. Nuance and subtlety become crucial elements of one's nascent theology of communion, which is actually what theologies of liturgy and the ecclesia are concerned with; how the new life of Christ is shared and manifest, entered into and habituated in concrete ways that are not superficially symbolic but sacramental in the richest sense possible.

This is the context in which the current generation of Catholic theologians, especially of a younger variety, struggle to fulfil their vocation. In places like Australia there is not an abundance of Catholic theological institutions, faculties or colleges, and therefore there are few opportunities for the development of a career in theological teaching and research. That does not mean we do not have quality theologians, simply that they are not always well recognized and their work is sometimes overlooked because it does not sit easily within the calcified categories of left and right that has become the dominant paradigm over at least two generations. That is to say, theologians who wish to pray and think with the Church, while retaining a critical and thoughtful voice attuned to cutting edge intellectual currents of the day are not simply liberal or conservative. They have a capacity to be genuinely counter-intuitive within the life of the Catholic communion, entering into debate with its thinkers and leaders without succumbing to something so banal as the zeitgeist. They live, and their minds are alive, and they wish to breathe life into the Church they love. To paraphrase GK Chesterton, only a dead thing swims with the tide; you must be alive to go against it.

It is therefore appropriate that the opening chapter of this book introduces the theme through an overview of the debates that have been raging since the pontificate of Pius XII (1939–58) to the present day, which all center on the nature and mission of the Church. In the middle of the ecclesiological debates that took hold with Pius XII's *Mystici Corporis Christi* (1943) and onwards is the topic I mention above, that of *communio* or "communion."

Tracey Rowland traces the main paths ecclesiologists have taken back to the University of Tübingen and the Oxford study of John Henry Newman, beginning with an overview of the provenance and pedigree of many of the Catholic ecclesiological ideas and questions which we find today. The provenance of contemporary ecclesiologies at work among Catholics help us to understand the kinds of polarizations that take place in ecclesial settings, including the parish and the diocese, and not just the academy or the seminary lunchroom. There are real tensions that work themselves out in the way we organize the local Church, in the bureaucracies we build, and in the manner in which resources are allocated. The pedigree identified by Rowland gives us the history and intellectual development behind tensions such as the People of God versus the Body of Christ, the Church as communion and as sacrament, the particular churches versus the universal Church, the hierarchy versus the Church of the people, and in the language of "communion" versus "synodality." Rowland argues there is a "division developing within the field of ecclesiology between what might be called a Lubacian appropriation of Tübingen ecclesiology and a Kasperian appropriation of Tübingen ecclesiology." If we are to overcome these tensions intelligently and charitably, we will need the boldness of John Paul II's invitation to "go out into the deep."

The following chapters enter into prominent themes in the terrain painted so clearly by Rowland. Fr Simon Wayte MGL draws on the work of Hans Urs von Balthasar to analyze the relationship between the local and the universal Church, particularly with reference to the public debate between Cardinals Joseph Ratzinger (subsequently Pope Emeritus Benedict XVI) and Walter Kasper. While the Ratzinger/Kasper conflict involves two leading German theologians who are deeply involved in the debates of the post-Conciliar era, Wayte clarifies the way that Balthasar's relationship between the whole and the part becomes a reasonable solution to a contemporary quandary through the influence of St Augustine's *totus Christus*. If we are serious about the Church in its totality, an Augustinian focus on the whole Christ orients us with a Christo-centric ecclesiology less prone to magnify the part over the whole or to marginalize the part by the whole.

Appropriately, Sr Isabell Naumann, ISSM, a noted Marian scholar, follows Wayte's Christo-centric chapter with her consideration of how the Second Vatican Council has given us a vision of the role of Mary that is intrinsically biblical and patristic. Perhaps the dimensions of Marian theology and spirituality highlighted by Sr Naumann are yet to take deep root in the Church, but if they can find nourishment in the seminaries and colleges that form our future leaders, we may find that the "task of Mary" truly becomes the "task of the Church" and therefore *our* task and *my* task. Chapter 8 of *Lumen Gentium* would seem not simply to allow for this way of thinking, but directs us in that manner.

The chapters by Bishop Tony Randazzo and Mariusz Biliniewicz take us to the leadership and pastoral care of the Church. Randazzo teases out the meaning of language which in the Church we take for granted—such as "accompaniment" (popularized by Pope Francis) and "aggiornamento" (a common term denoting the intentions of St John XXIII for the Second Vatican Council). Randazzo shows how the Italian versions of these words carry a meaning which can be fuller, communal and perhaps even incarnate, and develops these in light of the Pauline vision for the Church as the Body of Christ. There is nothing respectable or bourgeois about Randazzo's vision for Christian leadership here. Rather, it prompts us to live radically for the love of Christ and those he died for and to accept the Cross with devotion.

While Randazzo looks at leadership from an episcopal point of view, Biliniewicz considers the question of a "pastoral Magisterium" in relation to Pope Francis, a descriptor often used in connection with his distinctive style. Biliniewicz achieves a subtlety on this question often lacking in commentaries about the papacy because he considers the shape of the pontificate since St John XXIII and the nature of the petrine office as a service to the whole Church. In this way we are able to see that the Magisterium is, and always must be a pastoral ministry, and part of what the service of Peter in the Church achieves is an overcoming of false dichotomies (for example dogmatic versus pastoral). In this light Francis can be appreciated not as a great comforter to any of us, but a provocateur to deeper faith and a comprehensive commitment to the integrity of Catholic practice.

Anybody involved in the Catholic Church in recent decades will have a comment to make on the organizational structures of the local Church and subsequent allocation of resources. Sadly, many Catholics have found the manner in which diocesan offices are run have been inculcated, to varying degrees, with what Thomas Gourlay calls the "ethos of bureaucratic managerialism," an infective malaise that has risen to prominence in (post)modern liberal Western culture. I would want to be particularly clear that Gourlay is not arguing against professionalism, or good stewardship, or models of best practice in the local Church and ecclesial institutions (whether in healthcare, social services, education and so forth). Rather, the ethos that Gourlay rales against is the usurpation of the biblical ecclesiology of the Body of Christ as an inherently mystical communion that derives from, and finds its telos, in the person of Christ Jesus. If our mindset is inherently bureaucratic rather than mystical, or if it is managerial rather than evangelistic, we have embraced a non-biblical and entirely non-Catholic ecclesiology. With reference to the work of David L. Schindler, Gourlay reminds us that "success" is not a gospel category, but 'holiness" certainly is.

With the aim of holiness in mind, it is appropriate that Fr James Baxter OP casts light on the distinction, and specifically the difference in degree, between the ministerial priesthood and the priesthood of the faithful. Baxter situates this analysis firmly on the basis of *Lumen Gentium* and the vision of the Second Vatican Council for the Church's mission ahead. It is a bold chapter because it enters into a context that is confused and often uninformed, and in which there is a need for clarity and witness.

Matthew Tan is equally bold when he leads us into the world of social media, a "lifeworld grounded in celebrity, competitive one-upmanship and hyperreality." One hopes this is not the life-world of the Church, but in many ways we come to replicate in the ecclesia the patterns of inter-relatedness we learn to cultivate in the worlds in which we most typically engage. Tan defends a liturgical account of time and space that owes much to Francis, Benedict XVI and John Paul II, and bequeaths us a way of responding to the false ecclesiology of social media with the witness of the Body of Christ as communion. Powerfully, Tan ushers us back, perhaps surprisingly, to the terrestrial parish in which such communion can be manifest.

In Western societies it is not uncommon to find that many families do not frequent their parish for regular attendance at Mass, but they still bring their children to the parish for the Sacraments of Initiation. Sr Moira Debono RSM gives an enlightening lesson in perhaps the least understood sacrament (for Western Catholics at least), that of Confirmation. Recent

Magisterial teaching on Confirmation is considered, as well as particular interventions by Pope Francis, and a grounded theology of the ecstatic sacramentality of St Thomas Aquinas. In looking again at the parish, we will need to look even more closely at the sacramental experience of young people there, and how Confirmation can enliven one's part in the Body of Christ.

If we are called to a deeper communion as well as a new missional awareness of our aspirations in the Church, Fr Gerard Kelly fine-tunes our consciousness of the ecumenical task since the 1960s. Fundamentally, the Catholic Church has moved from a juridical mindset to a predominantly Christological and pneumatological one. Yves Congar is a crucial voice for helping to understand this shift, as well as a historical perspective on what actually took place in the Reformation with the debate on the theology of justification. For Kelly, we can draw hope in the goal of organic unity between separated Christians and communities through the receptive ecumenism project, but cannot lose sight of the concreteness of ecclesial and Christian contexts in which unity is manifest and becomes a living reality.

Talking of living realities, the corpus of writings bequeathed to the Church by Pope Benedict XVI contains many jewels not yet widely appreciated. Peter McGregor reflects on *Deus Caritas Est* with its emphasis on caritas as the center and wellspring of Christian mission. For Benedict, the human heart is the "integration of the intellect, will, passions, and senses, of the body and the soul," as McGregor puts it, and thus our mission, and the beating heart of the Church, is the means by which we live and interact as disciples of Christ.

Before the book finishes with a contextual study of ecclesiology and the university in Australia, Kevin Wagner takes us on pilgrimage to Alexandria, home to Clement, Origen, Athanasius, Theophilus, and Cyril, with its roots in the apostolic witness of St Mark the Evangelist. There he introduces the modern reader to a church facing no shortage of challenges, and the practice of the festal letter by St Cyril, from whom we have twenty-nine letters in posterity. Wagner identifies a contemporary fracture between "dogmatic" and "pastoral" theology that can be remedied by the creativity and perseverance of Cyril.

Michael Quinlan leans heavily on his extensive experience in the law and in Australian academic life to construct a fulsome argument for the place and the leading role of the Catholic university in Australia (of which there are two), with special regard for the part played by a faculty of law in a Catholic university setting. Quinlan does not shy from the new context of secular drift and diminished religious practice, and of a move from apathy about religion to hostility towards religious practitioners. For larger institutions that prevail against the odds to serve the nation with an identity that is robustly Catholic, this means there is a need for constant vigilance to protect religious freedom.

In light of the penetrating study manifest in these chapters, it is worth returning to the opening account of our present situation described by Rowland. At the heart of these writers' ecclesiology, and therefore of the present volume, is a desire for the Church to be manifest as the Church, and not as some bureaucratic entity that blindly repeats the self-replicating methods of postmodern managerialism towards which it has become so prone in recent decades. The gospel is still good news for every person, and the Church is still that body called to cultivate a love and discipleship with its head, Christ Jesus, who asks that we joyfully share that good news. This is an ecclesiology that consciously rejects ideology, with an eye on what is hoped for without being blind to the realities of the world. As Fr James Baxter says: "Everyone who practices the Catholic faith must at some stage come to terms with the gap between the ideal and the reality." How we come to terms with that gap will depend largely on our reading of scripture, our care for the living tradition in which we humbly participate, and our orientation to Christ. In other words, the Church is a call to communion in Him, who draws all men and women to himself through his sacrificial giving on the Cross and shares with us the new life of the Resurrection. As Rowland says:

> People can only encounter the love of Christ through others who act as completely whole integrated persons with intellects and wills, indeed with their whole hearts, engaged with the encounter with that other person.

May this work of theological reflection be an encounter—thoughtful, critical and challenging—with Christ and with others in the communion of the Church.

Ecclesiology at the Beginning of the Third Millennium

—Tracey Rowland

> *This chapter surveys the major themes and debates in Catholic ecclesiology from the pontificate of Pius XII (1939–1958) with its landmark ecclesiology document Mystici Corporis Christi (1943) until the present. It argues that Catholic ecclesiology at the beginning of the third millennium is heavily indebted to ideas developed by theologians at the University of Tübingen in the nineteenth century, though the appropriation and development of Tübingen school ecclesiology has not been uniform. In particular, there are different understandings of the concept of "Communio" or "communion" to be found in the magisterial teaching and academic works of John Paul II and Benedict XVI on the one side and the academic work of Walter Kasper on the other. The chapter concludes by identifying the sociological trend towards the adoption of business management theory for the governance of Church agencies, and the political pragmatism of the Vatican Diplomat Corps, as two contemporary 'hot issues' in Catholic ecclesiology.*

Since its foundation in 1817, the Faculty of Roman-Catholic Theology of the University of Tübingen has given rise to a number of important Catholic theologians. Among these were Johann Sebastian von Drey and Johann Adam Möhler in the nineteenth century, and more recently,

Cardinal Walter Kasper and to some degree his nemesis Joseph Ratzinger/Benedict XVI. So much that has happened in the field of Catholic ecclesiology over the past two centuries can be traced back to Tübingen scholarship. Even scholars prominent in the field of ecclesiology who were never students or professors in Swabia are cited as heirs to the Tübingen legacy or described as people who were running on parallel lines. Most notable among these are: Blessed John Henry Newman who reached similar conclusions to Möhler about the role of tradition in the life of the Church; Henri de Lubac SJ, the author of three ecclesiological works, *Catholicisme* (1938), *Méditation sur l'Eglise* (1953), and *Les églises particulières dans l'Église universelle, suive de La maternité de l'église* (1971), who received the Tübingen patrimony via Maurice Blondel and Georges Goyau; Yves Congar OP who credited Möhler with placing an accent on the primacy of the Church's supernatural ontology and with understanding that the whole ecclesial community is an organ of tradition; Louis Bouyer who directly engaged with the ideas of the Tübingen scholars in his ecclesiological work *The Church of God: Body of Christ and Temple of the Spirit*, and Hans Urs von Balthasar who was also influenced by Möhler's ecclesiological masterpiece published in English as *Unity in the Church or the Principle of Catholicism*.[1] In short, most of the roads in Catholic ecclesiology at the beginning of the third millennium start either in Swabia or in Newman's study in Oxfordshire.

In offering a "state of the question" style chapter there are at least three possible ways of proceeding: first one can trawl through the magisterial documents, second one can trawl through the publications of the big names, and thirdly one can examine the concrete issues that have arisen. The approach of this chapter is to ambitiously attempt all three, although priority will be given to the magisterial teaching as a foundation for understanding the contemporary issues.

In the twilight years of the second millennium the most significant of the magisterial documents for the field of ecclesiology was the encyclical *Mystici Corporis Christi* of Pope Pius XII promulgated in 1943. This document affirmed the Pauline teaching that the Church is the mystical body of Christ. In its introduction Pius XII stated that there were three wrong approaches to ecclesiology: the first he described as a false rationalism which ridicules anything which transcends human genius. According to this mentality the Church is merely a human institution, there is nothing supernatural about it. Its ecclesial offices, including the papacy and the

---

1. Lee, "Shaping Reception," 693–72.

college of bishops, are mere human artefacts. The second wrong approach is that of popular naturalism which views the Church as nothing but a juridical and social union. Its conclusions are almost identical to those of the rationalists. It also occludes the supernatural dimension of the Church. The third wrong approach was described by Pope Pius as a "false mysticism" that "attempts to eliminate the immovable frontier that separates creatures from their creator."

In emphasizing that the Church is the mystical body of Christ Pius XII affirmed the accent on the supernatural which was strong in Tübingen ecclesiology and in the works of Blessed John Henry Newman. Pius XII also sought to affirm the principle argued by St Robert Bellarmine, a Church Doctor of the Counter-Reformation era, that the Church is a visible reality notwithstanding the importance of her mystical or invisible dimension. Paragraph 65 of *Mystici Corporis Christi* claims that there can be no real opposition or conflict between the invisible mission of the Holy Spirit and the juridical commission of Ruler and Teacher received from Christ (which is associated with the more visible dimensional of the Church) since they mutually complement and perfect each other—as do the body and soul in the human person. Arguably this is the ideal situation while in practice the exercise of juridical authority by the organs of the visible Church can sometimes fall far short of this ideal. This is a major reason why the sixteenth-century schisms occurred and why the Church in first world countries is currently under scrutiny for its handling or mishandling of the child abuse crisis, and why the visible Church has lost so much of her moral authority. Paragraph 66 concedes that at times there will appear to be imperfections in the body of Christ, but that such weakness should not be attributed to the Church's juridical constitution, to her structure as such, but to the regrettable inclination to evil to be found in each individual.

This tension between the visible and the invisible, the mystical and the all too fleshly human, will no doubt form a common topic of ecclesiological scholarship at the beginning of the third millennium. Not only is there the fall-out from the sex abuse crisis, but there is the fact that serious sexual and financial corruption exists within the Curia, manifested in tens of millions of "missing" Euros and the operation of a "lavender mafia" network. When reports appear in the mainstream press of a cocaine fueled gay orgy involving curial officials being closed down by police inside the Vatican, one is reminded of Dorothy Day's comment that though the Church does sometimes play the harlot she will always be her mother.[2] The metaphors of

---

2. "As to the Church, where else shall we go, except to the Bride of Christ, one flesh with Christ? Though she is a harlot at times, she is our Mother" (Day, "In Peace," 2).

"mother" and "harlot" stand in stark juxtaposition and the task of untangling that relationship will no doubt be a concern of Catholic scholars in the years that lie ahead.[3]

Mystici Corporis Christi was followed in 1964 by the Second Vatican Council's Dogmatic Constitution on the Church known as *Lumen Gentium* which is a reference to Christ (not the Church herself) as the Light of the Nations. Chapter 1 took up *Mystici Corporis Christi's* emphasis on the mystery of the Church. Paragraph 6 noted that just as in the Old Testament the revelation of the Kingdom is often conveyed by means of metaphors today the inner nature of the Church is made known in different images taken either from tending sheep or cultivating the land, from building or even from family life and betrothals.

The second chapter is titled "The People of God" and it presents the members of the Church as a new spiritual community analogous to the Chosen People of the Old Testament. Paragraph ten holds that the baptized, by regeneration and the anointing of the Holy Spirit, are consecrated as a spiritual house and a holy priesthood. The common priesthood of all the faithful, otherwise known as the Royal Priesthood, is said to be distinguished from the ministerial and hierarchical priesthood in essence and not only in degree. The organic structure of the priestly community both royal and sacerdotal is said to be brought into operation by the sacraments. Both the members of the Royal Priesthood and those of the ministerial priesthood participate in the prophetic, priestly and kingly ministry of Christ though they do this in different ways since the two priesthoods are essentially different. However the precise nature of this difference is not explained in any depth. It is also acknowledged that the individual People of God have been blessed with different gifts for the service of the ecclesial body and that what are called in the English translation "particular churches" will retain their own traditions and that these "legitimate differences" will be protected by the Petrine Office. However there is almost no attention given to an analysis of what constitutes a legitimate difference of a particular church. The reference to lower case 't' traditions would seem to imply that the Council Fathers had in mind things like different liturgical languages and devotional practices. Today however, some theologians, including Cardinal Kasper, would extend the ambit of the concept of "legitimate differences" to a far broader range of issues.

Paragraph fifteen offers an olive branch to Christians who remain outside the Church by acknowledging that they share a Christian baptism,

---

3. For a history of the "harlot" metaphor, see Nichols, *Figuring out the Church*. See also Balthasar, *Spouse of the Word*; Biffi, *Casta Meretrix*.

belief in the Trinity and respect for the Sacred Scriptures while paragraph sixteen addresses those of other faiths in very irenic phrases. Jews are told that they remain most dear to God, Muslims are affirmed for professing that they follow the faith of Abraham, those who through no fault of their own do not know the gospel of Christ but sincerely try to do God's will as it is known to them through the dictates of conscience are said to be capable of attaining salvation. Nonetheless the Council Fathers affirm Christ's great commission to preach the gospel to every creature and state that the Church is compelled by the Holy Spirit to do her part that God's plan may be fully realized, whereby He has constituted Christ as the source of salvation for the whole world. The obligation of spreading the faith is said to be imposed on all the faithful, not exclusively upon members of the ministerial priesthood.

The third chapter of *Lumen Gentium* is entitled "On the Hierarchical Structure of the Church and in Particular on the Episcopate." In this section bishops are described as the successors of the Apostles whom Christ willed to be shepherds in his Church while the Petrine Office is said to have been established by Christ so that the episcopate itself might be one and undivided. The relationship between the Petrine Office and the College of Bishops is addressed in paragraph 22. We are told that "just as in the Gospel, St Peter and the other apostles constitute one apostolic college, so in a similar way the Roman Pontiff, the successor of Peter, and the bishops, the successors of the apostles, are joined together." Moreover, the pope is said to have "full, supreme and universal power over the Church," while the order of bishops is also said to have full, supreme power but only when acting with the consent of the pope. This paragraph has been criticized for offering little practical guidance about the relationship between what today is commonly called, in the parlance of liberation theology, the center and the periphery, or the Roman Curia and the local church.

The third chapter of *Lumen Gentium* deals with the issue of papal infallibility. This is described as limited to matters of faith and morals and this jurisdiction extends only "as far as the deposit of Revelation extends, which must be religiously guarded and faithfully expounded." In other words the power of the pope and the college of bishops is said to be circumscribed by Revelation itself as it has been written in the Gospels or orally handed down. For those with artistic interests there is a representation of this principle in a fresco by Fra Angelico in the Niccoline Chapel inside the Vatican Museum.[4] The principle has also recently been emphasized in an essay by Cardinal Gerhard Müller in the journal *First Things*. Cardinal Müller declared:

---

4. Salatino, "Frescoes of Fra Angelico."

> In the exercise of its teaching ministry, it is not enough for the Church's Magisterium simply to appeal to its judicial or disciplinary power as if its teachings were nothing but a matter of legal and doctrinal positivism. Rather, the Magisterium must seek to present a convincing case, showing how its presentation of the faith is in itself coherent and in continuity with the rest of Tradition. The authority of the papal Magisterium rests on its continuity with the teachings of previous popes. In fact, if a pope had the power to abolish the binding teachings of his predecessors, or if he had the authority even to reinterpret Holy Scripture against its evident meaning, then all his doctrinal decisions could in turn be abolished by his successor, whose successor in turn could undo or redo everything as he pleased. In this case we would not be witnessing a development of doctrine, but the dire spectacle of the Barque of Peter stranded on a sandbank.[5]

The fourth chapter of *Lumen Gentium* is simply entitled "the Laity" and is unremarkable but for the fact that it does emphasize that lay people are also called to participate in the mission of the Church and thus they are not simply sheep to be protected or, to quote Monsignor Talbot, one of Cardinal Newman's sparring partners, people whose sole responsibility is to "hunt, to shoot and to entertain."[6] The notion that the lay faithful are also called upon to be evangelizers is a good segue to chapter 5 which promotes the idea of the universal call to holiness.

The sixth chapter is addressed to religious. It affirms the evangelical counsels of poverty, chastity and obedience as a particularly fruitful path to holiness but this chapter is often criticized for not offering anything particularly new or creative. Chapter 7 is similarly without novelty. It addresses the issue of eschatology and reiterates the Church teaching that all will be judged by Christ and that eternal damnation for some is a possibility.

The final chapter deals with the relationship between Mariology and ecclesiology. Here the teaching of St Ambrose is positively endorsed according to which Mary is a type of the Church in the order of faith, charity and perfect union with Christ. It is said that the Church is rightly called mother and virgin and that Mary stands out in eminent and singular fashion as exemplar both of virgin and of mother.[7]

---

5. Müller, "Development of Corruption?"
6. Talbot, "Letter to the Archbishop of Westminster."
7. Quoting from the Mozarabic Rite: "The one gave salvation to the nations, the other gives the nations to the Saviour. The one carried life to her womb, the other carries it in the sacramental font. What was once accorded to Mary in the carnal order is now accorded spiritually to the Church. She conceives the Word in her unfailing faith,

Lumen Gentium concludes with an appendix Pope Paul VI requested be inserted. At the theoretical level the appendix is about the meaning of the word "college" as used in the phrase "the college of bishops." Practically the effect of the appendix is to underscore the principle that bishops are not to act independently of the pope. In theological language the principle is that "without hierarchical communion the ontologico-sacramental function [of the bishops] which is to be distinguished from the juridio-canonical aspect, cannot be exercised."

These themes were later amplified in the 1998 document of the Congregation of the Doctrine of the Faith entitled *The Primacy of the Successor of Peter in the Mystery of the Church*. According to this document the purpose of the Petrine office is "the unity of faith and communion." The ministry of St Peter's successor is said to be inscribed in the heart of each particular Church and thus does not reach it from the outside. Rather, this interiority of the Bishop of Rome's ministry to each particular Church is said to be an expression of the mutual interiority between the universal Church and particular Church. Against what Pius XII would identify as rationalist or naturalist readings of the Petrine primacy, the CDF document states that "the primacy differs in its essence and in its exercise from the offices of governance found in human societies. It is not an office of coordination or management, nor can it be reduced to a primacy of honor, or be conceived as a political monarchy." Moreover, like the faithful, the pope is said to be subject to the Word of God as presented in the Scriptures and interpreted by Tradition. His power is circumscribed by divine law itself and thus he is "the rock which guarantees a rigorous fidelity to the Word of God against arbitrariness and conformism." This CDF document, which bears more than a few Ratzinger watermarks, includes the clause "hence the martyrological nature of the primacy." It has been argued by Bishop Voderholzer of Regensburg that Joseph Ratzinger's view of the papacy was strongly martyrological and that Ratzinger regards Cardinal Reginald Pole's essay *De Summo Pontifice Christi in Terris Vicario Eiusque Officio Potestate Liber Vere* (cited in its short form as *De summo Pontifice*) as "one of the most profound theologies of papal primacy."[8]

The Second Vatican Council also passed the decree *Christus Dominus* on the Pastoral Duties of Bishops and *Presbyterorum ordinis*, a decree on

---

she gives birth to it in a spirit freed from all corruption, she holds it in a soul covered with the Virtue of the Most High."

8. Voderholzer, "Joseph Ratzinger's Martyrological Understanding," a paper delivered at Mundelein Seminary, October 19th, 2017. Pole (1500–1558) was the last Catholic Archbishop of Canterbury. He composed *De summo Pontifice* during the conclave of 1555.

the ministry and life of priests. In 1967 Pope Paul VI released an encyclical entitled *Sacerdotalis Caelibatus* in which he described priestly celibacy as a brilliant jewel and he defended the practice theologically by reference to the intensely christological nature of the priesthood. St John Paul II and Benedict XVI were also strongly supportive of maintaining the practice of celibacy. This is made explicit in John Paul II's Post-Synodal Apostolic Exhortation *Pastores Dabo Vobis*—on the formation of priests in the circumstances of the present day—at paragraph 29. Benedict XVI addressed the subject as a private theologian in his interview with Peter Seewald published as *Salt of the Earth*. In that interview he stated that celibacy has a christological and an apostolic meaning at the same time. As he expressed the idea: "The point is not simply to save time—so I then have a little bit more time at my disposal because I am not a father of a family. That would be too primitive and pragmatic a way to see things. The point is really an existence that stakes everything on God and leaves out precisely the one thing that normally makes a human existence fulfilled with a promising future."[9] As Pope Benedict XVI, Ratzinger also made some off the cuff statements on the subject of celibacy in a Q and A session with priests in June, 2010. In this discussion he added the argument that there is an eschatological dimension to priestly celibacy. As he expressed the idea, celibacy is an anticipation of the world of the resurrection. The subject of "celibacy and priesthood" was also the theme of an address delivered by Cardinal William Levada in the Archdiocese of Belo Horizonte in 2011 when he was the Prefect for the Congregation of the Doctrine of the Faith. Following John Paul II and Ratzinger/Benedict, Levada also defended the practice of celibacy by reference to the Christological character of the priesthood. Significant academic publications where the issue has been treated include: *Celibacy and the Crisis of Faith* by Dietrich von Hildebrand in 1971, *Theology of Priestly Celibacy* by Stanley Jaki in 1997 and *The Case for Clerical Celibacy: Its Historical Development and Theological Foundations* by Cardinal Alfons Stickler in 1995.[10] For a more ambivalent perspective recourse can be had to Edward Schillebeeckx's *Clerical Celibacy Under Fire* (1968).[11]

At the beginning of the third millennium there is a tendency among scholars to accept that celibacy will continue to be the norm for Latin Rite Clergy but to ask questions about how to better prepare seminarians for a celibate life which is perceived as something good, as a spiritual gift no less,

---

9. Ratzinger, *Salt of the Earth*, 195.

10. Hildebrand, *Celibacy and the Crisis of Faith*; Jaki, *Theology of Priestly Celibacy*; Stickler, *Case for Clerical Celibacy*.

11. Schillebeeckx, *Clerical Celibacy Under Fire*.

rather than simply as a cross one stoically learns to carry. Among clergy the issue has resurfaced in the form of rumors that Pope Francis favors a liberalization of canon law to allow for married clergy in some select regions of the world, such as Brazil, while Cardinal Marx of Munich-Freising is encouraging a re-opening of the debate about clerical celibacy in a situation where the number of those entering seminaries in particular dioceses in Europe, such as his own, is beyond a crisis. In 2016 the great Bavarian Catholic Archdiocese of Munich-Freising received only one new seminarian.

Returning to the magisterial teaching, in 1985 John Paul II called an extraordinary Synod to reflect on the reception of the teaching of the Second Vatican Council. A central theme to emerge from this meeting was that one of the most significant Conciliar achievements was the ecclesiology of *Lumen Gentium*. By this time it had been labelled "Communio ecclesiology." This ecclesiology emphasizes the relationships of communion within the Church. In another CDF document, *Letter to the Bishops of the Catholic Church on Some Aspects of the Church Understood as Communion*, published in 1992, the concept of *communion* is described as a "key for the renewal of Catholic ecclesiology." Paragraph 3 states:

> If the concept of *communion*, which is not a univocal concept, is to serve as a key to ecclesiology, it has to be understood within the teaching of the Bible and the patristic tradition, in which *communion* always involves a double dimension: the *vertical* (communion with God) and the *horizontal* (communion among men). It is essential to the Christian understanding of *communion* that it be recognised above all as a gift from God, as a fruit of God's initiative carried out in the paschal mystery. The new relationship between man and God, that has been established in Christ and is communicated through the sacraments, also extends to a new relationship among human beings.

However paragraph 8 of the document goes on to say that some approaches to ecclesiology "suffer from a clearly inadequate awareness of the Church as a *mystery of communion*, especially insofar as they have not sufficiently integrated the concept of *communion* with the concepts of *People of God* and of the *Body of Christ*, and have not given due importance to the relationship between the Church as *communion* and the Church as *sacrament*." Moreover, sometimes, "the idea of a 'communion of particular Churches' is presented in such a way as to weaken the concept of the unity of the Church at the visible and institutional level." This occurs when "it is asserted that every particular Church is a subject complete in itself, and that the universal Church is the result of a *reciprocal recognition* on the part of the particular

Churches." The CDF document declares that such "ecclesiological unilateralism, which impoverishes not only the concept of the universal Church but also that of the particular Church, betrays an insufficient understanding of the concept of communion." Prescriptively, paragraph 9 declares that "the universal Church cannot be conceived as the sum of the particular Churches, or as a federation of particular Churches." It is not the result of the communion of the Churches, but, in its essential mystery, it is a reality *ontologically and temporally* prior to every *individual* particular Church.[12]

The document goes on to say that indeed, according to the early Church Fathers, ontologically speaking, the Church precedes creation and gives birth to the particular Churches as her daughters. Thus, there is the tradition of referring to France as "the eldest daughter of the Church."[13] The document also affirms the long-standing teaching that the Church was first manifested, *temporally*, on the day of Pentecost in the community of the one hundred and twenty gathered around Mary and the twelve Apostles. This one hundred and twenty are described as representatives of the one unique Church and the founders-to-be of the local Churches, who have a mission directed to the world: from the first the Church *speaks all languages.*

Much of the theological analysis offered in this CDF document can be found in Henri de Lubac's work *The Motherhood of the Church*. Speaking of what he called the "problem of ecclesial nationalism" de Lubac remarked that bishops must resist such psychological action—from voodoo worship to the profession of an Aryan Christianity.[14]

What might be called the Lubac-Ratzinger interpretation of *Communio* ecclesiology has not received a sympathetic reception from Cardinal Kasper. In the first decade of the third millennium the hottest topic in ecclesiology was the so-called "Ratzinger-Kasper" debate, an exchange between

---

12. Cf. De Lubac, *Motherhood of the Church*, 199–200: "The particular church is not merely an administrative division of the total Church, she does not result from a partition which would fragment the expanse of the universal Church, but from a concentration of Church exercising her own capacity for fulfilment. She is not a section of a vaster administrative body, one part fitted to other parts in order to form a larger whole, each of these parts remaining exterior to the others, in the way the French provinces, for example, are fitted to each other in order to form the administrative body of the State. It is for this reason that some would even have wished to proscribe from ecclesiastical language the word 'diocese' which can by its origin evoke the idea of a circumscription analogous to the ancient dioceses of the Roman Empire."

13. This point had been made by de Lubac in his work, *The Splendor of the Church*. De Lubac argued that prior to the Incarnation, the Church was betrothed to Christ and that this betrothal will to a 'certain extent' remain in place until the end of time when the Church will finally be united with the Lord in the bridal chamber of the heavenly kingdom.

14. De Lubac, *Motherhood of the Church*, 228–29.

two German Cardinals initially appearing in the German journal *Stimmen der Zeit* and then in *America* and the London *Tablet*. Kasper rejects the idea that the universal Church was first made manifest at Pentecost. He follows the judgement of Michael Theobald who claims that at Pentecost the focus was not on the nascent universal Church but upon the Jewish diaspora. Kasper was critical of Ratzinger for approaching issues intellectually from the perspective of systematic theology and not from what he called a pastoral perspective. Kasper even offered a psychological explanation for Ratzinger's stance saying that Ratzinger thinks in a Platonic world of ideas rather than in an Aristotelian world of facts.[15] At the time of the outbreak of the debate Cardinal Avery Dulles, author of the very popular *Models of the Church* book, weighed in on the side of Ratzinger.[16]

Notwithstanding this debate, throughout the pontificates of John Paul II and Benedict XVI, the reigning ecclesiology was very much *Communio* ecclesiology with intellectual debts to Newman and Möhler and de Lubac for the understanding of the supernatural nature of the Church, with debts to Yves Congar in the understanding of tradition and its mediation in history, with debts to Louis Bouyer in the understanding of foundational principles for ecumenism and a debt to Balthasar for his creative defense of the Petrine Office which had suffered a high level of flak from Hans Küng. A synthesis of these many contributions can be found in the 2014 publication of Benoît-Dominique de la Soujeole entitled *Introduction to the Mystery of the Church*.[17] This work is likely to be used as an ecclesiological "primer" in many Catholic academies since it brings together in the one place a number of elements of *Communio* ecclesiology.

Balthasar's defense of the papacy was presented in his book *Der antirömische Affekt* published in 1974 as a foil to Küng's best-seller *Infallible? An Inquiry* published in 1971. The English translation of Balthasar's book appeared as *The Office of Peter and the Structure of the Church*. It began with a few missile shots declaring the recent attacks on the papacy as a peasant rebellion driven by Germanic guilt over the obedience given to Adolf Hitler. In the 1960s and 70s not only Hans Küng but members of the Frankfurt School of Social Theory were busy attacking the whole idea of hierarchies

---

15. For an extensive analysis of Kasper's "Platonic criticism," see Rowland, "Reception of *Einführung*," forthcoming in the University of Notre Dame's Proceedings on the Conference to mark the 50th anniversary of Joseph Ratzinger's publication of *Introduction to Christianity*.

16. Kasper, "On the Church," 927–30; Ratzinger, "Local Church and the Universal Church"; Dulles, *Models of the Church*. Dulles famous five models were: (1) Institution, (2) Mystical Communion, (3) Sacrament, (4) Herald, and (5) Servant.

17. De la Soujeole, *Introduction to the Mystery of the Church*.

and authority figures as a symptom of what they called "false consciousness." Some people were said to suffer from this condition because they were being unwittingly coerced by cultural leaders, others were deemed to suffer from the malady because they themselves were the agents of coercion. Either way authority figures and hierarchies have been regarded with suspicion by intellectual elites imbued with various forms of Marxist ideology of which the Frankfurt School of Social Theory represents the most sophisticated and influential example.

Balthasar was not moved by any of these elements in the *zeitgeist* of the 1960s and 70s. He regarded leadership and thus hierarchies as a necessary part of the human condition. The Church, he said, was not a pure spirit nor an angelic idea. This would not be appropriate for an institution of the Incarnation. Creatively Balthasar argued that ecclesial leaders were of four basic types, representing four particular charisms or missions. In some places he called them the four pillars of the Church, in other places he referred to a Christological constellation or network of figures surrounding Christ who were prototypical of future ecclesial leaders. Specifically, he spoke of the pillar of St Peter which in practice becomes the Petrine ministry focused on ecclesial governance, the pillar of St John or the Johannine ministry linked to the contemplative life of the Church, the pillar of St James dedicated to guarding the tradition, and finally the Pauline pillar which is associated with the newness of grace and perpetual ecclesial renewal. Balthasar also spoke of the Marian archetype of the Church and used nuptial imagery to affirm both the femininity of the Church and the masculinity of the priesthood.

According to Balthasar these four pillars represent ecclesial missions that are always held in tension. The good of the Church depends upon their harmonious interaction, if one or other gains the upper hand to such a degree that the other three are suppressed or marginalized, the body of Christ suffers. For example, Balthasar suggested that Johannine love can "degenerate into orthopraxis or a universal humanitarian benevolence that takes its values from a 'change in social structures' which would redistribute goods more equitably."[18] Although he did not use the words "liberation theology" this is what he seems to be gesturing towards in this statement. Broadly it is the mentality that all we need is love and social justice and that orthodoxy should be subordinated to orthopraxy. More specifically Balthasar spoke of the problem of theologians who want to break up the concrete unity of the *Catholica* into an abstract unity of *humanitas*.[19] By this he meant that some theologians are tempted to give priority to the so-called brotherhood

18. Balthasar, *Office of Peter*, 328.
19. Balthasar, *Office of Peter*, 43.

of man rather than the community of those who are bound together by the one baptism and one faith. As a caricature one might say that such types are often more excited by the project of realizing the dreams of the French Revolution than the project of carrying out the Great Commission and indeed that their mistake is precisely to conflate the two.

While the Johannine section of the ecclesial orchestra needs to guard against the temptation to chant the Beatles' "All we need is Love" mantra, the pillar of St James, or that section of the ecclesial orchestra responsible for maintaining the integrity of the tradition, needs to guard against what Balthasar called a "reactionary clinging to obsolete forms."[20] This kind of problem is often associated with traditionalist movements where people will go to war over cultural practices like whether or not to wear a mantilla. Traditionalists are correct when they make the point that cultural practices are not theologically neutral—that different practices convey different meanings, including different theological meanings and accents—but this valid insight can become problematic, if, for example, communities end up divided on issues like whether Gothic vestments are to be preferred to Baroque or vice-versa. Meanwhile the Pauline charism to be "all things to all men" can become, in Balthasar's words "a diplomatic *aggiornamento* to all that is popular and fashionable."[21] This is the mentality of those who want to accommodate the practices and culture of the Church to whatever is fashionable in the world at large. Ratzinger referred to this problem when he said that the Church is not a haberdashery shop that updates its windows for each new fashion season. Balthasar diplomatically refrained from defining the pathological operation of the Petrine pillar saying that the "Petrine distortions have been too often exposed to need further mention."[22] As a general principle Balthasar argued that there needs to be an "eschatological center of gravity" provided by the gospel of Christ which holds together these pillars or tensions within the body of Christ.

Balthasar died in 1998 and thus did not live to read the CDF declaration *Dominus Iesus: On the Unicity and Salvific Universality of Jesus Christ and the Church*, promulgated in 2000. Nonetheless, given all the above, especially his warnings about watering down the *Catholica* in favor of the abstract unity of the *humanitas*, it's safe to say that Balthasar would have concurred with the central teachings of *Dominus Iesus*. These include: the declaration in paragraph 6 that the theory of the limited, incomplete, or imperfect character of the revelation of Jesus Christ, which would be

---

20. Balthasar, *Office of Peter*, 329.
21. Balthasar, *Office of Peter*, 329.
22. Balthasar, *Office of Peter*, 329.

complementary to that found in other religions, is contrary to the Church's faith; the declaration in paragraph 12 that the action of the Spirit is not outside or parallel to the action of Christ and the declaration in paragraph 16 that the Catholic faithful *are required to profess* that there is an historical continuity—rooted in the apostolic succession—between the Church founded by Christ and the Catholic Church. Paragraph 16 also states that when *Lumen Gentium* held that the fullness of revelation subsists in the Catholic Church, governed by the Successor of Peter and by the Bishops in communion with him, the expression *subsistit in,* was used to harmonize two doctrinal statements: on the one hand, that the Church of Christ, despite the divisions which exist among Christians, continues to exist fully only in the Catholic Church, and on the other hand, that "outside of her structure, many elements can be found of sanctification and truth," that is, in those Churches and ecclesial communities which are not yet in full communion with the Catholic Church. But with respect to these, it needs to be stated that "they derive their efficacy from the very fullness of grace and truth entrusted to the Catholic Church." A concrete example of ecumenism conducted with respect for these principles was the establishment of the Anglican Ordinariate under the Apostolic Constitution *Anglicanorum coetibus* during the pontificate of Benedict XVI.

Before leaving the Wojtyła-Ratzinger era it should also be mentioned that in 1994 John Paul II promulgated the Apostolic Letter *Ordinatio Sacerdotalis* wherein he declared that the Church had no authority whatsoever to confer priestly ordination on women. This followed upon the CDF Declaration of 1976 titled *Inter Insigniores: On the Question of the Admission of Women to the Ministerial Priesthood*. Both documents emphasize that Christ did not include any women among his chosen 12 apostles, not even his mother. *Inter Insigniores* adds the argument that since the "whole sacramental economy is based upon natural signs or symbols imprinted on the human psychology" and since Christ's role in the Eucharist is to be expressed sacramentally, the "natural resemblance" which must exist between Christ and his minister would not be present if the place of Christ were to be taken by a woman. This is often referred to in the theological literature as the anthropological argument, while the fact that the twelve apostles were all male and that they themselves did not chose to ordain women is described as the argument from tradition. Speaking as a private theologian Joseph Ratzinger also remarked that for him it was theologically significant that priestesses were highly popular in Old Testament times. They abounded in many ancient religions, but not in the religious practices of the Jews who were the people to whom God first chose to reveal himself. A further argument one often finds in the academic literature is that the use of masculine "Father" language for God and the masculinity of God the Son is appropriate since it points to the transcendent nature of God in relation to the world. The world is willed by God but it is not an emanation of God. As Aidan Nichols OP expresses the idea: "A mother goddess is too continuous with the world, too much like the womb from which we came, to stand for the divine reality revealed in the Old Testament, a reality that is decisively other than the world, different from the world, discontinuous with the world."[23]

Nonetheless, notwithstanding the arguments from tradition and from anthropology the whole sub-field of theology known as feminist theology stands opposed to the restriction of the priesthood to men. There is not space in this chapter to offer a profile of every sub-species of feminist theologian, even though, like Australian parrots, they do come in an interesting array of colors.[24] There are, for example, the differences between first, second, third and fourth wave feminism, and between essentialist feminists and constructivist feminists, and between structuralist and post-structuralist feminists, to name but a few of the most common intellectual species. Suffice to say that the differences between feminist theologians (regardless of which particular philosophy or social theory drives their theological analysis) and magisterial teaching usually lie deep in the territory of fundamental theology. Feminists come with their own feminist scriptural hermeneutics, their own feminist social theories and sometimes even their own linguistic philosophies. Since Catholic theology is not a fideism but rather a partnership of faith and reason, what happens in the realm of reason, more specifically today in the realm of social theory, has huge repercussions for theology. The debates between feminist theologians and non-feminist theologians in the field of ecclesiology are the epiphenomena of debates thrown up by different approaches to fundamental theology. Concretely the argument from anthropology makes no sense if one believes that femininity and masculinity are mere social constructs that have no ontological foundations. Conversely if one reads the words in the Book of *Genesis* "male and female he created them" as positing that humanity is divided into two distinct forms, a male form and a female form, and holds this as theologically significant, as part of the data of revelation no less, then this also has huge implications for one's understanding of sacramental theology and ultimately ecclesiology. It also follows as a matter of logic that if one starts from a theological baseline of believing that a priest is primarily the minister and sacramental representative of Christ, that is to say that he celebrates the sacraments *in persona*

---

23. Nichols, *Holy Order*, 149–50.

24. See, for example, Parsons, *Cambridge Companion to Feminist Theology*; McClintock and Briggs, *Oxford Handbook of Feminist Theology*.

Christi then the anthropological argument is much more important than if one holds to a different understanding of the nature of the priesthood. It is precisely for this reason that advocates for the ordination of women often try to argue that a priest also represents the Holy Spirit, or alternatively they argue for a change to the whole understanding of Eucharistic theology so that the sacrificial dimension is muted which makes a sacerdotal priesthood less necessary.

As we move from the era of Wojtyła-Ratzinger to that of Bergoglio-Kasper there is a definite change in ecclesial metaphors. There is far less talk about the mystical body of Christ and sacramental relationships and much more talk about the field hospital and diplomatic relationships. The new buzz word in ecclesiology is not "Communio" but "Synodality," not sacramentality but dialogue. "People's Theology" (in Spanish *Teologia del Pueblo*)—which is the Argentinian strain of liberation theology—embodies what might be called a "preferential option for the view from the periphery." *Teologia del Pueblo* has been described in both the academic and popular press as a form of liberation theology which is Peronist not Marxist. The adjective Peronist is derived from the political platform of the Argentinian General Juan Peron who was three times elected President of Argentina in the years between 1946–1955 and 1973–74. Peronism as a political agenda was both intensely nationalist and intensely anti-intellectual. The nationalist elements within the *Teologia del Pueblo* dovetail well with Cardinal Walter Kasper's desire to give ontological priority to the local Church over that of the universal Church. This means in turn that a contemporary "hot area" in the field of ecclesiology is that of the powers of Synods and national and regional Bishops' Conferences.[25]

For those who seek to give ontological priority to the local Church—and here the big names are Walter Kasper and the late Jean-Marie Tillard OP—national or regional bishops conferences are held in very high regard.[26] Vatican II's *Decree on the Pastoral Office of Bishops in the Church* (pars. 37–38) described an episcopal conference as "a kind of assembly (*coetus*) in which the bishops of some nation or region discharge their pastoral office in collaboration, the better to promote the good which the Church offers to people, and especially through forms and methods of apostolate carefully designed to meet contemporary conditions." In 1966 in the decree *Ecclesiae sanctae*, Blessed Paul VI mandated the establishment of episcopal conferences wherever they did not already exist. In 1988 St John Paul II

---

25. For a history of the issues in this context, see Sullivan, "Teaching Authority of Episcopal Offices," 472–93.

26. For a bibliography of Tillard's works, see Ruddy, *Local Church*, 235–39.

issued the Motu *Apostolos suos* in which paragraph 22 declared that bishop's conferences could only make statements about matters of faith and morals if they were unanimous in their decision or otherwise had the approval of the Holy See.

In *The Ratzinger Report* interview of 1985, Cardinal Ratzinger was not very complimentary about bishops' conferences. His basic argument was a point about group dynamics. Whenever there is a document put together by a committee it inevitably becomes a flattened kind of document representing the lowest common denominator of agreement. He observed that during the Nazi era the best documents were produced by individual heroic bishops not by the German bishops as a collective. In *The Motherhood of the Church*, de Lubac also down-played the theological status of national meetings of bishops. He drew a distinction between a collective act of bishops and a collegial act of bishops with the former not having the same weight as the latter.[27] He declared:

> The primary objective of episcopal conferences is an immediately practical one; and their efficacy is connected to this limited character. Their most usual activity, devoted to local affairs, does not in itself constitute an exercise in collegiality. All the more reason that this must be said of the activity of the commissions and the various bureaus of secretariats they assign to themselves.[28]

Episcopal Synods clearly have more theological status than Episcopal conferences but even here their precise powers vis-à-vis the papacy remains a subject of on-going theological reflection. In his *Church, Ecumenism and Politics: New Essays in Ecclesiology*, Joseph Ratzinger argued that it is in governing the particular churches that bishops share in the governance of the universal church and not the other way around:

> The idea that it is only by being represented at the center that they will have significance for the whole represents a fundamental misjudgement of the nature of the Church; it is the expression of a centralism which the Second Vatican Council in fact wanted to overcome. If one wanted to pursue this idea in order to overcome papal centralism, then all that would be introduced would be a new and much coarser centralism which would bring the Church's real nature to disappearing-point and

---

27. De Lubac, *Motherhood of the Church*, 259–60.
28. De Lubac, *Motherhood of the Church*, 259–60.

subordinate it to the logic of contemporary political theories of the state.[29]

Ratzinger further argued that Synods require time to responsibly deal with issues. Where Church teaching is at stake complex theological problems should not be discussed in sound-bites like a high school debate or a current affairs Q and A program on television. However the longer the duration of Synods the less time bishops can spend in their own diocese. If a permanent Synod were to be established it would take bishops away from their dioceses and in effect create a second tier of Curial government which would increase centralization and lead to a neglect of dioceses. Paradoxically Ratzinger's argument is that the enthusiasm for Synods leads to centralism even though it is a form of governance promoted to give greater voice to the non-Curial bishops.

Not all Synods are however comprised entirely of bishops. When lay people are invited to participate this raises another contemporary "hot topic"—that of how to understand the *sensus fidelium* of the laity. The International Theological Commission (ITC) released a document on the subject of Synodality in 2018, while a document on the *sensus fidelium* was published by the ITC in 2014.

The 2014 ITC document entitled "Sensus Fidei in the Life of the Church" linked the *Sensus Fidei* to the prophetic mission of the laity. This concept does not appear anywhere in scripture but was developed by John Henry Newman is his essay, "On Consulting the Faithful in Matters of Doctrine" (1859). Newman sought to demonstrate that the faithful have their own active role to play in conserving and transmitting the faith. This idea was taken up and developed by Yves Congar in his account of the role of the Holy Spirit in the life of the faithful and it found its magisterial endorsement in *Lumen Gentium*. In paragraph 48 of the ITC document, the *sensus fidei fidelis* is defined as a sort of spiritual instinct that enables the believer to judge spontaneously whether a particular teaching or practice is or is not in conformity with the gospel and with apostolic faith. This "spiritual instinct" is in turn linked to grace and the theological virtues. Paragraph 57 states that the *sensus fidei fidelis* is proportional to the holiness of one's life and paragraph 55 acknowledges the corollary of this, that "in the actual mental universe of the believer the correct intuitions of the *sensus fidei* can be mixed up with various purely human opinions, or even with errors linked to the narrow confines of a particular pastoral context. . . . Not all the ideas which circulate among the People of God are compatible with the faith." For this reason it is the responsibility of the magisterium to judge "whether opinions

---

29. Ratzinger, *Church, Ecumenism, and Politics*, 52.

which are present among the People of God, and which may seem to be the *sensus fidelium*, actually correspond to the truth of the Tradition received from the Apostles."[30] Chapter 4 of the ITC document therefore concludes with a list of dispositions needed for an authentic participation in the *sensus fidei*. These are active participation in the life of the Church, listening to the word of God, openness to reason, adherence to the magisterium, holiness, and seeking the edification of the Church. It is also noted in chapter 4 that throughout the Church's history it has been the minority not the majority of the baptized who have witnessed to the faith.

In *The Office of Peter and the Structure of the Church*, Balthasar was of the view that the trend toward what he called "provincialization" would simply lead to a multiplication of bureaucratic structures to such a degree that the "church militant" would become the "photocopying church."[31] He suggested that individual bishops swamped with paper—reports from this and that subcommittee—may even find themselves calling upon the pope "as a defender of freedom against a more or less anonymous bureaucratic machine."[32] He further drew attention to the sociological fact that Church Councils, Synods, conferences and the like are never peaceful events. They are intensely confrontational with different theological factions and different personalities trying to politically out-maneuver one another. Balthasar remarked:

> Ecumenical councils have had a lively history. At some, people were bribed; at others, they were beaten up; at others, shots were fired. Political pressures of all kinds were the order of the day. Nevertheless—*Dei providential et hominum confusione*—some gains were made for Christianity. On the other hand, the immense expenditures in time, health, money and materials on the part of national synods have not yet been justified. In all the bustle one thing stands out: as never before, the Church is preoccupied with herself, and, in particular, the clergy are preoccupied with themselves. They struggle for identity (which is a clinical problem), they practice individual and collective "navel-gazing," and the greater the confusion of voices, the less the national church knows who she really is.[33]

Balthasar also observed that the great reform movements in the Church have never been initiated by boards and panels but by saints, and thus he

---

30. ITC, "Sensus Fidei" par 77.
31. Balthasar, *Office of Peter*, 40.
32. Balthasar, *Office of Peter*, 40.
33. Balthasar, *Office of Peter*, 41–42.

suggested that the question our ecclesial leaders should be asking is: how does a people produce a saint? One might add: if we are to have more lay participation in ecclesial decision-making, how do we structure things so that the holiest people are those consulted and not those who are the noisiest self-promoters or most highly efficient bureaucratic paper shufflers? How do we make sure that ecclesial governance does not become a parody of the British comedy *Yes, Minister* where the common way for problems to be solved is to call a meeting of all the protagonists, issue a report which shows that the problems are intractable and then set up a quango to study the report and appoint leading protagonists to the quango? The protagonists do often feel happy about this outcome. Their appointments give them another line on their *curriculum vitae*, and the more boards they sit on, the higher their chances of receiving a civil honor. The problems however remain unresolved.

This issue of the Church mimicking contemporary bureaucratic ways of managing conflict relates to another ecclesial hot issue—that of the excessive corporatization of church agencies—the attempt to run church agencies according to the most fashionable business management theories, as if the Church has no ideas of her own about management. Lyndon Shakespeare's *Being the Body of Christ in the Age of Management* offers an extensive analysis of this problem.[34] In sociological terms the corporatization of the pastoral work of the Church means the demise of charismatic authority and its replacement with rational-bureaucratic authority. In practice it also often means turning dioceses into miniature corporations, delegating legitimate episcopal authority to people with degrees in accounting and business management who confuse evangelization and the salvation of souls with strategic plans and key performance indicators. Real Catholic pastoral work, educational formation and evangelization can only take place when there is a personal encounter with Christ mediated by one faithful Catholic to another person, either someone who has the faith but needs the maternal care of the Church in some way, or to someone who is only at the beginning of his or her journey of faith. People can only encounter the love of Christ through others who act as completely whole integrated persons with intellects and wills, indeed with their whole hearts, engaged with the encounter with that other person. The corporatization of the Church's agencies has the effect of planting roadblocks in the path of such real heart to heart encounters. This is because risk-management theory identifies personal encounters as danger zones, as situations which might give rise to litigation. Every effort is therefore taken to minimize the possibility that any one person can take

---

34. Shakespeare, *Being the Body of Christ*.

personal responsibility for any "delivery of a service." Service has to be "depersonalized" and decision-making has to be relegated to committees so that no individual exercises his or her prudential judgment. No individual as an individual can be called to account for any practice, policy or program. In this system responsibility is so diffused that there is no opportunity for real leadership and real heroism and real charismatic office bearing. The grace of the Incarnation is thwarted, the Holy Spirit has no room to breathe.

It is arguably of theological interest that the apostle who betrayed Christ was the one responsible for the money. It is not surprising that there is no place in Balthasar's "four pillars" for someone whose primary job description is accountant or business manager. There is also no special place for someone whose job description is diplomat. There is no mention anywhere in the Gospels of one of the apostolic band being given responsibility for negotiations with the Sanhedrin or the court of the Roman governor. This raises the question about the place of the Vatican Diplomatic Corps. Arguably it is *not* one of those parts of the ecclesial structure for which it can be said that it was established by Christ and foreshadowed in the Old Testament. There was no sacred league of diplomats travelling the roads of the ancient biblical world paying court to the powerful.

At present one of the most serious issues in ecclesiology, real and practical, not merely theoretical, is the fate of Catholics in China who worship in the underground church. Vatican diplomats are bending over backwards to obtain diplomatic recognition from the Chinese government which is demanding, as a condition, significant influence over the appointment of bishops. Cardinal Zen has said that for the Vatican to accede to the Communist Party's demands would be to condemn faithful Chinese Catholics to life in a "Communist cage."[35] It is also a breathtaking disregard of the "white martyrdom" of the late Bishop Kung of Shanghai, the Servant of God, who was sentenced to life imprisonment because he opposed the Communist Party's demand to control episcopal appointments. It has been further argued that the whole idea of ceding episcopal appointment authority to the Chinese government is contrary to the Second Vatican Council's decree *Christus Dominus*—On the Pastoral Office of Bishops in the Church.[36] In that document the Council fathers said: "In order to safeguard the liberty of the Church and more effectively to promote the good of the faithful, it is the desire of the sacred Council that for the future no rights or privileges be conceded to the civil authorities in regard to the election, nomination, or presentation to bishoprics." That Conciliar desire was then given legislative

---

35. Wu, "Cardinal Says Vatican-China Deal." See also Zen, *For Love of My People*.
36. Weigel, "Pope Francis Is Playacting Realpolitik."

effect in the 1983 Code of Canon Law. One of Cardinal Newman's arguments in favor of the superiority of the Catholic Church over that of the Church of England was precisely that the Petrine Office served to protect Catholics from being governed by local civil authorities.[37] However in the last century time and again the members of the Vatican Diplomatic Corps have capitulated to tyrannical governments with the effect that the Catholic martyrs and other heroes living under the tyranny are sold out by the very institution which is most able to help them and to which they have offered their own lives in humble service. The Vatican's *Ostpolitik* strategy for dealing with Communist leaders in the countries of Central and Eastern Europe, especially in Czechoslovakia and Hungary, provides a case study of how to undermine the morale of an oppressed people and destroy their faith in the visible Church.[38]

In summary one might say that a contemporary issue in ecclesiology is precisely that of how to distinguish a Christian form of governance from popular bureaucratic, corporate and, in the context of the work of the Diplomatic Corps, pragmatic ends-justify-the-means models? A related issue is the operation of the Petrine Office itself.

The papacies of Karol Wojtyła and Joseph Ratzinger have been criticized on the grounds that during these years we had professor popes who were great scholars but who were not very good at the day to day management of the Curia. More positively in the academic literature it is said that these two men exercised the Petrine ministry in a very Pauline way in

---

37. "Our ears ring with the oft-told tale, how the temporal sovereign persecuted, or attempted, or gained, the local Episcopate, and how the many or the few faithful fell back on Rome. So it was with the Arians in the East and St Athanasius; so with the Byzantine Empress and St Chrysostom; so with the Vandal Hunneric and the Africans; so with the 130 Monophysite Bishops at Ephesus and St Flavian; so was it in the instance of the 50 Bishops, who, by the influence of Basilicus, signed a declaration against the Tome of St Leo; so in the instance of the Henoticon of Zeno; and so in the controversies both of the Monothelites and the Inconoclasts. . . . In later and modern times we see the same truth irresistibly brought out; not only, for instance, in St Thomas's history, but in St Anselm's, nay, in the whole course of English ecclesiastical affairs, from the Conquest to the sixteenth century, and, not with least significancy, in the primacy of Cranmer. Moreover, we see it in the tendency of the Gallicanism of Louis XIV, and the Josephism of Austria. Such, too, is the lesson taught us in the recent policy of the Czar towards the United Greeks, and in the present bearing of the English Government towards the Church of Ireland. In all of these instances, it is a struggle between the Holy See and some local, perhaps distant, government, the liberty and orthodoxy of its faithful people being the matter in dispute; and while the temporal power is on the spot, and eager, and cogent, and persuasive, and dangerous, the strength of the assailed party lies in its fidelity to the rest of Christendom and to the Holy See" (Newman, *Certain Difficulties*, 184–86).

38. See, for example, O'Grady, *Turned Card*.

the sense that St Paul is associated with theological leadership. With reference to Balthasar's four pillars it could also be said that the two papacies showed a Jacobite interest in the defense of the tradition, especially the papacy of Ratzinger/Benedict. However with the move to the papacy of Bergoglio-Francis we have a move away from professor popes to something more like a General Pope. Instead of something like Balthasar's "four pillars" of ecclesial governance. Bergoglio-Francis offers what in his Apostolic Exhortation *Evangelii Gaudium* he called four "principles for building a people." These are: time is greater than space, unity prevails over conflict, reality is more important than ideas, and the whole is greater than the sum of its parts. It is said that he extracted these principles from a letter written by the nineteenth-century Argentinian dictator Juan Manuel de Rosas (1793–1877) to the caudillo Facundo Quiroga (1788–1835) in 1834.[39] One gets a sense from these principles and from the history of the Bergoglio papacy to date, that Pope Francis does not regard conflict as necessarily a bad thing. One also gets a sense that he is much more inclined to look at issues in ecclesiology from the position of Walter Kasper than from the position of Joseph Ratzinger. We do not know what he thinks of the historical fact that his Apostolic Exhortation *Amoris Laetitia* is interpreted in different ways in different dioceses throughout the world. The fact that a practice can be a mortal sin in one country and a mere irregular situation in another may or may not be of concern to him. He may find it stressful or he may take the view that it is a problem to which one can simply apply the principles—time is greater than space, reality is more important than ideas, unity will prevail over conflict and the whole is greater than the parts. It is however a cause of much stress for those in the Church who see this sociological fact as evidence of a breakdown of the unity of the Church—an attack on the Church's Catholicity no less. Cardinal Kasper would argue that there is no such attack because the issues in dispute are mere matters of church discipline, not matters of faith and morals. However it is precisely this point that is hotly disputed. This in turn raises the issue of the relationship between ecclesiology and sacramental theology, especially eucharistic theology, and then the relationship between eucharistic theology and moral theology. When members of the faithful and professional theologians and bishops speak about these relationships and seek to explain how a decision in one field of theology will have repercussions in others, the advocates for Cardinal Kasper's position usually reply that people are being too logical, too systematic, not pastoral. The word pastoral seems to be code for not rational. As Fr Antonio Spadaro famously tweeted, "2 plus 2 in theology can

---

39. Scannone, "El papa Francisco," 31–50.

make 5." This proposition however is hard for many Catholics to swallow when they have been taught to believe that the Catholic faith is built on *both* reason and revelation, and that love and reason are the "twin pillars" of all reality, no less. Love without reason is blind, reason without love is cold. The Catholic preference is always for an integration of love and reason and of reason and revelation, not a choice for one rather than the other. What is reasonable is never contrary to what is pastorally appropriate.

One of Pope Francis's favorite metaphors to describe the Church is the field hospital. Field hospital work is certainly something that the Church provides, but like so many appropriate metaphors the idea of the Church as a field hospital highlights only one aspect of her reality.[40] Field hospitals can only do so much. Catholics certainly want to bandage the broken hearted, the spiritually wounded, provide consolation to the sick and the dying and the unemployed and those is all manner of dysfunctional family situations. However one cannot think of ecclesiology without considering eschatology and here the idea that part of the mission of the Church is to restore all things in Christ means that the mission is not limited to pouring ointment on wounds, but includes a thorough-going impregnation of every human act and every social practice with the grace of the Incarnation. This is the task of both priests and laity. As St John Paul II wrote in his Apostolic Exhortation, *Christifideles Laici*, "the lay faithful are called to restore to creation all its original value. In ordering creation to the authentic well-being of humanity in an activity governed by the life of grace, they share in the exercise of the power whereby the Risen Christ draws all things to himself and subjects them along with himself to the Father, so that God may be everything to everyone." If this eschatological reading of the mission of the Church is correct then the Church cannot be a "mere booth in the fairground of postmodernity" (to use Robert Spaemann's expression) or just another institution trying to provide social welfare.[41]

---

40. For a work on this concept, see Cavanaugh, *Field Hospital*.

41. In relation to the topic of the laity as a royal priesthood, de Lubac quotes Hugh of St Victor—"The incarnate Word is our king: now, He came into this world to give battle to the devil, and all the saints who lived before his coming are, as it were, soldiers who form the advance guard of the royal army; those who have come since then, and are to come up to the end of the world, are the soldiers who march behind their king. The king Himself takes His place at the center of His army, and he advances surrounded by the defensive wall which His troops form around Him. And although all sorts of different arms can be seen in so great a multitude—for the sacraments and observances of the ancient peoples are not the same as those of the new—still, all are fighting for the same king and under the same standard, pursue the same enemy and are crowned by the same victory" (Hugh of St Victor quoted in Lubac, *Splendor of the Church*, 185).

If the Church were to present herself to the world as a mere booth, just another philanthropic association with Jesus Christ as her inspirational founder, then few would have any objections. However it is precisely her claim to have an eschatological mission that is the source of so much of the hostility she faces. It is for this reason that the Church often finds herself out of favor with governments, and in particular, out of favor with contemporary western governments and institutions like the European Union, that see themselves, not the Church, fulfilling a salvific function. As William Cavanaugh has argued, the modern liberal state operates as a parody of the Body of Christ.[42] Thus, yet another contemporary "hot issue" in ecclesiology is the relationship between the Church and the modern liberal state and in particular the state's claims to occupy a "neutral" stance towards all moral and theological principles. This particular "hot issue" is the subject of a document on religious freedom due to be released by the International Theological Commission in 2019.

This chapter began with a reference to the influence of the Tübingen theologians. Certainly it would seem if one trawls though the magisterial documents and the academic debates that the ideas at issue often have a Swabian pedigree. However just as we speak of Left-Wing Hegelians and Right-Wing Hegelians there seems to be a division developing within the field of ecclesiology between what might be called a Lubacian appropriation of Tübingen ecclesiology and a Kasperian appropriation of Tübingen ecclesiology. The papacies of John Paul II and Benedict fostered the first, the papacy of Francis is fostering the second. There are some points of overlap but also elements of difference. Whether the universal Church has ontological priority over the local church, whether bishop's conferences and lay assemblies are an affirmation of diversity or an exercise in increased bureaucratization and centralization, whether we should mute the eschatological button for the sake of social peace, whether bishops should be gentlemen bureaucrats who do paper work or social leaders who do people work, whether the powers of the Petrine Office trump everything or whether the Petrine Office is itself subject to revelation and to the judgments of the Jacobite pillar, to use Balthasar's idiom, are all hot topics in the field of ecclesiology at the beginning of the third millennium. So too is the issue of the corporatization of the Church's pastoral mission and the principles by which the Vatican Diplomatic Corps operates. Indeed some commentators have called for a total re-consideration of the structure of the Diplomatic Corps and the education of its members. Until these many and varied issues

---

42. Cavanaugh, "City Beyond Secular Parodies," 182–201.

are resolved the barque of Peter may very well find herself "stranded on a sandbank" (to borrow Cardinal Müller's metaphor).

Bibliography

Balthasar, Hans Urs von. *The Office of Peter and the Structure of the Church*. San Francisco: Ignatius, 1986.
———. *Spouse of the Word*. Vol. 2. San Francisco: Ignatius, 1991.
Benedict XVI. *Anglicanorum coetibus*. Rome: Libreria Editrice Vaticana, 2009.
Biffi, Giacomo. *Casta Meretrix, The Chaste Whore: An Essay on the Ecclesiology of St Ambrose*. Farnborough: St Austin, 2000.
Bouyer, Louis. *The Church of God: Body of Christ and Temple of the Spirit*. San Francisco: Ignatius, 2011.
Cavanaugh, William. "The City Beyond Secular Parodies." In *Radical Orthodoxy*, edited by John Milbank et al., 182–201. Oxford: Blackwell, 1999.
———. *Field Hospital: The Church's Engagement with a Wounded World*. Grand Rapids: Eerdmans, 2016.
Congregation for the Doctrine of the Faith (CDF). *Dominus Iesus: On the Unicity and Salvific Universality of Jesus Christ and the Church*. Rome: Libreria Editrice Vaticana, 2000.
———. *Inter Insigniores: On the Question of the Admission of Women to the Ministerial Priesthood*. Rome: Libreria Editrice Vaticana, 1976.
———. *Letter to the Bishops of the Catholic Church on Some Aspects of the Church Understood as Communion*. Rome: Libreria Editrice Vaticana, 1992.
———. *The Primacy of the Successor of Peter in the Mystery of the Church*. Rome: Libreria Editrice Vaticana, 1998.
Day, Dorothy. "In Peace Is My Bitterness Most Bitter." *Catholic Worker* 33.4 (1967) 1–2.
Dulles, Avery. *Models of the Church*. New York: Doubleday, 1978.
Francis. *Amoris Laetitia*. Rome: Libreria Editrice Vaticana, 2016.
———. *Evangelii Gaudium*. Rome: Libreria Editrice Vaticana, 2013.
Hildebrand, Dietrich von. *Celibacy and the Crisis of Faith*. Chicago: Franciscan Herald, 1971.
International Theological Commission. "*Sensus Fidei* in the Life of the Church." Rome: Libreria Editrice Vaticana, 2014.
———. *Synodality in the Life and Mission of the Church*. Rome: Libreria Editrice Vaticana, 2018.
Jaki, Stanley. *Theology of Priestly Celibacy*. West Chester, PA: Christendom, 1997.
John Paul II. *Apostolos Suos*. Rome: Libreria Editrice Vaticana, 1988.
———. *Christifideles Laici*. Rome: Libreria Editrice Vaticana, 1988.
———. *Pastores Dabo Vobis*. Rome: Libreria Editrice Vaticana, 1992.
Kasper, Walter. "On the Church: A Friendly Reply to Cardinal Ratzinger." *The Tablet*, June 23, 2001, 927–30.
Lee, James Ambrose, II. "Shaping Reception: Yves Congar's Reception of Johann Adam Möhler." *New Blackfriars* 92 (2016) 693–72.
Lubac, Henri de. *Catholicism: Christ and the Common Destiny of Man*. San Francisco: Ignatius, 1988.
———. *The Motherhood of the Church*. San Francisco: Ignatius, 1993.

———. *The Splendor of the Church*. San Francisco: Ignatius, 1999.
McClintock, Mary, and Shelia Briggs, eds. *The Oxford Handbook of Feminist Theology*. Oxford: Oxford University Press, 2014.
Möhler, Adam. *Unity in the Church, or, The Principles of Catholicism: Presented in the Spirit of the Church Fathers of the First Three Centuries*. Washington, DC: Catholic University of America Press, 2016.
Müller, Gerhard. "Development or Corruption?" *First Things*, February 20, 2018. Online. https://www.firstthings.com/web-exclusives/2018/02/development-or-corruption.
Newman, John Henry. *Certain Difficulties Felt by Anglicans in Catholic Teaching Considered*. London: Longmans, Green & Co., 1894.
Nichols, Aidan. *Figuring Out the Church: Her Marks, and Her Masters*. San Francisco: Ignatius, 2013.
———. *Holy Order: Apostolic Priesthood from the New Testament to the Second Vatican Council*. Dublin: Veritas, 1990.
O'Grady, Desmond. *The Turned Card: Christianity Before and After the Wall*. Chicago: Loyola, 1997.
Parsons, Susan F., ed. *The Cambridge Companion to Feminist Theology*. Cambridge: Cambridge University Press, 2002.
Paul VI. *Ecclesiae sanctae*. Rome: Libreria Editrice Vaticanaa, 1966.
———. *Sacerdotalis Caelibatus*. Rome: Libreria Editrice Vaticana, 1967.
Pius XII. *Mystici Corporis Christi*. Rome: Libreria Editrice Vaticana, 1943.
Pole, Reginald. *De Summo Pontifice Christi in Terris Vicario Eiusque Officio Potestate Liber Vere*. Upper Saddle River, NJ: Gregg, 1969.
Ratzinger, Joseph. *Church, Ecumenism, and Politics: New Essays in Ecclesiology*. New York: St Paul, 1988.
———. "The Local Church and the Universal Church: A Response to Walter Kasper." *America* 185.16 (2001) 7–11.
———. *The Ratzinger Report*. San Francisco: Ignatius, 1985.
———. *Salt of the Earth: The Church at the End of the Millennium, Interview with Peter Seewald*. San Francisco: Ignatius, 1997.
Ruddy, Christopher. *The Local Church: Tillard and the Future of Catholic Ecclesiology*. New York: Herder and Herder, 2006.
Salatino, Kevin. "The Frescoes of Fra Angelico for the chapel of Nicholas V: Art and Ideology in Renaissance Rome." PhD diss., University of Pennsylvania, 1992.
Scannone, Juan Carlos. "El papa Francisco y la teologia del pueblo." *Razón y Fe* 217 (2015) 31–50.
Schillebeeckx, Edward. *Clerical Celibacy Under Fire*. London: Sheed and Ward, 1968.
Second Vatican Council. "Christus Dominus: Decree Concerning the Pastoral Office of Bishops in the Church." October 28, 1965. Online. http://www.vatican.va/archive/hist_councils/ii_vatican_council/documents/vat-ii_decree_19651028_christus-dominus_en.html.
———. "Lumen Gentium: Dogmatic Constitution on the Church." November 21, 1964. Online. http://www.vatican.va/archive/hist_councils/ii_vatican_council/documents/vat-ii_const_19641121_lumen-gentium_en.html
———. "Presbyterorum Ordinis: Decree on the Ministry and Life of Priests." December 7, 1965. Online. http://www.vatican.va/archive/hist_councils/ii_vatican_council/documents/vat-ii_decree_19651207_presbyterorum-ordinis_en.html.

Shakespeare, Lyndon. *Being the Body of Christ in the Age of Management*. Eugene, OR: Cascade, 2016.

Soujeole, de la Benoit-Dominique. *Introduction to the Mystery of the Church*. Washington, DC: Catholic University of America Press, 2017.

Stickler, Alfons. *The Case for Clerical Celibacy: Its Historical Development and Theological Foundations*. San Francisco: Ignatius, 1995.

Sullivan, Francis A. "The Teaching Authority of Episcopal Offices." *Theological Studies* 63 (2002) 472–93.

Talbot, George. "Letter to the Archbishop of Westminster, 25 April, 1867." In Vol. 2 of *Life of Cardinal Manning: Archbishop of Westminster*, by Edmund Sheridan Purcell. London: Macmillan & Co., 1896.

Voderholzer, Rudolf. "Joseph Ratzinger's Martyrological Understanding of Papal Primacy: A Key for Unresolved Ecumenical Problems." In *Joseph Ratzinger and the Healing of the Reformation-Era Divisions*, edited by Matthew Levering et al., 1–17. Steubenville, OH: Emmaus Academic, 2019.

Weigel, George. "Pope Francis is Playacting Realpolitik." *Foreign Policy*, February 15, 2018. Online. https://foreignpolicy.com/2018/02/15pope-francis-is-playacting-realpolitik.

Wu, Venus. "Cardinal Says Vatican-China Deal Would Put Catholics in Communist Cage." *Reuters*, February 10, 2018. Online. https://ww.reuters.com/article/us-china-vatican/cardinal-says-vatican-china-deal-would-put-catholics-in-Communist-cage.

Zen, Joseph. *For Love of My People I Will Not Remain Silent: On the Situation of the Church in China*. San Francisco: Ignatius, 2019.

2

Leadership in the Body of Christ

—Anthony Randazzo

Proceeding from the Pauline image of the Church as the Body of Christ (cf. 1 Cor 12), this chapter will explore the promises of the image for mission, pastoral practice and leadership among the baptized. Having outlined the purpose and orientation of the Pauline image, the chapter also highlights some areas of practice where development is needed, as observed from an episcopal vantage point, and square it up against the Pauline image. Areas for discussion include the role of laity, religious, women, and in the context of Australia, migrants. In doing so, it is hoped that this will open up areas of formation for further theological discussion, research and development in the area of leadership, which is in turn geared towards supporting the pastoral ministry of the bishop more specifically, and the mission of the Church more generally.

On October 19, 1958, the Irish American author Flannery O'Connor wrote in a letter to Dr. T. R. Spivey:

> I suppose what bothers us so much about writing about the return of modern people to a sense of the Holy Spirit is that the religious sense seems to be bred out of them in the kind of society we've lived in since the eighteenth century. And it's bred out of them double quick now by the religious substitutes for

> religion. There's no where to latch on to, in the characters or the audience. . . . They are all so busy explaining away the virgin birth and such things, reducing everything to human proportions that in time they lose even the sense of the human itself, what they were aiming to reduce everything to.[1]

I raise this in the context of leadership in the Body of Christ because I cannot talk about leadership without first talking about what it means to be a Christian. There seems to be an idea that to be a Christian is to think rightly about Christianity, in other words, to have the right ideas. The problem is we face is that Christianity is *not* primarily about the right ideas, but about entering into the mystery of Christ, who is the Divine Word and as the *Logos* of all creation, is the foundation of all reality. To be Christian is to enter into the depths of reality, both in this world and the next. To be Christian is less about what I do or think but rather who I am meant to be as an icon—a true likeness—of the reality of the living God.

All this has implications for what leadership means in the Church. Leadership is not the kind one sees in the corporate world, for the aim of this kind of leadership is the static aim of generating profit for the company and for shareholders. The aim of corporate leadership is not the dynamic transformation of becoming an icon of God. If our task is entering into Christ, then leadership in the Church only makes sense when spoken of in the context of entering into and being transformed by the Body of Christ. We now have a question: What does this kind of leadership mean in practice?

Accompagnamento and *Aggiornamento*

To answer this, I would like to flag two words that are often used in English. The first, which has become very popular with Pope Francis is the word "accompaniment." In English usage, the word can denote "walking beside someone." This is a lovely but ultimately passive image. It misses other important, active, dimensions of leadership. By contrast, the Italian word for accompaniment, *accompagnamento*, involves not only a "walking besides," but active encompassing. This will make more sense if you permit me to indulge in an architectural analogy. When you build, say a cathedral in the Gothic style, the architect does not simply walk beside the site. The *accompagnamento* in the building process involves providing the right supports in every part of the building. *Accompagnamento* starts not from the sides, but

---

1. O'Connor, *Collected Works*, 1077.

from the very foundations underneath, mining the depths to form proper foundations, using the many layers of the earth that were built up before to form a steady base to take the weight of the Church's present day reality. *Accompagnamento* also involves an attention to what is outside of the Church, through the provision of buttresses which support the body and prevent the parts of the Church from collapsing on themselves. It also requires attention to what is above, by the provision of vaults to support the weight at the top, with that weight resting on the keystone located at the top of the structure. *Accompagnamento*, as you can see, is an active attention to every key aspect of the edifice. It is a dynamic interplay of the horizontal, the human relationships and also the vertical, those relations in the divine. Attention to that interplay must be constant, it must be vigilant to the movements and changes in conditions that require adaptations to continue to keep the structure upright.

Another concept that is relevant for our consideration of leadership is *aggiornamento*. Normally the word is used in English to mean "updating," which again is a passive observance and acceptance of what is going on around you. One updates in accordance with the fashionable trends of any given time, so that there is no distinction between what is within the Church and what is without. Again, the Italian language draws out more active nuances overlooked in the English usage. The actual Italian word has as one of its components the idea of *giorno*, which literally means the day, or in this case, the *new* day. A new day is not simply another day, for at one level it denotes a new beginning. The Christian understanding of the new day is one that is centered in Jesus Christ, who is the "light" (cf. John 1:4–5) and the "alpha" (cf. Rev 22:13) and so Christ is in front of all new beginnings. And the day, the *giorno* in *aggiornamento*, is prefixed by the preposition "*a*," which in Italian means "to move towards." While there may be an updating, it is an updating that makes the new dawn of Christ more apparent and enables us to better move to the new day in Christ. Both of these concepts outlined above are important in our understanding of leadership, because the role of a leader is not to talk at people, but to lead and accompany them on a journey of constant rediscovery. It is to delve deeper into the mystery of Christ, which we can only undertake *in* Christ. Before talking further about what leadership means in the Church, I need to speak briefly about the reality of the Church as the Body of Christ, in particular the thoughts on the Body of Christ that link up with ideas about leadership.

The Body of Christ in Paul

When speaking of the image Body of Christ, the image can generate a number of meanings. The simplest reading is the Stoic idea of everybody having a place in an order.[2] It is true that the Christian—and thus the Pauline—understanding of the Body of Christ does include this understanding. Every single cell in the Body of Christ has the dignity of playing a vital role in the mystery of salvation. Nothing is left out, nothing is irrelevant or unimportant. However, the Church runs the risk of an impoverished understanding if it goes no further than this Stoic understanding, because it is also a very static reading. It has strong connotations of "know your place." I have seen this attitude of "knowing your place" come in two forms. Outside the Church, it comes in the form of a militant secularism where the culture beyond the Church tells the Church to know its place and stay in a confined, pre-defined private sphere, though that is never a two-way street. Inside the Church, it comes in a silly form of feudalism where either clergy or congregation try to outdo one another in confining the other's involvement in the Church to a set, controlled, and ultimately impotent zone of activity. At its most benign, this equating of the Body of Christ to "know your place" runs the risk of creating silos within the Church. At its worst, it runs the risk of turning the Church into the old wine skin, unable to withstand the new wine that God constantly pours into his creation through Jesus Christ.

In contrast to this, the then Cardinal Ratzinger reminded us in *Called to Communion* that the Pauline image of the Body of Christ goes much further than the Stoic understanding. The Body of Christ builds on that, it expands that into a bigger, more dynamic reality. In my opinion, Ratzinger seems to suggest that at the heart of the Pauline image of the Body of Christ is the theme of opening up to realities far beyond my own understanding, expectations and plans. The faith is one where, in Ratzinger's words, "the seemingly uncrossable frontier of my 'I' is left wide open," and the Body of Christ in which my faith consists is also one that opens my horizons. Ratzinger uses this beautiful quote from the Psalms where he says that, in faith, the Lord takes me to "broad places" (Ps 31:9).[3] Entry into the Mystery of Christ does not shrink my world, but opens it up to proportions beyond my wildest imaginings. And this happens not just once, or a few times, but throughout my life in this world and the next.

In what way does my membership in the Body of Christ open me up? The first place to start is with the "I." You may think it strange that this

---

2. Ratzinger, *Called to Communion*, 34.
3. Ratzinger, *Called to Communion*, 144.

would be starting point, especially given how prone to self-centeredness the current culture is. In their own way, an array of diverse thinkers from Karl Rahner[4] to John Paul II[5] note that the experience of the "I" is vital to the life of faith and life in the Church, but the sad reality is that we have entered a crisis of the "I." We now live in a society that has closed in on itself, perpetuating individuals that also close in on themselves. We now see anything outside of ourselves as a threat to our freedom, failing to see that it is the other in our community that helps us in articulating our "I." We then end up with a tragedy of an emaciated "I." What compounds this crisis of the "I" is that Christians have brought this emaciated version of the closed off individual into our being in the Church. When we start conceiving of ourselves as individual Catholics first and not as part of the Body of Christ.

Christ, however, does not leave this "I" closed off and autonomous. According to Ratzinger, in Christ the "I" is opened up and widened.[6] Christ is the one who initiates this expansion of the "I," first by becoming one of us, and in the Incarnation, fusing the "I" of humanity with the "I" of the Godhead. This is why communion is not just a feeling of fellowship between individuals, a fellowship that one can just take or leave as they choose to go back to their original individual selves. Communion, Ratzinger says, is where my once hermetically-sealed self is opened up by a fusion of existences, a fusion between my existence to that of Christ. Ratzinger goes on to say that in Christ I am opened up to the whole, that is, the universal church,[7] fusing my existence with that of everyone in the Body of Christ. The Body of Christ designates a "corporate personality," and Ratzinger talks about how we are "a single Adam" in the Church.[8]

Desire and Renewal in the Body of Christ

The upshot of the above reflections on the Pauline image of the Body of Christ is that, in Christ, I am not exclusively my own person. At the same time, I am so much *more* than merely my own person. This is a highly counter-cultural claim, which is also tapping into the deepest desires of so

---

4. Rahner, *Foundations of Christian Faith*, 455.

5. Pope John Paul II once said, "Sometimes even Catholics have lost or never had the chance to experience Christ personally: not Christ as a mere 'paradigm' or 'value,' but as the living Lord, 'the way, and the truth, and the life' (John 14:6)." See John Paul II, "New Catechism," 3.

6. Ratzinger, *Called to Communion*, 37.

7. Ratzinger, *Called to Communion*, 100.

8. Ratzinger, *Called to Communion*, 35.

many in that culture, in particular our young people who, even if they do not admit it, desire so much more than what the current culture has to offer. This desire for more is a crucial moment, brothers and sisters, because this is the very moment when a window into the soul is opened, a window through which the light of Christ can shine. The church's task is not to crush that bruised reed of desire (cf. Isa 42:3). The church's task is to provide an avenue for that growth in desire, and channel that desire in the Body of Christ. This is so that desire may grow even further in Christ, and that desire for more in life may participate in Christ's promise of "life to the full" (John 10:10).

When my desire is opened up in the Body of Christ, Christ then makes me aware of new realities that lie outside my normal frame of reference, including my *own* understanding of being in the Body of Christ. When Psalm 104 speaks of the Spirit renewing the face of the earth (cf. Ps 104:30), it is because the Spirit draws all things to Christ, and Christ is the one promised by God through the prophet Isaiah and is the one who fulfils that promise in the Book of Revelation to "make all things new" (Rev 21:4). In Christ, new realities are not outside the Church simply because they are outside *my understanding* of the Body of Christ. Remember that Ratzinger cautions—and I would also caution—against equating the Church to *my* church.[9]

Ratzinger goes on to remind us of our need to be aware of the continual emergence of new realities. He does this by using a very subtle link between the Body of Christ and the Bride of Christ, which ties ecclesiology to the nuptial mystery.[10] At first glance this looks like a strange link to make. That is until you stop to consider how the Bride is *distinct* from the groom, yet is not so distinct as to be *separate* from the groom. Christ the Groom and his Bride the Church—the head and his body—are simultaneously one flesh and also distinct from each other. It is precisely this distinction that enables the expression of love between the spouses, which in turn enables the two to become one flesh. When we speak of married couples, our primary frame of reference is not what the husband and wife individually *do*, but what the one couple *becomes* together. In a similar way, our primary frame of reference for leadership in the Church ought to be what the Church as a whole does rather than about what one function or person does isolated from another. Furthermore, a single expression of love can never adequately express the love between the spouses, and every expression of love is never a carbon copy of the one that came before, for if it is, that love becomes stale. Being in the Church is not about static membership, and so *communion* is not about a common formal membership. Rather, it is a common union in Christ, and

---

9. Ratzinger, *Called to Communion*, 139–40.
10. Ratzinger, *Called to Communion*, 38–40.

a common call to love *in* the Body of Christ. In this vocational sense, not in the sense of being formally all the same, that we are all equal in the Body of Christ.

Ratzinger adds that "it is precisely the mystery of love, seen as a nuptial mystery, that indicates both our task and the Church's capacity to fall short of it."[11] Consequently, Ratzinger's important link between the Body of Christ and the nuptial mystery shows that the Church is "never complete but is perpetually in need of renewal."[12] One area where renewal is most pressing is in our understanding of what unity in the Church means. Ratzinger does speak of unity of the Body, and says there is always an emphasis on unity in the Body of Christ. But unity is not a kind of conformity. Instead, there is what Ratzinger calls a "vital exchange of the whole," that is, an exchange of gifts that give life to the whole organism.[13] In a place like Sydney, the opportunities for this vital exchange are immense, much more so than in many other cities in the world. For instance, in the western region for which I have responsibility, there are 140 nationalities and 150 languages spoken. Each community housed within these nationalities and languages brings a unique inflection of the Church, a unique journey within the Body of Christ and a unique way of living Christ's command to "take up your cross and follow me." All these are potential gifts for the building, growth and enlivening of the Church, so long as we do not dismiss them out of hand as something irrelevant simply because they are something different.

Expanding Realities

I would now like to have a quick overview of these new expanding realities that I have observed as a priest and now a bishop, realities in which leadership in the Body of Christ, defined by *accompagnamento* and *aggiornamento*, can be applied.

The first of these realities pertains to Australian migrants. We are a country that depends on migrants, receiving and welcoming them from all walks of life into Australia. The first thing they try to do is find themselves a home and, once that is found, gainful employment. Migrants see in our country an experience of a new dawn. Yet with this new dawn comes all sorts of adjustments and flux. What this means for many, if not most migrants, is that looking for a home will involve more than just housing. For many, that constant home has been their faith and their church. If you look

11. Ratzinger, *Called to Communion*, 39.
12. Ratzinger, *Called to Communion*, 40.
13. Ratzinger, *Called to Communion*, 100.

at the results of the 2017 National Church Life Survey, you will find that the typical Catholic in Sydney is not only older, but also a migrant. I think we in the Church fall short when we treat migrants as little more than additional people in the pews, and the prime pastoral question focuses on how many more hosts we need to provide or how much more revenue we are going to collect at Mass. This kind of treatment is a barrier for the Catholic migrant to exercise their specific vocation in our parishes. Where we also fall short is when we tell migrants to get used to what we are currently doing, using the age-old excuse of "we were here first." Migrants bring an enthusiasm to and new initiatives in the Church, which many may regard as being foreign to the Church. To this, Ratzinger in *Called to Communion* reminds us that being open to new initiatives is all part of what he calls the vital exchange of the different gifts within the Body of Christ.[14] It may be new, and yet we are assured in the Letter to the Hebrews that underpinning all this is Christ, who is the same yesterday, today and forever (cf. Heb 13:8).

Another long overdue area of concern for the Church is properly drawing out the charisms of lay women and men in the Church. First, I cannot overstress the importance of drawing on a massive pool of gifts and talents that women have in the Church. In very practical terms, women are the ligaments in the Body of Christ. From the home to the parish to the chancery, women are undertaking vital work in holding things together, very often unnoticed and unacknowledged. I have seen in my ministry both as a priest and as a bishop that there is a perception of the Church as male dominated, maybe not in terms of numbers, but certainly in mindset. It is marked by a tendency to be suspicious of the particular charisms of women. Likewise, I have encountered many women who had to prove their unique abilities and charisms against the backdrop of constant struggle. The result of this struggle is that proving of the charism has become unnecessarily mixed with a kind of combative determinism that can only inhibit the creation of a common society within the Church. Where the Church as a whole can encourage the particular genius of women *as women* to shine through in the context of ecclesial leadership is always an ongoing concern.

At the same time, another concern I have as vicar for formation of clergy is the neglect of lay men. I mentioned before the risks of bringing a secular mindset into the thinking within the Church, and one area where I see this happening is in using the yardstick of formal equity where success is measured in terms of numbers. This is a problem because a purely numerical measure depersonalizes the Body of Christ and subordinates the particular gifts and talents of each person within it to a ratio. The pursuit

---

14. Ratzinger, *Called to Communion*, 100.

of a ratio at the expense of the pursuit of communion will end up turning the life-giving and self-giving Body of Christ into a space for self-seeking and mutual suspicion. Lying at the heart of this problem is the lack of a proper appreciation of the centrality of Christ, a failure to recognize that our charisms and gifts are given by Christ and that they are gifts to us to build the Church and proclaim Christ. I have often said that the norm for determining membership and thus candidacy for leadership is not a number, but baptism. Through baptism, each of us has a mandate to bear witness to Jesus, a mandate that comes from being baptized and confirmed in His Body. The only legitimate competition in the Body of Christ as Paul says, ought to be in the race to meet Christ and building each other up in His Body.

Finally, I would like to turn now to the situation of our consecrated men and women. It is an often-neglected part of the Body and in recent times, our thinking of the consecrated has been reduced to one of function, and largely confined to education and care of the sick in hospitals. When we reduce the place of the consecrated in the Body of Christ to mere functions, which more often than not are the product of historical accident, then we must take a step back and ask what our role is in that forum, particularly if it is such a secular one. When we reduce the role of the consecrated to functions, consecrated life at its worst becomes a form of social work. We forget that at its best, consecrated life is a vibrant witness to the abundance borne out of full surrender to Christ. They are enriched by a simple life in communion, they are loved through their embrace of chastity, and their hearts are lightened through obedient service. I see so much scope to expand this service, and doing so in accordance to the Second Vatican Council's Decree on the renewal of religious life, *Perfectae Caritatis*, which says that the founder's spirit and aims should always be faithfully set before them.[15] In so doing, consecrated men and women do what *Lumen Gentium* reminds us that the whole Body of Christ is meant to do, which is to provide a foretaste of heaven through their particular characteristics, works and gifts.[16] The foundations of the institutes of consecrated men and women lies in discerning and meeting the mission's demands and needs at any given time and place. These women and men can show leadership by indicating to the rest of the Church where new mission fields lie in our local area, instead of remaining stuck in the silos of historical accident. They can also show leadership through simply living their life in community, which reveal more clearly here, the heavenly realities mentioned above.

15. Second Vatican Council, "Perfectae Caritatis" no. 2; cf. *CCC*, 931; *Code of Canon Law*, 783.
16. Second Vatican Council, "Lumen Gentium" no. 44.

Conclusion

Let me bring together the various threads I have laid out with a single image, which is the image of the Cross. Ratzinger said that life in the Body of Christ is an expanding reality, and so life in the local church should orient me to the life of the Apostle.[17] Life in the Church should bring into my view the life of mission and of witnessing to Christ, rather than the expectation of the privileges of a respectable club member. Life in the Church lived rightly runs the risk of being anything but respectable. We also know what happened to the status of those early disciples who proclaimed what St Paul called the Christ crucified: foolishness to some, a scandal to others (cf. 1 Cor 1:23).

With all our talk about leadership, one image we must never leave behind is that of the crucified Christ. The cross gives us a vivid visual reminder of the vertical and the horizontal aspects coming together in the person of Jesus Christ, but it is the Body of Christ who hangs on the cross and gives that cross meaning. On the one hand, life in the Body of Christ is a call to discipleship, but St Paul also says that the call to discipleship is a call to be "crucified to the world" (Gal 6:14). Our leadership ought to be a leadership in imitating Christ, who did not cling to his life, but emptied it for the sake of those below him. This is not a masochistic sentiment but the blueprint of life itself, because it is the blueprint of someone who not only entered death, but conquered death. Without Christ, the cross is just two pieces of dead wood. In the Body of Christ, however, the cross becomes not the end of existence. Rather, as Hans Urs von Balthasar tells us, it is the definition of existence, a growth of one's own existence into the very existence of Christ.[18]

Bibliography

Balthasar, Hans Urs von. *Seeing the Form*. Vol 1 of *The Glory of the Lord: A Theological Aesthetics*. 2nd ed. San Francisco: Ignatius, 2009.
Catechism of the Catholic Church (CCC). Washington, DC: United States Conference of Catholic Bishops, 1995.
Code of Canon Law. New York: Collins, 1983.
John Paul II. "New Catechism Will Promote National Recatechising Effort." *L'Osservatore Romano*, March 24, 1993.
O'Conner, Flannery. *Collected Works*. New York: Literary Classics of the United States, 1988.

---

17. Ratzinger, *Called to Communion*, 85.
18. Balthasar, *Seeing the Form*, 224.

Second Vatican Council. "Lumen Gentium: Dogmatic Constitution on the Church." November 21 1964. Online. http://www.vatican.va/archive/hist_councils/ii_vatican_council/documents/vat-ii_const_19641121_lumen-gentium_en.html.

———. "Perfectae Caritatis: Decree on the Adaptation and Renewal of Religious Life." October 29, 1965. Online. http://www.vatican.va/archive/hist_councils/ii_vatican_council/documents/vat-ii_decree_19651028_perfectae-caritatis_en.html.

Rahner, Karl. *Foundations of Christian Faith*. New York: Crossroads, 1985.

Ratzinger, Joseph. *Called to Communion: Understanding the Church Today*. San Francisco: Ignatius, 1996

3

"Pastoral Magisterium"?
The Teaching Office of the Church in the Pontificate of Pope Francis

—MARIUSZ BILINIEWICZ

After five years of the pontificate of Pope Francis there is little doubt that the predominant, mainstream narrative about his tenure as Bishop of Rome focuses on change and reform. Among the alleged changes introduced by Pope Francis into papacy is a change of understanding of the role of papal magisterium. When describing the way Francis exercises his teaching office the expression "pastoral magisterium" is sometimes used. This chapter presents the main characteristics of this 'pastoral magisterium' and critically reflects on them.

Introduction

After more than five years of the pontificate of Pope Francis there is little doubt that the predominant, mainstream narrative about his tenure as Bishop of Rome focuses on change and reform. As early as October 2013, six months into the Bergoglio pontificate, Cardinal Theodore McCarrick, Archbishop Emeritus of Washington, DC, in a talk given at Villanova University in Philadelphia, Pennsylvania recalled a pre-2013 conclave conversation which he held with some influential man in Rome. This man, whom the Cardinal chose not to identify, tried to convince him that in five years Bergoglio would "make the Church over again" and "put it back on target."[1] In July 2013 another Cardinal, Cormac Murphy O'Connor, the former Archbishop of Westminster, shortly after the election of Francis made a similar prediction and stated that "four years of Bergoglio would be enough to change things."[2] Today, expressions such as "Great Reformer," "Radical Pope"[3] or "Revolutionary Pope"[4] in many places have become a part of the everyday language used for describing the 266th Successor of St Peter.[5]

Are these past and present judgements correct? Are we really witnessing epochal changes in the pontificate of Francis? With the passage of time a growing number of observers admit that the pontificate of Jorge Mario Bergoglio does bring something genuinely new. Admittedly, every new pope introduces something new to the way the papacy is perceived and enriches the office with his own personality and style. Are changes that come with Francis also simply a matter of style and personality, or is perhaps something more at stake here?

This lengthy topic cannot be analyzed here in detail, especially since the most appropriate time for a sound analysis will come after the conclusion of this particular tenure of the Bishop of Rome. In this chapter, however, one particular shift brought about by the Argentinian pontiff so far will be discussed, namely an apparent change in the understanding of the role of the teaching office of the Church, especially when it is exercised by the Supreme Pontiff.

There are authors who argue that the pontificate of Francis brings a real novelty in this regard. They see a new way of exercising the papal teaching office in the arrival of pope's daily homilies which are often delivered without notes and "of the cuff,"[6] his unauthorized interviews, such as those presented by Eugenio Scalfari in which the pope, among other things, was reported to deny the existence of hell[7] or state that there is no such thing as objective good and evil,[8] and his famous press conferences in airplanes

1. See McCarrick, "Francis Will 'Change' Church."

2. Vallely, "Pope Francis."

3. Ivereigh, *Great Reformer*.

4. Piqué, *Pope Francis*.

5. For more critical analyses of the pontificate, see Lawler, *Lost Shepherd*; Douthat, *To Change the Church*.

6. Even the official Vatican channels begin to use this expression in relation to Pope Francis's interventions. See, for example, the distinction between "The Holy Father's off-the-cuff address" and the official "Address of the Holy Father" made in Holy See Press Office, "Summary of Bulletin."

7. Scalfari, "Quel che Francesco."

8. Scalfari, "Pope."

or his private conversations and phone calls which his interlocutors often made public shortly after the conversation. Authors who argue for novelty believe that this phenomenon is not simply a matter of style of teaching of a particular pope, but more a matter of what papal teaching, or broader magisterial teaching, really is.

Such is the position of Richard R. Gaillardetz, the Joseph Professor of Catholic Systematic Theology at Boston College. Professor Gaillardetz asks whether what we are witnessing with Francis is "simply a refreshingly different style of leadership, but one easily left behind with the next conclave" and which could be considered as "simply a curiosity, an historical anomaly," or "is the pope subtly reconfiguring the papacy in a way that might have a lasting impact on the exercise of the papal office itself?"[9] Gaillardetz opts for the latter. He argues that along with the possibility proposed by John Paul II in his encyclical *Ut Unum Sint* (1995) of finding "a way of exercising the primacy which, while in no way renouncing what is essential to its mission, is nonetheless open to a new situation,"[10] Pope Francis "is not just bringing to the Church a refreshing new papal 'style'" but "is refashioning what we have traditionally referred to as the papal magisterium."[11] He believes that "Pope Francis is modelling a fresh understanding of the role of doctrine in the Church" by enacting a kind of magisterium which is different to the one to which we are used.[12] Following Christoph Theobald's emphasis on "the pastorality of doctrine,"[13] he calls this new way of exercising the teaching office "a pastoral magisterium."[14]

What Is a "Pastoral Magisterium"?

Professor Gaillardetz begins his explanation of the novelty brought by Pope Francis by looking at the recent history of the way the papal magisterium has been exercised. Following Klaus Schatz's analysis[15] and his own works[16] he concludes that with the arrival and popularization of the genre of papal

---

9. Gaillardetz, "Pope Francis."
10. John Paul II, "Ut Unum Sint" no. 95.
11. Gaillardetz, "Pope Francis."
12. Gaillardetz, "Pope Francis."
13. Theobald, "Theological Options of Vatican II."
14. See Gaillardetz, "Pope Francis"; "More Pastoral Magisterium" (a shorter version of that presentation).
15. Schatz, *Papal Primacy*.
16. See Gaillardetz, *Teaching with Authority*; *By What Authority?*; "Reception of Doctrine"; "Prudential Judgment and Catholic Teaching"; "Doctrine Air."

encyclical during the pontificates of Gregory XVI (1831-46) and Pius IX (1846-78) the understanding of the role of the papal magisterium shifted from being "the court of final appeal on pressing doctrinal matters" to being "a major contributor to, and final arbiter of, contemporary theological conversation."[17] This process gathered great momentum during the papacy of Leo XIII (1878-1903) and reached its peak in the pontificate of Pius XII (1939-58). It was after the pontificate of Pius XII and in reaction to this recent trend that pope John XXIII (1958-63), during his Opening Speech to the Second Vatican Council, known as *Gaudet Mater Ecclesia*, emphasized that the teaching authority always needs to have primarily pastoral character.[18] According to Gaillardetz, pope John's call for a "pastoral magisterium" was only partially taken up by popes Paul VI (1963-78), John Paul II (1978-2005) and Benedict XVI (2005-13) and only with the pontificate of Francis we are witnessing it "being taken up and developed with unprecedented vigor."[19]

What is this "pastoral magisterium"? Gaillardetz lists its seven (or six, depending on which source is consulted) basic characteristics.[20]

The first one is that a pastoral magisterium serves a synodal church. Gaillardetz refers to Francis's opinion that only on the way of synodality can we find the pathway that God expects from the Church of the third millennium[21] and that "a synodal church must be, whole and entire, a listening church governed by the practice of mutual listening."[22] A pastoral magisterium, therefore, is exercised by employing a broad practice of consultation which "is more than gathering together safe voices that function as little more than an ecclesiastical echo chamber" and which includes attending

---

17. Gaillardetz, 'Are We Seeing Changes?"

18. John XXIII, "Opening Speech," 715.

19. Gaillardetz, "Pope Francis." See also Gaillardetz, "Pastoral Orientation of Doctrine," 76, where he states that in the pontificates of Paul VI, John Paul II, and Benedict XVI, "significant conciliar themes were either neglected entirely or given only a cursory nod." On the other hand, Francis, in his opinion, "has boldly returned to the foreground a broad range of neglected conciliar teachings and foremost among them is the Council's pastoral orientation toward doctrine." This orientation, according to Gaillardetz, is to be found in Francis's relating of doctrine to the fundamental Christian message and in his insistence that doctrine must be always interpreted in the pastoral context.

20. Gaillardetz, "Pope Francis," has seven characteristics listed, however Gaillardetz, "More Pastoral Magisterium," has six. In the latter, the principle of "appropriate doctrinal humility" seems to be merged with the magisteriums "self-criticism."

21. Francis, "Ceremony."

22. Gaillardetz, 'Pope Francis."

"to a wide range of voices, including those in ecclesial exile."[23] A pastoral magisterium, therefore, is consultative.

The second characteristic of a pastoral magisterium is that it teaches more by a symbolic gesture than by a juridical act. Gaillardetz finds a link here between the pontificate of Francis and of John Paul II who, in his opinion, mastered the use of symbolic gesture and realized much more than his predecessors, and also his immediate German successor, how powerful is the language of gesture in a media-saturated culture. The pastoral magisterium of Pope Francis, therefore, does not focus on producing new documents but on communicating key Christian values through such symbolic actions as his

> request that the people of Rome bless him when he appeared on St Peter's loggia immediately after his election, his eschewal of ostentatious baroque vestments, his dramatic transformation of the Holy Thursday washing of feet ritual (visiting a juvenile detention facility and washing the feet of women and even Muslims), his establishment of Vatican showers for the homeless and his decision to have refugees accompany him on a return trip to Rome.[24]

In the opinion of Gaillardetz, Francis follows on the Polish pope's successful employment of symbolic gestures, however without adopting Wojtyła's "more punitive"[25] or "heavy handed"[26] exercise of authority within the Church. A pastoral magisterium, therefore, speaks more by actions than by words.

The third feature of a pastoral magisterium Gaillardetz sees is ecclesial decentralization. Francis states that "not all discussions of doctrinal, moral or pastoral issues need to be settled by interventions of the magisterium"[27] and insists on "the need to promote a sound 'decentralization.'"[28] He thinks that "excessive centralization, rather than proving helpful, complicates the Church's life and her missionary outreach."[29] A pastoral magisterium, therefore, needs to emphasize the teaching role of regional episcopal conferences and elaborate more on providing them with "specific attributions, including

---

23. Gaillardetz, "Pope Francis."
24. Gaillardetz, "Pope Francis."
25. Gaillardetz, "Pope Francis."
26. Gaillardetz, "More Pastoral Magisterium," 19.
27. Francis, "Amoris Laetitia" no. 3.
28. Francis, "Evangelii Gaudium" no. 16.
29. Francis, "Evangelii Gaudium" no. 32.

genuine doctrinal authority."[30] A pastoral magisterium is, therefore, based on the principle of subsidiarity.

Fourth, a pastoral magisterium should exhibit "appropriate doctrinal humility" which, in the opinion of Professor Gaillardetz, characterized the Second Vatican Council.[31] This doctrinal humility recognizes the historical conditioning of all church teaching (including dogmatic teaching) and considers authoritative pronouncements not as dogmatic endpoints forestalling further debate, but as utterances which

> are continually involved in an unfinished and never to be completed process which itself is not actually inaugurated and cannot be completely controlled by the magisterium and the results of which in the future cannot clearly be foreseen [32]

Gaillardetz points to Francis's reluctance in speaking about "absolute truth" and links this with the fact that "truth is always encountered in history."[33] This means that all church teaching is inseparably linked to the historical period in which it emerged "Indeed, "church teaching should not be used as an excuse for suppressing disagreement and doubt"[34] since doubts have positive values and are far better than false certitude. "If one has the answers to all the questions—that is the proof that God is not with him,"[35] says Francis and Gaillardetz concludes that Francis's exercise of magisterium is based on the notion of the "hierarchy of truths" about which Vatican II spoke in *Unitatis Reintegratio*.[36] A pastoral magisterium, we are told, "has to concentrate on the essentials on what is most beautiful, most grand, most appealing and at the same time most necessary."[37] It "must shift away from the 'policing' function to which it has become habituated in the modern period" and present not a conglomeration of disjoint doctrines but a holistic vision.[38] A pastoral magisterium needs to be conscious of its own limitations not only *toward* doctrine (due to limitations of human reason in approaching and expressing divine realities) but also *about* doctrine (due to dynamic

---

30. Francis, "Evangelii Gaudium" no. 32, quoted in Gaillardetz, "Pope Francis."
31. He develops this topic in Francis, "Vatican II."
32. Rahner, "Magisterium and Theology," 62, quoted in Gaillardetz, "Pope Francis."
33. Francis, "Letter to an Unbeliever," quoted in Gaillardetz, "Pope Francis."
34. Gaillardetz, "Pope Francis."
35. Francis, "Big Heart Open to God."
36. Second Vatican Council, "Unitatis Redintegratio" no. 11.
37. Francis, "Evangelii Gaudium" no. 35, quoted in Gaillardetz, "Pope Francis."
38. Francis, "Letter to an Unbeliever," quoted in Gaillardetz, "Pope Francis."

understanding of Tradition's development and historical conditioning of the Church's teaching).[39]

The fifth characteristic of a pastoral magisterium is that it is self-critical on the part of the Church leadership. As an example of this self-criticism of the magisterium Gaillardetz gives Francis's frequent admission that members of the clergy often fail to live up to their calling to be pastors of souls and lose the spirit of humility by developing various "spiritual diseases."[40] These pastors often fail the people by imposing on them dry and rigid rules which are permeated by the spirit of legalism and which do not take into account the many complexities of people's everyday lives. Pastors should not pretend to have "the monopoly of solutions for the many challenges that modern life presents to us"[41] and should recognize that lay people often know better than they what to do and say.[42] A pastoral magisterium, therefore, renounces clericalism, empowers the laity and calls for less theoretical and more practical approach to the ministry of serving the People of God.

Six, a pastoral magisterium serves the practice of discernment and the formation of conscience. It needs to stop treating Catholics as if they were children and start treating them as adults who are capable of carrying out their own discernment in their own circumstances; circumstances which often require more than "rigorous application of juridical norms."[43] The famous chapter 8 of the post-synodal apostolic exhortation *Amoris Laetitia* and Francis's response to the question about Lutherans receiving Communion at Catholic Masses given during his visit to the Evangelical Lutheran Church of Rome on November 15, 2015[44] are used here as examples of how this discernment works in practice. Gailladretz denounces "a kind of paternalism that assumes that *we* [i.e., the pastors] understand a moral situation better than the persons to whom we are ministering" and calls Francis's teaching about the inclusion of those Catholics who are divorced and civilly remarried into the life of the Church contained in *Amoris Laetitia* "the most comprehensive, astute and balanced guide to the exercise of moral discernment that one will find in an official church document."[45]

---

39. Gaillardetz, "More Pastoral Magisterium," 20; Cornille, *Im-possibility of Interreligious Dialogue*, 27–28, quoted in Gaillardetz, "Vatican II," 100. Catherine Cornille attributes this idea to Vatican II's *Dei Verbum*.

40. Francis, "Christmas Address" quoted in Gaillardetz, "Pope Francis."

41. Francis, "Letter to Cardinal Marc Ouellet," quoted in Gaillardetz, "Pope Francis."

42. Gaillardetz, "Pope Francis."

43. Gaillardetz, *By What Authority*, 131.

44. Francis, "Evangelical Lutheran Church of Rome."

45. Gaillardetz, "Pope Francis."

Finally, a pastoral magisterium refuses to offer premature doctrinal pronouncements on controverted issues. Francis's insistence that "there should be no preemptive effort to remove controversial topics from consideration," his reluctance to use such expressions as "heresy" or "dissent" and his preference for the word "disagreement" instead, as well as his overall approach of welcoming diversity of opinions and an "honest dialogue" bring Gaillardetz to his conclusion that Francis's pontificate "marks a new stage in the development of the Petrine ministry, a stage first announced by pope John and then only haltingly enacted in the post-conciliar papacy prior to Francis."[46] This new form of exercising the magisterium is "explicitly dialogical, improvisational and provisional" and it "creates an expanded ecclesial space for Catholics to engage the pope's positions in a more open and dynamic fashion."[47]

In summary, Professor Gaillardetz believes that Pope Francis helps us to move away from "thinking of the magisterium in a largely juridical key, focused too much on the matter of formally pronouncing on matters of doctrine."[48] Using Eamon Duffy's judgment that "'definitive' papal utterances are not oracles providing new information, but adjudications at the end of a wider and longer process of doctrinal reflection, consultation, and debate, often extending over centuries"[49] he concludes that "a pastoral magisterium does not claim to have all the answers nor does it provide definitive solutions to every controverted issue" but it "acknowledges the here and now, normative character of current church teaching while always keeping open the possibility of further insight."[50] In another place, he summarizes his argument thus:

> In the synodal, listening church of Pope Francis, we are witnessing the gradual emergence of a new exercise of papal teaching, one that is more patient, persuasive and dialogical. It is an exercise of papal teaching particularly attentive to the complexities and challenges of living the Gospel within the concrete conditions of daily life. It is teaching put directly to the service of discipleship.[51]

---

46. Gaillardetz, "Pope Francis."
47. Gaillardetz, "Pope Francis."
48. Gaillardetz, "Pope Francis."
49. Duffy, "Who Is the Pope?"
50. Gaillardetz, "Pope Francis."
51. Gaillardetz, "Are We Seeing Changes?"

What Can Be Said about "Pastoral Magisterium"?

What can be said about Professor Gaillardetz' analysis? Is he correct in attributing to Pope Francis the idea of changing the way we think about church's magisterium? What can be said about the particular characteristics of it? Does the expression "pastoral magisterium" adequately represent the way Francis exercises his teaching office? Is Francis's "pastoral magisterium" really a fulfilment of the desires of St John XXIII?

With regard to the alleged change of not only the exercise but also of understanding of the teaching office, Gaillardetz's argument is convincing—Francis does seem to execute his magisterium somehow differently than his predecessors. His style of writing and preaching is less systematic and academically rigorous; his answers to questions of journalists at press conferences are spontaneous (they are not prepared in advance, as it was the case with the previous popes) and are delivered in a colloquial, personal tone; he gives more interviews than any previous pope and he is obviously not interested in authorizing them before publication (see the Scalfari interviews). He often prefers making very general remarks over going into particulars and even in the official, magisterial documents frequently chooses not to be as specific as his interlocutors would seem to expect and as the previous popes used to be. He often talks about his ignorance in various matters, even theological, and he seems to consider certain teachings and policies of his predecessors more as a matter of historically conditioned opinion than as an unalterable, binding point of reference (more will be said about this below). He prefers direct, casual conversations over delivering pre-meditated lectures prepared ahead of time. In this way, he seems to be treating his teaching office more "lightly" than his immediate predecessors.

Moreover, Gaillardetz's conviction that "perhaps the pope's penchant for informal and unscripted interviews reflects in microcosm a broader attitude regarding the very exercise of church teaching"[52] is shared by other commentators. These commentators do not share Gaillardetz's enthusiasm about this new way of teaching (or refraining from teaching) but they do not disagree about its existence. What Gaillardetz calls "pastoral magisterium" of Pope Francis, Raymond de Souza calls "magisterium by stealth,"[53] Sandro Magister a "fluid magisterium,"[54] Brian Harrison, OS, a "hearsay magisterium"[55] and Phil Lawler admits that the only explanation which he

---

52. Gaillardetz, "Are We Seeing Changes?"
53. de Souza, "Debating 'Amoris Laetitia.'"
54. Magister, "Yes, No, I Don't Know."
55. Harrison, "Cardinal Schönborn's Interview."

is able to find for Francis's words and actions is that the pope himself deliberately wishes to diminish the authority of the papal magisterium.[56] If John O'Malley, SJ, is correct in stating that "the style is the man" and that how we say things is never without influence on what exactly is being said,[57] then indeed something important is taking place in this pontificate.

What can be said about the particular characteristics of this new "pastoral magisterium"? Without a doubt, many of the principles laid out by Professor Gaillardetz are sound, worth considering, and in line with the expectations of pope St John XXIII and the Second Vatican Council. For example, the call for helping the faithful in developing an upright, well-formed conscience which is able to discern what to do in complex situations in which no immediate, straightforward answer to a moral dilemma can be found, is certainly worth pursuing. The call for caution in addressing, by the magisterium, issues which are still a matter of debate is also worth listening to, as is the call for not absolutizing any particular theological system which, however noble and useful, can never exhaust the mystery of God who is always greater. Without a doubt the importance of symbolic gesture and social imagination is also worth keeping in mind in times when nearly everything that a pope says or does today goes viral within minutes.

At the same time, certain proposals regarding the "pastoral magisterium" can raise doubts when looked at from a greater perspective. Reservations about them can be raised both on the grounds of theory and of practice.

An example of such reservations is the first characteristic of the "pastoral magisterium," the principle of synodality. The idea that even "the teaching church" (*ecclesia docens*) is primarily "the learning church" (*ecclesia dicens*) and that every ecclesial authority should carry out its mission in the spirit of listening to various, even conflicting points of view, is undoubtedly noble in principle. However, just how difficult this is to realize in practice is seen in Francis's own policies. It is often argued that during the pontificates of John Paul II and Benedict XVI a particular theological vision was promoted through the channels of the magisterium as the "official theology of the Church" and that critical voices were not listened to carefully enough. Leaving aside the question of whether this assessment is fair or not, the inevitable question which imposes itself here is: is the pontificate of Francis really that different to that of his predecessors in this regard? Are critical, non-mainstream voices listened to more carefully than they have

---

56. Lawler, "Is Pope Francis Deliberately Subverting?"

57. See O'Malley, "Style of Vatican II"; "Vatican II"; *What Happened at Vatican II*, 1–14, 290–313.

been before? Pope Francis *also* has a distinct theological and pastoral vision and with the passage of time it becomes more and more obvious that those who do not share that vision and who raise concerns about it are gradually sidelined. The most evident examples of ecclesial and academic figures who respectfully expressed their criticisms about various aspects of Pope Francis's pontificate, first privately and then publicly, and who, as a result, were consequently demoted/removed from their positions of influence include Cardinals Raymond Leo Burke and Gerhard Müller in the Vatican and Professors Peter Seifert and Thomas Weinandy, OFM, Cap. outside it. Without a doubt, every authority, also ecclesial, has a right to surround itself with people who share its vision and are likely to cooperate in putting it into practice. However, the problem here is not that, for example, the four *dubia* cardinals' (Burke, Caffarra, Meisner and Brandmüller) point of view on *Amoris Laetitia* has not been included in Francis's teaching, but that their questions have not even been answered, either formally or informally (the cardinals claim that they were never granted an audience with Pope Francis although they had repeatedly asked for it).[58] Refusal to engage with genuine questions is hardly an example of a magisterium which engages in "real, not just ceremonial consultations."[59]

Louis J. Cameli believes that Francis is not answering the *dubia* because they are not answerable.[60] While it is true that not all questions are answerable with a simple "yes" or "no," the question which begs asking here is: if this is the case, why cannot the pope's response be elaborated and nuanced in order to address the possible complexities and complications involved? If even providing a more lengthy reply is not possible (although it would be hard to imagine why), then why can this "unanswerability" of the *dubia* not be communicated to those who ask? Popes might be under no juridical (canonical) obligation to answer any questions that are put to them by anyone, however they do have a moral obligation to address concerns raised by the faithful. This is especially important when these concerns are presented to them by cardinals, and when all this happens in the context of so much emphasis being placed on the principle of collegiality, synodality, and the need for open speech in the Church, as it is in this pontificate.

These practical deficiencies might point to something more than just human failure to live up to the proclaimed ideas. What needs to be remembered is that consultation which encompasses all conceivable points of view on the given topic is never going to be entirely possible. When a thesis and

---

58. Magister, "Another Letter."
59. Francis, "Big Heart Open to God"; Gaillardetz, "Francis Moment," 73.
60. Cameli, "Pope Francis."

an anti-thesis meet, a satisfactory and coherent synthesis encompassing both points of view (cf. Hegel) will not always be worked out. Even the most synodal church will have to leave some voices out, and by saying "yes" to one way of thinking about a given matter, it will inevitably say "no" to at least few others. If a pastoral magisterium is to be built on the principle of synodality understood as something more than "gathering together safe voices that function as little more than an ecclesiastical echo chamber,"[61] it will require development of some criteria and mechanisms which will help to determine the way conclusions are arrived at and disagreements are managed. Recent history shows that without such criteria and mechanisms, "synodality" in practice can simply mean listening to voices other than those which have been listened to so far, yet with the same attitude of refusal to engage with critics; the attitude which the enthusiasts of Francis's magisterium often accuse his immediate predecessors of having.

Another example of a concept related to a "pastoral magisterium" which is not unproblematic is the call for "sound decentralization." There is little doubt that the principle of subsidiarity in many ecclesial matters is solid and worth promoting. Few would argue that ecclesial discipline needs to be exactly the same in every place around the world since various cultural, social or even geographical contexts sometimes call for a variety of ways of applying the same, unchanging principles. However, when Pope Francis, and following him Professor Gaillardetz, talk about national episcopal conferences possessing "genuine doctrinal authority,"[62] it begs the question of what this "genuine doctrinal authority" would actually look like. According to John Paul II's Apostolic Letter issued *motu proprio Apostolos Suos* (1998), the only doctrinal authority which the local churches possess pertains to issuing catechisms. Scripture translations and statements which are accepted by the members of the given episcopal conferences unanimously, always in communion with the Holy See.[63] When Gaillardetz quotes the passage in *Evangelii Gaudium* in which Francis addresses this issue (no. 32), he states that when the Argentinian pontiff talks about insufficient elaboration of an understanding of the doctrinal authority of episcopal conferences in the post-Vatican II era, he makes reference to *Apostolos Suos*. In Gaillardetz's opinion this might be "a thinly veiled judgement of the theological inadequacies of that document."[64] If he is correct and if Francis really does consider provisions of John Paul II for national episcopal conferences

61. Gaillardetz, "Francis Moment," 73.
62. Francis, "Evangelii Gaudium" no. 32.
63. John Paul II "Apostolos Suos."
64. Gaillardetz, "Francis Moment," 75.

insufficient (and there are good reasons to believe that this indeed is the case), then what exactly are the new boundaries proposed? "Genuine doctrinal authority" of local episcopal conferences seems to suggest a possibility of some kind of "genuine doctrinal pluralism." This, however, raises some serious concerns—could the doctrinal teaching of the Church in one Catholic region differ from doctrinal teaching in another? How could this be squared with the fundamental principle of the unity of the one church?

The idea of doctrinal pluralism not only compromises the principle of the unity of the Church but also undermines the credibility of the magisterium. The question of sacramental policies regarding divorced and civilly remarried Catholics, the example used by Gaillardetz,[65] seems to be an apt example of this kind of problem. If the Catholic faithful in one region hear from their pastors that there are rules which allow no exceptions in following the Ten Commandments and the faithful in another region hear that "there are rules, but exceptions are also possible," this creates a real problem, especially in today's world of the "global village" where Catholics travel, migrate and have constant access to information. Are we not all a part of the universal (catholic) church? How "pastoral" is it to give the impression that God's demands in relation to the most fundamental moral truths differ from one nation or geographical region to another? The famous maxim "*in necessariis unitas, in dubiis libertas, in omnibus caritas*" ("unity in things necessary, freedom in things doubtful, charity in all things") does not really apply in this case since the principle of liberty related to "the doubtful things" refers to theology, not doctrine. In doctrine ("the necessary things") the Church is and needs to be united.

Another characteristic feature of the "pastoral magisterium" which is not unproblematic is the call for "doctrinal humility." It is certainly true that orthodoxy is not constrained to a system and that Revelation always transcends the language in which it is expressed. However, "doctrinal humility" can be, and practice shows that it often is, understood in a rather minimalistic way in which so much attention is given to the fact that various church teachings mature in historical circumstances that not enough recognition is given to the fact that many of these teachings, however strongly embedded in history, are still definitive, certain and irreversible because they are true. If the magisterium is to be really "doctrinally humble," this humility must consist not only of self-restraint, but also of a humble reception of the magisterial pronouncements of previous ages; pronouncements which were often preceded by lengthy discussions, consultations, and a prayerful,

---

65. Gaillardetz, "More Pastoral Magisterium," 19–20.

pastoral discernment of which Eamon Duffy, and following him Richard Gaillardetz, speak in this context.

This is why talking about the "doctrinal humility" of the magisterium makes most sense in relation to new issues arising rather than issues which have already been discussed in the past. There are times when the magisterium might have an "explicitly dialogical, improvisational and provisional" character, as Professor Gaillardetz would like it to have.[66] However, the magisterium cannot pretend that it does not know the answers to questions which have already been asked and answered. Nevertheless, in the pontificate of Pope Francis this often seems to be the case. An example of such situation is Francis's statement about intercommunion with members of the Lutheran community from his visit to a Lutheran church in Rome on 15 November 2015, another example used by Gaillardetz in his papers about the "pastoral magisterium." When Francis was asked the question about intercommunion in a mixed Catholic-Lutheran marriage, he gave a lengthy response in which he did not address the issue directly but, in a not untypical fashion for him, he gave a number of hints which could be interpreted in various ways. Among other things, he said that

> on the journey [towards the New Jerusalem], I wonder—and I don't know how to answer, but I am making your question my own—I ask myself: "Is sharing the Lord's Supper the end of a journey or is it the viaticum for walking together? I leave the question to the theologians, to those who understand."[67]

He concluded his answer to this rather straightforward question by recalling that Catholics and Lutherans share the same baptism, by stating that he is unable to give any general permission and by seemingly leaving it to the decision of the individual person involved.[68] If this is an example of "doctrinal humility" and a magisterium which is "dialogical, improvisational and provisional," then such understanding of humility raises serious concerns. Pope Francis states that he does not know the answer to the question, but he surely must know that his predecessors, including his immediate predecessors, *did* know the answer to this question and that they presented it publically on many occasions and with their magisterial authority.[69] Gaillardetz argues that Francis "was careful not to challenge the formal Catholic doctrine and policy regarding intercommunion, but instead appealed to the

66. Gaillardetz, "More Pastoral Magisterium," 21.
67. Francis, "Evangelical Lutheran Community of Rome."
68. Francis, "Evangelical Lutheran Community of Rome."
69. See, for example, John Paul II, "Ut Unum Sint" nos. 45–46; "Ecclesia de Eucharistia" nos. 43–46; Benedict XVI, "Sacramentum Caritatis" no. 56.

practice of discernment."⁷⁰ But precisely by appealing to the practice of discernment and leaving it to the decision of the individual persons Francis did just that—he challenged the current official Catholic doctrine and policy which specifies the conditions of when and how a non-Catholic Christian can be admitted to the Eucharist. He chose not to mention these conditions ("danger of death . . . or other grave necessity," "proper disposition" and "manifestation of Catholic faith in this sacrament," see canon 844.4 in the current Code of Canon Law) and in fact played them down by dismissing the differences between the Catholic and non-Catholic understandings of the Eucharist and stating that "life is greater than explanations and interpretations [of the doctrine of the Eucharist]."⁷¹ He chose to give the impression that the well-known teaching of his predecessors about the Eucharist being not the means of ecumenism but its goal is simply an opinion and that other opinions could also be legitimately held. Similar remarks can be made about his treatment of sacramental discipline for divorced and civilly remarried Catholics in *Amoris Laetitia* where John Paul II's and Benedict XVI's teachings are not explicitly reiterated but instead replaced with open-ended formulae which seem to leave decisions about receiving Communion to the individuals involved.⁷²

"Doctrinal humility," if it is to be exercised in a truly pastoral way, should not consist of self-restraint in presenting certain unpopular teachings and giving the impression that Catholics should not take them all that seriously because they were historically conditioned. It should consist of a humble reception of the whole, entire doctrine of the Church, in both its reassuring and its challenging aspects. If the Church teaching is presented only partially, ignored, treated just as a matter of opinion, or passed over in silence and left unsaid, then what Professor Gaillardetz calls "doctrinal humility" can easily turn into doctrinal minimalism, or even doctrinal agnosticism, which is certainly not pastoral. It is true that history always plays an important part in formulating doctrines and practices of the Church. However, true "doctrinal humility" should recognize not only this, but also the fact that in the case of many doctrinal issues certain routes have been taken and others rejected (for good reasons) and there simply might be no going back. Is it conceivable, for example, that in the name of "doctrinal humility" a pastoral magisterium would go back to pre-Nicaea I times and reconsider Arianism? Or to pre-Nicaea II discussions about iconoclasm and reconsider the tradition of venerating images of Christ and the saints? Or

---

70. Gaillardetz, "Pope Francis."
71. Francis, "Evangelical Lutheran Community of Rome."
72. I treat this topic in greater detail in Biliniewicz, *Amoris Laetitia*.

to pre-Tridentine discussions about the number of the sacraments or the books of the Bible? It is true that the issues mentioned above have a dogmatic character and contemporary sacramental practices do not. However, sacramental discipline is often so closely related to dogmas that understanding of those dogmas without reference to the sacramental discipline is not possible. For example, the Catholic teaching about Apostolic Succession, Holy Orders, Real Presence or Sacrament of Penance will not be intelligible if Lutherans are admitted to the Catholic Eucharist on a regular basis and simply on account of being married to a Catholic spouse. Similarly, the Catholic teaching about the Sacrament of Marriage will not be fully intelligible if divorced and civilly remarried Catholics are admitted to the Eucharist without the requirement of living in sexual abstinence.

Professor Gaillardetz refers to Eamon Duffy's statement that "magisterial teaching should *conclude* our tradition's lively engagement with a particular question, not pre-empt its consideration."[73] In the context of "doctrinal humility," Gaillardetz argues:

> A pastoral magisterium does not claim to have all the answers, nor does it provide definitive solutions to every controverted issue. Rather, it acknowledges the normative character of current church teaching but keeps open the possibility of further insight. It is committed to cultivating an ecclesial atmosphere in which controverted questions can be freely debated, new insights can emerge, and the Spirit can work through the shared discernment of the whole People of God.[74]

However, the fact that the magisterium does not have all the answers to *all* questions does not mean that it does not have answers to *some* questions. Questions related to sacramental discipline of Catholics living in irregular unions or in mixed marriages have already been answered by the magisterium, often after a lengthy process of consultation and reflection. Some of these pronouncements go back to the period on the Reformation, others even further back. Is passing over these answers in silence, as if they were simply a matter of opinion, really an exercise of humility and of good pastoral care?

In the same context of "doctrinal humility" Gaillardetz states that church leaders exercise their mission of being faithful to our doctrinal heritage by "heeding Pope Francis's injunction to abandon a place of the safety and certitude, and move from the center to the peripheries of human

---

73. Gaillardetz, "More Pastoral Magisterium," 21.
74. Gaillardetz, "More Pastoral Magisterium," 21.

existence."[75] This call is certainly worth serious attention, however is it really appropriate in the context of safety and certitude with which the *gospel* provides us? No one would disagree that we should always be prepared to leave our comfort zones and go out to the peripheries, but we cannot go there with empty hands. What the peripheries need is the liberating message of Christ presented in its fullness. The human language in which it is expressed might be insufficient and limited, but it is not useless. A truly pastoral magisterium certainly recognizes both the moral failures of those who proclaim it and the fact that God is always greater than anything that we can say of him. At the same time, a truly pastoral magisterium is also humble enough to accept and present the Church's teaching in its totality, including both its reassuring and challenging aspects. As said before, Pope Francis stresses the importance of proclaiming the Catholic faith in its fullness. This fullness, however, includes also the teaching of his many predecessors.

Perhaps the greatest difficulty involved in talking about the idea of "a pastoral magisterium" is that very often the word "pastoral" is not clearly defined in this context. In everyday language used in many Catholic places it often seems to mean something that is easily digestible, welcoming, not too demanding and devoid of anything that could sound controversial or too upsetting for anyone. However, this is not what the word "pastoral" really means.

Alcuin Reid, OSB, in the context of the calls for "a pastoral liturgy," explains that the word "pastoral" should be read in the context of Psalm 23 which presents us with the "image of the Lord leading his people, like sheep, to green pastures' [Ps 23:2]."[76] He states that "the indication that this new pasture is to be 'forever' [Ps 23:6], gives an explicitly eschatological content to this reality." He argues that the image of the Good Shepherd who leads his flock to eternal life is confirmed by Christ's self-description in the tenth chapter of St John's Gospel, which has a decidedly eschatological character.[77] In the context of the Church's teaching office, "pastoral magisterium," therefore, is such an exercise of the office which contributes best to the eternal salvation of men and women. Leading sheep to green pastures means not only showing the right path but also warning about the dangers of wandering off into the desert or to rocky places where no food or drink can be found. A truly pastoral magisterium certainly focuses on the positive aspect of the Good News, but it also courageously calls to conversion and warns about routes which are to be avoided. In other words, it presents the *totality* of the Church's teaching and does not shy away from its unpopular aspects by hiding behind fears of an incomplete or partial understanding.

75. Gaillardetz, "Pope Francis."
76. Reid, "Pastoral Liturgy Revisited."
77. Reid, "Pastoral Liturgy Revisited."

John XXIII and "Pastoral Magisterium"

This brings us to the question of whether Pope Francis's "pastoral magisterium" and the criteria outlined by Professor Gaillardetz really put into practice pope John XXIII's call for exercise of a "magisterium which is primarily pastoral in character."[78] As mentioned above, some of them certainly do. The "Good Pope" without a doubt would welcome extensive consultations before making pronouncements about new issues arising, the importance of symbolic gestures, "sound decentralization" based on the principle of subsidiarity in terms of policies and practical matters, critical self-reflection on the part of pastors regarding their teaching and preaching methods, or the call for formation of mature, responsible consciences of the faithful. Would he be equally happy with "doctrinal humility," the proposed self-restraint of the magisterium and its flight from the role of universal teacher to the role of ultimate arbiter of theological quarrels?

Professor Gaillardetz is certainly correct in stating that pope John XXIII in *Gaudet Mater Ecclesia* talked about the need for updating the way the Church teaching was being presented at that time. However, John XXIII's recommendations need to be placed in the context of what he considered to be the most important task of the Council, that is, "that the sacred deposit of Christian doctrine should be guarded and taught more efficaciously."[79] Pope John's intention in convoking the Council was, in his own words, "to assert once again the magisterium (teaching authority), which is unfailing and perdures until the end of time."[80] This teaching authority takes into account "the errors, the requirements, and the opportunities of our time"[81] and it needs to "transmit the doctrine, pure and integral, without any attenuation or distortion."[82] John XXIII insisted that what was necessary at that time was that the teaching of the Church be presented in its entirety and preciseness and that "a doctrinal penetration and a formation of consciousness in faithful" be done in "perfect conformity to the authentic doctrine."[83] This same, unchangeable, and authentic doctrine, however, can be expressed in various ways and it is here that renewal was needed, according to the pope. Therefore, pope John's address does not justify the call for the magisterium to limit its teaching function and go back to being the last court of resort between disputing theologians. Neither can one find in his speech any call

78. John XXIII, "Gaudet Mater Ecclesia," 715.
79. John XXIII, "Gaudet Mater Ecclesia," 713.
80. John XXIII, "Gaudet Mater Ecclesia," 710.
81. John XXIII, "Gaudet Mater Ecclesia," 715.
82. John XXIII, "Gaudet Mater Ecclesia," 715.
83. John XXIII, "Gaudet Mater Ecclesia," 715.

for revisiting the actual content of the Church's teaching in the light of contemporary historical consciousness. These proposals might be interesting and worth engaging, but they cannot be derived from pope John's Opening Speech. There is no indication that John XXIII envisaged "doctrinal humility" understood as playing down the universality and timelessness of the Church's expressions of faith and sacramental practices. If John XXIII emphasized the pastoral character of the magisterium, it seems that what he primarily had in mind was updating of the language, the manner of speaking in which the Church's faith was presented, not questioning the intelligibility of the Church's teachings outside the cultural contexts in which these expressions emerged. It is true that there is no one way in which the gospel can be expressed. At the same time, what seems to be missing in Professor Gaillardetz's call for "doctrinal humility" of the magisterium is the emphasis that however we express the one doctrine of the Church, in terms of content we need to be saying the same thing. The principle of non-contradiction needs to be applied here and various expressions of the same doctrine, however needed and mutually completing, cannot be self-contradictory.

The examples given by Professor Gaillardetz in the section about formation of conscience, that is, the alleged allowing Lutherans to receive Communion at Catholic Masses and the alleged permission given to divorced and civilly remarried Catholics to receive the sacraments of Penance and Communion without the absolute requirement of continence, are a good illustration of this problem. Gaillardetz, and many other commentators, take pains in arguing that Pope Francis does not change any doctrine here but simply opens new possibilities and leaves it to the consciences of the faithful. However, *this alone* is a change, since before Francis many of these possibilities did not exist as they do now and both Lutherans and divorced and remarried Catholics were not allowed to partake in the sacrament of the Eucharist without meeting certain specific criteria. Now, apparently, they can since a great deal of judgement is left to them. It is true that Francis does not give any blanket permissions or change official policies and one could only agree with Professor Gaillardetz that doing so would simply not match his style of exercising the magisterium. However, Francis *does* introduce a change and does it, among other things, by not repeating the previous teachings of the magisterium and instead by replacing them with ambiguous, open-ended statements which can be interpreted in diverse, often contradictory ways. Is his silence about the teachings and disciplinary measures of the Church an example of "doctrinal humility"? If it is, then at least it needs to be clearly said that using John XXIII as a supporter of this kind of magisterium is an over-interpretation. It is clear from pope John's intervention that if he talked about a "pastoral magisterium" he meant finding new ways of speaking about doctrine, not ignoring it, leaving it behind (as in the case of Communion for divorced and civilly remarried) or putting it into question (as in the case of Communion for Lutherans).

What both John XXIII and Paul VI meant when they spoke about development in the way the magisterium of the Church is to be carried out was finding a proper balance between condemning error and promoting sound doctrine. They thought that in the decades before the Council the magisterium focused too much on the former at the cost of the latter and they wished to regain the harmony between the two. However, it does not mean that these conciliar popes would consider the conciliar idea of "pastorality of doctrine," or even of "the hierarchy of truths" as a justification for silencing or ignoring certain well-established, traditional teachings of the magisterium and the practical solutions (policies) which logically follow from them.

Conclusion

In the conclusion it needs to be said that the teaching office of the Church is and always has to be, by its definition, pastoral. Reclaiming of the word "pastoral" and re-examining it in the light of its actual meaning, which is not simply "as pleasant to hear as possible," seems to be one of the most important tasks for the Church these days. In this way, Pope Francis's way of exercising of his magisterium and the label "pastoral" which is attached to it can serve as a very positive stimulus for the whole church, and especially for theologians, to revisit the idea of what is really "pastoral" and what is not. What needs to be stated clearly is that any opposition between "doctrinal" or "dogmatic" on the one hand, and "pastoral" on the other, has no place in the Catholic tradition, and even if one disagrees with some of Professor Gaillardetz's conclusions and recommendations, one can only applaud him for making this clear in his works on Francis's "pastoral magisterium."[84] There is no division between Christ the teacher and Christ the pastor since such a division would comprise some form of Nestorianism, as Cardinal Gerhard Müller remarked at one time. The Second Vatican Council reminds us that teaching of the gospel in its totality is at the very center of pastoral activity of the Church, always and everywhere.[85] If this is true, then "pastoral magisterium" did not start in March 2013 with the pontificate of Pope Francis, but has always been present in the Church when the liberating truth of the gospel was courageously proclaimed and lived.

84. E.g., Gaillardetz, "Pastoral Orientation of Doctrine," 77.
85. E.g., Second Vatican Council, "Lumen Gentium" no. 25.

Bibliography

Benedict XVI. "Sacramentum Caritatis." Post-Synodal Apostolic Exhortation. February 22, 2007. Online. http://w2.vatican.va/content/benedict-xvi/en/apost_exhortations/documents/hf_ben-xvi_exh_20070222_sacramentum-caritatis.html.

Biliniewicz, Mariusz. *Amoris Laetitia and the Spirit of Vatican II: The Source of Controversy*. London: Routledge, 2018.

Cameli, Louis J. "Pope Francis Still Hasn't Responded to the Dubia. He has Good Reason Not To." *America*, January 5, 2017. Online. https://www.americamagazine.org/faith/2017/01/05/pope-francis-still-hasnt-responded-dubia-he-has-good-reason-not.

Cornille, Catherine. *The Im-possibility of Interreligious Dialogue*. New York: Crossroad, 2008.

de Souza, Raymond. "Debating 'Amoris Laetitia': A Look Ahead." *National Catholic Register*, December 30, 2016. Online. http://www.ncregister.com/daily-news/debating-amoris-laetitia-a-look-ahead.

Douthat, Ross. *To Change the Church: Pope Francis and the Future of Catholicism*. New York: Simon and Schuster, 2018.

Duffy, Eamon. "Who is the Pope?" *New York Times Review of Books*, February 19, 2015. Online. http://www.nybooks.com/articles/archives/2015/feb/19/who-is-pope-francis.

Francis. "Amoris Laetitia." Post-synodal Apostolic Exhortation. March 19, 2016. Online. https://w2.vatican.va/content/dam/francesco/pdf/apost_exhortations/documents/papa-francesco_esortazione-ap_20160319_amoris-laetitia_en.pdf.

———. "A Big Heart Open to God." *America*, September 30, 2013. Online. http://americamagazine.org/pope-interview.

———. "Ceremony Commemorating the 50th Anniversary of the Institution of the Synod of Bishops." Adress. October 17, 2015. Online. http://w2.vatican.va/content/francesco/en/speeches/2015/october/documents/papa-francesco_20151017_50-anniversario-sinodo.html.

———. "Christmas Address to the Roman Curia." December 22, 2014. Online. https://w2.vatican.va/content/francesco/en/speeches/2014/december/documents/papa-francesco_20141222_curia-romana.html.

———. "Evangelical Lutheran Church of Rome: Responses to the Questions." Address. November 15, 2015. Online. https://w2.vatican.va/content/francesco/en/speeches/2015/november/documents/papa-francesco_20151115_chiesa-evangelica-luterana.html.

———. "Evangelii Gaudium." Apostolic Exhortation. November 24, 2013. Online. https://w2.vatican.va/content/francesco/en/apost_exhortations/documents/papa-francesco_esortazione-ap_20131124_evangelii-gaudium.html.

———. "Letter to Cardinal Marc Ouellet." March 19, 2016. Online. https://w2.vatican.va/content/francesco/en/letters/2016/documents/papa-francesco_20160319_pont-comm-america-latina.html.

———. "Letter to an Unbeliever." September 4, 2013. Online. http://w2.vatican.va/content/francesco/en/letters/2013/documents/papa-francesco_20130911_eugenio-scalfari.html.

Gaillardetz, Richard R. "Are We Seeing Changes in the Teaching Ministry of the Pope?" *America*, September 15, 2017. Online. https://www.americamagazine.org/faith/2017/09/15/are-we-seeing-changes-teaching-ministry-pope.

———. *By What Authority? A Primer on Scripture, the Magisterium, and the Sense of the Faithful*. Collegeville, MN: Liturgical, 2003.

———. "The 'Francis Moment': A New Kairos for Catholic Ecclesiology." *CTSA Proceedings* 69 (2014) 63–80.

———. "A More Pastoral Magisterium: Papal Authority in the Francis Era." *Commonweal*, January 27, 2017. 18–21.

———. "The Pastoral Orientation of Doctrine." In *Go Into the Streets!: The Welcoming Church Of Pope Francis*, edited by Thomas P. Rausch. e-book ed. New York: Paulist, 2016.

———. "Pope Francis and the Rise of a Pastoral Magisterium." Lecture presented at the Louis G. Vance Lecture in Oblate School of Theology, March 27, 2017. Online. https://ost.edu/pope-francis-rise-pastoral-magisterium.

———. "Prudential Judgment and Catholic Teaching." In *Voting and Holiness: A Catholic's Guide to the Political Process*, edited by Nicholas Cafardi, 66–80. Mahwah, NJ: Paulist, 2012.

———. "The Reception of Doctrine: New Perspectives." In *Authority in the Roman Catholic Church*, edited by Bernard Hoose, 95–114. London: Ashgate, 2002.

———. *Teaching with Authority: A Theology of the Magisterium in the Church*. Collegeville, MN: Liturgical, 1997.

———. "Vatican II and the Humility of the Church." In *The Legacy of Vatican II*, edited by Massimo Faggioli and Andrea Vicini, 87–108. Mahwah, NJ: Paulist, 2015.

Harrison, Brian. "Cardinal Schönborn's Interview: How Credible is a 'Hearsay Magisterium'?" *One Peter Five*, July 18, 2016. Online. https://onepeterfive.com/cardinal-schonborns-interview-how-credible-is-a-hearsay-magisterium.

Holy See Press Office. "Summary of Bulletin. Audience with the Delegation of the Forum of Family Associations." June 16, 2018. Online. https://press.vatican.va/content/salastampa/en/bollettino/pubblico/2018/06/16/180616f.html.

Ivereigh, Austen. *The Great Reformer: Francis and the Making of a Radical Pope*. New York: Holt and Co., 2014.

John Paul II. "Apostolos Suos." Apostolic Letter. May 21, 1998. Online. http://w2.vatican.va/content/john-paul-ii/en/motu_proprio/documents/hf_jp-ii_motu-proprio_22071998_apostolos-suos.html.

———. "Ecclesia de Eucharistia." Encyclical Letter. April 17, 2003. Online. http://www.vatican.va/holy_father/special_features/encyclicals/documents/hf_jp-ii_enc_20030417_ecclesia_eucharistia_en.html.

———. "Ut Unum Sint." Encyclical Letter. May 25, 1995. Online. http://w2.vatican.va/content/john-paul-ii/en/encyclicals/documents/hf_jp-ii_enc_25051995_ut-unum-sint.html.

John XXIII. "Opening Speech to the Council [Gaudet Mater Ecclesia]." In *The Documents of Vatican II*, edited by Walter M. Abbott, 710–19. New York: America, 1966.

Lawler, Philip F. "Is Pope Francis Deliberately Subverting Papal Teaching Authority?" *Catholic Culture*, September 15, 2016. Online. https://www.catholicculture.org/commentary/otn.cfm?id=1176.

———. *Lost Shepherd: How Pope Francis Is Misleading His Flock.* New Jersey: Regnary Gateway, 2018.

Magister, Sandro. "Another Letter From the Four Cardinals To the Pope. This Too With No Response." *L'Espresso*, December 20, 2018. Online. http://magister.blogautore.espresso.repubblica.it/2017/06/20/another-letter-from-the-four-cardinals-to-the-pope-this-too-with-no-response/?refresh_ce.

———. "Yes, No, I Don't Know, You Figure It Out: The Fluid Magisterium of Pope Francis." *L'Espresso*, May 13, 2016. Online. http://chiesa.espresso.repubblica.it/articolo/1351297bdc4.html?eng=y.

McCarrick, Theodore. "Francis Will 'Change' Church in 5 Years." *Youtube* video, 6:01. February 19, 2019. https://www.youtube.com/watch?v=NnM3959OzTc&feature=youtu.be.

O'Malley, John. "The Style of Vatican II." *America*, February 24, 2003. Online. https://www.americamagazine.org/issue/423/article/style-vatican-ii.

———. "Vatican II: Did Anything Happen?" *Theological Studies* 67 (2006) 3–33.

———. *What Happened at Vatican II.* Cambridge, MA: Harvard University Press, 2010.

Piqué, Elisabetta. *Pope Francis: Life and Revolution: A Biography of Jorge Bergoglio.* Chicago: Loyola, 2014.

Pope, Stephen J., and Richard R. Gaillardetz. "Doctrine Air: Room to Breathe on Church Teaching." *Commonweal* 143 (2016) 11–12.

Rahner, Karl. "Magisterium and Theology." In vol. 18 of *Theological Investigations*, by Karl Rahner, 54–73. New York: Crossroad, 1983.

Reid, Alcuin. "Pastoral Liturgy Revisited." In *T&T Clark Companion to Liturgy*, edited by Alcuin Reid. London: T&T Clark, 2015. https://ebookcentral.proquest.com/lib/unda/detail.action?docID=4000349#.

Scalfari, Eugenio. "The Pope: How the Church Will Change." *La Repubblica*, October 1, 2013. Online. http://www.repubblica.it/cultura/2013/10/01/news/pope_s_conversation_with_scalfari_english-67643118.

———. "Quel che Francesco può dire all'Europa dei non credenti." *La Repubblica*, March 15, 2015. Online. http://www.repubblica.it/politica/2015/03/15/news/quel_che_francesco_puo_dire_all_europa_dei_non_credenti-109542750.

Schatz, Klaus. *Papal Primacy: From Its Origins to the Present.* Translated by John A. Otto and Linda M. Maloney. Collegeville, MN: Liturgical, 1996.

Second Vatican Council. "Lumen Gentium: Dogmatic Constitution on the Church." November 21, 1964. Online. http://www.vatican.va/archive/hist_councils/ii_vatican_council/documents/vat-ii_const_19641121_lumen-gentium_en.html.

———. "Unitatis Redintegratio: Decree on Ecumenism." November 21, 1964. Online. http://www.vatican.va/archive/hist_councils/ii_vatican_council/documents/vat-ii_decree_19641121_unitatis-redintegratio_en.html.

Theobald, Christoph. "The Theological Options of Vatican II: Seeking an 'Internal' Principle of Interpretation." *Concilium* 4 (2005) 87–107.

Vallely, Paul. "Pope Francis Puts People First and Dogma Second. Is This Really the New Face of Catholicism?" *Independent*, July 31, 2013. Online. http://www.independent.co.uk/voices/comment/pope-francis-puts-people-first-and-dogma-second-is-this-really-the-new-face-of-catholicism-8740242.html.

4

Catholic Inc.

On the Mechanized, Managerial Body of Christ

—Thomas V. Gourlay

In an era where many once proudly Catholic institutions scramble to retain and promote some semblance of Catholic "mission and identity," the ecclesiological reality of the Church as the mystical Body of Christ is often usurped by secular organization and management theory. Developing David L. Schindler's conception of the mechanistic ontology of modern (liberal) societies, this chapter will examine the ways in which managerial language and processes of secular corporate bodies commandeer the order of grace in the ecclesial body hindering the Church's mission to be "salt and light" (Matt 5:13–16). The chapter will then seek to provide some kind of remedy to the malignant managerialism in returning to the Christocentric Communio ecclesiology exemplified in the work of Schindler and others associated with the Communio journal and the related theological milieu.

Introduction

The phenomenon of decline in the general religiosity of Western societies, particularly since the mid-1960s, has been well documented. The drift towards secularism is felt across a variety of social spheres even, and perhaps most acutely within those institutions, such as schools, hospitals, or other social outreaches that were founded and staffed by members of once flourishing venerable religious orders and congregations. As these often established and considerably well-heeled Catholic institutions scramble to retain and promote some semblance of Catholic "mission and identity" or "mission integration," the ecclesiological reality of the Church as the mystical Body of Christ is often usurped by the employment of secular organization and management theory.

An ethos of bureaucratic managerialism has arisen in (post)modern liberal Western culture and has slowly begun to penetrate further beyond its traditional home in the business sector. For many who work in church organizations, which are decidedly outside of the business sector, managerial techniques and practices can often be viewed as mere organizational tools, devoid of any moral content and thus adopted without problem for use in a wide variety of spheres. Cardinal Joseph Ratzinger identified this managerial creep as a problem for the Church in his short but potent primer on Catholic ecclesiology, *Called to Communion*. He wrote, "The more administrative machinery we construct [in the Church], be it the most modern, the less place there is for the Spirit, the less place there is for the Lord, and the less freedom there is." He then went on to exhort his readers, that, "we ought to begin an unsparing examination of conscience on this point at all levels in the Church."[1]

With the aid of the work of David L. Schindler, this chapter will argue that such managerialism bears within it a latent metaphysic and onto-logic that commandeers or usurps all other conceptions of reality. It therefore, insofar as such managerialism has been adopted within the Church, is not only stripping the Church of moral and ethical values but also inhibiting the development of authentic *communio*. This chapter will conclude by arguing that for the Church, success will always bear a cruciform character, and as such, its measures for success will be fundamentally different from other institutions. We will argue that the Church's capacity to successfully fulfil its mission lies not in its ability to incentivize individual activity, streamline its operations, or meet particular external goals, but to adopt a fundamentally receptive and contemplative posture, and to offer witness that takes the martyr as its interior form.

---

1. Ratzinger, *Called to Communion*, 146–47.

Secular Management Theory and Practice
outside and inside the Church

In a significant recent work in this field, *Being the Body of Christ in the Age of Management*, Episcopalian priest and scholar Lyndon Shakespeare defines managerialism as "an ideology based upon the assumption . . . that any and all organizations benefit from a deployment of a managerial grammar and purpose-driven logic, for the mechanisms implicit are viewed as value-free in as much as each individual organization develops its own 'world' through this grammar and logic."[2]

Examples of this ideological creep abound in the spheres of politics, education, and also in the Church. The Australian cultural critic and former speechwriter for Prime Minister Paul Keating, Don Watson, has described this phenomenon as increasingly evident in Australian society and in Western culture more broadly. Through a variety of pointed descriptions he shows that we are witnessing the "blurring of the corporate (or managerial) with more traditional (or primitive) human activity creating confusing environments."[3]

In clever and often humorous ways, Watson's books, lexicons, lectures, and websites have drawn attention to the insidious nature of managerialism and the change in language that accompanies it. While Watson's critique focuses on how this phenomenon of managerialism has led to a diminution in language's capacity to communicate meaning, his observations point to a more fundamental diminution of the mind that coincides with the adoption of managerial logic which at its most basic level results in the incapacity to see the particular in relation to the whole. This is evidenced in his commentary on the Black Saturday fires in Victoria of 2009, which saw over 170 deaths, 3500 buildings destroyed including 2029 houses, and the inability of the fire managers to communicate effectively.[4]

The widespread adoption of managerial language evidences an even more pervasive adoption of managerial and bureaucratic structures across a wide variety of sectors from politics, through to education and healthcare. Moreover, while the collapse in meaning arising from the adoption of such language may be profoundly deleterious, it in fact betrays a deeper loss arising from the adoption of managerial and bureaucratic structures across these various strata in society. In the Church too, one can see how the employment of these kinds of structures impacts both on the kind of language

---

2. Shakespeare, *Being the Body of Christ*, 55.
3. Watson, *Death Sentence*, 17.
4. See Watson, "Vital Lessons."

used, but also more fundamentally on the thinking allowed to occur across a variety of levels within the Church as such. This is evidenced, for example, in the concoction of parish mission or vision statements that demonstrate the commitment "To build an active community enabling everyone to be united in connecting life with faith to build a better world."[5] It is also particularly apparent in the attempt to reduce the charism of dying religious orders to a series of propositional statements of "core values" that will guide newly established lay professional boards to carry on the apostolate of the order in the absence of any members.

Obviously, this is an incredibly complex reality facing many of these venerable Orders, and there is no doubt that the establishment of lay professional boards to oversee the governance of these institutions and to carry on the charism of order is a difficult task. In drawing attention to this phenomenon, our intention is simply to highlight the danger in what might be considered reducing the charism of a Religious Order, which is fundamentally a way of living in relationship with the Trinitarian God of Love through the Incarnate Word, Jesus Christ, and of mediating that love to the world, to a kind of propositional statement of identity—an extrinsic, primarily moral, and essentially voluntaristic formulation of "Catholic" identity.[6]

The problem of a creeping managerialism within church structures is one recognized at the highest levels of governance in the Church often noted, for example, in the writings or interviews of Joseph Ratzinger-Pope Benedict XVI. While Ratzinger-Benedict XVI has not developed a comprehensive critique of the trend to uncritically incorporate secular management theories into the Church, his often pithy and perhaps even biting remarks found in his book length interviews evidence a concern for the influence that such theories have on the resulting operational ecclesiology. Beyond this, they point to a deeper critique of an underlying ontology that informs this essentially inadequate ecclesiology that is at odds with an authentic *Communio* ecclesiology.

For Ratzinger, "the reality of the Church is far greater than what you can tabulate in statistics or achieve by decisions. The reality is a living organism, whose life cycle derives from Christ himself."[7] He continues:

---

5. The name of the parish which makes use of this mission statement has been withheld, not wanting to tarnish the name of an otherwise exceptional parish community. For an insightful commentary on the phenomenon of parish mission statements, see Jones, "Parish Mission Statements."

6. The complexity of this phenomenon is wonderfully illustrated in an essay by the Roman Catholic Archbishop of Sydney, Anthony Fisher, OP, which can be found in Fisher, *Catholic Bioethics*, 275–301.

7. Ratzinger and Seewald, *God and the World*, 343.

> It seems to be a particular temptation for our very active and rational society to try to make the Church accessible by means of commissions and boards and consultations. People would like to make her handier and more practical, to some extent make her a human construction in which, in the end, some majority or other will decide what we should actually believe or what we cannot believe, and so forth. But we would only distort her by doing this, moving her farther away from her true self. She would no longer be a living thing-and certainly not something divine.[8]

The brevity of statements like these lead many readers to miss the radical nature of such criticisms. In such statements, Ratzinger does not go into great depths illustrating the resulting ecclesiology implied in the circumstances that he criticizes, he simply draws attention to a growing phenomenon and indicates that it is unfitting for the Church as both *communio* and as Body of Christ to adopt a view of itself that is impersonal, dead, mechanical, and bureaucratic.

To deepen this criticism, we turn now to another prominent author from within the *Communio* theological milieu, long-time editor of the English language edition of the journal, American theologian and philosopher David L. Schindler.

David L. Schindler and a Communio Critique of Liberal Modernity

A common thread in much of Schindler's vast and diverse work has been an underlying concern for the Church's mission to the world. His careful study of the culture of modernity in its dominant liberal form has borne fruit in an acute awareness of the dangers that such a culture presents to the faith. As a result, he is decidedly cautious of proposals by some Catholic scholars who would advocate for the wholesale and uncritical adoption of certain secular theories and structures within the Church.

In his work, Schindler develops a root and branch critique of the culture of liberal modernity, showing that despite its putative metaphysical and theological neutrality it always–already bears within it a metaphysic and a theology that is at odds with an authentic Christianity. Schindler's critique is worked out in three primary areas: in politics, with a commentary that particularly engages in issues of the Church's relationship with the state; in economics, which particularly develops Catholic thought in light of the Church's openness to particular economic structures, both capitalist

---

8. Ratzinger and Seewald, *God and the World*, 343.

and Marxist; and, culturally or more specifically within the academy, where Schindler develops a critique of particular attempts to adopt the liberal model of the academy by Catholic institutions. So, while Schindler does not explicitly tackle the insidious rise of managerial and bureaucratic logic within the Church, his broader project critiquing the (anti)culture of liberalism encompasses a strident critique of such theories and practices. Of course, it is obvious that managerialism and bureaucratization are fully compatible with both collectivism and Marxism, however, as we will see, they operate clearly in contemporary Western modernity as expressions of liberal individualism, and as such, Schindler's critique of liberalism is most useful in this context.

Contemporary liberal theorists such as John Rawls and Judith Shklar claim that liberalism evolved in response to the Wars of Religion that followed the Protestant Reformation as a mechanism for keeping peace amongst warring religious factions.[9] As the Christian religion splintered into multiple factions following the Protestant reformation, liberal theory, so the story goes, sought to create a metaphysically and theologically neutral space from which important decisions about governance, economic life and so on could be made peacefully. Generally speaking, liberal theorists claim that liberalism itself is a theory absent of metaphysical and therefore theological claims.[10] Liberalism seeks to operate outside of tradition, suspending or bracketing out preconceived and often contested notions of the good, attempting to operate from a neutral *tabula rasa*.[11] It proposes and aims to create a secularized public space which is absent of confessional theological and/or metaphysical precursors and is therefore "neutral," promoting peace amongst peoples with varying accounts of the good life.

Schindler, however, argues that at the heart of liberalism lies a pernicious and hidden mechanistic ontology, one that displaces an authentically Catholic ontology rooted in the Catholic doctrines of creation, Incarnation, and redemption. He writes, that "What the language of the machine brings out is the preoccupation with power (understood in terms of physical force or displacement of physical bodies) and technique, and control

---

9. Cavanaugh, *Theopolitcal Imagination*, 21. See also Rawls, "Justice as Fairness"; Shklar, *Ordinary Vices*.

10. The most explicit articulation of this tenet of liberalism is offered by influential liberal theorist John Rawls. See particularly his essay—mentioned above—Rawls, "Justice as Fairness."

11. According to Alasdair MacIntyre, "Liberalism is the only meta-narrative that has convinced the world that it is not a meta-narrative." MacIntyre made this comment during a talk on Edith Stein given at the Lumen Christi Institute in 1998, quoted in Chapp and Howsare, "David L. Schindler," 207.

or manipulation." He goes on to state that "the language of the machine indicates the materialization of relations, in a Cartesian sense of matter: things and persons are approached as though they had only an "outside" as it were."[12]

Importantly Schindler sees that this liberal/mechanistic ontology has something of an infectious character, commandeering other ontological stances vis-à-vis the world—it "pre-empts the debate," much like Alasdair MacIntyre would argue.[13] Importantly for Schindler, this is not a way of conceiving of reality that simply effects non-Catholics or non-Christians, increasingly, it effects those of us within the Church. Indeed, Schindler has made something of a career out of often vigorously critiquing otherwise good, orthodox Catholics for capitulating (often, he readily admits, unwittingly) to the supposed metaphysical neutrality of the mechanistic structures of liberal modernity.[14]

Schindler argues that a liberal/mechanistic onto-logic has influenced the vast majority of modern Western thought, and has greatly affected the way in which Catholics conceive of the Church and its relation to the world. He reserves a particularly strong critique for those who would advocate that the Church and her members could simply adopt secular liberal structures and processes without compromising the faith and without tacitly accepting a liberal worldview. For Schindler, this is particularly dangerous because these structures and mechanisms, he argues, are always and already imbued with a latent ontology and metaphysic at odds with the Christian faith As such, it is imperative that Christians become aware of the underlying ontology imbedded within the structures that they seek to employ, lest the faith become a mere voluntarism, "painted on" so to speak, over what is otherwise a simply secular institution.[15]

We see then how Schindler's cautions can be brought to bear on the adoption of secular management theories and structures within the Church. Nobody, including Schindler, would negate the Church's duties towards

12. Schindler, "Grace," 18.

13. Schindler, like MacIntyre, is mindful that liberalism is generally successful in "preempting the debate by reforming quarrels and conflicts within liberalism, putting in question this or that particular set of attitudes or policies, but not the fundamental tenets of liberalism with respect to individuals and the expression of their preferences" MacIntyre, *Whose Justice? Which Rationality?* 392.

14. For a particularly insightful overview of the debates from a perspective that is sympathetic towards Schindler, see Deneen, *Catholic Showdown*. For a reading of these engagements that is less sympathetic towards Schindler, see Lowery, "Dialogue."

15. Schindler offers a variety of examples of how this has come to pass. Of particular value here is Schindler's critique of the vision of Fr Theodore Hesburgh, long-time president of Notre Dame, Indiana. See Schindler, *Heart of the World*, 143–76.

those employed in her institutions, or her responsibilities towards the vulnerable ones in her care, or the fact that the Church is required to provide excellent stewardship of the earthly resources gifted to her. What Schindler argues however, is that one must be critically aware of the latent metaphysical content within the theories and structures employed or utilized by the Church and her institutions, and how such structures can come to infect one's way of conceiving of the Church and reality as such.

This is of particular importance for the mission of the Church in the world. If the Church, however unconsciously, comes to be conceived of first as a managed or bureaucratic body, and thus in terms of managerial authority, any direct influence it has on the world cannot but tend to be systematic, cold and mechanistic. In the instance where a mechanized managerial ecclesiology takes hold, the only influence that the Church can have on society could only be in terms of the mechanized and managerial logic that seems to define the "greater" managerial machinations of secular society more broadly.[16]

It is imperative that those in positions of ecclesial governance have an awareness of the latent ontology embedded within secular managerial structures. What is needed is a kind of "Catholic Critical Theory" that empowers bishops, priests, and lay leaders in ecclesial institutions or apostolates to critically evaluate the concealed but potent ontologies operative in the various management theories or mechanisms employed in other facets of human society.[17] The hidden but robust mechanistic onto-logic of managerial thought usurps one's conception of reality as such, imposing an individualistic, cold and mechanical ontology thereby blocking authentic communion and impairing the Church's capacity to enact its mission.

A Communio Alternative

Taking heed of Schindler's warning, it is evident that the danger that accompanies the rise of managerialism within the Church and her institutions is that the Church herself comes to be understood as coming into existence as the result of human action, or that it can be measured by standards set outside of its relationship with God. Under the tyranny of managerial structures concepts such as Key Performance Indicators (KPIs), Risk Assessment and Management Plans (RAMPs), costs, efficiencies, profits and competition

---

16. On this point we refer you to the excellent essay, Rowland, "Authority of 'Experts,'" 744–70.

17. I am indebted to Dr. Wanda Skowronska for this notion of a Catholic Critical Theory.

come to dominate modes of thought and activity leaving anything that is not easily quantified undervalued or abandoned.

As Ratzinger pointed out, however, "the reality of the Church is far greater than what you can tabulate in statistics or achieve by decisions."[18] The church does not extend its mission by merely meeting various KPI's formulated in parish councils, priest zone meetings, School boards, Bishops conferences and synods, or questionnaires formulated in a dubious attempt to provide bishops with the *sensus fidei*. To think that it does, betrays a fundamental misunderstanding of the nature of church as communion.[19]

There are two essential characteristics of the Church understood as communion that we would like to propose to form a basic counter balance to the managerial, bureaucratized modes of ecclesial existence that we have sketched above. These include a fundamental posture of receptivity and contemplation, as well as a commitment to the mission of the Church as witness bestowed upon her by Jesus Christ [see Matt 28:19], ultimately bearing the form of the martyr.

Receptivity and Contemplation

Schindler, following St Paul, describes the Church as the ongoing presence of Jesus in the world, and as the means of man's relation with God. "The church," he writes, "is not in the first instance a community of people who establish their identity as church as it were 'from below,' in and by themselves. On the contrary, the Church, in and by means of the Holy Spirit, is already—from the beginning—identitfied with Jesus: it *is* his Body and hence *is* his message." Schindler continues to emphasize both the given and the relational aspect of this: "The church of its own inner essence—that is, as established by God through Christ in the Holy Spirit—really participates in the relation of unity with the Father which Christ himself is."[20] The church is the means of humanity's relationship with God.

Schindler emphasizes that human creativity is analogous to the creativity of the Father, only in the receptivity of the Son.[21] Schindler writes;

> The notion here of a love that is first received is Crucial: "this is the love I mean: not our love for God, but God's love for us"

18. Ratzinger and Seewald, *God and the World*, 343.

19. See CDF, "On Some Aspects."

20. Schindler, "Catholicity and the State of Contemporary Theology," 429. Schindler's description here bears a striking resemblance to that of Luigi Giussani. See particularly Giussani, *Why the Church?*

21. Schindler, *Heart of the World*, 37.

(1 John 4:10). Creatures are first *from God:* they image the divine *communio personarum* through the initiative of God in Jesus Christ, and are thus born of God's love—indeed, in the order of history, they are receivers of God's love through the archetypical *fiat* of Mary and of Christ's Bride, the Church. The meaning and the dignity of creatures therefore lie most fundamentally not in something creatures themselves do but in what they *are*: in the very *be*ing that they first *receive*. Being receptive of God's love is the fundamental fact about created being, the constitutive condition *of* being, the inner-anterior condition of all creaturely doing and making.[22]

This notion of receptivity is a constant trope in the work of theologians associated with the *Communio* ecclesiological framework.

Immediately it becomes evident how this stands at odds with the fundamental liberal assertion of man as first/primarily radically creative or self-asserting. In his own disputation with Catholic neoconservatives, Schindler points out that, while creativity is indeed an important element in a Christian anthropology, it is not and cannot be primary. Instead, Schindler emphasizes that the primary mode, or posture, of the creaturely being must be first receptive prior to it being creative.

Schindler's insistence on receptivity as the most adequate and fundamental creaturely posture (as exemplified particularly by the Blessed Virgin Mary) is objectionable to the modern liberal, who praises the independent functionary. The receptive dependence advocated by Schindler negates, for the liberal thinker, any real autonomy on the part of the creaturely being leaving them with little more than a fabricated freedom wherein being itself remains bound in a humiliating passively receptive relation to God. Schindler however, is careful to assert that contrary to being a source of humiliation for the creature, a primary mode or posture of active receptivity is what in fact allows the creature to then participate in the generative/creative gift giving proper to its nature. Schindler describes this receptivity as primarily and at once both Christological (as in the case of Christ's *fiat* in the Garden of Gethsemane, see Matt 26:38) and Marian, and develops this with recourse to the *fiat* and subsequent *Magnificat* of the Blessed Virgin Mary.[23]

"My proposal," states Schindler,

hinges most directly and decisively on a double affirmation by the pope [John Paul II]: that Jesus Christ "fully reveals man to

---

22. Schindler, *Heart of the World*, xv.

23. Importantly, Mary's receptive *fiat* is related analogically to receptivity in the Trinity, because Mary receives something totally other to her (beyond her nature).

himself" (*GS*, 22); and that, "totally dependent on Christ and completely directed toward him, Mary is the most perfect image of freedom and of the liberation of humanity and for the universe" (*Redemptoris Mater*, 37). This summary affirmation entails a unified Gospel spirituality: there is a single *basic* spirituality for all Christians, and Mary is the model of that spirituality. Or, as Balthasar puts it: "The Marian *fiat* is the '*Urakt*': the primary or originating act that serves as the ground of all Christian life and action."[24]

Schindler is not advocating a view of creaturely being (i.e., the human person) as a passive automaton. In pointing to Mary as the archetype of creaturely receptivity, Schindler illustrates a receptivity that is active.[25] Her *fiat* is no mere flaccid acceptance of the inevitable, but a free and efficacious volition to accept and bear the Word within her.

It is in this sense that, in the *active* receptivity of her *fiat*, Mary becomes the archetype of all creation and of the Church. It is in her *fiat*, states Schindler, that Mary "reveals in all of its profundity what it means to be a creature."[26] Furthermore, Schindler argues, "The *fiat* expresses the dependent relation on God that discloses the inner meaning of all of reality as gift, [and] which in turn disposes one towards service. All that I am I have been *given*—by God in Jesus Christ; and what has been given is to be shared."[27] Here one can see clearly the operation of *fiat*/*Magnificat* dynamic within a Christian spirituality that first receives, and then creatively shares. Schindler goes on to assert that "a self formed in the *fiat* and the *Magnificat* is a self whose disposition of grateful receiving informs all of its doing, having, and making—a self that recognizes that it is, *strictly*, never the owner of its being and acting."[28]

In commenting on this Marian dimension of Schindler's ontology, English author Stratford Caldecott writes that "Mary's 'letting be'—conventionally described as obedience or submission—can be traced back all the way to the Trinity itself."[29] In asserting thus, Caldecott describes how Schindler supersedes what he sees as a "defect" (Schindler's term) in the Aristotelian-Thomistic metaphysics, which would prohibit appropriating

---

24. Schindler, *Heart of the World*, 92.
25. Schindler, *Heart of the World*, 232–33.
26. Schindler, *Heart of the World*, 93.
27. Schindler, *Heart of the World*, 93.
28. Schindler, *Heart of the World*, 93.
29. Caldecott, "Marian Dimension of Existence," 288.

receptivity as an attribute of God, regarding receptivity as a deficiency.³⁰ Caldecott argues that for Schindler, "the capacity to receive is a necessary complement to self-communication in and between the divine persons." Thus, he continues: "One might say, perhaps, that the *fiat* of Jesus does not merely show him as receptive in his human nature to the divine will, but expresses a quality in the divine nature itself. (Jesus is not simply obedient to *his own* divine will, but precisely as Son is obedient to the will *of the Father.*)"³¹

Importantly, Schindler asserts that man images this receptive character operative within the Trinitarian relations *prior* to his imaging of the creativity of God in his (man's) creativity:

> Man images the *creativity of God the Father and Creator only in and through the* receptivity of Jesus Christ and his mother Mary. The divine creativity of which human creativity is the image, in other words, is first that of Sonship and not that of Fatherhood. We are "sons in the Son": we represent the creativity of the Father only through the Son (cf. Col 1:15–16), and indeed through the archetypal creature, Mary—the freedom or love of both of whom consists first in receptive obedience.³²

For Schindler, as demonstrated above, the Marian/receptive form of creation as such is related analogously to the Trinity itself.³³ "Crucial to Schindler's gift-ontology," writes Caldecott, "is the fact that created being, too, has a

---

30. Schindler's work here bears the marked influence of Jesuit Father W. Norris Clarke, SJ. An important discussion on divine and creaturely receptivity and the notion of receptivity as a perfection is taken up in a lively discussion carried out on the pages of the *Communio* journal (Spring 1994), between Norris Clarke, Steven A. Long, George A. Blair, and David L. Schindler. See Schindler, *Heart of the World*, 275–311. As the late Stratford Caldecott has noted: "This theology [which speaks of receptivity in God] is controversial in Thomist circles, not least because of the notion that there is "receptivity" in God. But as David L. Schindler and Norris Clark have shown, receptivity here is not an imperfection, and not to be confused with passivity or potentiality. It is in fact a kind of activity" Caldecott, "Theology of Gift," n12. For another series of relevant arguments, see also the debate between W. Norris Clark, Kenneth Schmitz, and Steven A. Long. Clarke, "Reply to Steven Long," 617–24; Long, "Personal Receptivity and Act," 1–31; Schmitz, "Created Receptivity," 339–71.

31. Caldecott, "Marian Dimension of Existence," 289.

32. Schindler, *Heart of the World*, 118. Here Schindler cites Balthasar, *Theology of History*, 25–33; *Unless You Become Like This Child*.

33. As always, Schindler is clear that in any discussion of analogy between creator and creature allowance be made for the *maior dissimilitudo* clarified in the Lateran IV Council. "Because between the Creator and the creature there cannot be a likeness so great that the unlikeness is not greater" Schroeder, *Disciplinary Decrees of the General Councils*, 337.

triadic structure because it participates in this Trinitarian form—it is 'from,' 'in,' and 'for' (or 'toward')—with receptivity fundamental to its nature as gift."[34] Schindler explains,

> Creatures are first *from God*: they image the divine *communio personarum* through the initiative of God in Jesus Christ, and are thus born of God's love—indeed, in the one and only order of history, they are receivers of God's love through the archetypical *fiat* of Mary and of Christ's Bride, the Church. The meaning and the dignity of creatures therefore lie most fundamentally not in something creatures themselves do but in what they *are*: in the very *being* that they first *receive*. Being receptive of God's love is the fundamental fact about created being, the constitutive condition *of* being, the inner-anterior condition of all creaturely doing and making.[35]

Schindler emphasizes the importance of receptivity in the life of the individual believer, but also corporately in the life of the Church as *communio*. In this Mary is an exemplary type of the Church, first receptive and contemplative, and only then active. Her *fiat* precedes her *Magnificat* not only chronologically but also ontologically. Strikingly, this model of receptive-contemplative-active is inverted in a managerial approach described above, where primacy of action is prized far over and above contemplation, often to its exclusion. This managerial tendency so rife in modern liberal culture results in extroversion, mechanism, and instrumentalism.

For Schindler the characterization of the Church as feminine is also of crucial importance. Much more than mere rhetorical nicety, it is an ontological perfection. The church can only adequately respond to Christ's spousal invitation as feminine, epitomized by Mary by whose *fiat* He first came into the world, and through whom His grace is mediated.[36]

Importantly, this primacy of contemplative receptivity does not negate the need to act. Nevertheless, it is crucial that we understand contemplation as the anterior condition, both prior and immanent, for all human action. Schindler argues that "the contemplative life must be intrinsically ordered toward activity. But action must take its form from within contemplation."[37] On the fundamental level of the organization and management of parish life, this could be achieved for example in a prayerful contemplative mode of decision making that emerges not out of functionary policies and procedures

---

34. Caldecott, "Marian Dimension of Existence," 289.
35. Schindler, *Heart of the World*, xv.
36. See Schindler, *Heart of the World*, 39.
37. Schindler, *Heart of the World*, 233.

that do not account for individual and collective interests, but out of time collectively spent in adoration of Our Eucharistic Lord, or engaged in some other pious practice. This prevents action from being a harsh, extroverted, and superficial doing and making, and it keeps contemplation from becoming a navel gazing, barren theorizing. Contemplation must always be ordered to action, which must always receive its impetus from contemplation. This paradoxical relationship is brought to light by another author from within the *Communio* setting, Hans Urs von Balthasar, who writes:

> Whoever desires greater action needs better contemplation; whoever wants to play a more formative role must pray and obey more profoundly; whoever wants to achieve additional goals must grasp the uselessness and futility, the uncalculating and incalculable (hence "unprofitable") nature of the eternal love in Christ, as well as of every love along the path of Christian discipleship. Whoever wants to command must have learned to follow in a Christ-like manner; whoever wants to administer the goods of the world must first have freed himself from all desire for possession; whoever wants to show the world Christian love must have practiced the love of Christ (even in marriage) to the point of pure selflessness. . . . Every program of mission to the world must at all times contain what Guardini called "the discernment of what is Christian."[38]

Witness

Beyond this primary and fundamentally constitutive ecclesiological posture of receptivity and contemplation, another essential element of the Church that is particularly occluded following the managerial creep described above is that of the Church as missionary—as authentic witness to the truth (cf. Matt 29:19).

As has been articulated consistently by the pontificates of the late twentieth/early twenty-first century, the call to proclaim the gospel in contemporary times must be much more than the presentation of rational propositions to which the assent of the intellect is required. Pope Benedict XVI expressed this sentiment with characteristic eloquence when he wrote that "being Christian is not the result of an ethical choice or a lofty idea, but the encounter with an event, a person, which gives life a new horizon and a decisive direction."[39] This has found particular resonance with Pope

---

38. Balthasar, *My Work*, 52.
39. Benedict XVI, "Deus Caritas Est," 1.

Francis, who like Benedict XVI and John Paul II before him, has sought to emphasize with a particular priority the mercy/love of God incarnated in the context of the person to person relationship, noting with specific emphasis the person of Jesus as the Incarnation, or enfleshment, of the the Father's mercy/love.[40] The mission of the Church to proclaim the gospel to all nations is achieved by incarnating the mercy of God personally, and as such, involves what the Second Vatican Council referred to as a gift of self.[41] This gift of self, something of a recurrent theme in the pontificate of St John Paul II, implies a particular vulnerability, a significant risk, to the point of losing ones' life [cf. Matt 10:39].

This ideal of witness as articulated in the Gospels and in the life of the Church is one that is only possible in the flesh, so to speak—person to person. It is, however, precisely such personal contact that is inhibited in the operations of the mechanisms of bureaucratic structures. So, while managerial structures may be employed for a variety of reasons, such as ensuring professionalized governance, streamlining the activities of an organization, or ensuring that risks to persons or the assets of institutions are appropriately mitigated, these structures effectively depersonalize any potential or actual encounters between persons inhibiting opportunities for authentic witness in the context of said encounter. These aims of professionalization, economic rationalization, and risk management might be pursued in good faith, but when they are transposed uncritically into ecclesial settings, such activity stifles the achievement of the elemental mission of the Church [cf. Matt 28:19]. Instead of authentic human contact, managerial machinations erect a buffer around individuals and organizations that, while offering protection and reducing risk, inhibits one's capacity to be vulnerable to another or to open oneself in genuine compassion towards another. While authentic service to the mission of the Church always bears a cruciform character and must come by way of the Cross, the buffered environment established as a result of the employment of managerial, bureaucratized structures operates at all times to minimize the risk of vulnerability. If the witness of individuals and of institutions hoping to bear the name Christian must, as articulated in the Dogmatic Constitution on the Church, *Lumen Gentium,* embrace the form of the martyr as the form of Christian existence,[42] this becomes increasingly difficult, perhaps even impossible in environments dominated by managerial and bureaucratized structure.

40. In addition to the Extraordinary Jubilee of Mercy 2016, initiated by Pope Francis in 2016, see Francis, *Name of God.* See also John Paul II, "Dives in Misericordia," 7: "For mercy is an indispensable dimension of love; it is as it were love's second name."

41. Paul VI, *Gaudium et Spes,* 24.

42. See Second Vatican Council, *Lumen Gentium,* 42.

Beyond this, it is evident that such managerial and bureaucratic structures have an implicitly formative character on the people embedded within these institutions who act as functionaries and managers. As has been argued above, these liberal, managerial structures project an apparent metaphysical neutrality and as such, they are perceived merely as dumb tools. This projected and perceived structural neutrality entices well-meaning Christians to attempt to co-opt these putatively empty structures, with the intention of imbuing them with "gospel values," unaware of the perniciously powerful and even evangelical nature of the metaphysics hidden within.[43]

So while secular managerial structures might be engaged as simple tools at the service of the promotion of the success of church institutions or diocesan chancelleries, "success," to quote David L. Schindler, "is not a Gospel category."[44] Schindler may here be accused of something of a self-sabotaging martyr complex, but such claims are little more than an ill-informed caricature of his position. For in his affirmation of the radically different measures for success for ecclesial and non-ecclesial spheres, Schindler is decidedly Christological. Success, in the end, is embodied in a holiness that is fundamentally and inescapably cruciform. In emphasizing this his thinking bears a striking resemblance to that of Joseph Ratzinger/Pope Benedict XVI who stated that "what the Church needs to respond to the needs of man in every age is holiness and not management."[45]

This, of course, is not to say that a manager cannot be holy or that the grace of God cannot overcome manmade managerial and bureaucratic structures. Rather it is to point out first, that holiness, a deeply personal and interior reality, simply cannot be transposed into managerial structures that are fundamentally mechanistic/extrinsic and depersonalized; and second, that such managerial and bureaucratic structures implicitly form those who work within them such that the risk inherent not only in Christian mission/

---

43. While a great deal of this analysis relies on the work of David L. Schindler, it is important to note that Schindler himself does not speak of liberal structures as "evangelizing" *per se*, although there is much in his work that would seem to be in agreement with the use of this particular term to describe the effect that liberal structures have on persons and institutions that make use of, or attempt to co-opt them. My use of the term in this context is indebted to the work of Reformed theologian and philosopher, James K. A. Smith, whose analysis is in many ways similar to that of Schindler, notwithstanding important divergences. Smith's description of the evangelical potency of secular liturgies bears a striking resemblance to Schindler's own critique of secular-liberal structures. See Smith, *Desiring the Kingdom*; *Imagining the Kingdom*; *You Are What You Love*, 27–55.

44. Chapp and Howsare, "David L. Schindler," 211.

45. Ratzinger and Messori, *Ratzinger Report*, 52–53.

witness, but in authentic human interaction more generally comes to be viewed as something to be avoided at all costs.

Conclusion

The managerial logic described above and experienced in the day to day of modern Western cultures, does a fundamental damage to the human person's capacity to open himself or herself up to relationship, and consequently, to participate in the mission of the Church—a mission characterized most fundamentally by *communio*, by friendship with Christ (cf. John 15). Managerialism stifles relationships, prioritizing processes over persons, and conceives of any relationships between persons as fundamentally extrinsic to them as persons. Managerial logic is first active, rather than receptive; it is cold, impersonal, and dead, rather than cordial and living; it is characterized by externality of relations, rather than an intrinsic openness to the other.[46]

For the most part, we can be safe in our assumption that the application of secular management theories and practices within the Church is attempted in good faith—most often such application is done with little reflection at all. Following Schindler however, one can see the veiled metaphysical content of such theories and practices which are often presented as mere tools that are empty of such metaphysical content and as such can be utilized uncritically for the betterment of the Church, and the serving of its mission. Our aim has been to demonstrate first that such theories, structures, and practices are in fact imbued with definite metaphysical content, and that such content prohibits authentic relationality—it inhibits communion.

Bibliography

Balthasar, Hans Urs von. *My Work: In Retrospect*. San Francisco: Ignatius, 1993.
———. *A Theology of History*. New York: Sheed and Ward, 1963.
———. *Unless You Become Like This Child*. San Francisco: Ignatius, 1991.
Benedict XVI. "Deus Caritas Est: On Christian Love." December 25, 2005. Online. http://w2.vatican.va/content/benedict-xvi/en/encyclicals/documents/hf_ben-xvi_enc_20051225_deus-caritas-est.html.
Caldecott, Stratford. "The Marian Dimension of Existence." In *Being Holy in the World: Theology and Culture in the Thought of David L. Schindler*, edited by Nicholas J. Healy and D. C. Schindler, 281–94. Grand Rapids: Eerdmans, 2011.

---

46. Of course, an ethos of non-receptive voluntarism and mechanistic bureaucracy are fully compatible with collectivism and Marxism, but the focus of this chapter has been Western modernity in its dominant liberal form.

———. "A Theology of Gift: The Divine Benefactor and Universal Kinship." *Imaginative Conservative*, December 9, 2018. Online. https://theimaginativeconservative.org/2018/12/theology-gift-divine-benefactor-kinship-stratford-caldecott.html.

Cavanaugh, William T. *Theopolitcal Imagination: Discovering the Liturgy as a Political Act in an Age of Global Consumerism*. London: T&T Clark, 2002.

Chapp, Larry S., and Rodney A. Howsare. "David L. Schindler and the Order of Modernity: Toward a Working Definition of Liberalism." In *Being Holy in the World: Theology and Culture in the Thought of David L. Schindler*, edited by Nicholas J. Healy and D. C. Schindler. Grand Rapids: Eerdmans, 2011.

Clarke, W. Norris. "Reply to Steven Long: A Re-Evaluation of the Notion of 'Receptivity' as a Positive Ontological Perfection in the Thoughts of Thomas Aquinas." *The Thomist* 61 (1997) 617–24.

Congregation for the Doctrine of the Faith (CDF). "On Some Aspects of the Church Understood as Communion." May 28, 1992. Online. http://www.vatican.va/roman_curia/congregations/cfaith/documents/rc_con_cfaith_doc_28051992_communionis-notio_en.html.

Deneen, Patrick J. "A Catholic Showdown Worth Watching." *American Conservative*, February 6, 2014. Online. http://www.theamericanconservative.com/2014/02/06/a-catholic-showdown-worth-watching.

Fisher, Anthony. *Catholic Bioethics for a New Millennium*. New York: Cambridge University Press, 2012.

Francis. *The Name of God Is Mercy*. Translated by Oonagh Stransky. New York: Pan Macmillan, 2017.

Giussani, Luigi. *Why the Church?* Translated by Viviane Hewitt. Montreal: McGill-Queen's University Press, 2001.

John Paul II. "Dives in Misericordia." November 30, 1980. Online. https://w2.vatican.va/content/john-paul-ii/en/encyclicals/documents/hf_jp-ii_enc_30111980_dives-in-misericordia.html.

Jones, Brian. "Parish Mission Statements and Authentic Ecclesiology." *Catholic World Report*, September 12, 2013. https://www.catholicworldreport.com/2013/09/12/parish-mission-statements-and-authentic-ecclesiology.

Long, Steven A. "Personal Receptivity and Act: A Thomistic Critique." *The Thomist* 61 (1997) 1–31.

Lowery, Mark. "The Dialogue between Catholic 'Neoconservatives' and Catholic 'Cultural Radicals': Toward a New Horizon." *Catholic Social Science Review* 3 (1998) 41–61.

MacIntyre, Alasdair. *Whose Justice? Which Rationality?* Notre Dame, IN: University of Notre Dame Press, 1988.

Paul VI. *Gaudium et Spes—Pastoral Constitution of the Church in the Modern World*. Vatican City: Libreria Editrice Vaticana, 1965.

Ratzinger, Joseph. *Called to Communion: Understanding the Church Today*. Translated by Adrian Walker. San Francisco: Ignatius, 2010.

Ratzinger, Joseph, and Vittorio Messori. *The Ratzinger Report: An Exclusive Interview on the State of the Church*. Translated by Salvator Attanasio and Graham Harrison. San Francisco: Ignatius, 1985.

Ratzinger, Joseph, and Peter Seewald. *God and the World: Believing and Living in Our Time: A Conversation with Peter Seewald*. Translated by Henry Taylor. San Francisco: Ignatius, 2002.

Rawls, John. "Justice as Fairness: Political Not Metaphysical." *Philosophy and Public Affairs* 14 (1985) 223–51.
Rowland, Tracey. "The Authority of 'Experts' and the Ethos of Modern Institutions." *Communio: International Catholic Review* 28 (2001) 744–70.
Schindler, David L. "Catholicity and the State of Contemporary Theology: The Need for an Onto-Logic of Holiness." *Communio: International Catholic Review* 14 (1987) 426–50.
———. "Grace and the Form of Nature and Culture." In *Catholicism and Secularization in America: Essays on Nature, Grace, and Culture*, edited by David L. Schindler, 10–30. Huntington, IN: Our Sunday Visitor, 1990.
———. *Heart of the World, Center of the Church: Communio Ecclesiology, Liberalism and Liberation*. Grand Rapids: Eerdmans, 1996.
Schmitz, Kenneth. L. "Created Receptivity and the Philosophy of the Concrete." *The Thomist* 61 (1997) 339–71.
Schroeder, H. J. *Disciplinary Decrees of the General Councils: Text, Translation and Commentary*. St Louis: B. Herder, 1937.
Second Vatican Council. *Lumen Gentium: Dogmatic Constitution on the Church*. Vatican City: Libreria Editrice Vaticana, 1965.
Shakespeare, Lyndon. *Being the Body of Christ in the Age of Management*. Edited by Conor Cunningham and Eric Austen Lee. Eugene, OR: Wipf and Stock, 2016.
Shklar, Judith. *Ordinary Vices*. Cambridge, MA: Harvard University Press, 1984.
Smith, James K. A. *Desiring the Kingdom: Worship, Worldview and Cultural Formation*. Vol. 1 of *Cultural Liturgies*. Grand Rapids: Baker Academic, 2009.
———. *Imagining the Kingdom: How Worship Works*. Vol 2 of *Cultural Liturgies*. Grand Rapids: Baker Academic, 2013.
———. *You Are What You Love: The Spiritual Power of Habit*. Grand Rapids: Brazos, 2016.
Watson, Don. *Death Sentence: The Decay of Public Language*. Sydney: Penguin, 2004.
———. "Vital Lessons from the Day Words Fell Short." *The Age*, September 19, 2009. Online. https://www.theage.com.au/politics/federal/vital-lessons-from-the-day-words-fell-short-20090918-fvfr.html.

5

The Baptismal Priesthood
Confusion and Potential

—Fr James Baxter, OP

> *Paragraph 10 of Lumen Gentium contains a well-known description of the common priesthood of the faithful and the ministerial priesthood as differing from one another "in essence and not only in degree." Much attention since the Second Vatican Council has been focused on explaining the essential difference between the two priesthoods, but little attention has been paid to the difference in degree. Some scholars have even suggested that the phrase means that there is no difference in degree at all between the two priesthoods. In this chapter I discuss some of the reasons for hesitation in asserting a difference between the priesthoods, and I argue that there is indeed a difference in degree between them. I set out what that difference consists in, by analyzing them both with reference to the one priesthood of Jesus Christ.*

Everyone who practices the Catholic faith must at some stage come to terms with the gap between the ideal and the reality. In everything from personal holiness, to the Catholic intellectual tradition, liturgical worship, and parish life, church documents set forth an ideal of how things are meant to be in the life of the Church. Reality is often otherwise. This gap is nowhere vaster than in certain of the documents of the Second Vatican Council. The vision for liturgy, for example, in *Sacrosanctum*

Concilium has gone famously unrealized. One reads in that document of an expectation that the chief hours of the Divine Office, particularly Vespers, should be celebrated in common in church on Sundays and on the more solemn feasts.[1] A grand idea, and one hardly ever implemented. It is, though, about one particular way among many in which people are encouraged to pray. The document on the Church, *Lumen Gentium*, deals with more fundamental question, touching on basic questions of identity: What does it mean to belong to the Church? What are the implications of being baptized?

If one were to approach a selection of Catholics on the steps of the Church on a Sunday, and ask them the question, "What happened when you were baptized?" most would probably know that that was when they joined the Church. The more theologically well-formed might be able to expound on the life of grace, or their adoption as children of God. But rare would be the Catholic who could explain—or who could even recall ever hearing—that through baptism they were incorporated into a priesthood, a priesthood that is a participation in the one priesthood of Jesus Christ.

The intention at Vatican II was otherwise. In *Lumen Gentium*, the Council Fathers gave an expansive teaching on the priesthood. Following the scriptural teaching particularly found in the Letter to the Hebrews (5:1–5), *Lumen Gentium* teaches that there is one priesthood, the priesthood of Jesus Christ.[2] There are, though, two ways in which human beings participate in this priesthood. The most well-known way is through the ministerial priesthood, received by the sacrament of holy orders. But the most common way is through the priesthood that is possessed by all the baptized, known as the "common priesthood" or the "baptismal priesthood." The scriptural basis for this teaching is the First Letter of Peter, in which early Christians are addressed as a "royal priesthood" (1 Pet 2:9), and are encouraged to be built into "a spiritual house, to be a holy priesthood" (1 Pet 2:5). This priesthood is exercised in the offering of "spiritual sacrifices acceptable to God through Jesus Christ" (1 Pet 2:5) and of declaring "the wonderful deeds of him who called you out of darkness into his marvelous light" (1 Pet 2:9). The Council taught that it is in virtue of their priesthood that all the faithful join in offering the Eucharist, and "exercise that priesthood in receiving the sacraments, in prayer and thanksgiving, in the witness of a holy life, and by self-denial and active charity."[3]

---

1. Second Vatican Council, "Sacrosanctum Concilium" no. 100.
2. Second Vatican Council, "Lumen Gentium" no. 10.
3. Second Vatican Council, "Lumen Gentium" no. 10.

The Development of the Modern Teaching

Lumen Gentium's teaching on the baptismal priesthood resulted from a lengthy movement to acknowledge and develop the role of the laity in the Church. Although the baptismal priesthood is not identical to the laity (given that priests also possess the baptismal priesthood), it is nevertheless the case that the laity comprises the great majority of the baptismal priesthood, and discussions of the baptismal priesthood are often commingled with those of the laity. The writings of John Henry Newman in the mid-nineteenth century were critical for the modern development of the role of the laity. As Newman's ideas were disseminated among Catholic Europe in several waves into the twentieth century, his writings on the laity grew in influence. The liturgical movement, ecumenism, and heightened lay apostolic involvement in the Church, for example through Catholic Action, were other forces that coalesced to influence a rediscovery, largely lost after the Protestant Reformation, of the importance of the baptismal priesthood.

In the twentieth century, teaching on the baptismal priesthood began to emerge in documents issued by the magisterium. In 1922, Pius XI gave the following encouragement to bishops in his encyclical *Ubi Arcano*:

> Tell your faithful children of the laity that when, united with their pastors and their bishops, they participate in the works of the apostolate, both individual and social, the end purpose of which is to make Jesus Christ better known and better loved, then they are more than ever "a chosen generation, a kingly priesthood, a holy nation, a purchased people," of whom St Peter spoke in such laudatory terms.[4]

Even though Pius XI would on more than one occasion remind his readers of the priesthood possessed by all the faithful, he still saw it in terms highly auxiliary to the ministerial priesthood. In a revealing passage in his 1935 encyclical on the priesthood, *Ad Catholici Sacerdotii*, he praises the work of lay Catholics participating in Catholic Action. Although he commends Catholic Action as a work of the baptismal priesthood, for Pius XI the best exercise of that priesthood is through producing (ministerial) priestly and religious vocations:

> For by Catholic Action the laity share in the hierarchical apostolate of the Church, and hence it cannot neglect this vital problem of priestly vocations. Comfort has filled Our heart to see the associates of Catholic Action everywhere distinguishing

---

4. Pius XI, "Ubi Arcano" no. 58. See also Pius XI, "Miserentissimus Redemptor" no. 9.

> themselves in all fields of Christian activity, but especially in this. Certainly the richest reward of such activity is that really wonderful number of priestly and religious vocations which continue to flourish in their organizations for the young.... Let [members of Catholic Action] be persuaded that, *in no better way than by this work for an increase in the ranks of the secular and regular clergy, can the Catholic laity really participate in the high dignity of the "kingly priesthood"* which the Prince of the Apostles attributes to the whole body of the redeemed.[5]

We see then that in the 1920s and 1930s, magisterial teaching on the baptismal priesthood was in a state of development. Its importance was being reasserted, but its highest value lay in the numbers it added to the ministerial priesthood. The teaching would continue to develop with Pius XII, who in *Mediator Dei* stressed that the faithful also offer the Eucharistic sacrifice with the ministerial priest:

> Nor is it to be wondered at, that the faithful should be raised to this dignity. By the waters of baptism, as by common right, Christians are made members of the Mystical Body of Christ the Priest, and by the "character" which is imprinted on their souls, they are appointed to give worship to God. Thus they participate, according to their condition, in the priesthood of Christ.[6]

Pius XII gave a different emphasis to the baptismal priesthood than his predecessor had, less on apostolic works than on liturgical worship. He saw a prayerful self-offering in the sacrifice of the Mass as the truest meaning of a "spiritual sacrifice," which then in turn makes one's faith more ready to work through charity.[7]

Also during the pontificate of Pius XII, there began to be greater discussion among theologians of what was initially termed the "lay priesthood." The term itself demonstrates that theologians were still negotiating how best to speak of the baptismal priesthood. A Jesuit sacramental theologian, Paul F. Palmer wrote at length of the historical development of the baptismal priesthood.[8] The titles of his articles—*The Lay Priesthood: Real or Metaphorical?*; *Lay Priesthood: Towards a Terminology*—give some indication of how much of the discussion of the baptismal priesthood at this time comprised the attempts of theologians almost tangibly feeling their way around the subject. Palmer relates the puzzlement of theologians as

---

5. Pius XI, "Ad Catholici Sacerdotii" no. 79 (emphasis added).
6. Pius XII, "Mediator Dei" no. 88.
7. Pius XII, "Mediator Dei" no. 99.
8. Palmer, "Real or Metaphorical," 574–613; "Towards a Terminology," 235–50.

to what kind of priesthood the lay priesthood actually is. In 1948, a panel discussion at the American Catholic Theological Society was devoted to the question "In what sense is the layman priestly?" a question to which they did not seem to reach a resolution.[9] Palmer brought some welcome clarity to the debate when he made the distinction that although the laity share in the priesthood of Christ, in no way do they share in the ministerial priesthood which is conferred in the sacrament of orders: "The priesthood of the laity and that of orders differ not only in degree but also in kind."[10]

Difference of degree

By the time of Vatican II, the teaching had developed such that *Lumen Gentium* contained a fuller teaching on the baptismal priesthood than had previously been seen in a magisterial document. But, as Palmer had earlier anticipated, it was a teaching that brought with it an obvious question—what is the difference between the priesthoods? That is what the Council Fathers sought to clarify in paragraph 10 of *Lumen Gentium*, with this statement:

> Though they differ from one another in essence and not only in degree, the common priesthood of the faithful and the ministerial or hierarchical priesthood are nonetheless interrelated: each of them in its own special way is a participation in the one priesthood of Christ.[11]

The statement is clear enough that there is a difference between the priesthoods, but what is the difference in essence? What is the difference in degree? The difference of essence lies in the fact that the baptismal and ministerial priesthoods are two distinct realities. The ontological basis for each is a separate sacrament, giving rise also to distinct modes of sacrifice. The essential difference between the priesthoods is most evident at the offering of the Eucharistic sacrifice, where although all present join in the offering of the sacrifice, only the ministerial priest does so acting in the person of Christ. Here, though, there is also a difference of degree. Christ is the head of the body, the Church, and the Mass is the offering of both Christ and his church. But since the ministerial priest—who as a baptized Christian is a member of the body—acts in the person of Christ, he also represents Christ to the faithful as the head of the body.[12]

---

9. Palmer, "Real or Metaphorical," 235n2.
10. Palmer, "Real or Metaphorical," 237–38.
11. Second Vatican Council, "Lumen Gentium" no. 10.
12. For an extensive explanation of differences of degree in the *tri munera* offices of

Much of the theological commentary since the Council has sought to explain the difference in essence, and how the two priesthoods are ordered to each other. The difference of degree is rarely treated, and when it is, it is often given a surprising angle, one that that brings confusion where there was supposed to be clarity. One would think that the sentence "they differ from one another in essence and not only in degree," necessarily implies that there is a difference of degree. Degree of *what* is a separate question, but that there is a difference of degree seems beyond question.

But questioned it is, and even outright rejected. Michael Richards, for example, argues that the ministerial priesthood does not differ in degree *at all* from the baptismal priesthood. He writes:

> it is affirming "essence" and setting "degree" aside. It is saying that if you want to understand what difference ordination makes, you must look for an *essential* difference, a difference *in kind* not a mere difference of degree: degree simply does not enter into it.[13]

In support of Richards is Daniel Donovan, who states that, "The relation between the priesthoods is not one of degree. . . . The ministerial priesthood does not fit in at a particular point on the scale of holiness, but is rather of a different order."[14] Likewise, Jean-Pierre Torrell, in one of the most substantial modern works on the baptismal priesthood, also rejects a difference in degree:

> If one says that the two priesthoods differ *not only in degree*, one is suggesting that they *also* differ in degree. But there is nothing of that here. The difference between them is not a simply one of more or less, as if they were situation along the same ascending line.[15]

Note that none of these authors is simply favoring the explanatory power of an essential difference over a difference in degree. Each is dismissing a difference in degree entirely. Their position seems so radically at odds with the plain and ordinary meaning of the text that it deserves detailed examination.

---

priest, prophet, and king, see De La Soujeole, "Différence d'essence," 621–38.

13. Richards, "Hierarchy and Priesthood," 229.
14. Donovan, *What Are They Saying*, 8.
15. Torrell, *Priestly People*, 137.

Latin Phraseology

Among the common arguments against a difference in degree, the reasoning takes three general forms. The first is an argument from the phrase used to express the difference in the original Latin text. The phrase in question is *non gradu tantum* ("not only in degree") in *essentia et non gradu tantum differant* ("they differ in essence and not only in degree"). According to Richards, the choice of *non gradu tantum* instead of other possible phrases was a deliberate one from the Council, to avoid the suggestion that there is a difference *both* in essence *and* in degree:

> The Council could have said 'both . . . and' (*et . . . et*); it could have said 'not only . . . but also' (*non tantum . . . sed etiam*); and it could have said 'together with' (*una cum*; a favorite conjunction in the documents of Vatican II). But it did not. It chose to use a precise form of words which in Latin indicates that the given alternative is to be excluded as irrelevant.[16]

This latter claim would have greater heft had Richards offered examples from Latin literature, each of them obviously excluding a both/and interpretation, but no examples are offered. Moreover, while *Lumen Gentium*, as a conciliar document, carries a level of authority exceeding that of documents from the ordinary magisterium, it nevertheless must be read within the magisterial tradition. It is therefore significant that both before and after *Lumen Gentium* we find magisterial documents that, using different turns of phrase, clearly express a difference both in essence and in degree. The first is the 1954 papal allocution *Magnificate Dominum*, in which Pius XII reiterated that Christ's faithful have a kind of "priesthood" (the inverted commas are his). But, he warned,

> whatever is the full meaning of this honorable title and claim, it must be firmly held that the "priesthood" common to all the faithful, high and reserved as it is, differs not only in degree, but in essence also [*non gradu tantum, sed etiam essentia differre*], from priesthood fully and properly so called.[17]

With his use of *sed etiam* ("but also"), Pius gives a clear both/and reading of the differences in essence and degree, and the Council Fathers cited this allocution as a footnote in support of *Lumen Gentium* 10. Antonio Aranda Lomeña, who opposes a translation of "not only in degree" acknowledges the connection between the expressions of difference in *Magnificate*

---

16. Richards, "Hierarchy and Priesthood," 229.
17. Pius XII, "Magnificate Dominum," 669.

Dominum and *Lumen Gentium*.[18] He nevertheless points to a difference in context, spirit, and accent between the choice of phrases that should lead us to interpret them differently. But that is an argument that could go the other way—that a difference in degree was affirmed despite these extraneous factors. It is improbable that a Council, departing from the teaching of a recent pope (though a teaching carrying only the authority of an allocution) would then cite that very teaching in support of its departure. Even if we grant that as a possibility, it is a possibility that should be set aside once we examine the magisterial teaching on this subject that most closely followed *Lumen Gentium*. While the Council was still underway, Paul VI issued the encyclical *Mysterium Fidei*, in which *sed etiam* made a reappearance. Paul expressed the difference between the priesthoods as one "not only of degree but also of essence" (*distinctione non gradus solum sed etiam essentiae*).[19] *Lumen Gentium* is flanked by magisterial teaching that affirms a both/and difference in essence and degree. It is crucial that this shapes the manner in which the conciliar teaching is interpreted. To read a conciliar document in abstraction from surrounding magisterial documents will inevitably risk interpreting the document inconsistently with the tradition.

Apples and Oranges

The second form of reasoning is an apples and oranges argument—there simply cannot be a difference in degree if there is a difference in essence. It is one or the other. To assert a difference of essence is to reject a difference of degree. Avery Dulles explicitly employs the apples and oranges analogy:

> The distinction is not between two kinds of person but two kinds of priesthood. The council refuses to attribute a higher grade or degree to the ministerial, as though the common priesthood ranked lower that it on the same scale. Instead, it situates the two kinds of priesthood in different categories, like oranges and apples.[20]

At first glance Dulles's analogy seems to demonstrate that a difference of essence, or kind, must exclude a difference of degree. But the dichotomy between personhood and priesthood betrays the problem with the analogy.

---

18. Lomeña argues that the Spanish "tantum" (so much) should replace "solo" (only), so that the difference would be one "not so much in degree as in essence" ("no tanto gradual cuanto esencial"), or "not so much gradual as essential." See Lomeña, "El sacerdocio de Jesucristo," 365–404.

19. Paul VI, "Mysterium Fidei" no. 31.

20. Dulles, *Priestly Office*, 11.

An apple is not simultaneously an orange. A person, though, can simultaneously possess the baptismal and ministerial priesthoods. The man who is ordained to the ministerial priesthood does not simply undergo an intensification of his baptismal priesthood. If he did, a difference of degree would suffice. Nor does he lose his baptismal priesthood on ordination to the ministerial priesthood. If he did, a difference of essence would suffice. It is because the ministerial priest participates doubly in the priesthood of Christ that both degree and essence must be invoked to explain the difference between the priesthoods. It would be a different matter altogether if the essences in question were the lay priesthood and the ministerial priesthood, but they are not. As has been seen above, there is no strictly "lay" priesthood that would be replaced by the sacrament of orders. The common priesthood is common not to all the laity but to all the baptized.

A further problem with using apples and oranges as an analogy is that any discussion of what an apple or orange is does not require reference to a third essence. While it is not greatly meaningful outside a metaphysics class to consider an apple or an orange as a participation in something like "fruitness," the baptismal and ministerial priesthoods cannot be understood as isolated essences but only with reference to the priesthood of Christ, in which each is a participation. So what might be a more appropriate analogy? A tempting candidate would be friendship, if only because Aristotle, in his discussion of friendship in his *Ethics*, points out that things of different kinds can also differ in degree. He dismisses the claim that, because friendship admits of degree, all friendship must therefore be of the same kind.[21] But there is another analogy to be found in the different ways of being a scholar, engaged in the scholarly enterprises of study, reading, reflecting, and learning. Two ways to be a scholar are to be a student and a professor. As the two priesthoods are ordered to one another, the student and professor are ordered to one another in the common pursuit of learning. There is a difference in kind, which their different roles and tasks demonstrate, but as scholars there is also a difference in degree in the years of study that separates them (which is sometimes measured by the word "degree"), often also in the extent to which they are invested in the life of a scholar. But just as the ministerial priest does not lose his baptismal priesthood, the professor never stops being a student. Though the years of sitting in class may be in the past, the basic scholarly commitment to reading, reflecting, and learning never ends. A substantive explanation of the difference between professor and student must draw on essence as well as degree. So, too, with the priesthoods.

---

21. Aristotle, *Nichomachean Ethics*, 1155b8–29.

There is, though, a potential—though not real—problem with this analogy. It may seem to elevate the ministerial priesthood to a professorial elite, and to keep baptismal priests in their place, sitting passively behind their desks, the better to take in the wisdom of their elders and betters. The force of the analogy will be affected by one's experience of having been a student and/or a professor. Anyone who has been taught by a professor who is at the service of the students, ready to learn from their insights, expecting to be questioned, prepared to be challenged, should have no concerns with the analogy.

If/Then

The third approach—the most common—is what may be termed an "if/then" approach: if there is a difference in degree, then that would have unwanted implications. This objection was raised during the debates of the Council, when bishops from the Scandinavian and German-speaking conferences called for *tantum* (the word translated as "only") to be deleted from the phrase "licet essentia et non gradu tantum differant" (in essence and not only in degree). Their concern was that if *tantum* remained, the Protestant complaint would not be silenced, which saw Catholic teaching as judging that priests are placed in a "higher grade" in comparison with lay people in all respects, and that personal holiness is of less importance than hierarchical rank.[22] The word remained in the text, but the concern remained as well, that a difference of degree implies a difference of status. Yves Congar, writing after the Council, claimed that a difference of degree would make the ordained priest a "super-Christian."[23] This finds an echo in the work of Christoph Schönborn:

> If the difference between the two forms of participating in Christ's priesthood were a difference of degree, the ministerial priesthood would be a sort of superior form of perfection. It would follow that becoming a priest would be becoming a superior Christian. Priestly ordination would confer on the priest the status of an elite Christian, a being superior to the so-called common faithful.[24]

It is well to name this if/then argument for what it is—a fear of clericalism, which has lurked in the background or stood firmly in the foreground

---

22. Second Vatican Council, *Acta Synodalia Sacrosancti*, 781.
23. Congar, "Quelques problèmes touchant les ministères," 790.
24. Schönborn, *Joy of Being a Priest*, 18–19.

of discussions of the ministerial priesthood since Vatican II. In his article expounding the reasons for a difference *in essence* between the priesthoods (note: not a difference in degree), Thomas Guarino notes the uneasiness that the language of "essential difference" can cause in egalitarian contemporary theology, given that all Christians are "first and foremost disciples of Jesus Christ, sharing a common vocation to holiness":

> The very idea of an essentially different ministerial priesthood appears, at least on the surface, to purvey a kind of elitism and social stratification characteristic of the *ancien régime*, an idea entirely outdated given our long experience of egalitarian democracy. Isn't it truer to the nature of the Church to emphasize the equality of all the baptized on their pilgrim journey to the heavenly Jerusalem? Is it proper to speak of one Christian priesthood as substantially distinct from another without reverting to an obsolete ecclesiology?[25]

Guarino simply notes these concerns and, undeterred, goes on to explain the essential difference, but in other authors clericalism looms substantially larger. Michael Richards begins his article on 'Hierarchy and Priesthood' with an anecdote about the visit of a Cardinal Archbishop of Westminster to St Edmund's College. The archbishop climbed out of his chauffeured limousine and declared to the staff and students who were there to greet him, "This is the summit of my career."[26] The problem with Richards's article, and with Congar and Schönborn's fear of the priest-as-super-Christian, is that elitism, pride, superiority, and personal advancement may accompany the reception of all sacraments. Those who receive the baptismal priesthood could think of themselves as superior human beings on account of the higher, supernatural life that is now theirs. The confirmed and the married could lord it over the unconfirmed and unmarried; those who have received the sacrament of anointing might cast a superior glance towards those in adjacent hospital beds. But the meaning of a sacrament should not turn on how it can be misunderstood or misused, but what the intention of the Church is in conferring the sacrament, both considered objectively but also in the demands it makes subjectively of the recipient of the sacrament.

---

25. Guarino, "Essentia," 560–61.
26. Richards, "Hierarchy and Priesthood," 228.

What Is the Degree?

Much confusion about the difference of degree can be removed by asking what the difference of degree consists in. Degree of what? It is helpful to let the ghost of clericalism return to his rest by stating what the difference in degree is *not*. It is not a degree of importance, status, worthiness, or personal holiness between ordained and non-ordained. When Donovan states that the ministerial priesthood "does not fit in at a particular point on the scale of holiness," he is certainly not speaking in error, but a degree of holiness is not the only possible degree. Neither is the grace of baptism. In contrasting difference in kind to difference of degree, Sara Butler comments:

> A difference in "degree" suggests the fuller or more intense possession of something that is common to all, in this case, the grace of Baptism. If the ministerial priesthood differed from the common priesthood only in "degree," it would suggest that the ordained differ from the non-ordained as the "virtuoso" Catholic differs from the "average" Catholic. All hope that candidates for ordination are exemplary Christians, but their ordination does not confer the "fullness" of Baptism.[27]

Even though the grace of baptism is common to all the baptized, so is the priesthood of Christ, and this is the only degree that is at issue when considering the objective difference between the priesthoods. There is no need to look elsewhere, whether to baptism or holiness or worthiness, other than the priesthood of Christ for the basis of the difference of degree. The difference lies in the degree of participation in Christ's priesthood, and the fear of clericalism should not cause us to baulk from saying so.

The difference of degree of priesthood, though, does carry implications for other possible differences of degree. Here we arrive at the priest's subjective response to the objective difference of degree in priesthood. If both priesthoods are a participation in the priesthood of Christ, when a man is ordained to the ministerial priesthood the Church's expectation is not that the man's participation in the priesthood of Christ will remain static, fixed as it was when he exercised solely the baptismal priesthood. The whole purpose of ordination is that the ordained priest will participate more deeply in the priesthood of Christ, becoming configured more closely to Christ the Priest. One of the few authors who does support a difference of degree, Peter Fink, points to the commissions that the Church gives in its various ordination rites, and comments: "The difference of degree can be located right here. Degree of closeness, degree of intensity, degree of

---

27. Butler, *Catholic Priesthood and Women*, 55–56.

personal investment in the Word, the sacrifice, and the pastoral care of Jesus Christ himself."[28] This is precisely why ordination is a daunting prospect. It is not simply a matter of the usual concerns about celibacy and the forgoing of a secular career, but it is about the degree of personal commitment and conformity to Christ as priest that is required of a man once he is ordained. The church expects more of a man who is ordained or preparing for the priesthood. As Fink points out, the Church asks new questions of his intentions at every stage of the Sacrament of Holy Orders.[29] Thus, for example, the ordinand promises "to be united more closely every day to Christ the High Priest." Although he may have sought this unity in the exercise of his baptismal priesthood, the Church is calling him to an ever-closer unity as a ministerial priest.

In its official teachings, too, the Church reminds ministerial priests of the greater demands placed upon them. These demands can be about something as specific as the priest's intellectual formation.[30] More generally, though, the demand is for a greater degree of personal holiness. This, however, is a demand made in consequence of the greater degree of priesthood that is conferred. Every major twentieth-century document on the priesthood touches on the holiness to which the ministerial priest is called. Pius XI in 1935 taught that "so holy an office demands holiness in him who holds it. A priest should have a loftiness of spirit, a purity of heart and a sanctity of life befitting the solemnity and holiness of the office he holds."[31] In the 1950 apostolic exhortation *Menti Nostrae*, Pius XII relates the teaching of Christ that the perfection of Christian life consists in the love of God, and of one's neighbor, and so a man should direct his intentions and actions towards this end in whatever circumstances he is placed in. But, he says, a priest is bound to do this by his very office, because he must follow Christ the Priest "who during his life on earth had no other purpose than to bear witness to his most ardent love for His Father and to bestow on men the infinite treasures of his heart."[32] Because of the high dignity of the priesthood, then, the priest should tend with ever-increasing efforts to perfection of life. Pius addresses the priest: "Your life, which should be completely immune from sin, should be more hidden with Christ in God than the lives of Christian layfolk."[33]

---

28. Fink, "Priesthood of Jesus Christ," 77.
29. Fink, "Priesthood of Jesus Christ," 76–77.
30. See John Paul II, "Pastores Dabo Vobis" no. 51.
31. Pius XI, "Ad Catholici Sacerdotii" no. 33.
32. Pius XII, "Menti Nostrae" no. 12.
33. Pius XII, "Menti Nostrae" no. 9.

Such passages are exhortations, rather than descriptions of guaranteed reality. It is obviously not the case that ministerial priests necessarily exceed lay Catholics in personal holiness. John Paul II taught as much in *Pastores dabo vobis*, first noting that "the ministerial priesthood does not of itself signify a greater degree of holiness with regard to the common priesthood of the faithful."[34] He then pointed out, following the conciliar document *Presbyterium Ordinis*, that the sacrament of holy orders brings with it a "specific" vocation to holiness.[35] It is certainly the case that on ordination to the ministerial priesthood, the priest should aim to be holier than he was before, as a response to the call and the gift that he has received. It is quite possible, too, that an ordained priest who does not live in the grace of the sacrament might be less holy than he was before ordination. Regrettable as this is, he would still share in Christ's priesthood to a greater degree. The objective difference of degree exists independently of the priest's subjective response. Again, though, the expectation of the Church is for greater holiness. Pius XI noted that because "be perfect as your Heavenly Father is perfect" was said to all Christians, "how much more then should the priest consider these words of the Divine Master as spoken to himself, called as he is by a special vocation to follow Christ more closely."[35] Thus in the Prayer of Ordination, the bishop prays for the ordinand that the Father will "renew deep within him the Spirit of holiness." This renewal of holiness is prayed for, and greater demands are asked of the priest, precisely because he is being given more—a greater degree of participation in the priesthood of Christ.

All-Round Confusion

Why is it necessary, when discussing the baptismal priesthood, to spill so much ink on the demands of the ministerial priesthood? The first reason is to demonstrate the connection between priesthood and holiness. They are supposed to go together. This positive correlation between priesthood and holiness, when the priesthood is gratefully and faithfully lived out, was recognized by Paul VI at the end of the Council. Less than a year after *Lumen Gentium* was promulgated, he commented on its teaching on the baptismal priesthood:

> We cannot help being filled with an earnest desire to see this teaching explained over and over until it takes deep root in the

---

34. John Paul II, "Pastores Dabo Vobis" no. 17.
35. John Paul II, "Pastores Dabo Vobis" no. 20.
36. Pius XI, "Ad Catholici Sacerdotii" no. 38.

hearts of the faithful. For it is a most effective means of fostering devotion to the Eucharist, of extolling the dignity of all the faithful, and of spurring them on to reach the heights of sanctity, which means the total and generous offering of oneself to the service of the Divine Majesty.[37]

Paul's enthusiasm for the potential of the baptismal priesthood is evident—if only this teaching were to be widely understood, greater Eucharistic devotion and holiness would be the result. But in yet another instance of a gap between ideal and reality, this certainly did not happen. Partly this is because most people are baptized as infants, so unless the meaning of their baptism is well-explained later in life in the family, parish, or school, they usually cannot articulate much at all about the meaning of their baptism. Even if someone is baptized as an adult, a large amount of their preparation for the sacrament is spent is on learning the basic content of revelation and preparing to live the sacramental life. But there has been a further problem. A condition for a teaching to be heard, let alone be understood and take "deep root," is that it be conveyed with clarity, and clarity has been notably missing from discussion of the baptismal priesthood. This is second reason for the need to have clarified the difference of degree between the priesthoods. As we have seen, however, there is a lack of clarity as to whether it is legitimate to speak of any differences at all. Even if the baptismal priesthood had been "explained over and over," as Paul VI desired, people receive teachings through making distinctions: "one of these things is not like the other." When differences are obscured, or any discussion of them is implicitly *verboten*, the conditions for a teaching to be received are not favorable.

If the only topic of confusion after the Council was the question of differences between the priesthoods, perhaps Paul VI's desire could still have been realized. But the ministerial priesthood itself has been the object of immense confusion ever since the Council, as has been well documented.[38] David Power refers to a series of articles in the *Irish Times* in the late 1960s suggesting that "priests today are anxious about the precise role of the ordained priesthood in the Church."[39] Some bishops at the 1971 Synod on the Ministerial Priesthood called for an exact definition of what the essential difference was.[40] Ideological tussles abounded. Thomas Rausch tells of the

37. Paul VI, "Mysterium Fidei" no. 31.
38. For a survey of the contributions of Hans Küng and Edward Schillebeeckx, see Dulles, *Priestly Office*, 2–4.
39. Power, "Church's Pastoral Ministry," 99.
40. Michalski, *Relationship*, 67–72. The response of the Synod was, among other things, to point to ordained priests' share in the apostolic ministry. This did not prevent continuing confusion through the 1970s and beyond.

word "priesthood" being at least tacitly banned in some theological centers, to avoid giving offence to those studying for ministry who could not be ordained: "The result is not infrequently a loss of identity for those preparing to be priests."[41] Avery Dulles described the situation in the mid-1990s: "Even today, many of the Catholic intelligentsia of Western Europe and the United States either reject the concept of ministerial priesthood or refine it in ways that make it scarcely distinguishable from the concept of ministry in Protestant Congregationalism."[42] It is hard to imagine Catholics coming into a greater understanding of the baptismal priesthood at the same time as understanding of the ministerial priesthood was being lost.

At this point we may recall that *Lumen Gentium* had taught that the two priesthoods are ordered to one another. This is a teaching with positive theological and pastoral significance. It means first that the two priesthoods have the common goal of Christ the Priest in gathering all humanity to the Father. The baptismal priesthood is usually brought into being and built up through the ministerial priesthood in the administration of the sacrament of baptism. Conversely, since ministerial priests are first of all members of the baptismal priesthood, they are offered for this priesthood from among the baptized faithful. The ministerial priesthood, through which Christ is made sacramentally present, also provides the means by which the members of the baptismal priesthood are called together into unity with Christ in the Eucharist. The necessity of the ministerial priesthood for the Church was emphasized in a 1997 Vatican instruction on the collaboration between the ordained and non-ordained in the ministry of the priest:

> The ministerial priesthood is therefore necessary for a community to exist as "Church." . . . Indeed, were a community to lack a priest, it would be deprived of the exercise and sacramental action of Christ, the Head and Pastor, which are essential for the very life of every ecclesial community.[43]

Although it is possible for the Church to continue for a time without ministerial priests, as it has had to do in times of persecution, it is not possible for the full sacramental life of the baptismal priesthood to be lived without ministerial priests, in particular the more intense communion that is shared

41. Rausch, "Priesthood Today," 207.

42. Dulles, *Priestly Office*, 3–4.

43. Congregation for the Clergy, "Instruction on Certain Questions." Richard Gaillardetz comments: "The document was issued to re-establish the distinction between the clergy and the laity which, in the minds of Vatican officials, has been blurred by recent pastoral initiatives, particularly in western and central Europe" (Gaillardetz, "Shifting Meanings," 115).

by those who are united in the Eucharist. The baptismal priesthood in turn provides the ministerial priesthood with its reason for existence. Priestly ordination makes the baptismal priesthood the orientation of a Catholic priest's life. Certainly, he is ordained to serve God, but to serve God through making Christ present to others in word, sacrament, and pastoral care. When priests serve the faithful in this way, it allows the baptismal priesthood to flourish, and when this happens the ordained priesthood flourishes in turn. When many in the Church are taking the sacramental life seriously, ordained priests can see that their ministry is effective and appreciated. The reflection of Bishop Kicanas is apposite here: "Some priests still see laity as needing to stay in their place. Some fear that the more lay ministry is emphasized, ordained ministry will diminish. That fear has never been demonstrated. I would rather emphasize that unless we grow together, nobody grows."[44]

Such is the positive relationship between the priesthoods. But there are negative implications, some of which are obvious and have become painfully evident in past decades. The mutual ordering means that ministerial priests cannot behave scandalously without the baptismal priesthood being negatively affected. Likewise, confusion about one of the priesthoods cannot exist without affecting the clarity of the other. To downplay differences between the priesthoods may seem to do a service to the baptismal priesthood and to strike a blow against clericalism. But just as genuine clericalism turns the ministerial priesthood in on itself, to the detriment of the baptismal priesthood, a disproportionate fear of clericalism can be toxic to both priesthoods. Neither of the priesthoods is well-served by a lack of clarity about the other.

Reviving the Baptismal Priesthood

Returning to the question posed to worshippers at the beginning of this chapter, does it actually matter if people on the steps of a church are unaware that they possess the baptismal priesthood? No doubt there have been multitudes of holy lay Christians through history, who lived out their faith in precisely the way *Lumen Gentium* envisaged for the baptismal priesthood (receiving the sacraments, prayer and thanksgiving, the witness of a holy life, self-denial and active charity), but who would never have considered themselves to possess a priesthood. There is, though, great potential for a reanimation of the Church if Christians realized that their baptism brought with it not simply membership of the Church, with the option of taking

---

44. Kicanas, "Vital Dimensions of Priesthood," 282.

it seriously, but the identity of a priest. In that case the obvious and non-negotiable purpose of the Christian life is to offer sacrifice—not merely in the sense of giving things up, but in the broader sense of "making holy," as the etymology of "sacrifice" suggests.

One person who serves as a model of consciously making one's life holy was the French laywoman Elisabeth Leseur (1866–1914). Her journal, published after her death, displays a rich interior life and an awareness of the need to live a life of sacrifice in ordinary life. Although there is no evidence that she specifically thought of herself as possessing the baptismal priesthood, it is possible to go through each of the spiritual sacrifices mentioned by *Lumen Gentium* and produce quotations from her journal that show how she lived that element of the baptismal priesthood. Three quotations will demonstrate the point. The first displays her understanding of the fundamental call to Christians to sacrifice:

> Christianity is based on the idea of sacrifice. Christians should imitate Jesus's model in their own times and make their sacrifice, amid human silence or indifference, to be joined to that of the Master. They should know Gethsemane or Calvary to the small degree that their strength supports.[45]

The second shows how Elisabeth's sacrifice was to make her whole life an offering to Christ:

> *Consecration*, total gift of myself to Jesus Christ. . . . Renewed *consecration* of my life to Jesus Christ. To live forever for him alone; to maintain my loves and friendships in him, more graced each day.[46]

The third is a resolution demonstrating that her self-offering was not simply a one-off and general offering, but was consciously renewed throughout each day:

> To offer the morning with its prayers, thoughts, words, actions, pains, sufferings, and deprivations for those who are to die that day.
>
> To offer the afternoon in the same way for the Church or souls.
>
> To offer the evening and night for all those I love, for their spiritual and temporal interests.[47]

---

45. Leseur, *Selected Writings*, 159.
46. Leseur, *Selected Writings*, 99–100.
47. Leseur, *Selected Writings*, 116–17.

If the baptismal priesthood is to be revived, catechesis and the kind of repetitive teaching that Paul VI called for are naturally essential. Encyclicals and pastoral letters on that sole topic could be greatly potent. Little changes should also not be underestimated. Something as small as recognizing the baptismal priesthood on baptismal certificates would go some way to bringing the baptismal priesthood, if not to the front of Christians' minds, at least to the back, rather than not at all. But more important are models of the baptismal priesthood, since in the Church, as elsewhere, people learn more from example than from words. To revive the baptismal priesthood, Elisabeth Leseur's is the kind of life to be held up as a model.

* * *

The decades since the Council have not been good ones for people's understanding of priesthood. Just as the potential of the baptismal priesthood was being recognized by no less a figure than Pope Paul VI, there followed great confusion about the ministerial priesthood and the relationship between the priesthoods. Any clarity that can be restored to the discussion on any aspect of priesthood is welcome and necessary. A disproportionate fear of clericalism risks obscuring the call to greater holiness that comes with a share in Christ's priesthood. What always accompanies the great gift of the ordained priesthood, as well the sacrament of baptism, is a call to give of oneself—to offer sacrifice. And the words of Christ remind us of what is at stake in responding to a share in his priesthood: "Much is expected of those to whom much is given" (Luke 12:48).

Bibliography

Aristotle. *The Nichomachean Ethics*. Translated by J. A. K. Thomson. New York: Penguin, 1976.

Butler, Sara. *The Catholic Priesthood and Women: A Guide to the Teaching of the Church*. Chicago: Hillenbrand, 2007.

Congar, Yves. "Quelques problèmes touchant les ministères." *Nouvelle Revue Théologique* 93 (1971) 785–800.

Congregation for the Clergy. "Instruction on Certain Questions Regarding the Collaboration of the Non-Ordained Faithful in the Sacred Ministry of Priest." August 15, 1997. Online. http://www.vatican.va/roman_curia/pontifical_councils/laity/documents/rc_con_interdic_doc_15081997_en.html.

De La Soujeole, Benoît-Dominique. "Différence d'essence et différence de degré dans le sacerdoc." *Revue Thomiste* 109 (2009) 621–38.

Donovan, Daniel. *What Are They Saying About the Ministerial Priesthood?* Mahwah, NJ: Paulist, 1992.

Dulles, Avery. *The Priestly Office: A Theological Reflection*. Mahwah, NJ: Paulist, 1997.

Fink, Peter E. "The Priesthood of Jesus Christ in the Ministry and Life of the Ordained." In *Priests: Identity and Ministry*, edited by Robert J. Wister, 71–91. Wilmington, DE: Michael Glazier, 1990.

Gaillardetz, Richard R. "Shifting Meanings in the Lay-Clergy Distinction." *Irish Theological Quarterly* 64 (1999) 115–40.

Guarino, Thomas G. "'*Essentia et non Gradu Tantum Differant*': A Note on the Priesthood and Analogical Predication." *The Thomist* 77 (2013) 559–76.

John Paul II. "Pastores Dabo Vobis." Apostolic Exhortation. March 25, 1992. Online. http://w2.vatican.va/content/john-paul-ii/en/apost_exhortations/documents/hf_jp-ii_exh_25031992_pastores-dabo-vobis.html.

Kicanas, Gerald. "Vital Dimensions of Priesthood Accented by a Time of Crisis." *Origins* 32 (2002) 277–83.

Leseur, Elisabeth. *Selected Writings*. Edited and translated by Janet K. Ruffing. Mahwah, NJ: Paulist, 2005

Lomeña Antonio Aranda. "El sacerdocio de Jesucristo en los ministros y en los fieles: Estudio teológico sobre la distinción 'essentia et non gradu tantum.'" *Scripta Theologica* 22 (1990–92) 365–404.

Michalski, Melvin. *The Relationship between the Universal Priesthood of the Baptized and the Ministerial Priesthood of the Ordained in Vatican II and in Subsequent Theology*. Lewiston, NY: Edwin Mellen, 1996.

Palmer, Paul F. "The Lay Priesthood: Real or Metaphorical." *Theological Studies* 8 (1947) 574–613.

———. "The Lay Priesthood: Towards a Terminology." *Theological Studies* 10 (1949) 235–50.

Paul VI. "Mysterium Fidei." Encyclical Letter. September 3, 1965. Online. http://w2.vatican.va/content/paul-vi/la/encyclicals/documents/hf_p-vi_enc_03091965_mysterium.html.

Pius XI. "Ad Catholici Sacerdotii." Encyclical Letter. December 20, 1935. Online. http://w2.vatican.va/content/pius-xi/en/encyclicals/documents/hf_p-xi_enc_19351220_ad-catholici-sacerdotii.html.

———. "Miserentissimus Redemptor." Encyclical Letter. May 8, 1928. Online. https://w2.vatican.va/content/pius-xi/en/encyclicals/documents/hf_p-xi_enc_19280508_miserentissimus-redemptor.html.

———. "Ubi Arcano." Encyclical Letter. December 23, 1922. Online. http://w2.vatican.va/content/pius-xi/en/encyclicals/documents/hf_p-xi_enc_19221223_ubi-arcano-dei-consilio.html.

Pius XII. "Magnificate Dominum." Allocution. November 2, 1954. *Acta Apostolica Sedis* 46 (1954) 666–77. English: *The American Ecclesiastical Review* 132 (1955) 55.

———. "Mediator Dei." Encyclical Letter. November 20, 1947. Online. http://w2.vatican.va/content/pius-xii/en/encyclicals/documents/hf_p-xii_enc_20111947_mediator-dei.html.

———. "Menti Nostrae." Apostolic Exhortation. September 23, 1950. Online. http://www.ewtn.com/library/papaldoc/p12clerg.htm.

Power, David N. "The Church's Pastoral Ministry." *Irish Theological Quarterly* 36 (1969) 99–112.

Rausch, Thomas P. "Priesthood Today: From Sacral to Ministerial Model." *Irish Theological Quarterly* 55 (1989) 206–214.

Richards, Michael. "Hierarchy and Priesthood." *Priests & People* 7 (1993) 228–32.

Schönborn, Christoph. *The Joy of Being a Priest: Following the Curé of Ars*. Translated by Michael J. Miller. San Francisco: Ignatius, 2010.

Second Vatican Council. *Acta Synodalia Sacrosancti Concilii Oecumenici Vaticani II*. Vol 2/1. Vatican: Typis Polyglottis Vaticanis, 1971.

———. "Lumen Gentium: Dogmatic Constitution on the Church." December 21, 1964. Online. http://www.vatican.va/archive/hist_councils/ii_vatican_council/documents/vat-ii_const_19641121_lumen-gentium_en.html.

———. "Presbyterorum Ordinis: Decree on the Ministry and Life of Priests." December 7, 1965. Online. http://www.vatican.va/archive/hist_councils/ii_vatican_council/documents/vat-ii_decree_19651207_presbyterorum-ordinis_en.html.

———. "Sacrosanctum Concilium: Pastoral Constitution on the Liturgy." December 4, 1963. Online. http://www.vatican.va/archive/hist_councils/ii_vatican_council/documents/vat-ii_const_19631204_sacrosanctum-concilium_en.html.

Torrell, Jean-Pierre. *A Priestly People: Baptismal Priesthood and Priestly Ministry*. Translated by Peter Heinegg. Mahwah, NJ: Paulist, 2013.

6

Communio After Social Media

—Matthew John Paul Tan

> *This chapter will explore several aspects in which the conception of the Church as Communion is affected by its pilgrimaging through a social sphere saturated by social media. Whilst affirming the necessity for the Church to traverse such a landscape, it will also challenge the treatment of this landscape as a neutral canvas. This chapter will show how social media filters the gospel by reformatting the Church These fissures become particularly acute when set against the Communion ecclesiology as outlined in Lumen Gentium and expanded upon in the thought of Popes Benedict, John Paul II and Francis. The main reference points would be authority, communication and encounter as aspects of the lifeworld of communion ecclesiology The chapter will then use these themes to identify the ecclesiological fault lines with social media, a lifeworld grounded in celebrity, competitive one-upmanship and hyperreality. By way of conclusion, this chapter will highlight the potential of a liturgical apprehension of social media as a way of faithful traverse through and redemptive transformation of the lifeworld of social media.*

Introduction

This work is part of an ongoing project that touches on the relationship between the Church's engagement with social media and the changes in its self-understanding as a polity.[1] A golden thread running through this works concerns how Christian engagement with social media more specifically—and the internet more generally—should be based not on our understanding as individuals, which would make matters of technique the prime consideration. Rather, the prism of our engagement with social media ought to be as members of a polity called the Body of Christ. Whilst affirming the necessity for the Church to traverse such a landscape, my work also challenges the convention adopted by many in the Church whereby this landscape is treated as a neutral canvas on which the gospel can be unproblematically transmitted. Indeed, this chapter will highlight stark ecclesiological fissures that social media puts into place, via a lifeworld which filters the gospel by reformatting the Church that passes through its territory. These ecclesiological fissures become particularly acute when set against the lifeworld of *Communio* ecclesiology as outlined in *Lumen Gentium* and expanded upon in the thought of Joseph Ratzinger's *Called to Communion*. The present study will take as its two main reference points the themes of selfhood and the relationship between that self and community. From these anthropological and communal touchstones the inquiry will branch out to cover themes of authority, communication and encounter as aspects of the lifeworld of communion ecclesiology. The chapter will then use these themes to identify the ecclesiological fissure points with social media, a lifeworld grounded in celebrity, competitive one-upmanship and hyperreality.

The Self

First, to the anthropological. Implicit in my previous projects is the claim that the appeal of social media to Christians lies in the seemingly significant area of anthropological overlap between the faith (conceived of as being part of the communion of the Church) and social media. Both mediums seem to expand the modern self that is conceived of in Lockean terms, that is a hermetically sealed individual unit that is prior to any communal belonging. In contrast to the autonomous individual, the self in social media is one that is, at least in its initial operation, deeply communal, even in the expression of individual selfhood. A sign of this compound self can be gleaned by the most common reason for which one uses social media, which is the sharing of experiences as a criterion of individual experience itself—think of the variations of the phrase "if it did not happen on facebook, it did not

---

1. See Tan, "Bobblehead Church"; "Faith in the Church of Facebook."

happen." In the age of social media, it is not enough for experience to be confined to an individual, but for it to be shared with others in order for it to be a legitimate experience, even for the self.[2]

I raise this anthropological point because a similar point is made in Joseph Ratzinger's *Called to Communion*. There, Ratzinger speaks of being part of the *Communio* as an opening experience, one where the "I" is expanded and the hermetically sealed walls of the autonomous "I" are broken down.[3] This expansion of the self is put in sharper relief when one considers the late Avery Dulles's article on the "ecclesial dimension of faith."[4] There, Dulles said that faith was not an individual possession that one expresses solely through the individual's act of volition. Instead, Dulles argued that faith is an act of the Church, "the great believer" in which the individual's faith participates Dulles argument sharpens a similar point in paragraph 9 of Vatican II's Dogmatic Constitution on the Church, *Lumen Gentium*, which says that God

> does not make men holy and save them merely as individuals. . . . Rather has it pleased Him to bring men together as one people, a people which acknowledges Him in truth and serves Him in holiness.[5]

Dulles cites two examples that demonstrate the corporate nature of the Christian faith. The first is the Eucharistic liturgy, in which the decisive factor for our salvation is not the sins of those within the Church, but the faith of the Church itself. The second is sacrament of Baptism for infants, where the decisive factor is not the individual faith of the infant, but the Church's imputation of its faith, that in turn makes the individual's articulation of the faith possible.[6] Once faith is understood as fundamentally an *ecclesial* act in which the individual *participates*, then we can understand why Ratzinger regards faith as the act of an expanded "I," encompassing the people gathered *by* God to find their "I" in the "I" of Jesus of Nazareth. Jesus of Nazareth then mediates this "I" through the Twelve and then the seventy.[7] At one level then, faith in the Communion of the Church thereby expands the horizons of the "I" by orienting it to Jesus, then to all those who mediate Him within His body—past, present and future.

---

2. See, for example, Munzel and Kunz, "Sharing Experiences via Social Media."
3. Ratzinger, *Called to Communion*, 37.
4. Dulles, "Ecclesial Dimension of Faith."
5. Second Vatican Council, "Lumen Gentium" no. 9.
6. Dulles, "Ecclesial Dimension of Faith," 420.
7. Ratzinger, *Called to Communion*, 40–45.

Whilst we should be aware of the great similarity in the expansion of the subject by both the Church and social media, we should be even more aware of a subtle and important divergence when social media expands the self. While there is a desire for experiences to be shared, such a desire is interwoven with the narcissistic desire to be seen.[8] The importance of identifying this narcissistic difference lies in the fact that it counteracts the opening orientation of *communio*, by becoming a self-referential vortex, that expands by absorbing others for its own ends. Whilst *communio* expands the self towards others as other, narcissism contracts it by instrumentalizing others to aggrandise the self. The other that one opens up to and engages in social media is not a whole person. It is more accurately a commodified portion of that other, because what is sought from the other in the act of sharing is their gaze, filtered through metrics of views, likes and shares. What is more, the self that is aggrandised a step removed from the self as a whole person. What is aggrandised is also as commodified as the gaze of the other, an online avatar of the self, a profile made out of strings of data and statistics. The communion engendered on social media is a communion made of selves expanded via the process of alienation, and opened up only insofar as it facilitates a curving in on oneself.

Contracted Communio

As can be seen above, how the subject is conceived greatly affects the terms of engagement with the other in a communal context. By extension, a forum that preloads a user with a tendency to curve in on itself ends up with a contracted sociality, both in terms of a thinned out mode of communion and in terms of a form of communion that is circumscribed by terms and conditions. As the self becomes expanded toward the other, the mutation of desire in social media outlined above causes the corporate reality of being in the *communio* of the Church to contract and ultimately fragment. One can observe this when one looks at one of the less fashionable elements of *communio*, namely authority.

To look at authority, we must return to a theme touched upon earlier, namely the ecclesial nature of faith. *Lumen Gentium* makes clear that authority does not arise from the person of the office holder, but arises from the context of the whole church, founded upon the Apostles by Christ. Having been reminded of the common Christic and apostolic grounding of authority within the Church, notice how that authority plays itself out. In Paragraph 8 of *Lumen Gentium*, we see that after the resurrection, Christ

---

8. Biolcati and Passini, "Narcissism and Self-Esteem."

left the Church for "Peter to shepherd" and "the other apostles to extend and direct with authority."[9]

This is an incredibly important ecclesiological paragraph when it comes to authority. It implies that within the Body of Christ, headship is simultaneously centralised and dispersed. It is not just Peter that exercises the function of oversight, but the other Apostles as well in communion with Peter. This communal authority qualifies the idea of the exclusive authority of a single figure, and this is demonstrated by the authority of a bishop. The conception of apostolic authority in *Lumen Gentium* is such that the authority of any one bishop does *not* arise from the charisma of the individual office bearer, nor is the authority that comes with episcopal office itself an acquisition that becomes the sole personal property of that office bearer. Rather, episcopal authority derives from the sacramental life of the Church as a whole, making the bishop's authority an *ecclesial* function. Furthermore, it is an ecclesial function given to the College of Bishops *as a whole*. In the words of paragraph 21 of *Lumen Gentium*, episcopal authority "of its very nature, can be exercised only in hierarchical communion with the head and the members of the College."[10] Even as the Apostles are sent to all the world to tell the Good news (cf. Matt 28:19), authority does not become dispersed into independent centers. Authority may be exercised in a variety of localities, but that authority is always orienting each of those localities towards unity. This unity pertains both to every other local church in the present, and also with the whole Church past, present and future.

While *communio* demands ecclesial unity, Ratzinger acknowledges that this unity does not equate to what he called a "false uniformity." Such a conformity, he says, is a "reduction" of the full reality of the Church. This is why Ratzinger's call for unity is coupled with a call for "room for the doubtless often troublesome multiplicity of God's gifts."[11] These are the diverse particular local adaptations of the universal grammar of the universal Church, with each local church having differing charisms, assets and afflictions that each participate in the singular organism of the Body of Christ. That said, these diverse articulations are never ends in themselves. While they are diverse with respect of their locality, they are also governed by what Ratzinger calls the "criterion of unity of faith," that is, every local iteration is always oriented towards the Church as a whole, which is made manifest by, in Ratzinger's words, a "vital exchange of the whole."[12] What this requires in

9. Second Vatican Council, "Lumen Gentium" no. 8.
10. Second Vatican Council, "Lumen Gentium" no. 21.
11. Ratzinger, *Called to Communion*, 100.
12. Ratzinger, *Called to Communion*, 100.

practice is coupling the task of the mission of the Church *vis a vis* the world, together with "the immense task of reconciliation" among the differences within the Church,[13] making the Church an "open space of reconciliation."[14]

When opened up in the *communio* of the Church, difference does not become synonymous with infidelity. Rather, these differences become vital symbols of the inability of any single human intellect to encompass the full mystery of the Body of Christ. This is why Ratzinger says that the act of faith does not consist of merely the mental assent of cognitive categories, but also the "break[ing] the barriers of finitude and thus creat[ing] that open space that reaches into the unlimited."[15] Set in the context of *communio*, difference is not an obstacle to harmony, but a first step towards it, as the unique particularity of each difference—in and of itself—expresses the unity of the one Lord that generated that particularity.

Social media, on the other hand, is oriented towards another form of communion. Consequently, social media operates with another form of authority and another perception of difference in mind. The main material factor for this is the shift in the primary interface with the Church on social media, from temporal space to the virtual space of the screen of the desktop or mobile device. The screen thus subordinates the Church's most basic spatial unit, the parish, as the prime interface with the faith. In other words, social media disengages the faith from the life in the parish populated by other believers and is instead transferred to a life on the screen, populated by text, profiles and URL codes for blogs, documents and videos. The net result of this textualisation of the faith is a fragmentation of the body of believers, as the interface between the faithful and the Church becomes privatised to the individual reader or viewer. In a similar vein, authority becomes centered not on a common criterion of apostolicity (as laid out by Ratzinger above), but on the charismatic skillset of the individual social media entrepreneur or celebrity.

The fragmentation of authority one sees here is compounded when one considers the fragmentation of a common body, which is a complex organism made of many differing members, articulating the same faith in that common body. The internet sociologist Felicia Wu Song says in her book *Virtual Communities* that when immersed in social media, that complexity gives way to a whole collection of streamlined, hermetically sealed lifestyle enclaves.[16] The creation of the enclave is due to a number of factors includ-

13. Ratzinger, *Called to Communion*, 78.
14. Ratzinger, *Called to Communion*, 100.
15. Ratzinger, *Called to Communion*, 144.
16. Wu Song, *Virtual Communities*.

ing the disembodied nature of coming together around common textual formats within social media, the vast menu of texts to choose from, and the ease of establishing and breaking communion via a simple click of the mouse. The net result of these factors is that the brake against streamlining, which is the givenness of the complexity expressed within embodied communities, is now either an optional extra or not even present in an online format.

When this material complexity gives way to a dematerialised simplicity, Sherry Turkle points out that relations between the faithful are such that each can "imagine [each] other as you wish them to be, constructing them for your purposes."[17] In other words, the online platform, when cut off from the life of the parish, lends itself towards generating a fantasy of conformity. Communion and fidelity becomes redefined to a frictionless conformity with a set of ideas, and usually a narrow set of ideas set by group administrators at a given moment, rather than the width and breadth of the tradition lived through the centuries. What this means is that left on its own, each individual enclave on social media would have little if anything to do with other enclaves. Indeed, a faithfulness tied to conformity to abstract ideas risks creating a common currency of mutual suspicion between enclaves. Ratzinger's *communio*, that "open space of reconciliation," runs the risk of giving way to what Manuel Castells calls "communes of resistance identity,"[18] where the sustenance of the enclave is obtained, not from a participation in a common ecclesial faith, but from the drive to constantly resist what lies outside the conformity of the enclave. In other words, anything outside the enclave, even though they may share a common faith at the parish level, may nonetheless be relegated outside the borders of that faith, whether it is through the different choices of textual content, differing interpretations of the same textual content, or a decree of schism by the enclave's authority figures. Against a backdrop where fidelity becomes synonymous with conformity, the task of reconciliation between the differences outlined by Ratzinger is thus not only ignored, but actively fought against.

Conclusion

It is foolhardy to simply wish that *communio* reformatted by social media in the way I have described above is a passing phase and will just go away with the passage of time. What is key is realising the tendency towards the faith becomes filtered when it is immersed in a social media format. What is

17. Turkle, *Alone Together*, 188.
18. Castells, *End of the Millennium*, 351.

also key is realising that one cannot simply combat this filtration with nothing more than good intentions, since the process of filtration is built into the format itself. Whilst *communio* as conceptualised by Ratzinger bears a capacity for the expansion of the self toward the other as other, social media reformats that expansion towards that other as a tool for the self. While Ratzinger's *communio* expands the range of possibilities for the articulations of faith *and* bears within it the capacities to reconcile those possibilities within the Body of Christ, that body in social media honeycombs into ghettos where difference and reconciliation are anathema, and conformity and conflict are the dominant vocabularies of sociality.

What allows for this expansion, complexification and reconciliation of the Body of Christ is actual embodiment, and actual embodiment is primarily realisable in real space and time. The marvellous density of the Church as *communio* requires attention, not only to the transcendent Trinity that generates it. What is also crucial is attention to the material sites in space and time that undergird it. What this means is not a rejection of social media as a sign of fidelity, but rather a realisation that its tendency towards reformatting means that it cannot remain an ecclesial center of gravity. What this means is an attention to the digital outreach for the dissemination of the gospel must also be coupled with an even keener attention to the terrestrial parish as the privileged site of *Communio*. It requires an attention to the liturgical spaces and church halls, and also those other ecclesial elements orbiting round the parish, such as the forms of intentional communities where persons, not avatars, define the communion of saints. For the Church as *communio,* in particular as the the communion of saints, is what expresses the myriad declensions of the grammar of the communion of the whole Church in every place, age and time.

Bibliography

Biolcati, Roberta, and Stefano Passini. "Narcissism and Self-Esteem: Different Motivations for Selfie Posting Behaviors." *Cogent Psychology* 5 (2018). Online. https://doi.org/10.1080/23311908.2018.1437012.

Castells, Manuel. *The End of the Millennium*. London: Blackwell, 1998.

Dulles, Avery. "The Ecclesial Dimension of Faith." *Communio* 22 (1995) 418–32.

Munzel, Andreas, and Werner Kunz. "Sharing Experiences via Social Media as an Integral Part of the Service Experience." *SSRN Electronic Journal*, August 8, 2013. Online. https://doi.org/10.2139/ssrn.2307120.

Ratzinger, Joseph. *Called to Communion: Understanding the Church Today*. San Francisco: Ignatius, 1996.

Second Vatican Council. "Lumen Gentium: Dogmatic Constitution on the Church." November 21, 1964. Online. http://www.vatican.va/archive/hist_councils/ii_vatican_council/documents/vat-ii_const_19641121_lumen-gentium_en.html

Tan, Matthew John Paul. "Bobblehead Church: The Ecclesiological Effects of Catholic Online Celebrity." In *Authority and Leadership: Values, Religion, Media*, edited by Miriam Diez Bosch, et al., 69–78. Barcelona: Observatori Blanquerna de Comunicaciao, Religio i Cultura, 2017.

———. "Faith in the Church of Facebook." *Journal of Moral Theology* 4 (2015) 25–35.

Turkle, Sherry. *Alone Together: Why We Expect More From Technology and Less From Each Other*. New York: Basic, 2011.

Wu Song, Felicia. *Virtual Communities: Bowling Alone, Online Together*. New York: Peter Lang, 2009.

7

The Sacrament of Confirmation and Its Role in the Ecclesiology of Communion

—Moira Debono, RSM

> *As a Sacrament of Initiation, Confirmation incorporates the Catholic more firmly into the Church. This incorporation is a dynamic reality that not only effects a spiritual maturity for the person but strengthens the Body of Christ. Aquinas notes that with Confirmation a Catholic is no longer living an "individual life," but is meant to be in relationship with others and is spiritually strengthened for this.[1] This chapter will briefly explore magisterial documents which consider the ecclesiology of communion and the sacrament of Confirmation and this statement of Aquinas, and conclude with distinguishing the role of Confirmation in strengthening communion within the Church.*

As a Sacrament of Initiation, Confirmation incorporates the Catholic more firmly into the Church. This incorporation is a dynamic reality that not only effects a spiritual maturity for the person but strengthens the Body of Christ. Aquinas notes that with Confirmation a Catholic is no longer living an "individual life," but is meant to be in relationship

---

1. Aquinas, *ST* III.72.1.

with others and spiritually "arrives at the 'perfect age.'"[2] In other words, a Catholic, already an integral member of the Body of Christ by Baptism, is effectively brought into active relationship with other members of the Body; that is, in a new kind of communion with others through the sacrament of Confirmation. This new way of relationship within the Church for the individual cannot but enhance the communion the Church lives and expresses.

However, magisterial documents do not often highlight Confirmation in discussions regarding communion ecclesiology, a significant theme of the Second Vatican Council. For example, the Dogmatic Constitution of the Church of the Second Vatican Council, *Lumen Gentium*, mentions Confirmation a total of three times, but it does not elaborate in relation to communion ecclesiology.[3] The *Final Relatio* of the Extraordinary Synod of Bishops of 1985 which discussed Vatican II twenty years on from its conclusion does not associate Confirmation with a role in communion ecclesiology either, and neither does the Congregation for the Doctrine of the Faith (CDF) document on "Some aspects of the Church understood as communion," *Communionis Notio* of 1992. However, a 2016 letter of the CDF, "Regarding the Relationship Between Hierarchical and Charismatic Gifts in the Life and the Mission of the Church," *Iuvenescit Ecclesia*, cites the *Final Relatio* of 1985 and makes a bit of a corrective by including Confirmation in between Baptism and Eucharist as elementary to the notion of communion.[4] Still, it does not elaborate. Is there something that can be added to this topic? I hope to do that in some initial way in this chapter.

Reception of the sacraments is to bring us into contact with the Paschal Mystery of Christ; more specifically, the Christian is to encounter Christ and through that encounter to be transformed and more conformed to Him in one's being and ultimately that is made known or visible through one's actions.

The sacramental journey begins with Baptism. After the initial character and graces received in Baptism, the Catholic is confirmed. Whether this "after" should be before receiving one's First Holy Communion or later, I will leave out of the current discussion.[5] Suffice to say that in the Roman

---

2. Aquinas, *ST* III.72.1.

3. Second Vatican Council, "Lumen Gentium" no. 11, 26, 33. On the other hand, Baptism and Eucharist are cited between sixteen and twenty times in "Lumen Gentium."

4. CDF, "Iuvenescit Ecclesia" no. 13.

5. Pope Benedict XVI encouraged Conferences of Bishops to align pastoral practice with dogmatic understanding of the sacraments of initiation in his 2007 post-synodal apostolic exhortation, Benedict XVI, "Sacramentum Caritatis" no. 18.

Rite, after Baptism is received as a child, Confirmation typically is not to be celebrated earlier than at the age of reason.[6]

Due to the parameters of this chapter, communion ecclesiology will be only briefly explored from the limited number of representative magisterial documents, then we will address the sacramental effects of Confirmation received by an individual, and how those effects can influence the life of a Catholic. In conclusion, it will be noted how Confirmation and the ecclesiology of communion are linked.

A Selection of Magisterial Documents

The ecclesiology of communion was illustrated through the principle of sacramentality in *Lumen Gentium* of the Second Vatican Council: "The Church, in Christ is like a sacrament or as a sign and instrument both of a very closely knit union with God and of the unity of the whole human race."[7] The Church in her various dimensions helps us to see beyond the visible. Both the faithful and those not of the Church are meant to see the relationship of the *communio personarum* of the Trinity through a Church faithful to her Lord. The Church, made up of persons made in *imago dei*, is not simply an institution with levels of hierarchy and various agencies, but a living reality which is enlivened by the Spirit of God dwelling within her members. The "very closely knit union with God" is described in *Lumen Gentium* with images from the Scriptures. The biblical images of the vine and the shepherd with his flock in *LG* are two which illustrate this organic completeness. The Old Testament nuptial images of the Lover calling his beloved, the People of God, Israel (cf. Hos 2:14) are fulfilled in the New Testament images of the Church, the New People of God as the Bride of Christ (cf. Eph 5:25–38) called to be in spousal intimacy with their God.[8] The communion of God and his people is matched by the necessary relationship of each part of the Body with each other and not only with the Head (1 Cor 12:14–26).

Gaudium et Spes, the Pastoral Constitution of the Church, was promulgated a year after *Lumen Gentium* and the communion of persons was highlighted from the outset of that document as well. *Gaudium et Spes* 12 states: "For sacred Scripture teaches that man was created 'to the image of God.'... God did not create man a solitary being. From the beginning 'male and female he created them' (Gen 1:27). This partnership of man and woman

---

6. "Code of Canon Law" 889.
7. Second Vatican Council, "Lumen Gentium" no. 1.
8. Second Vatican Council, "Lumen Gentium" nos. 6, 7.

constitutes the first form of communion between persons." *Gaudium et Spes* ties the relationship between being made in *imago dei* with man's relationship with one another. However, *Gaudium et Spes* is quick to point out that it was our first parents' actions that not only disrupted the communion with God, but with each other.[9]

The *Final Relatio* of the Extraordinary Synod of Bishops 1985 summarizes the ecclesiology of communion as presented in the Second Vatican Council documents. The significance of the interiority of communion with one another is highlighted as well as acknowledging the foundational communion with "God through Jesus Christ in the Holy Spirit, first of all" and that it comes about through the Scriptures and a sacramental life.[10] Thus, "unity and pluriformity"[11] can exist because of the communion that is shared. This unity is remarkably manifested in the diversity of Churches in communion, the collegiality of bishops, the responsibility that is shared by the episcopate with the presbyterate, diaconate, religious and the lay faithful, and the Church's work in ecumenism and inculturation. As mentioned earlier, while Baptism and Eucharist are indicated as instrumental in this communion, Confirmation is not mentioned.

A year after the *Final Relatio*, St John Paul II released his 1986 encyclical on the Holy Spirit *Dominum et Vivificantem*. While not directly addressing the theme of communion ecclesiology, he deepens one of the topics of the *Final Relatio*. Whereas the *Final Relatio* describes the mission of service that extends from communion, St John Paul II notes the supernatural foundation for its efficacy:

> The bishops in turn by the Sacrament of Orders render the sacred ministers sharers in this spiritual gift [grace of the Holy Spirit] and through the Sacrament of Confirmation, ensure that all who are reborn of water and the Holy Spirit are strengthened by this gift. And thus, in a certain way, the grace of Pentecost is perpetuated in the Church.[12]

Here we have the Holy Father noting the communion that originates in the bishop, and is extended to his priests and confirmandi who all have a role in continuing the Pentecost event. He goes on:

---

9. Second Vatican Council, "Gaudium et Spes" no. 13. There is no mention of any of the sacraments in "Gaudium et Spes," except for matrimony, which is addressed both as a sacrament and non-sacramentally. See Second Vatican Council, "Gaudium et Spes" no. 46–51.

10. Extraordinary Synod of Bishops, "Final Relatio" no. 1.

11. Extraordinary Synod of Bishops, "Final Relatio" no. 2.

12. John Paul II. "Dominum et Vivificantem" no. 25.

> Christ's prophecies in the farewell discourse found their most exact and direct confirmation on the day of Pentecost, in particular the prediction which we are dealing with: "The Counselor . . . will convince the world concerning sin. . . . 'And they were all filled with the Holy Spirit and began to speak in other tongues, as the Spirit gave them utterance' (Acts 2:4) thus bringing back to unity the scattered races and offering to the Father the first-fruits of all the nations."[13]

As *Gaudium et Spes* emphasized the introduction of sin into the world by the breaking of communion, St John Paul II associates the gift of the Holy Spirit with the re-establishment of communion through the works of the Redemption. This will be recalled when we consider the effects of Confirmation.

And further:

> For this reason the early Christians, right from the days immediately following the coming down of the Holy Spirit, "devoted themselves to the breaking of bread and the prayers," and in this way they formed a community united by the teaching of the Apostles (cf. Acts 2:42). Thus "they recognized" that their Risen Lord, who had ascended into heaven, came into their midst anew in that Eucharistic community of the Church and by means of it.[14]

John Paul II reiterates what was stated in *Lumen Gentium* 2, that the "Church is like a sacrament." The interior communion among the members of the Church is made known through the exterior actions of the faithful thus allowing, such as the first members of the Church, "the favour of all the people. And the Lord added to their number day by day those who were being saved" (Acts 2:47, RSV). The *communio personarum* of the Trinity is made visible.

John Paul II later described communion ecclesiology in his post-synodal exhortation *Christifidelis Laici*: "The Church [is a] communion with its inseparable dimensions: the communion of each Christian with Christ and the communion of all Christians with one another."[15] To speak of

---

13. John Paul II, "Dominum et Vivificantem" no. 30.

14. John Paul II, "Dominum et Vivificantem" no. 62.

15. John Paul II, "Christifidelis Laici" no. 19. "*The reality of the Church as Communion is*, then, the integrating aspect, indeed *the central content of the 'mystery,'* or rather, the divine plan for the salvation of humanity. For this purpose ecclesial communion cannot be interpreted in a sufficient way if it is understood as simply a sociological or a psychological reality. The Church as *Communion* is the 'new' People, the 'messianic' People, the People that 'has, for its head, Christ . . . as its heritage, the dignity and

communion ecclesiology is not to just be speaking about working together well, but underlined once again is the vertical dimension of an individual's union with the Trinity through Christ's Paschal Mystery in Baptism and the horizontal dimension then of every member of the baptized with each other. Further, the living God is made present through sincere lives of service of the members of the Church:

> *Church communion then is a gift, a great gift of the Holy Spirit,* to be gratefully accepted by the lay faithful, and at the same time to be lived with a deep sense of responsibility. This is concretely realized through their participation in the life and mission of the Church, to whose service the lay faithful put their varied and complementary ministries and charisms.[16]

In his last encyclical, Saint John Paul II wrote in *Ecclesia de Eucharistia*, 17:

> And in the *Roman Missal* the celebrant prays: "grant that we who are nourished by his body and blood may be filled with his Holy Spirit, and become one body, one spirit in Christ" [Eucharistic Prayer III]. Thus by the gift of his body and blood Christ increases within us the gift of his Spirit, already poured out in Baptism and bestowed as a "seal" in the sacrament of Confirmation.[17]

Here, John Paul II links the second epiclesis of the Eucharistic Prayer (a petition for ecclesial communion) with Baptism and its intensification in Confirmation. The sacramental effects of all three sacraments of initiation are indicated as being the basis for expressing the Church as communion, "one body, one spirit in Christ."

In his first encyclical, *Deus Caritas Est*, Benedict XVI makes the distinction that not only is there a vertical and horizontal communion in the Church, but there is a drawing out of oneself through reception of Holy Communion to arrive at that communion:

> Union with Christ is also union with all those to whom he gives himself. I cannot possess Christ just for myself: I can belong to him only in union with all those who have become, or who will

---

freedom of God's Children . . . for its law, the new commandment to love as Christ loved us . . . for its goal, the kingdom of God . . . established by Christ as a communion of life, love and truth.' (*Lumen Gentium* 9) The bonds that unite the members of the New People among themselves—and first of all with Christ—are not those of 'flesh and blood,' but those of the spirit, more precisely those of the Holy Spirit, whom all the baptized have received (cf. Jœl 3:1)" (John Paul II, "Christifidelis Laici" no. 19).

16. John Paul II, "Christifidelis Laici" no. 20.
17. John Paul II, "Ecclesia de Eucharistia" no. 17.

> become, his own. Communion draws me out of myself towards him, and thus also towards unity with all Christians. We become "one body," completely joined in a single existence.[18]

Whereas Confirmation is not addressed in this encyclical, the ecclesiology of communion, self-gift and kenosis are presented. There is a close alignment with the quote above from *Ecclesia de Eucharistia*. This will be further developed in the discussion of the effects of the sacrament of Confirmation.

In the encyclical, *Laudato Sí*, Pope Francis frequently speaks of the communion that all of nature shares. More specifically, he writes:

> The human person grows more, matures more and is sanctified more to the extent that he or she enters into relationships, going out from themselves to live in communion with God, with others and with all creatures. In this way, they make their own that trinitarian dynamism which God imprinted in them when they were created. Everything is interconnected, and this invites us to develop a spirituality of that global solidarity which flows from the mystery of the Trinity.[19]

Here, while it is not explicitly communion ecclesiology, Pope Francis emphasizes communion with God and the global reality of communion to which humanity is called to embrace. At the same time, he uses the phrase "going out from themselves," which flows from Benedict's earlier statement that one's self-gift invites communion.

The CDF promulgated the Letter, *Iuvenescit Ecclesia* in 2015 which considered the relationship of hierarchical and charismatic gifts in the Church. This quote, though long, is worth presenting:

> Within the Church, men are called together to become members of Christ and within the ecclesial communion they are united in Christ, as members of each other. Communion is always "a vital double participation: the incorporation of Christians into the life of Christ, and the diffusion of charity itself amongst the whole faithful in this world and the next. Unity with Christ and in Christ; and unity between Christians in the Church." In this sense, the mystery of the Church shines "in Christ like a sacrament or as a sign and instrument both of a very closely-knit union with God and of the unity of the whole human race." From this, one can see that the Church as a mystery of communion has a sacramental root: "Fundamentally this means communion with God through Jesus Christ, in the Holy Spirit.

---

18. Benedict XVI, "Deus Caritas Est" no. 14.
19. Francis, "Laudato Sí" no. 240.

> This communion is effected in the Word of God and in the sacraments. Baptism"—in close union with Confirmation—"is the entrance to and foundation of the communion of the Church."[20]

This letter appears to more clearly align Confirmation with communion ecclesiology than earlier documents and even to emphasize Confirmation's role by the way the sentence has been given. As in *Ecclesia de Eucharistia*, the supernatural foundation of communion through sacramental effects is evident.

In 2018 during an audience on Confirmation, Pope Francis said, "In Confirmation it is Christ who fills us with his Spirit, consecrating us as his witness, participants in the same principle of life and of mission, according to the design of the heavenly Father."[21] Here, we have an emphasis on the interior communion that Confirmation grants us. In the following week's audience continuing the theme, the pope quoted an earlier writing of his, as he encouraged the faithful to "reflect Jesus Christ in today's world."[22] Here we have something similar to *Lumen Gentium* and the sacramentality of the Church being expressed.

In summary, these few and varied documents that developed communion ecclesiology explicitly or implicitly have been briefly considered. Levels of communion were noted, ranging from exterior communion of hierarchical status to the actions that manifest a communion among individuals to the ultimate foundation of communion being a participation in the Paschal Mystery beginning with Baptism. Confirmation, a sacrament of initiation was widely, but not quite universally, overlooked in these documents as contributing to a deepening of the communion of the members of the Church.

The Church as a kind of sacrament is the image of the Communion of Persons of the Trinity *and* the image of the eschatological communion towards which the New People of God are on journey. This current age of the Church is the "time of the already and the not yet." The power of the Paschal Mystery is made present in the sacraments. Yes, we experience communion, but the fullness of communion will only be in the age to come.

---

20. CDF, "Iuvenescit Ecclesia" no. 13.

21. Francis, "Audience [May 23, 2018]."

22. Francis, "Audience [May 30, 2018]," in which Pope Francis quoted from his apostolic exhortation *Gaudete et Exultate*. He was not alluding to Confirmation specifically in the exultation, but to the work of the Spirit.

The Effects of Confirmation

As described by Liam Walsh, the effects of Confirmation have to be "something distinctive in the gift of the Spirit that is made visible in the rite."[23] We saw that in *Dominum et Vivificantem*, John Paul II describes the gift of the Spirit, not only with Confirmation, but Holy Orders. The question for Walsh is: we know that the Spirit is given, but in what specific way? The *Catechism of the Catholic Church* at 1302 grants that there is "a special outpouring of the Holy Spirit." This special outpouring is then said to be an "increase and deepening of Baptismal grace." As such, it is an intensifying of divine sonship, a firmer conformity to Christ, a more complete bond with Church, an increase of the gifts of the Holy Spirit and a "special strength" to witness to the faith.[24]

Are these effects simply a "step up" from Baptism? With the use of comparative vocabulary (intensifying, firmer, etc.) in the documents examined earlier, it would seem so. However, if we return to the work of the Angelic Doctor as a base, the uniqueness of Confirmation is manifested. Firstly, Thomas speaks of Baptism as spiritual regeneration.[25] It follows, then, as there is growth of the physical life, so this is true with the spiritual life. As we know that the effects of the sacraments are specific to times of life, we see that the spiritual rebirth of Baptism is supernatural life in Christ, entry into a relationship with the Trinity and the Church are effects of Baptism. There is forgiveness of original sin, and personal sin when appropriate, reception of the sacramental character, the supernatural virtues and sanctifying and sacramental graces available so that the Catholic can live as a child of God. Aquinas identifies Confirmation with another task.

While Thomas defines *physical* or *chronological* "perfect age" in another place,[26] he is not interested in physical age when he discusses Confirmation. He maintains that with the reception of Confirmation "the perfect age, as it were, of the *spiritual life*" is attained.[27] Thomas is careful not to give a chronological age. For him, the perfect age of the spiritual life is when "he [the believer] begins to have communication with others." He says this in contradistinction in regard to Baptism and the time before being confirmed: as "having been living an individual life . . . as if 'confined' to himself."[28]

23. Walsh, *Sacraments of Initiation*, 196.
24. *CCC*, 1303.
25. Aquinas, *ST* III.69.1 (I answer that).
26. Thomas Aquinas says in his *Catechetical Instructions*: "Perfect age, which is of thirty-two or thirty-three years" (Aquinas, *Catechetical Instructions* art. 11).
27. Aquinas, *ST* III.72.2 (I answer that).
28. Aquinas, *ST* III.72.2 (I answer that).

What does this mean? I venture to say that the effects of Baptism are for that "spiritual child" to come into his own. The effects of Baptism are to assist individuals to know the God who loves them—as an individual who is a Child of God and to grow in that understanding and most importantly, in that relationship. This would include beginning to know themselves with privileges and responsibilities as a member of the Church, part of the family of God.

In other terminology, we speak of being conformed to Christ. At Baptism, the Christian enters into not only a communion with the Trinity through life with Christ, but thus also enters into the mission of the Church which is an extension of the Mission of Christ which has priestly, prophetic and kingly dimensions.

With the celebration of Confirmation, the "perfect age" has arrived for the one confirmed. Just as Pentecost was the coming-of-age of the Church, as O'Neill calls it,[29] the same occurs in the confirmed individual. The spiritual strengthening for the sake of others was given to those disciples in the Upper Room. Before the tongues of fire rested on them, there was a personal relationship that they were nurturing with their Lord, according to O'Neill.[30] In the Pentecost event, the young Church was spiritually galvanised as a community for the sake of the mission of Christ. Christ had promised them: "you shall receive power when the Holy Spirit has come upon you; and you shall be my witnesses" (Acts 1:8). The sacramental character of Confirmation gives Catholics not only a similar responsibility for the salvation of the world, but the spiritual means (gifts and graces) to carry out the mission of Christ that continues to this day.

A key element is that the Catholic is both given a new role and the means to carry out this new role. We are not discussing at this point the Catholic's engagement with the new rank and "fullness of grace" that the believer has received. The fullness of grace is the "fullness of age" or perfect age.[31] Confirmation is the coming of the Spirit to a Christian in this time of the "already and not yet." In this Messianic age, the Catholic is more conformed to Christ, with the increase of graces and gifts, and, thus, is more responsible to continue the redemptive work of Christ, *quasi ex officio*, according to Thomas.[32] However, there is not a specification of what an individual's role is in this mission until there is collaboration on the part of the believer.

29. O'Neill and Cessario, *Meeting Christ*, 152.
30. O'Neill and Cessario, *Meeting Christ*, 152.
31. O'Neill and Cessario, *Meeting Christ*, 150.
32. Aquinas, *ST* III.72.5.ad2.

Fruitful Engagement with the Effects of Confirmation

An individual's engagement with the understanding of their Baptism as a beginning of their relationship with God can be similar to a kind of a "me, me, me" phase, a necessary phase of natural human development. In typical human development, a child's concerns are for food and comfort and at first sees others simply in that light. For the child, he/she is the center of it all. As the child continues to develop, they begin to differentiate that there are others like "me" out there. Those who gauge human development expect positive interaction with others as a sign of ongoing maturing. Even so, Saint Thomas would say this child was imperfect; there will be a completeness to the individual when they reach adulthood as the individual becomes more developmentally complete or perfected than as a child.

As an individual matures spiritually, they come to understand that a personal God loves them. As time goes on, "God loves you" becomes more descriptive as Christ's loving life, saving death, and glorious Resurrection is learned and embraced. The individual comes to know themselves beloved and to begin to consider what that means. In the course of development, a next step for an individual who comes to know about a gift given that is beyond expectation, is to ask: "How do I respond in return?"

So, as one comes to a clearer understanding of who they are within the Body of Christ, there grows within them a desire to respond to God's love gratuitously given throughout their life. How does one give thanks for the gift of supernatural life won by Christ through his self-gift manifested most clearly in his Paschal Mystery? The effects of having arrived at the "perfect age" helps an individual respond to that question which demands an answer.

The Ecclesiology of Communion and Confirmation

Now that a number of magisterial documents with descriptions of communion ecclesiology and the effects of Confirmation have been briefly outlined, it is possible to draw initial conclusions. The Church's understanding of communion is first of all situated in a vertical dimension of God and his people. Flowing from this relationship, is the Church. While there is a hierarchical order to the institution of the Church, every baptised member is in communion with one another as a child of God and a member of the Body of Christ. Thus, there is an external communion as well as an interior communion.

Confirmation strengthens the Catholic's relationship with God, as one is more closely conformed to Christ through the sacramental character. We are given a new rank or role in the Church to more visibly extend the Mission of Christ to bring the saving Good News of Christ to others. The power to accomplish this is also made available to us.

Firstly, simply by the reception of Confirmation, the communion within the Body is strengthened. However, it is the Catholic's engagement with the Gift, the fullness of grace, that will continue to perfect the communion that is possible.[33] Just as at Pentecost when the disciples moved outward to respond to the crowd who was drawn to them, it was because of the Spirit that enlivened them all to the mission of Christ in which they all had a part. In recognising one's increased conformity to Christ, one sees ever more clearly with the eyes of faith and hears with the ears of faith how to be for others.

The graces of Confirmation help the Catholic to focus on this outwardness or response to be a self-gift that arises within. The gifts of the Holy Spirit, already received in Baptism, are given in a new way for the spiritual maturity the individual has sacramentally entered into. The gifts given at Confirmation are for the sake of others.

Having reached the perfect age/been spiritually energised by the Holy Spirit, they realise the power of the Paschal Mystery within them to make the choices needed to spread the Kingdom of God. Assisted by a faithful life of prayer as baptised into the common priesthood of Christ, individuals can be confident in their participation in the kingly dimension of Christ. The same spirit of mission has been given to them to be His witnesses.

The responsibility to be a faith-filled disciple of Christ requires a profound commitment to maintain. It requires the theological and natural virtues of faith, hope and love. It will be lived out through the distinctive natural characteristics of the person enriched by grace. The permanence of the sacramental character of Confirmation speaks to this ongoing reality. The exuberance of the first Pentecost was not a childish excitement, but the enthusiasm that admitted of having received a gift that is meant to be shared.

In union with the other sacraments that accompany the Catholic on their journey to the eschatological banquet, Confirmation empowers one to discern one's particular mission in the redemptive mission of Christ and to carry it out. However, it is this mystery of an ever-more profound strengthening of the relationship of the disciple with the Lord that ultimately also impacts the communion of the Church and her witness, her worship and her service.

---

33. Recall St John Paul II's use of the second epiclesis of the Eucharistic Prayer III to point to this strengthening.

Bibliography

Aquinas, Thomas. *Catechetical Instructions*. Online. http://www.documentacatholicaomnia.eu/03d/1225-1274,_Thomas_Aquinas,_Catechismus,_EN.pdf.

———. *Summa Theologica*. Translated by the Fathers of the English Dominican Province. 2nd and rev. ed. Online. http://www.newadvent.org/summa/4072.htm#article2.

Benedict XVI. "Deus Caritas Est." Encyclical Letter. December 25, 2005. Online. http://w2.vatican.va/content/benedict-xvi/en/encyclicals/documents/hf_ben-xvi_enc_20051225_deus-caritas-est.html.

———. "Sacramentum Caritatis." Post-synodal Apostolic Exhortation. February 22, 2007. Online. https://w2.vatican.va/content/benedict-xvi/en/apost_exhortations.index.html.

Catechism of the Catholic Church (CCC). 2nd ed. Strathfield: St Pauls, 1997.

"Code of Canon Law." Online. http://www.vatican.va/archive/cod-iuris-canonici/cic_index_en.html.

Congregation for the Doctrine of the Faith (CDF). "Communionis Notio: Some Aspects of the Church Understood as Communion." May 28, 1992. Online. http://www.vatican.va/roman_curia/congregations/cfaith/documents/rc_con_cfaith_doc_28051992_communionis-notio_en.html.

———. "Iuvenescit Ecclesia: Letter on the Relationship between Hierarchical and Charismatic Gifts in the Life and Mission of the Church." May 15, 2016. Online. http://www.vatican.va/roman_curia/ congregations/cfaith/documents/rc_con_cfaith_doc_20160516_iuvenescit-ecclesia_en.html#_ftn45.

Extraordinary Synod of Bishops. "Final Relatio." 1985. Online. https://www.ewtn.com/library/curia/synfinal.htm.

Francis. "Audience." May 23, 2018. Online. http://w2.vatican.va/content/francesco/en/audiences/2018/documents/papa-francesco_20180523_udienza-generale.html.

———. "Audience." May 30, 2018. Online. http://w2.vatican.va/content/francesco/en/audiences/2018/documents/papa-francesco_20180530_udienza-generale.html.

———. "Laudato Sí." Encyclical Letter. May 24, 2015. Online. http://w2.vatican.va/content/francesco/en/encyclicals/documents/papa-francesco_20150524_enciclica-laudato-si.html.

John Paul II. "Christifidelis Laici" Post-synodal Apostolic Exhortation on The Vocation and the Mission of the Lay Faithful in the Church and in the World." December 30, 1988. Online. http://w2.vatican.va/content/john-paul-ii/en/apost_exhortations/documents/hf_jp-ii_exh_30121988_christifideles-laici.html.

———. "Dominum et Vivificantem." Encyclical Letter. May 18, 1986. Online. http://w2.vatican.va/content/john-paul-ii/en/encyclicals/documents/hf_jp-ii_enc_18051986_dominum-et-vivificantem.html.

———. "Ecclesia de Eucharistia." Encyclical Letter. April 30, 2003. Online. http://www.vatican.va/holy_father/special_features/encyclicals/documents/hf_jp-ii_enc_20030417_ecclesia_ eucharistia_en.html.

O'Neill, Colman, and Romanus Cessario. *Meeting Christ in the Sacraments*. New York: Alba, 1991.

Second Vatican Council. "Gaudium et Spes: Pastoral Constitution on the Church." December 7, 1965. Online. http://www.vatican.va/archive/hist_councils/ii_vatican_council/documents/vat-ii_cons_19651207_gaudium-et-spes_en.html.

———. "Lumen Gentium: Dogmatic Constitution on the Church." November 21, 1964. Online. http://www.vatican.va/archive/hist_councils/ii_vatican_council/documents/vat-ii_const_19641121_lumen-gentium_en.html.

Walsh, Liam. *Sacraments of Initiation*. 2nd ed. Chicago: Hillenbrand, 2011.

8

The Indivisible Totus Christus and the Universal Church

—SIMON R WAYTE, MGL

> *The relationship between the local and universal churches is examined in this chapter using the principle from Hans Urs von Balthasar that the whole is present in the part. This illuminates certain aspects of the debate between Ratzinger (Pope Emeritus Benedict XVI) and Kasper on the ontological priority of the universal church. Balthasar's principle together with the connection between Christ and the Church based on Augustine's concept of the totus Christus enables a deeper understanding of the relationship between the local and universal churches. It is found that the indivisibility of the totus Christus resolves some key difficulties in this debate. This indivisibility of the one totus Christus is brought into focus using the analogy of a hologram where the whole is quintessentially in the part. This leads to some fundamental implications for the ministry of priest and bishop.*

Introduction

The flowering of communion ecclesiology since Vatican II has not been without its challenges. Noticeable evidence for this came in 1992 with the issuing by the Congregation for the Doctrine of the Faith (CDF) of the document "Letter to the Bishops of the Catholic Church on

Some Aspects of the Church Understood as Communion."[1] This document sought to bring clarification to the topic of the Church understood as communion given that some approaches to communion ecclesiology were seen by the CDF to be inadequate. By presenting an understanding of the relationship between the universal church and particular or local churches that gave ontological and temporal priority to the universal church this document began an important debate between Cardinals Kasper and Ratzinger (now Pope Emeritus Benedict XVI) on the precise nature of the relationship between the local and universal church. This debate covered a number of points in ecclesiology, but at its heart was the contention by Cardinal Kasper regarding the teaching by Pope St John Paul II through the CDF that the universal church had ontological priority over individual particular or local churches.[2]

The Whole in the Part

In seeking to address this issue raised in the debate new insight can be gained by developing a principle found at the heart of the work of Hans Urs von Balthasar. This is the principle of the whole present in the part. The profound power of this principle can be missed if it is not properly interpreted. The idea that a part contributes to the whole and therefore in a way represents the whole so that the whole is present in the part is an incorrect enunciation of this principle. Further, the idea that the part contains a microcosmic reflection of the whole also incorrectly interprets this principle. Correctly interpreted the presence of the whole in the part has such a radical character that the whole becomes essentially indivisible. The whole can be present in the part because the whole transcends the normal understanding of whole and part.

Given that this experience of the whole and the part together with the resultant indivisibility of the whole runs counter to much of our everyday experience the application of the Balthasarian principle of the whole in the part, and the subsequent indivisibility of the whole, is best developed methodologically using analogies. A suitable analogy provides not only

---

1. CDF, "Communionis Notio."

2. Particular and local will be used as synonyms when referring to particular churches notwithstanding the distinction of De Lubac (see De Lubac, *Particular Churches*, 194–95) since the socio-cultural relational differences in local churches are part of what enables the particular churches to possess mutual interiority with the universal church.

correspondence between differing realities, but also inferential power to reveal hidden aspects of the reality for which the analogy is employed.

Balthasar leads his multi-volume magnum opus with the clear aim "to develop a Christian theology in the light of . . . the beautiful."[3] Fundamental to this development of an aesthetic theology is the use by Balthasar of the German concept *Gestalt*. David C. Schindler indicates that there is a sense in which the title of Balthasar's book "*Das Ganze im Fragment*, the whole in the part" can be understood as "in a certain sense the definition of Gestalt."[4] For Balthasar the *Gestalt Christi* is "present to faith as an indivisible . . . figure or form."[5] Philosophically Balthasar draws this from Goethe who was fascinated by the metamorphosis of plants where one has "the whole reflected in each separate part."[6] Nurseries often take cuttings from plants to propagate more instances of the plant to sell. Each potted plant is a different instance of the plant variety, but essentially the same plant. The whole reality of the plant variety is present in the part cut from the original plant and placed in a new pot. The whole is present in the part and one can say that the plant is essentially indivisible since cutting it does not destroy it, but allows it to continue growing in more than one place.

An analogy with greater inferential power in the application of the principle of the whole in the part is a hologram. Figure 1 shows the hologram of a crucifix made using red laser light.

---

3. Balthasar, *Seeing the Form*, 9.
4. Schindler, *Dramatic Structure of Truth*, 172.
5. Balthasar, *Spirit of Truth*, 203.
6. Goethe, *Metamorphosis of Plants*, 3.

Figure 1. Hologram of a crucifix[7]

Unlike a photograph, the hologram of an object does not have a one-to-one correspondence between the object and the image. The information about each point of the object is spread over the whole film or glass plate. In a hologram, created by the use of laser light, the pattern created by the laser encodes in a relational form the information about the object across the whole glass plate. When examined in ordinary daylight the pattern on the glass plate looks like a chaotic pattern of light and dark patches. However, when viewed using a laser, the image is revealed. Since the chaotic pattern contains the information of the object in relational form across the entire glass plate, any portion of the glass plate can show the whole image. Therefore, when the glass plate is cut into pieces (as seen in Figure 2) each of the pieces shows the whole image. They are not copies of the one image in the uncut hologram, but the very same image in different places (although from slightly different perspectives).

7. Commissioned image produced by Triple Take Holographics.

Figure 2. The crucifix hologram cut into four pieces[8]

The images in the cut hologram are not similar images, but one and the same image. The glass plate has been cut, but the image has not been divided. The whole image is present in any part of the glass plate. The image is in essence indivisible no matter how much the glass plate is cut. The greater inferential power of the holographic analogy over the plant analogy comes from the explanation for the manifestation of the whole in the part and the resultant indivisibility. The recording on the glass plate of the information about the image takes a plate wide *relational* form rather than a one-to-one substantial form. This relational form across the whole plate explains the capacity for the holographic image to be wholly present in any part of the glass plate. This makes the image essentially indivisible. In a hologram, the image becomes present through the light of a laser (the same laser that earlier created the image) interacting with the seemingly chaotic relational

8. Commissioned image produced by Triple Take Holographics.

pattern of light and dark patches on the glass plate. What is on the glass plate is this seemingly chaotic relational pattern rather than an actual image. This relational pattern replicates at every level across the glass plate so that even if only a portion of the glass plate is illuminated the whole image can be seen. This is the reason that even when the glass plate is cut the image remains present essentially indivisible. This differs from a photograph where cutting the photographic film would divide the image. A photograph only records the substantial intensity of light; it does not record a replicating relational pattern. The relational pattern is what brings about the presence of the whole in the part that consequently makes the holographic image indivisible.

The Indivisible Totus Christus

How does this consideration of the whole in the part and indivisibility apply to the Church? Does the insight from the holographic analogy that indivisibility arises from relationality apply in the case of the Church? If it does, then, what insight does indivisibility arising from relationality give to the issue of the ontological priority of the universal church?

A first step must be to consider what is meant by the term universal church. Is this the whole church militant, suffering, and triumphant currently constituted? Is it instead the whole church on earth over the entire course of its history? Is it rather the whole eschatological church in God's eternal plan? Alternatively is it simply the current visible worldwide church? To get to the heart of the matter it is necessary to go back to Ignatius of Antioch. Historically Ignatius of Antioch is the first to apply the term καθολική (catholic) to refer to the whole church. However, there is some debate about what Ignatius means when he says, "Wherever the bishop appears, there let the congregation be; just as wherever Jesus Christ is, there is the whole [καθολική] church."[9] Does Ignatius mean the universal church that is worldwide, orthodox in doctrine or organically unified? A careful examination by William Schoedel suggests that Ignatius means "not the universal church opposed to heresy, but the whole church resistant by its very nature to division."[10] Therefore, before other meanings accumulate to the term universal church its primary meaning must be the whole church as an indivisible reality.

Immediately, however, this text from Ignatius raises the issue of the relationship between Christ and the Church—"wherever Jesus Christ is, there

---

9. Schoedel, *Ignatius of Antioch*, 238.
10. Schoedel, *Ignatius of Antioch*, 244; cf. Clement of Alexandria, *Stromata* 17.107.

is the whole [καθολική] church."[11] The revelation of the indivisible nature of the Church comes not from a consideration of the Church as a substantial reality in itself, but in the context of its relationship to Jesus Christ. Augustine delves deeply into the reality of the Church in its relationship with Christ through his concept of the *totus Christus* which he develops from the Pauline texts regarding the body of Christ and being "in Christ."[12] Thus a consideration of the *totus Christus* may open up the precise basis for the indivisibility of the Church as introduced by Ignatius.

Augustine used the concept of the whole Christ or *totus Christus* to make sense of scriptural passages (like Matt 25:40; Acts 9:4) where Christ identifies with his disciples.[13] How can Christ be so united with the Church that he identifies with his church (e.g., "Saul, Saul, why do you persecute me?" Acts 9:4), while at the same time remaining distinct from his church as its Lord. Augustine speaks of the *totus Christus* as "both head and body."[14] Augustine, following Paul, speaks of Christ the Lord as the head and the Church as his body (1 Cor 12:12–27; Eph 1:10; Col 1:18). The *totus Christus* of Augustine is without spatial or temporal limitation. The *totus Christus* includes in the one body of Christ all the just over the whole world and across all time.[15] The concept of the *totus Christus* does not mean that Christ needs believers to complete his totality, but acknowledges that Christ chose to incorporate believers into himself.[16]

What type of incorporation is this and how does it come about? In Augustine's concept of the *totus Christus* the incorporation is not by nature, but by participation through faith.[17] The unity between Christ as head and his body is a personal unity.[18] This unity occurs "with Christ in his humanity and not in his divinity."[19] This unity brings about a personal communion so intimate that Augustine refers to Christ as "one man consisting of head and body."[20] In the act of incorporation this unity achieved is not at the level of nature, but at the level of personal communion.[21] The personal

---

11. Schoedel, *Ignatius of Antioch*, 238.
12. Bavel, "'Christus Totus' Idea," 85.
13. Meconi, *One Christ*, 194.
14. Augustine, "Sermones" 133.8; 341.11.
15. Augustine, "Sermones" 341.11.
16. Meconi, *One Christ*, 204.
17. Augustine, "Epistulae ad Galatas" 27.
18. Meconi, *One Christ*, 197.
19. Meconi, *One Christ*, 197, 211, 233.
20. Augustine, "Enarrationes in Psalmos" 61.4.
21. Meconi, *One Christ*, 212.

communion between the divine person of the Son and human persons is mediated through the assumed human nature of the Son. Through communion we see that the mysterious unity of the *totus Christus* is not a union of substantial natures, but a union of personal relations. It is not an absolutely complete identification, for believers are not absorbed into Christ.[22] Even in the personal unity Augustine does not totally collapse the Church into the person of Christ. He makes a distinction by speaking of Christ's own person and the person of the Church.[23] Even when he speaks of "the single person that is Head and body," he uses the image of bridegroom and bride which preserves a distinction within the personal unity.[24] In being incorporated into Christ, believers not only enter into communion with Christ himself, but they also enter into communion with each other, and hence are unified into a body—an ecclesial body.[25] In describing the Church as a body Augustine identifies the connection as charity.[26] This charity, in a sense, is the content of communion. Charity is not simply a moral connection, but an ontological one in which one part of the body shares the power of the whole through its incorporation into the whole.[27] The Holy Spirit is the one who achieves this incorporation. The Holy Spirit engenders charity in the believers who choose to accept the life of Christ through faith. Thus, the active life of Christ is communicated by the Holy Spirit to believers. In this way, the Holy Spirit conforms believers to Christ, and incorporates them into the *totus Christus*. The unity of the *totus Christus* flows from this action of the Holy Spirit within the relations of personal communion manifesting Christ, Lord and head, present in his body, the Church. Thus the principle of the whole present in the part, applied ecclesiologically, reveals in particular the fundamental indivisibility of the Church when understood within the framework of the *totus Christus*, and this indivisibility arises from the relational character of ecclesial communion through which Christ becomes present.

Holographic Development of the Totus Christus

The holographic analogy highlights the way Christ, Lord and head, is present in his body, the Church. As seen earlier, a holographic image becomes

22. Meconi, *One Christ*, 210, 213.
23. Augustine, "Enarrationes in Psalmos" 61.4, 142.3.
24. Augustine, "Enarrationes in Psalmos" 30.2.4.
25. Meconi, *One Christ*, 207–8.
26. Augustine, "Sermones" 162A.5.
27. Augustine, "Sermones" 162A.5.

present through the light of a laser interacting with a seemingly chaotic relational pattern on a glass plate or film. This pattern with information encoded relationally rather than substantially is what makes the holographic image indivisible. Similarly, the relations of personal communion are what make the *totus Christus* indivisible. The Holy Spirit can make present Christ, Lord and head, anywhere the ecclesial relations of personal communion are found (e.g., Matt 18:20). During Christ's earthly life, he worked in union with the Holy Spirit to form among his disciples the relations of personal communion, which continue to be a living reality across the Church today. The Holy Spirit acting upon these relations can today reveal the risen Lord Jesus present and active in a new mode within his church. The concrete ecclesial relations embody this pneumatological mode of Christ's risen presence. In this way, Christ, the risen Lord, becomes present in a transcendent way through the Holy Spirit working within the Church. Due to this embodiment in the ecclesial relations of communion, Christ can never be separated from his body, so even when the ecclesial body is apportioned into parts the Holy Spirit can still make Christ the head present in any of those parts thereby manifesting the indivisibility of the *totus Christus*. Therefore, an understanding of the universal church cannot be understood without reference to Christ in whom the Church finds its unity. Since Christ himself is the referent, this unity transcends the world. A discussion on the unity of the Church limited to the relationship between the universal church and the local or particular churches risks emphasizing either the universal or the particular to the detriment of the other. In whatever way the term universal church is used, the unity of the Church does not rely in an absolute sense on the visible structures of the Church, but on the one Christ.[28] Therefore, when speaking of the relationship between the particular churches and the universal church all that is necessary is to agree that both find their unity in Christ.

Thus, when the term universal church, from Ignatius of Antioch's reference to the whole church, is understood as the Church indivisible by its nature, the term universal church refers principally to the relational structures of personal communion through which the Holy Spirit makes Christ, Lord and head present in his body. This universal church can then manifest in particular expressions. These particular expressions can include the current visible worldwide church, or whole church on earth over the entire course of its history, or even the whole eschatological church.

---

28. Structures are important not because they determine the eschatological unity of the Church, but because they reflect this unity and constitute it in history.

Debate on the Ontological Priority of the Universal Church

This leads us to look in detail at the debate mentioned earlier between Cardinals Kasper and Ratzinger (now Pope Emeritus Benedict XVI) on the ontological priority of the universal church.[29] Following the publication of *Communionis Notio* regarding communion ecclesiology and further reflection in *L'Osservatore Romano* a year later, Kasper and Ratzinger engaged in a debate centered on the question of the ontological priority of the universal church with respect to the particular (or local individual) churches. Kasper found difficulty in the claim within these two documents that the universal church is ontologically prior to the particular churches, since that seemed to be at odds with the teaching of *Lumen Gentium* that particular churches are true churches and that "in and from these particular churches there exists the one unique catholic church."[30] Indeed, the claim of ontological priority for the universal church seemed to be at odds with the claim in the *L'Osservatore* article itself that "the mutual interiority between the universal Church and the particular Churches" is the hermeneutical key to *Communionis Notio*.[31] If they are mutually interior to each other how can the universal church be ontologically prior? Kasper emphasized his understanding of this mutual interiority by speaking of the simultaneous interiority or *perichoresis* of the universal church and the particular churches.[32] Ratzinger agreed with Kasper that "the local church and the universal church are internal to one another; they penetrate each other and are perichoretic."[33] However, for Ratzinger this misses the point.[34] The point for Ratzinger is that of church unity—there can be "only one bride, only one body of Christ."[35]

Understanding the unity of the Church in terms of the one body of Christ requires a delicate nuancing of the relationship between Christ and his church. Ratzinger highlights the relational openness of Christ.[36]

---

29. CDF, "Communionis Notio"; "Church Unity Rooted in Eucharist," 4, 10; Kasper, "Zur Theologie und Praxis," 32–48; "On the Church," 8–14; "Present Situation and Future," 11–20; "Letters," 28–29; Ratzinger, "Ecclesiology," 5–8; "Local Church and the Universal Church," 7–11.

30. Second Vatican Council, "Lumen Gentium" no. 23, 26.

31. "Church Unity Rooted in Eucharist," 4.

32. Kasper, "Present Situation," 18; Sakowski, *Ecclesiological Reality*, 54.

33. Ratzinger, "Local Church and the Universal Church," 10. Kasper's words in the *Tablet* translation are: "The local Church and the universal Church live within each other: they interpenetrate each other in an interwoven relationship" (Kasper, "On the Church," 929).

34. Ratzinger, "Local Church and the Universal Church," 10.

35. Ratzinger, "Local Church and the Universal Church," 10.

36. Ratzinger, *Introduction to Christianity*, 179–80.

Thanks to this openness, being one in Christ when Paul says "you are all one in Christ Jesus" (Gal 3:28) refers to "a new, singular subject together with Christ."[37] Who or what is this new singular subject? In becoming one new subject with Christ "the separate individual is not extinguished" and neither does the Church become "a separate subject endowed with its own subsistence."[38] Rather Ratzinger affirms that "the new subject is much rather 'Christ' himself, and the Church is nothing but the space of this new unitary subject."[39] By "giving oneself over into the unity of the 'whole Christ,' the *totus Christus*, as Augustine beautifully puts it," the Christian embraces the openness of Christ "emerging from the confinement of the ego."[40] Even though Miroslav Volf misunderstands Ratzinger in places, he rightly affirms that Ratzinger makes clear that the relationship between Christ and the Church is a "dynamic union" rather than an absolute identification.[41] However, Volf questions "just how the Church can be a single subject with Christ and yet be distinguished from Christ."[42]

Like Ratzinger, Zizioulas also takes on board Augustine's concept of the *totus Christus*. Taking his point of entry from the liturgy, Zizioulas affirms a "total . . . identification of Christ with the Church" when in the Eucharistic Prayer the Church with Christ prays to the Father.[43] This leads Zizioulas to the idea of a corporate personality where Christ is "the corporate being par excellence," for he cannot be head without his body, the Church.[44] However, at the same time in the liturgy Christ stands with the Father receiving the prayer of the Church. "In the eyes of his people the bishop *is* Christ; but in his own eyes he is *not*: he prays *to* Christ *for himself*, but to the Father (as if he were Christ) *for the people*."[45] The only way for such an identification with Christ, in which distinction is still maintained, to make sense is through "the Spirit as *constitutive of the identity* of Christ."[46] The Spirit constitutes Christ as a relational being who cannot stand as an isolated individual either in his divinity or in his humanity.[47]

---

37. Ratzinger, *Nature and Mission of Theology*, 52.
38. Ratzinger, *Introduction to Christianity*, 179; *Nature and Mission of Theology*, 54.
39. Ratzinger, *Nature and Mission of Theology*, 54.
40. Ratzinger, *Dogma and Preaching*, 44.
41. Bidwell, *Church as the Image of the Trinity*, 122, 236; Volf, *After Our Likeness*, 34.
42. Volf, *After Our Likeness*, 34.
43. Zizioulas, "Mystery of the Church," 297.
44. Zizioulas, "Mystery of the Church," 299.
45. Zizioulas, "Mystery of the Church," 298.
46. Zizioulas, "Mystery of the Church," 298.
47. Zizioulas, "Mystery of the Church," 299.

Thus in speaking of the universal church the relationship between the Church and Christ cannot be passed over. Ratzinger and Zizioulas both highlight the intimate identification of Christ with his church while simultaneously holding to necessary distinctions between Christ and the Church. In their discussions on this topic both Ratzinger and Zizioulas hold to the basic idea in Ignatius of Antioch that the whole church is "resistant by its very nature to division."[48] However, as said earlier, this cannot be understood without reference to Christ in whom the Church finds its unity, but a unity that transcends this world.

Understanding the unity of the Church as a transcendent reality found in Christ, it can be affirmed that "the universal Church, the one Church, the one body, the one bride" must be ontologically prior to any empirical expression of it.[49] Kasper agrees with Ratzinger in this affirmation of "the priority of inner unity" of the Church.[50] Kasper believes that this has moved the debate from the ontological priority of the universal church to a position on "the priority of inner unity" of the Church which they can both agree on.[51] When seeming ambiguity is removed and the universal church is understood as "the one pre-existing and eschatological Church" rather than the current world-wide church, Kasper sees himself in agreement with Ratzinger.[52] However, subsequent statements by Ratzinger (as Pope Benedict XVI) indicate that there has been no substantial shift in his thought from the idea and language that "the universal church has ontological priority."[53]

Why does Ratzinger continue to speak of the ontological priority of the universal church without specification of the term, when in Kasper's view part of the difficulty came from a misunderstanding of the term universal church? A hint of the cause for difference between Ratzinger and Kasper this comes from the seemingly less important question of the temporal priority of the universal church also taught in *Communionis Notio*. In the debate with Kasper, Ratzinger acknowledges that the claim of temporal priority claim is "certainly more difficult" to affirm than ontological priority.[54] However, he never turns away from this affirmation. The later homilies of Ratzinger (as Pope Benedict XVI) reiterate the assertion from the *L'Osservatore*

48. Schoedel, *Ignatius of Antioch*, 244.
49. Ratzinger, "Ecclesiology," 6.
50. Kasper, "Letters," 29. Ratzinger actually says, "the inner priority of unity," but the meaning is essentially the same.
51. Kasper, "Letters," 29.
52. Kasper, *Catholic Church*, 275.
53. Benedict XVI, "Homiliae I," 368. See also Benedict XVI, "Homiliae IV," 332; "Homiliae III," 456–57.
54. Ratzinger, "Ecclesiology," 6.

article that "at Pentecost there is no 'mutual interiority' between universal and particular Church, because these two dimensions are not yet distinct," for "the Church which is born at Pentecost is not primarily a particular Community—the Church of Jerusalem—but the universal Church."[55] However, for Kasper "a historic precedence of the one Church before the many local churches . . . cannot be verified biblically or historically in the Early Church," and "thus, the Church within history must be regarded historically *and philosophically* as unity in the diversity of individual churches as well as diversity in the unity of the one Church."[56] Thus, for Ratzinger, the mutual interiority of the universal church and particular churches comes into play some time after the beginning of the Church, while for Kasper this mutual interiority has been present from the very beginning. Even if Ratzinger is right in claiming the Church began at Pentecost in one geographic location, Kasper is right to affirm this philosophical concept of mutual interiority from the beginning, for without this quality of mutual interiority in the universal church, particular churches could never arise as geographically separate entities and still remain in the catholic whole. Indeed, in contrast to the clarification in *L'Osservatore Romano*, even in the eschaton this quality will remain even though geography will cease to have any meaning.[57] This quality will remain, for it is the quality of catholicity—the indivisibility of the Church.

While Kasper is stronger on the mutual interiority of the universal and particular churches Ratzinger correctly focuses on church unity and the way "the universal Church, the one Church, the one body, the one bride" must be ontologically prior to any empirical expression of it.[58] In equating the universal church to "the one pre-existing and eschatological Church," rather than the whole church indivisible by nature Kasper replaces the universal church in its relationally constituted indivisible essence with a particular substantial expression of it and is thereby in fundamental disagreement with Ratzinger though it appears Kasper does not recognize it.[59] The worldwide church, the eschatological church and particular churches are all particular substantial manifestations of the universal church (a fundamentally relational reality) found in the indivisible *totus Christus*.

The risen Lord can become transcendently present in both the worldwide church at any point in time and in particular churches. As the Holy

---

55. "Church Unity Rooted in Eucharist," 4; Benedict XVI, "Homiliae I," 368.
56. Kasper, *Catholic Church*, 276 (emphasis added).
57. "Church Unity Rooted in Eucharist," 4.
58. Ratzinger, "Ecclesiology," 6.
59. Kasper, *Catholic Church*, 275.

Spirit makes the risen Lord present in and through the concrete relations of personal communion of the Church, the whole person of Christ becomes present in the whole eschatological church, in the worldwide church, and in any particular church. The whole is truly present in the part. The whole Christ as head can be truly present in any appropriate part of his body, the Church. Yet following the holographic analogy, when the parts come together there are not multiple presences of Christ, but only *one* presence of the risen Lord. The risen Christ's presence in the Church is "multiple, but not multiplied," for there is only one head.[60] Thus, Kasper is right to argue against the relegation of particular churches to departments of the universal worldwide church, for they are the Church in a particular place in which the risen Christ becomes truly present.[61] At the same time, Ratzinger is right to affirm the teaching of *Communionis Notio* against a reductionist communion ecclesiology.[62] "*The universal Church cannot be conceived as the sum of the particular Churches, or as a federation of particular Churches.*"[63] For when taken as a universal reality the Church does not multiply the presence of Christ and the particular churches do not add up to the worldwide church. As Afanassieff says "'one plus one is still *one*' in ecclesiology."[64] This unusual mathematics can be seen if the four pieces of the hologram seen in Figure 2 are rejoined as seen in Figure 3. If that occurs, then only one image (not four) is then seen since the image in the whole does not come from the sum of the images in the parts. The image is always one and indivisible.

---

60. Tillard, *L'église locale*, 75, quoted in Sakowski, *Ecclesiological Reality*, 402.
61. Kasper, "On the Church," 927.
62. Ratzinger, "Ecclesiology," 6.
63. CDF, "Communionis Notio" no. 9; John Paul II, "Itinera Apostolica," no. 3.
64. Afanassieff, "Church Which Presides in Love," 109.

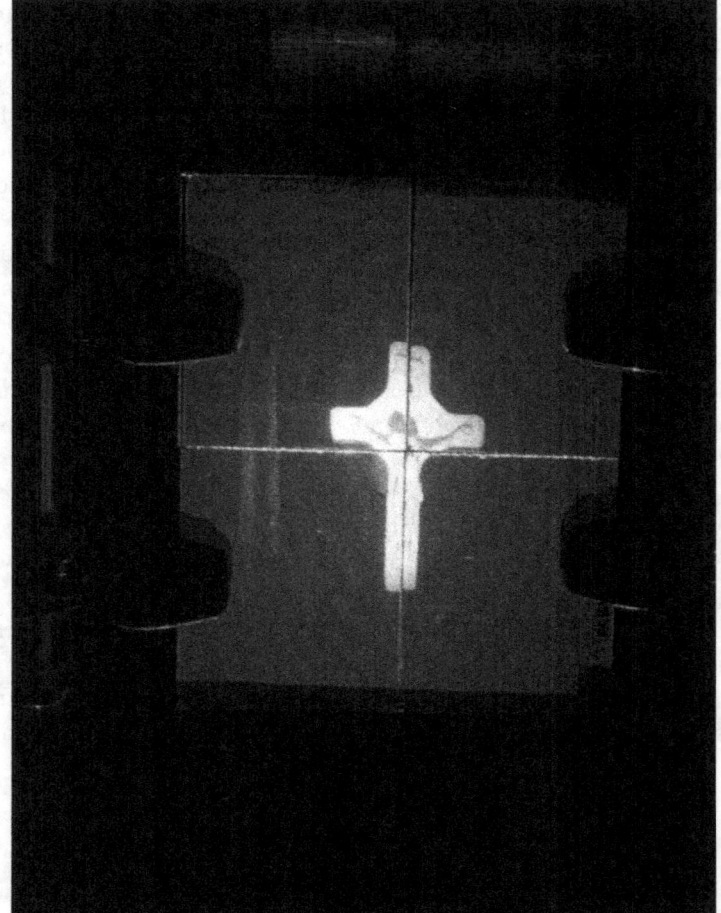

Figure 3. The four pieces of the crucifix hologram rejoined at a later date[65]

Now, the holographic analogy suggests that the quality of the whole present in the part arises at the very beginning of the Church. It is of the very nature of the Church as catholic—as unable to be divided. Therefore, in the indivisibility of the Church we can see the unity of the *totus Christus*. The holographic image can never be divided, no matter how many times the hologram is cut up. At the same time, when the parts come together again only one image is visible. So, individual particular churches manifest the one *totus Christus*, not only in themselves, but also when together. Therefore, the manifestation of the one *totus Christus* in particular churches is oriented towards the manifestation of the one *totus Christus* when they are together in the worldwide church, which itself is oriented towards the

65. Commissioned image produced by Triple Take Holographics.

manifestation of the one *totus Christus* in the whole eschatological church. For, "the presence of the whole in each of the parts gives each part an inner impulse towards universality."[66] Thus the concept of the universal church, through its relational structure manifesting the one *totus Christus* must have ontological priority over any particular expression for it grounds the indivisibility of the Church—its very catholicity.

Ecclesial Primacy and Episcopal Ministry

The holographic quality of the Church manifest in the relationship between the universal church and particular churches has an impact of the nature of primacy. A reflection of the holographic quality of the Church on the question of primacy can be found in the writings of Nicholas of Cusa, cardinal, philosopher, theologian, jurist, astronomer, and mystic (1401–64 AD). In his earlier works Nicholas promotes concordance in the Church and harmony between pope and council by taking an "intermediate position" between "coercive rulership" and "the election and consent of men and the Church."[67] Nicholas affirms that no one can go against the pope in matters affecting the universal church, and that without the agreement of the pope a synod has no authority.[68] However, he also affirms that "every Christian, even the Roman Pontiff, is subject to the universal council."[69] So, despite seeking a balance, his *De Concordantia Catholica* "is an unmistakable defense of the conciliar position."[70] In attempting to balance the authority of the pope and that of an ecumenical council Nicholas cannot avoid the either/or nature of the question because he seeks an intermediate position between the two. In seeking concord through an intermediate position on an either/or question, it is not surprising that later he switches to support the pope against the majority of the council of Basel in the matter of the location of a new council.[71] However, his move from conciliarist to papist becomes visible in his writings only after his return from Constantinople in 1437–38, when he experiences "a gift from the Father of Lights" by which he "was led to embrace incomprehensibles incomprehensibly in learned ignorance, by transcending those incorruptible truths that can be humanly known."[72] The change is most profound. While Nicholas does not "abandon

66. Benedict XVI, "Ecclesia in Medio Oriente," 769.
67. Nicholas of Cusa, *Catholic Concordance* 2.264.
68. Bond et al., "Presidential Authority," 33.
69. Bond et al., "Presidential Authority," 26.
70. Biechler, "Nicholas of Cusa," 5.
71. Bond et al., "Presidential Authority," 23.
72. Nicholas of Cusa, *De Docta Ignorantia* 3.263.

the theory of concordance, which was central to his conciliarism," he situates it within a new metaphysic based on the coincidence of opposites.[73] No longer does Nicholas seek an intermediate position. Now he develops a new metaphysic that enables him to completely transcend this idea of an intermediate position.

In his concept of the coincidence of opposites Nicholas seeks to find a way to hold contrarieties, such as the finite and the infinite, together without collapsing them into each other.

> For example, as finite figures the polygon and the circle are contradictory and incongruent, but when the notion of infinity is applied to them, they coincide and all contrariety desists. When the number of the sides of any polygon is multiplied by infinity, the polygon coincides with the circle, and their objective opposition resolved. However, though they coincide, "no multiplication of its angles, even if infinite, will make the polygon equal with the circle."[74]

Thus, the concept of the coincidence of opposites does not express a unity between elements on the same level as each other. Rather the coincidence of opposites expresses a unity of a higher order that transcends the elements to be unified.

This coincidence of opposites could be applied to the presence of the risen Christ in the Church. The risen Christ is truly present in his church such that he identifies with his church, just as the circle coincides with the infinite sided polygon, and yet the eschatological risen Christ is clearly to be distinguished from the Church, just as a circle is essentially different from a polygon. Thus one can understand the risen Christ present in the Church as the *totus Christus*, with the head united, yet distinguishable, from the members. Similarly, the holographic analogy presents the risen Christ present in the Church through the relational pattern between members, and yet the eschatological risen Christ transcends this relational pattern, and as head governs it through the Holy Spirit.

This leads to the question of the way in which the head and members of the *totus Christus* are united. As we saw earlier, Augustine identifies faith manifest in charity as the way in which the head and members of the *totus Christus* are united. Nicholas does not address this question directly. However, he does speak of the faithful being united to Christ "either by faith and love in this life or by attainment and enjoyment in the next."[75] In this union Nicholas notes that "each member will be present in Christ in such a way

---

73. Miroy, "From Conciliar Unity to Mystical Union," 171.

74. Bond, "Reconstruction of Theology," 92; Nicholas of Cusa, *De Docta Ignorantia* 1.3.10.

75. Nicholas of Cusa, *De Docta Ignorantia* 3.12.255.

that there is but one Christ from all the members."[76] However, this is not to collapse Christ and the Church into undifferentiated unity. The distinction between Christ and the Church can be preserved through the coincidence of opposites. In his general philosophy Nicholas relates the infinite one and the finite many in the coincidence of opposites through the concept of enfolding/unfolding (*complicatio/explicatio*) that he draws from Thierry of Chartres.[77] Applied here, Christ who is one and undivided enfolds the Church with its many members.

> Those who lay hold of the faith, wayfaring in hope with unifying love, evidently participate in their own way, in their varied diversity, the unique grace of Christ's being. Hence we call this Church mystically the body of Christ, because it is nothing but the grace of Jesus Christ unfolded.[78]

Thus the head and members are united through the grace of Christ. As Christ's two natures are united by "an absolute union, which is the Holy Spirit," so too the head and members of the *totus Christus* are united by the Holy Spirit at work among the many members.[79] Nicholas calls this work of the Holy Spirit among the members, the grace of Christ unfolded, though he does not identify (as the holographic analogy does) the personal relational structure between members as the manner of the unfolding. Adding this personal relational structure, we can say that the perichoretic relationship between Christ and the Holy Spirit enfolded in Christ himself unfolds in the world through the action of Christ and the Spirit during Christ's time on earth and draws human persons into this relational structure. This relational structure within the body of Christ has the unique quality that, when the Holy Spirit acts upon it, the person of the risen Christ becomes present. Thus the head and members of the *totus Christus* are united through the relational structure that Christ as head, and unfolded from him, set up with the Spirit during Christ's earthly life. The members are united with the head as they remain faithful to this relational structure through which the Holy Spirit makes Christ present. What does primacy look like within this relational structure? Nicholas suggests an answer by his discussion of the enfolding of the Church in Peter.

> Under the enfolding in Christ and as an image of it, Nicholas highlights the enfolding of the visible church in Peter.[80] Within the *totus Christus* and dependent on it the visible church finds

---

76. Nicholas of Cusa, *De Docta Ignorantia* 3.12.256.
77. Moran, "Nicholas of Cusa," 185.
78. Nicholas of Cusa, "Letter to Rodrigo Sánchez de Arévalo," 433.
79. Nicholas of Cusa, *De Docta Ignorantia* 3.12.262.
80. Izbicki, "Church in the Light of Learned Ignorance," 200.

its own integral unity "in the confession of Peter, which has its inception from Peter through supernal revelation."[81] Nicholas highlights Peter as the first to recognize that Jesus is the Christ.[82] So, just as the members of the Church unfolded from Christ are called Christians, so too the members of the Church unfolded from Peter are called "recognizers."[83] This confession of Peter, who enfolds the Church as recognizers of Christ, cannot be divided. Since, however, a multitude can participate unity only in a varied diversity, the Church cannot subsist, consequently, except in a varied participation of unity. For this reason, it is necessary for there to be various members of the one body of the Church, in whom there is that *one whole confession in the whole and in every part of it*. The Church, therefore, exists as a unity in a varied diversity.[84]

This implies that Peter and his confession of faith are reflected holographically (the whole in the whole and in every part) in the Church.

For Nicholas primacy has a similar holographic quality. "All princes in the Church participate in the principate of Peter, just as all the faithful participate in the faith of Peter."[85] Through his reference to the visible church being enfolded in Peter, Nicholas can speak of primacy without having to find an intermediate position between pope and council. Just as Christ stands as head in the *totus Christus*, present in his body which he governs but transcending it, so too Peter stands as the primary one who surrendered to Christ in the obedience of faith, present throughout the visible church, but distinct from it. Therefore, any prelate holds the same power as Peter, but only within the scope of the particular place the prelate stands in the unfolding.[86] Thus "each bishop acts as Peter for his diocese, but only for his diocese."[87] Similarly the pope acts as Peter for the whole world during his pontificate, but only for the time of his pontificate. Further, as a member of the college of bishops each bishop acts in this context not as Peter, but as an apostolic brother. The one exception is the pope who as the head of the college of bishops acts, also in this context, in the place of Peter to "strengthen

---

81. Nicholas of Cusa, "Letter to Rodrigo Sánchez de Arévalo," 437. Note that in Peter's confession of faith the confession cannot be separated from the person since faith itself is a personal act. See Ciraulo, "One and the Many," 52.

82. See Nicholas of Cusa, "Sermon 160," 479n2.

83. Nicholas of Cusa, "Sermon 160," 479 (emphasis added).

84. Nicholas of Cusa, "Letter to Rodrigo Sánchez de Arévalo," 437.

85. Nicholas of Cusa, "Sermon 160," 479.

86. Nicholas of Cusa, "Letter to Rodrigo Sánchez de Arévalo," 443.

87. Ciraulo, "One and the Many," 56.

his brothers" (cf. Luke 22:32). It must be remembered that this sharing in the power of primacy unfolded from Peter remains under the primacy of Christ, for only Christ himself as head has transcendent primacy across all places and all times where his body extends.

One can see a practical consequence of primacy understood holographically. When bishops act together as a college they place themselves under the protection of the primacy of the pope, this then allows them to speak candidly with all their uniqueness as parts of the whole. (Parts here are understood in the normal sense of sections that are less than the whole—not in the holographic sense. This can be understood if each of the four parts of Figure 2 are re-joined as seen in Figure 3. When re-joined each of the parts taken individually, show only a part of the holographic image.) In this mode the bishops, as it were, flesh out the face of Christ in the worldwide church. In this they reflect the social-cultural differences between local or particular churches that map out the various dimensions of Christ in the world. However, when the bishops return to their dioceses, they occupy the place of primacy in their dioceses and cannot speak in the same candid way as they did when they were together. This is more than a simple episcopal solidarity (like cabinet solidarity in western parliamentary democracy). They now reflect the oneness of Christ (and the oneness of Peter's confession of faith) in their dioceses, just as the pope reflects the oneness of Christ for the whole world. Unfolded from Peter, the pope reflects the oneness of Christ in his practice of primacy for the world, while the bishops reflect the oneness of Christ in their practice of primacy within their dioceses. So bishops can be forthright when they are together and faithful when apart. Peter and Paul are prime examples of this. When Peter came to Antioch Paul "opposed him to his face" (Gal 2:11), but Paul faithfully remained in concrete communion with the Jerusalem community throughout his travels (cf. 1 Cor 16:1–3) until finally Peter and Paul were united in martyrdom in Rome.

It is important to note that because of this holographic quality, the faithfulness of individual bishops in their particular churches may make it *appear* to others as though they are acting as departments of Rome, when in fact they are simply being faithful to their own charism of primacy in their local situation. If this faithfulness were to diminish, it would endanger the radiance of the presence of the risen Christ in that location since the relational structure through which the Holy Spirit makes Christ present would itself be damaged (but not destroyed). Nevertheless, this faithfulness should not restrict the forthright expression of bishops in dialogue with each other when gathering under the protection of *papal* primacy. It could be said that in recent centuries the Catholic Church has been strong on practicing primacy, both papal and episcopal, but weak on practicing collegiality both conciliar and synodic. Perhaps more notice should be taken of the injunction of the ecumenical council of Constance in session thirty-nine to have ecumenical councils at least every ten years in perpetuity.[88] This seeming impractical proposition in today's world highlights the importance of the practice since Vatican II of holding regular synods.

In an analogous way, this outlook regarding the ministry of bishops can be extended to priests. Priests can be forthright in their expression when they are together under the protection of episcopal primacy, but should remain faithful when they return to the people to whom they minister. This is not a suppression of the expression of conscience of the priest when they may disagree with their bishop, but an expression of their ministry standing in the person of Christ the head—one and indivisible.

Conclusion

Communion ecclesiology continues to make a positive contribution to the theology of the Church. The Balthasarian principle of the whole in the part has an important part to play in furthering this contribution. The application of this principle to the Church reveals the Church as essentially indivisible—essentially catholic. This indivisible nature of the Church depends on its intimate relationship with Christ. Christ stands in the midst of his body, the Church, with which he identifies, and yet in standing there in the midst, Christ transcends the Church as head in the *totus Christus*. The holographic analogy aids in the discovery of relationality as the foundation of this indivisibility of the *totus Christus*. Through the action of the Holy Spirit within the relational reality of the Church, Christ becomes present in the midst of the Church as head of his body.

The debate between Cardinals Kasper and Ratzinger (Pope Emeritus Benedict XVI) regarding the ontological priority of the universal church over local churches can be resolved when the universal church is seen in terms of this relational reality rather than in terms of a substance in a particular place (even if this place is the whole world). The worldwide church, the local churches and even the eschatological church are all particular expressions of the universal church understood in relational terms. In this way the universal church stands as indivisible and ontologically prior to any expression of it in either local churches or in the worldwide church.

A communion ecclesiology in which the Church exists as a relational and indivisible reality has implications for ecclesial primacy and episcopal ministry. In their relations bishops (and by extension priests) are called to be forthright and faithful in contexts appropriate to the life of the indivisible *totus Christus*. This mirrors the consideration in trinitarian theology of the

---

88. Council of Constance, *Frequens*, 438.

action of God *ad intra* and *ad extra*. Indeed, communion ecclesiology supported by the principle of the whole in the part can open up a fruitful way to consider the Church as a reflection of the triune life of God.

Bibliography

Afanassieff, Nicholas. "The Church Which Presides in Love." In *The Primacy of Peter: Essays in Ecclesiology and the Early Church*, edited by John Meyendorff, 91–143. Crestwood, NY: St Vladimir's Seminary, 1992.

Augustine. "Enarrationes in Psalmos 30." In *Expositions of the Psalms (1–32)*, edited by John E. Rotelle, 316–61. Translated by Maria Boulding. Works of Saint Augustine 3/15. Hyde Park, NY: New City, 2000.

———. "Enarrationes in Psalmos 61." In *Expositions of the Psalms (51–72)*, edited by John E. Rotelle, 202–28. Translated by Maria Boulding. Works of Saint Augustine 3/17. Hyde Park, NY: New City, 2001.

———. "Enarrationes in Psalmos 142." In *Expositions of the Psalms (121–150)*, edited by Boniface Ramsey, 344–59. Translated by Maria Boulding. Works of Saint Augustine 3/20. Hyde Park, NY: New City, 2004.

———. "Epistulae ad Galatas expositionis liber unus." In *Augustine's Commentary on Galatians*, edited by Eric Plumer, 124–236. Oxford: Oxford University Press, 2003.

———. "Sermones 133." In *Sermons: On the New Testament (94A–147A)*, edited by John E. Rotelle, 332–40. Translated by Edmund Hill. Works of Saint Augustine 3/4. Brooklyn, NY: New City, 1992.

———. "Sermones 162A." In *Sermons: On the New Testament (148–183)*, edited by John E. Rotelle, translated by Edmund Hill, 152–66. Translated by Edmund Hill. Works of Saint Augustine 3/5. New Rochelle, NY: New City, 1992.

———. "Sermones 341." In *Sermons: On Various Subjects (341–400)*, edited by John E. Rotelle, translated by Edmund Hill, 19–29. Translated by Edmund Hill. Works of Saint Augustine 3/10. Hyde Park, NY: New City, 1995.

Balthasar, Hans Urs von. *Seeing the Form*. Vol. 1 of *The Glory of the Lord: A Theological Aesthetics*. Edited by Joseph Fessio and John Riches. Translated by Erasmo Leiva-Merikakis. Edinburgh: T&T Clark, 1982.

———. *The Spirit of Truth*. Vol. 3 of *Theo-Logic: Theological Logical Theory*. Translated by Graham Harrison. San Francisco: Ignatius, 2005.

Bavel, Tarsicius J. van. "The 'Christus Totus' Idea: A Forgotten Aspect of Augustine's Spirituality." In *Studies in Patristic Christology*, edited by Thomas Finan and Vincent Twomey, 84–94. Portland, OR: Four Courts, 1998.

Benedict XVI. "Ecclesia in Medio Oriente." *Acta Apostolicae Sedis* 104 (2008) 751–96. Apostolic Exhortation. English translation. Online. http://w2.vatican.va/content/benedict-xvi/en/apost_exhortations/documents/hf_ben-xvi_exh_20120914_ecclesia-in-medio-oriente.html.

———. "Homiliae I: In Sollemnitate Pentecostes." *Acta Apostolicae Sedis* 100 (2008) 366–69. English translation. Online. https://w2.vatican.va/content/benedict-xvi/en/homilies/2008/documents/hf_ben-xvi_hom_20080511_pentecoste.html.

———. "Homiliae III: In Sollemnitate Pentecostes." *Acta Apostolicae Sedis* 103 (2011) 454–57. English translation. Online. https://w2.vatican.va/content/benedict-xvi/en/homilies/2011/documents/hf_ben-xvi_hom_20110612_pentecoste.html.

———. "Homiliae IV: In Sollemnitate Pentecostes." *Acta Apostolicae Sedis* 102 (2010) 331–35. English translation. Online. https://w2.vatican.va/content/benedict-xvi/en/homilies/2010/documents/hf_ben-xvi_hom_20100523_pentecoste.html.

Bidwell, Kevin J. *The Church as the Image of the Trinity: A Critical Evaluation of Miroslav Volf's Ecclesial Model*. Eugene, OR: Wipf and Stock, 2011.

Biechler, James E. "Nicholas of Cusa and the End of the Conciliar Movement: A Humanist Crisis of Identity." *Church History* 44 (1975) 5–21.

Bond, Lawrence H. "Nicholas of Cusa and the Reconstruction of Theology: The Centrality of Christology in the Coincidence of Opposites." In *Contemporary Reflection on the Medieval Christian Tradition: Essays in Honor of Ray C. Petry*, edited by George H. Shriver, 81–94. Durham, NC: Duke University Press, 1974.

Bond, Lawrence H., et al. "Nicholas of Cusa: 'On Presidential Authority in a General Council.'" *Church History* 59 (1990) 19–34.

"Church Unity Rooted in Eucharist." *L'Osservatore Romano* 27 (1993) 4, 10.

Ciraulo, Jonathan Martin. "The One and the Many: Peter and Peters." *Journal of Ecumenical Studies* 48 (2013) 45–57.

Clement of Alexandria. *Stromata*. In *Miscellanies Book VII: The Greek Text with Introduction, Translation, Notes, Dissertations and Indicies*, edited by Fenton John Hort and Joseph B Mayor. New York: Macmillan, 1902. Online. http://www.westcotthort.com/books/Hort_-_Clement_of_Alexandria_-_Miscellanies_Book_VII_(1902).pdf.

Congregation for the Doctrine of the Faith (CDF). "Communionis Notio: Litterae ad Catholicae Ecclesiae episcopos de aliquibus aspectibus Ecclesiae prout est communio." *Acta Apostolica Sedes* 85 (1992) 838–50. English translation. Online. http://www.vatican.va/roman_curia/congregations/cfaith/documents/rc_con_cfaith_doc_28051992_communionis-notio_en.html.

Council of Constance. "Frequens. On General Councils. October 9, 1417." In *Decrees of the Ecumenical Councils: Nicaea I to Lateran V*, edited by Norman P. Tanner, 438–39. London: Sheed and Ward, 1990.

De Lubac, Henri. *The Motherhood of the Church followed by Particular Churches in the Universal Church*. Translated by Sergia Englung. San Francisco: Ignatius, 1982.

Goethe, Johann Wolfgang von. *The Metamorphosis of Plants*. Cambridge, MA: MIT Press, 2009.

Ignatius of Antioch. "Letter to the Smyrnaeans." In *Ignatius of Antioch*, edited by Helmut Koester, 217–53. Philadelphia, PA: Fortress, 1985.

Izbicki, Thomas M. "The Church in the Light of Learned Ignorance." *Medieval Philosophy and Theology* 3 (1993) 186–214.

John Paul II. "Itinera Apostolica: Angelopoli, ad episcopos Civitatum Foederatarum Americas Septemtrionalis coram admissos." *Acta Apostolicae Sedis* 80 (1988) 787–805.

Kasper, Walter. *The Catholic Church: Nature, Reality, and Mission*. London: Bloomsbury T&T Clark, 2015.

———. "Letters: From the President of the Council for Promoting Christian Unity." *America* 185.17 (2001) 28–29.

———. "On the Church." *The Tablet* 255.8389 (2001) 927–30.

———. "On the Church: A Friendly Reply to Cardinal Ratzinger." *America* 184.14 (2001) 8–14.

———. "Present Situation and Future of the Ecumenical Movement." *The Pontifical Council for Promoting Christian Unity: Information Service* 109 (2002) 11–20.

———. "Zur Theologie und Praxis des bischöflichen Amtes." In *Auf neue Art Kirche sein: Wirklichkeiten—Herausforderungen—Wandlungen: Festschrift für Bischof Homeyer*, edited by Werner Schreer and Georg Steins, 32–48. Munich: Bernward bei Don Bosco, 1999.

Meconi, David Vincent. *The One Christ: St Augustine's Theology of Deification*. Washington, DC: Catholic University of America Press, 2013.

Miroy, Jovino. "From Conciliar Unity to Mystical Union." In *The Church, the Councils, & Reform: The Legacy of the Fifteenth Century*, edited by Gerald Christianson, et al., 155–73. Washington, DC: Catholic University of America Press, 2008.

Moran, Dermot. "Nicholas of Cusa and Modern Philosophy." In *The Cambridge Companion to Renaissance Philosophy*, edited by James Hankins, 173–92. Cambridge: Cambridge University Press, 2007.

Nicholas of Cusa. *The Catholic Concordance*. Edited and translated by Paul E. Sigmund. Cambridge: Cambridge University Press, 1991.

———. "De Docta Ignorantia." In *Selected Spiritual Writings*, edited by Lawrence H. Bond, 83–206. Mahwah, NJ: Paulist, 1997.

———. "Letter to Rodrigo Sánchez de Arévalo." In *Writings on Church and Reform*, edited by Thomas M. Izbicki, 430–49. Cambridge, MA: Harvard University Press, 2008.

———. "Sermon 160: 'Thou Art Peter.'" In *Writings on Church and Reform*, edited by Thomas M. Izbicki, 479–81. Cambridge, MA: Harvard University Press, 2008.

Ratzinger, Joseph. *Dogma and Preaching: Applying Christian Doctrine to Daily Life*. Edited by Michael J. Miller. Translated by Michael J. Miller and Matthew J. O'Connell. San Francisco: Ignatius, 2011.

———. "The Ecclesiology of the Constitution on the Church, Vatican II, 'Lumen Gentium.'" *L'Osservatore Romano* 38 (2001) 5–8.

———. *Introduction to Christianity*. Translated by J. R. Foster. London: Search, 1969.

———. "The Local Church and the Universal Church: A Response to Walter Kasper." *America* 185 (2001) 7–11.

———. *The Nature and Mission of Theology: Essays to Orient Theology in Today's Debates*. San Francisco: Ignatius, 1995.

Sakowski, Derek. *The Ecclesiological Reality of Reception Considered as a Solution to the Debate over the Ontological Priority of the Universal Church*. Rome: Editrice Pontificia Università Gregoriana, 2014.

Schindler, David Christopher. *Hans Urs von Balthasar and the Dramatic Structure of Truth: A Philosophical Investigation*. New York: Fordham University Press, 2004.

Schoedel, William R. *Ignatius of Antioch*. Edited by Helmut Koester. Philadelphia, PA: Fortress, 1985.

Second Vatican Council. "Lumen Gentium: Dogmatic Constitution on the Church." In *Decrees of the Ecumenical Councils: Trent to Vatican II*, edited by Norman P. Tanner, 849–900. London: Sheed and Ward, 1990.

Tillard, Jean-Marie R. *L'église locale: Ecclésiologie de communion et catholicité*. Paris: Cerf, 1995.

Volf, Miroslav. *After Our Likeness: The Church as the Image of the Trinity*. Grand Rapids: Eerdmans, 1998.

Zizioulas, John D. "The Mystery of the Church in the Orthodox Tradition." *One in Christ* 24 (1988) 294–303.

9

Ecclesiology and Ecumenism at the Beginning of the Third Millennium

—Gerard Kelly

> *The twentieth century has often been described as the ecumenical century, and there is no doubt that the achievements were remarkable. Nevertheless, the Church remains divided. The temptation at the beginning of the third millennium is to say that we have come as far as we can. To do this would be to deny Catholic ecclesiological principles. Pope John Paul II declared in the encyclical Ut Unum Sint that the work towards unity is not an appendix to church life, but is at the heart of the Church's pastoral activity. This must also be true of the Church's theological activity. There are many challenges at the beginning of the third millennium, and they are essentially ecclesiological. The Catholic Church cannot face these alone, but will do so in dialogue with her ecumenical partners. In this way the Catholic Church will be true to its very nature. This article examines three broad areas where common agreement does not yet exist.*

The twentieth century is often referred to as the ecumenical century. While the Catholic Church was a relative late-comer to the modern ecumenical movement, there is no doubt that the Church's ecumenical engagement has shaped and continues to shape the quest for the unity of the Church. It is also no coincidence that the ecumenical engagement of the Catholic Church coincides with and is a result of the Second Vatican Council. This was a Council that focused on renewal in Church life, and in this sense was preparing the Church for its mission into the third millennium. One of the Council's basic methods was the return to the sources. This method required an act of remembering; it allowed all in the Church to get in touch in a fresh way with the mystery of salvation and to frame more carefully the sacramental structure of the Church as the sacrament of the mystery of salvation.[1] The renewal generated by this methodology led to a deeper conversion to the apostolic faith. On the eve of the Council, in 1961 when the World Council of Churches held its Assembly in New Delhi, it was clearly stated that the unity of the Church would come about only by the death and re-birth of many forms of church life as we currently know them.[2] In other words, the ecumenical movement saw itself as a movement for renewal in church life.

The central thesis of this chapter is that renewal in the Catholic Church and renewal more broadly among our ecumenical partners go hand in hand. Pope John Paul II wrote in *Ut Unum Sint* that "ecumenism . . . is not just some sort of 'appendix' . . . to the Church's traditional activity," but is an organic part of the Church's life and work and must pervade all that the Church is and does.[3] This means that ecumenism must pervade the theological enterprise, and particularly the work of the ecclesiologist. We have all become quite comfortable saying that renewal is a constant imperative for the Church, but in the light of *Ut Unum Sint* we must also say that ecclesial renewal is ecumenical.

I will explore how this is happening and how it might develop into the third millennium by examining three areas that are a current focus in ecumenical dialogue and that are also important for ecclesial renewal in the Catholic Church. The first area is the notion, enunciated at the Second Vatican Council, that the Church of God *subsists in* the Catholic Church.[4] It might be many decades since this notion was worked out, but it continues to reverberate among our ecumenical partners. The second area I will consider is the sacramental nature of the Church. Again, this was enunciated clearly at the Council, but it is a stumbling block for many of our ecumenical

---

1. This understanding of the Church is most fully developed in the Second Vatican Council, "Lumen Gentium," esp. ch. 1.
2. Cf. Visser 't Hooft, *New Delhi Report*, 117.
3. John Paul II, *Ut Unum Sint* no. 20.
4. Second Vatican Council, "Lumen Gentium" no. 8; "Unitatis Redintegratio" no. 4.

partners, notably those who have their origins in the Reformation. Finally, the question of the papacy and how we might "find a way of exercising the primacy . . . that is open to a new situation" remains an imperative.[5] Pope John Paul II emphasized that the Catholic Church cannot work this out alone; we need our ecumenical partners.

In this article two things will be happening simultaneously. We will be considering renewal in ecclesiology both in the Catholic Church and in our ecumenical partners. But, importantly, we will be considering how these intersect and depend on each other.

Subsistit in

There is no doubt that the Second Vatican Council's choice of the phrase *subsistit in* to describe the connection between the Church of Jesus Christ and the Catholic Church was full of ecumenical significance. The story of the change in terminology from "is" (*est*) to "subsists in" (*subsistit in*) is well known. It has certainly been the subject of much scholarly debate.[6] It is not necessary to go into all the details of that debate or into the history. However, for the purposes of this article there are some basic points that need to be made.

The first is that, as the discussion in the theological commission working on the Council's texts made clear, the intention of the Council fathers was not to deny the doctrine whereby the Catholic Church is identified with the Church of God. The choice of *subsistit in* should be seen as a legitimate development in the doctrine of the Church.[7] This development takes into account the long-held fact that the Orthodox Churches were considered true churches in the proper sense of the word, even though they were not in juridical and canonical communion with the bishop of Rome.

A second point to note is that although a further argument supporting the change of wording was that there are found in other ecclesial communities "elements of the Church" (*elementa Ecclesiae*), theologically there is something more profound going on. This argument says that outside the

---

5. John Paul II, *Ut Unum Sint* no. 95.

6. See, for example, Sullivan, "Meaning of *Subsistit in*," 116–24; "Further Thoughts," 133–47; Paolo Gamberini, "Leap Forward," 362–84.

7. See Willebrands, "Vatican II's Ecclesiology of Communion," 179–91. "While recognizing the importance of the change of terminology from *est* to *subsistit in*, I think it must be said that the Council intended no break with the doctrine of the encyclical *Mystici corporis*. The Council fathers were, rather, looking for a development and deepening of the fundamental thought of the encyclical" (Willebrands, "Vatican II's Ecclesiology of Communion," 180).

boundaries of the Catholic Church the Spirit has been at work in these communities and that they therefore belong to the Body of Christ. In other words, the doctrine of the Church expressed by *subsistit in* is basically a doctrine of grace.[8] This too relies on an understanding that is deep in the Tradition and is evident in the recognition of the legitimacy and efficacy of baptism in those churches and communities not in communion with the Catholic Church. This goes back at least to St Augustine and the debate over heretical baptism.

This leads to the third point to make about the choice of *subsistit in*. It represents a clear break with an earlier ecclesiology which was focused predominantly on the juridical aspects of the Church. We now have a doctrine of the Church that is larger than its juridical determination. Christological and pneumatological considerations now determine the doctrine of the Church.

While the above can appear to be repeating insights that were present at the time of the Council, it is important to develop these ideas for two reasons. The first is that we must be continually receiving the doctrine of the Council. While we can agree with Yves Congar that the doctrine of the Council represents a return to a more traditional understanding of the Church, one that prevailed in the first millennium but that was eclipsed in the second millennium,[9] and while we can also agree with Pope John Paul II that the Church of the first millennium now serves as a kind of model,[10] we should not, nevertheless, underestimate the challenge of making the shift to a more theological and less juridical view of the Church. The reception of the Council is an on-going process. The second reason for looking again at the Council's doctrine of the Church is that we are still working out the ecumenical implications of this doctrinal development. There is no doubt that at the time of the Council the change of terminology from *est* to *subsistit in* was well received by Churches and ecclesial communities not in communion with the Catholic Church, but more than fifty years later many from these communities suggest that the phrase does not go far enough. We need think only of the disappointment among our ecumenical partners to the section in *Dominus Iesus* that stated "ecclesial communities which have not preserved the valid episcopate and the genuine and integral substance of the Eucharistic mystery are not Churches in the proper sense."[11] Perhaps

---

8. This was the understanding presented by J. M. R. Tillard. See Christory, *Dialogue et communion*, 40–44.

9. See Congar, *Fifty Years of Catholic Theology*, 40–44.

10. John Paul II, *Ut Unum Sint* no. 55.

11. CDF, *Declaration Dominus Iesus* no. 17. For some reaction to *Dominus Iesus*, see Pope and Hefeling, *Sic et non*; Sullivan, "Impact of *Dominus Iesus*," 8–11; van

we could ask whether the expectations around a further development in the Catholic doctrine of the Church were too high among these communities.

While this may be true, the more important question for Catholic ecclesiology is how the doctrine expressed by *subsistit in* has continued to shape the life of the Catholic Church. A point made by several commentators is that the doctrine of *subsistit in* represents a move away from a triumphalist ecclesiology to one that is humbler. This should be understood in the context of the prevailing theology of the Council, namely that the Church is a communion. In the ecumenical context this means that our ecumenical partners are part of the communion of the Church. If we take this seriously, then we must conclude that the Catholic Church cannot be her true self without those other churches and ecclesial communities who are part of the communion of the Church of God. The catholicity of the Church demands this. Other churches and ecclesial communities are not an appendix in Catholic ecclesiology; they are going to help the Catholic Church fulfil her mission of being the place where the Church of God subsists. This should act as a healthy antidote to any temptation for the Church to live in isolation.[12]

Of course, the temptation to isolation is experienced by most churches. It is inclined to arise when a church is under stress, particularly, but not exclusively, from outside sources. The doctrine of *subsistit in* cautions against this tendency. It is no longer possible, for example, to speak of or understand "Catholic identity" without taking account of our relationships with our ecumenical partners.

For this reason, the rise of a new ecumenical methodology, namely receptive ecumenism, is important. It is a methodology that is properly a twenty-first-century methodology. Its basic premise is that the ecumenical energies of the twentieth century have been exhausted and reached an impasse, so a new methodology is needed.[13] It is a method that focuses less on building stronger ecumenical relationships, and more on renewal in one's own church, and this renewal will be facilitated by our ecumenical partners. This is a methodology that focuses on ecclesial learning, i.e., my own church learning how to be more faithful to the communion that is the Church of God.

Wijnbergen, "Reactions to *Dominus Iesus*," 147–52.

12. Cf. Kasper, "Decree on Ecumenism," 26. He writes of *subsistit in*: "It no longer formulates the self-concept [self-image] of the Catholic Church 'in splendid isolation,' but also takes account of churches and ecclesial communities in which the one Church of Jesus Christ is effectively present."

13. See Murray, "Receptive Ecumenism and Catholic Learning," 5–25; "Introducing Receptive Ecumenism," 1–8.

I would like to argue in this chapter—and I haven't seen this argument presented elsewhere—that receptive ecumenism is a natural ecumenical methodology if you have received the doctrine of *subsistit in*. I base this argument on an insight from Cardinal Walter Kasper at a meeting to commemorate forty years since the *Decree on Ecumenism*. Speaking of the humble view of the Church found in the doctrine of *subsistit in*, he reminded his hearers that this doctrine, as expressed at the Council, allows not only for elements of the Church to be present outside the Catholic Church, but also acknowledges that sinful members and structures exist within the Catholic Church. He drew several consequences.[14] First, because of these sinful members and structures within the Catholic Church, "the spiritual essence of the Church does not rightly shed its light upon the separated brethren." Second, as the Decree on Ecumenism states, other churches and ecclesial communities "have on occasion better developed aspects of the revealed truth." Third, the two previous points indicate that "the Catholic Church, under the circumstances of division, is unable to accomplish its intrinsic catholicity." Finally, "the Church is in need of purification and renewal, and must constantly walk the path of penance." This requires the Church to be self-critical and penitent.

All of these consequences arise from and are related to the doctrine of *subsistit in*, which makes it imperative that the Catholic Church continually strive to be true to her calling and to demonstrate in concrete terms the true nature of the Church. No longer can the Church do this in isolation. Rather the Church should be attentive to the grace of the Holy Spirit active in our ecumenical partners, and recognize that this can help us to better express the catholicity of the Church.[15]

What we have discovered is that in an important way the doctrine of *subsistit in* takes us to the heart of the Catholic Church's more general approach to ecumenism, namely that the unity of the Church will come about by a renewal in church life among all churches and ecclesial communities. This approach is held in common with the wider ecumenical movement, as we saw above in relation to the Third Assembly of the World Council of Churches at New Delhi.

---

14. Kasper, "Decree on Ecumenism," 27.

15. For a helpful discussion of the grace of the Holy Spirit in a partner church, see Edwards, "Receptive Ecumenism," 457–67.

The Sacramental Structure of the Church

So far, I have been exploring the ways in which an understanding of the doctrine of *subsistit in* could enhance the relations between the Catholic Church and her ecumenical partners. This would involve a humble approach to the Catholic Church's self-understanding, which should shine through in her relations with other churches and communities. We must, however, take account of the criticism of this term by our ecumenical partners. A central part of their criticism of this doctrine is that it elevates the Catholic Church to something like a divine status; it expects the Church on earth to be more than it could ever be. Our ecumenical partners are not sure that there is any significant difference between *subsistit in* and the earlier phrase, *est*.

I hope I have already demonstrated that the intention of the doctrine is first to affirm that outside the boundaries of the Catholic Church there exist elements of the Church that indicate that other churches and communities truly belong to the body of Christ. Moreover, the doctrine also affirms the concrete reality of the Church of God; it is not simply a Platonic ideal that will be realized at the end time.[16] The church of God is to be found concretely in the Catholic Church. In this sense, the intent of the original word *est* is maintained.

The response from our ecumenical partners points to what has become the major ecumenical challenge at the present time, namely arriving at a common understanding of the Church. In a study that examined the results of all the theological dialogues in which the Catholic Church has taken part, Cardinal Walter Kasper suggested that the problem is highlighted by asking not only "What is the Church?" but also "Where is the Church and where is she realized in her fullness?"[17] For Catholics the latter question is about the sacramental nature of the Church. The alternative view, which we can broadly label as Protestant, tends to see the Church more as an event that exists wherever the gospel is preached and the sacraments are duly administered.[18] While there has been a growing consensus on *koinonia* as the fundamental characteristic of the Church,[19] sufficient connection has not yet been made between *koinonia* and the sacramental nature of the Church. Kasper described the sacramental view in terms that are familiar in Catholic ecclesiology: "the Church of Christ and her whole mystery . . . subsists in

---

16. Cf. Kasper, "Decree on Ecumenism," 25.

17. Kasper, *Harvesting the Fruits*, 155.

18. A classic expression of this is found in article 8 of the "Augsburg Confession." See Kolb and Wengert, *Book of Concord*, 42.

19. See, for example, a succession of documents from the Faith and Order Commission of the WCC, "Unity of the Church as Koinonia," 172–74; *Church*.

a concrete and permanent institutional structure, in communion with the bishop of Rome and the bishops in communion with him."[20]

Kasper believes that the problem has to do with the relationship of Christ—and ultimately the Trinity—to the Church. He formulates the question that he believes should be the focus of dialogue on this topic: "In considering the relationship between Jesus Christ and the Church, the fundamental question arises of the relationship of *solus Christus* to the Augustinian *totus Christus, caput et membra* (Christ as head of the Church in relation to the members of the Church as His Body)."[21] The *solus Christus* and the *totus Christus* represent the Protestant and Catholic conceptions respectively.

Without wanting to deny the difficulty of this question, I would like to set it up within a framework that I believe may help us move closer to a consensus on the matter. We need to go back to the Reformation and to the suspicions of the Church of the day held by Luther and those that followed him. On the one hand there was a suspicion that the Church had lost sight of its primary purpose regarding the salvation of humankind. The church seemed to have become so focused on itself that it lost sight of Christ and the salvation he brought. Hence the use of the slogan *solus Christus*. This was a slogan that wanted to focus attention on the saving mystery of Christ. Together with the other slogan *sola fide*, it formed the center piece of the doctrine of justification. For Luther and his successors, the context for talking about the Church was justification. Because this is the doctrine on which the Church stands or falls, there is within the theology of the Reformers, a call for a clearer articulation of the relationship between Jesus Christ and the Church.

The comment can be fairly made that when theological dialogues have studied the doctrine of justification, even with the *Joint Declaration on the Doctrine of Justification*, not much attention was paid directly to the ecclesiological implications of the topic. If we wish to make progress towards understanding the sacramental structure of the Church, it may be helpful to return to the agreement on justification and consider how it may be understood from the point of view of the Church as sacrament. The *Joint Declaration on the Doctrine of Justification* states the common understanding of Catholics and Lutherans:

> In faith we together hold the conviction that justification is the work of the triune God. The Father sent his Son into the world to save sinners. The foundation and presupposition of justification

20. Kasper, *Harvesting*, 204.
21. Kasper, *Harvesting*, 204–5.

is the incarnation, death and resurrection of Christ. Justification thus means that Christ himself is our righteousness, in which we share through the Holy Spirit in accord with the will of the Father. Together we confess: By grace alone, in faith in Christ's saving work and not because of any merit on our part, we are accepted by God and receive the Holy Spirit, who renews our hearts while equipping and calling us to good works.[22]

In professing the uniqueness of Christ's saving work (*solus Christus*), this statement situates it within the larger context of the Trinity, and includes a reference to the work of the Holy Spirit. The following paragraph goes on to note that all people are called to salvation in Christ and that we receive this salvation in faith, which is God's gift through the Holy Spirit. Moreover, the Spirit works through Word and Sacrament in the community of believers. The paragraph concludes by noting that the community of believers in whom the Spirit is at work is led by the same Spirit to a renewal of life that will be completed in eternal life.

These two paragraphs of the *Joint Declaration* (15 and 16) give us an opening for a reflection on the nature of the Church. While this is not a sacramental ecclesiology, I believe we can begin to interpret it against the background of the sacramental ecclesiology of the Second Vatican Council. *Lumen Gentium* opens with the statement that "the Church is in Christ as a sacrament or instrumental sign of intimate union with God and of the unity of all humanity."[23] The Council unfolds this understanding of the Church with a reflection on the plan of God from the beginning, a plan for the salvation of the whole world. It is a plan that humankind might share in the divine life, conformed to the image of the Son. This plan is fulfilled in Christ, in his life, preaching, mighty works, saving death, resurrection and ascension to the right hand of the Father. The mystery of this plan comes to completion with the sending of the Holy Spirt at Pentecost, where the Church is made manifest:

> [Christ] poured on his disciples the Spirit that had been promised by the Father. When, therefore, the Church, equipped with the gifts of its founder and faithfully keeping his precepts of love, humility and penance, receives the mission of announcing the kingdom of Christ and of God and of inaugurating it among all peoples, it has formed the seed and the beginning of the kingdom on earth. Meanwhile as it gradually grows, it aspires after

---

22. LWF and RCC, *Joint Declaration* no. 15.
23. Second Vatican Council, "Lumen Gentium" no. 1 (Tanner, *Decrees*, 2:849).

> the completion of the kingdom, and hopes and desires with all its strength to be joined with its king in glory.[24]

The church is the community filled with the Spirit who keeps alive the unfolding of the plan of God in the world. So, the Church is the Spirit-filled community that manifests the fulfilment of God's plan, and at the same time, it has the mission to be the means by which that plan continues to come to birth in the concrete circumstances of the world. We can express this in terms of the eschatological character of the Church, which abides in the "already" of the eschaton, but also holds out for the "not yet" of the eschaton.

The point about seeing the Church in the category of sacrament, as I have just described it, is that it highlights the fact that the plan of God is experienced concretely in the lives of people of all generations and all places. The church can be understood as part of the provident design of God who has endowed it with all that is necessary for its mission. That mission is to communicate the message of the saving plan of God and to draw people into communion with God. As sacrament, all that it is and does, and the quality of the relationships among its members should be signs of God's saving mercy. This is the point of that opening paragraph of *Lumen Gentium* that spoke of union with God and unity among people. Here the Council was reminding us that the Church is a communion. It is a sacrament of communion with God—described elsewhere as participation in the divine life.[25] It is also a sacrament of the unity of humankind—described in the Letter to the Ephesians as the breaking down of the dividing walls of hostility between divided peoples (cf. Eph 2:14). The plan of God is a universal plan; the mission of the Church is a universal mission.

It can be argued that this Catholic self-understanding, as expressed at the Second Vatican Council, represents a genuine ecclesiological reform. Furthermore, I will argue that the centrality of Christ and the Spirit in this ecclesiology overcomes the deficit perceived by the Reformers of the sixteenth century.

For the Catholic Church, this sacramental understanding of the Church is saying much more than that the Church is located wherever the gospel is preached and the sacraments are duly administered. While not denying that the preaching of the gospel and the celebration of the sacraments are central to the mission of the Church, Catholic ecclesiology also affirms that the whole life of the Church, including its institutional aspects, its ministry, its decision-making, and the fellowship among its members, are all

---

24. Second Vatican Council, "Lumen Gentium," no. 5 (Tanner, *Decrees*, 2:851).
25. See "Dei Verbum" no. 2 (Tanner, *Decrees*, 2:972).

part of its nature. They are not peripheral aspects, nor are they irrelevant to the essence of the Church. They are important because they are signs and instruments of the saving action of God in Christ. God's saving grace penetrates all aspects of the Church, thus we can speak of *totus Christus*.

Let me make two brief comments—a bit by way of a diversion. The first is that if the Catholic Church wishes to demonstrate more clearly what it means to speak of the Church as sacrament, then it must be careful not to separate into different compartments, as it were, various aspects of church life. To give just one example, many people have begun to set aside the institutional aspects of the Church's life, as if they are somewhat secondary to its nature and mission. And then there are others who are inclined to focus almost exclusively on the institutional aspects, as if this is the defining characteristic of Catholic identity. They see the institutional aspects simply in juridical terms and fail to understand them theologically, and specifically sacramentally. The problem with either of these approaches is that they miss the point that the institutional aspects of the Church's life can only properly be understood within the context of the Church as sacrament. Only in that context is their true significance understood.

The second comment is perhaps more difficult to deal with, and it concerns the problem of failure (or sin) in Church life, both personal and institutional. If the Church is like a sacrament how can we account for sin? *Lumen Gentium* addresses this matter in no. 8 when it says of the Church that it is "at the same time holy and always in need of purification" and that it thus "pursues unceasingly penance and renewal." This, in fact, should be understood as an aspect of its sacramentality: precisely as sacrament it demonstrates the need for renewal and purification. In other words, the Church is not the Savior; it is not self-sufficient because it always stands in need of God's mercy. In fact, if it is to be a sign of salvation, then it must demonstrate that we are always in need of God's mercy. The misunderstanding of those who are hesitant about speaking of the Church as a sacrament is that they presume that the Church is standing in the place of God. Rather the Church is a symbol—that is, sacrament—of God's mercy, and a means of encounter with that mercy. Yes, the Church is the body of Christ, but it is not Christ.

Let me now return to the doctrine of justification. I stated earlier that I believed one of the main impediments for Reformation churches to understand the sacramental nature of the Church was their perception that such an understanding would contravene the doctrine of justification, the doctrine, according to Lutheran teaching, on which the Church stands or falls. The reasons for this were twofold. First, that the Church was interpreted along the lines of works justification. According to such an understanding, the Church was seen as supplanting Christ as the source of justification.

Second, the Church would seem to be elevated to a status that would be at odds with it also being a sinner—what the Reformers call *simul iustus et peccator*. I believe that the understanding of the Church as presented in *Lumen Gentium* not only deals with these concerns, but also shows that these very concerns are not irrelevant to the sacramental understanding of the Church.

This approach was taken by the Lutheran-Roman Catholic Dialogue in Australia in its work on the papacy and serves to illustrate my argument. In facing up to the question of the papacy in relation to the centrality of Christ, the Catholic members of the dialogue proposed that the question must be considered within the hierarchy of truths. In the final text we read:

> The proper ordering of truths means that the Catholic Church cannot speak about the papacy without situating it in its relationship to other doctrines that bring out its relationship to the foundation of the Christian faith. In the first instance this means considering it within the context of the college of bishops. Further, the relationship of the college of bishops to Christ depends on an understanding of the Church and its relationship to Christ.[26]

The Lutheran Church of Australia welcomed this approach to a difficult question. To understand what is going on in this approach we need to recognize that it addresses the Lutheran emphasis on justification and *solus Christus*. However, in doing so, it also works out of a Catholic sacramental ecclesiology which implies the *totus Christus*.

The Bishop of Rome and Local Churches

This leads naturally into the third area that I wish to consider, namely the role of the papacy in the Church. There is no doubt that in recent years—at least since the promulgation of *Ut Unum Sint*—there has been much ecumenical work on the papacy. In that encyclical Pope John Paul II called for a patient and fraternal dialogue about ways in which the papacy could be exercised so that, without denying its essential character, it might be open to a new situation. Early in his papacy, Pope Francis commented that we do not seem to have made much progress on this front.[27]

While this is obviously a challenge for our ecumenical partners, as I have just demonstrated, we must also take account of the challenges the Catholic Church itself faces in this regard. There was wisdom in Pope John

---

26. Lutheran-Roman Catholic Dialogue, *Petrine Ministry* no. 89.
27. Francis, *Evangelii Gaudium* no. 32.

Paul II asking for assistance in finding a way of exercising the papacy for a new situation. This suggests that the reform of the papacy cannot happen in isolation. The Catholic Church needs other churches and ecclesial communities in order to undertake the necessary reform. This is a very clear area where receptive ecumenism can play a role. There are also a number of associated questions that have already arisen and will require further study if there is to be a genuine renewal in the Catholic Church as well as among other churches and ecclesial communities.

In the first place there is the relationship between the pope and the bishops of the world. Pope Francis seems to have made this a priority, as is evident both in his statements that too much centralization is dangerous, and in his practice of regularly quoting the documents of local bishops conferences. In *Evangelii Gaudium* no. 32 he opened the way, I believe, for a fresh examination of the meaning of the collegial spirit (*collegialis affectus*) that *Lumen Gentium* no. 23 had referred to when speaking of bishops' conferences.[28] He noted that the "juridical status of episcopal conferences which would see them as subjects of specific attributions, including genuine doctrinal authority, has not yet been sufficiently elaborated."[29] Here he calls for further study of collegiality which may possibly lead to doctrinal development. This seems to imply that we can no longer simply talk about a collegial spirit (*collegialis affectus*); we now must consider in what way we can talk about effective collegiality (*collegialis effectus*). In theological terms, to be able to do this would amount to a deepening of the doctrine of the collegiality of bishops.[30] Among most of our ecumenical partners there are strong practices of collegiality, or as it is usually called, synodality. The principal concern of the Orthodox Churches is that the principle of synodality is diminished in the Catholic Church. While renewal in the Catholic Church would not involve the adoption of any single one of these practices, the potential is there for the Catholic Church to learn from them, to gain insights from them and to develop what is right for the Catholic Church and in keeping with what is essential to the nature of the Church. To give a small example: by paying attention to the theology of the Orthodox Churches around the relationship between collegiality and primacy, we may notice what I believe has been largely unnoticed in *Ut Unum Sint*. Whereas the Second Vatican Council presented episcopal collegiality by emphasizing

---

28. "Episcopal conferences can today make a manifold and fruitful contribution to the concrete application of the spirit of collegiality (*collegialis affectus*)" (Second Vatican Council, "Lumen Gentium" no. 23 [Tanner, *Decrees*, 2:868]).

29. Francis, *Evangelii Gaudium* no. 23.

30. An important study on the collegiality of episcopal conferences is Tillard, "Conférences épiscopales," 523–39.

the communion of the college with its head,[31] the encyclical locates the exercise of the primacy in the heart of collegiality.[32] The difference is subtle but significant.

A second and related area for theological reflection is the relationship of the local church to the communion of local churches and indeed to the local Church of Rome. For some of our ecumenical partners the pope is still not properly understood as the bishop of a local church. It is probably fair to say that this is also the case among a large number of the Catholic faithful. This clouds the way the discussion about local church and the communion of local churches gets framed. The teaching of *Ut unum sint* is clear on this: "The Bishop of Rome is the Bishop of the Church which preserves the mark of the martyrdom of Peter and of Paul."[33] However, the teaching is still waiting to be received as part of the *sensus fidei fidelium*. A deepening of the teaching of the encyclical would seem to be an important element of ecclesiology in the third millennium.

This also goes to the more general question of the meaning of local church in the ecumenical community. A variety of approaches exists, including a congregation at worship, a parish territory, or a larger region. The Catholic understanding of the papacy and of bishops depends on a theology of local church. But even in the Catholic Church there is confusion about this at the level of ecclesiology, even if it might appear to be settled canonically. Let me illustrate the problem by giving two small examples from the work of Jean-Marie Tillard on the local church.[34] First, he notes that while the word "local" is sometimes used, another word, "particular," is also used and these two do not mean the same thing. Second, the question of the catholicity of the Church is raised when we see members of the Catholic Church living in the same territory without necessarily belonging to the same diocese. This is the case, for example, when Catholics in an Eastern rite eparchy live in the same territory as a Latin rite diocese. In such

---

31. See Second Vatican Council, "Lumen Gentium" no. 22.

32. Cf. John Paul II, *Ut Unum Sint* no. 95. "When the Catholic Church affirms that the office of the Bishop of Rome corresponds to the will of Christ, she does not separate this office from the mission entrusted to the whole body of bishops, who are also vicars and ambassadors of Christ. The Bishop of Rome is a member of the 'College,' and the bishops are his brothers in the ministry." This is the insight of Watine Christory in his study of the work of Jean-Marie R. Tillard. See Christory, *Dialogue et communion*, 55.

33. Cf. John Paul II, *Ut Unum Sint* no. 90. "The Catholic Church, both in her *praxis* and in her solemn documents, holds that the communion of the particular Churches with the Church of Rome, and of their Bishops with the Bishop of Rome, is—in God's plan—an essential requisite of full and visible communion" (John Paul II, *Ut Unum Sint* no. 97)

34. See Tillard, *L'Eglise locale*.

a situation there are two Catholic bishops who have jurisdiction over parts of the same territory. Yes, juridically they can be distinguished as particular churches, but theologically there is confusion about what constitutes a local church when there are two bishops in the same territory. The ancient tradition of the Church is very clear that there should only be one bishop in one place—otherwise there is schism and the Church is divided.[35] The problem is theological and sacramental: because the bishop is the sacrament of the unity of the Church, a place having more than one bishop becomes a sign of disunity.[36] This has huge ecumenical implications once we begin to ask what the future united church will look like. For example, might a city have a Catholic, an Orthodox and an Anglican bishop? This requires further study.

Conclusion

We could continue to build the ecclesiological and ecumenical agenda for the third millennium, but I believe I have identified enough elements to make the case that Catholic ecclesiology in the third millennium must be ecumenical. There are a few basic foundations for this claim. First, the statement by Pope John Paul II that ecumenism is not simply an appendix but an organic part of the Church's life demands that theology, which is part of the pastoral mission of the Church, must be ecumenical. Second, the phrase *subsistit in*, which was a theological development, further emphasizes that the Catholic Church cannot think of itself in isolation from its ecumenical partners. Consequently, there is a mutual accountability that must be attended to. Third, recovery of a sacramental understanding of the Church in twentieth-century theology and in church teaching has ensured that ecclesiology is properly theological rather than merely juridical. This remains a stumbling block for some of our ecumenical partners in the west.

During the second half of the twentieth century the prevailing ecumenical methodology was the joint study of the sources. This meant going back to the biblical and patristic sources, to the time of the undivided church. This led to important ecumenical advances. So, when Pope John Paul II wrote in *Ut Unum Sint* that the Church of the first millennium now serves as a kind of model for the unity of the Church, he framed some of the ecumenical questions in a new way. The method was not totally foreign

---

35. See Fourth Lateran Council, Constitution 9, which, after describing the problem of different people within the same city, addressed the appointment of a bishop: "We altogether forbid one and the same city or diocese to have more than one bishop, as if it were a body with several heads like a monster" (Tanner, *Decrees*, 1:239).

36. Cf. Wood, *Sacramental Orders*, 64–85.

to our ecumenical partners, even if the particular application may have been unfamiliar to many of them. For this reason, some of our Protestant ecumenical partners struggle to work with the methodology when, for example it touched on the episcopal structure of the Church and the role of the bishop of Rome. This suggests that the methodology which is a study of the sources has not been exhausted. The renewal of Catholic ecclesiology in the twentieth century thrived as a result of the study of the sources, so this is familiar territory to Catholic ecclesiologists. At the present time they surely have a responsibility to assist those less immersed in this methodology to become more familiar with it.

However, we must not forget that the joint study of the sources is not the end game of the search for unity. The unity of the Church is not achieved by a common ecclesiological statement. It will be something that is lived in the concrete circumstances of life and the world. For this reason, engagement with our ecumenical partners is itself a source of ecclesial renewal. Here the recent methodology of receptive ecumenism comes more clearly into play. It has the potential to define the ecumenical ecclesiological project at the beginning of the third millennium.

For the Catholic Church the goal is organic unity, the unity willed by Christ. Because of the advances of the last one hundred years we are much closer to that goal than previously. The most important questions that still divide us are ecclesiological. How we manage these will have significance for Catholic ecclesiology more broadly.

Bibliography

Congar, Yves. *Fifty Years of Catholic Theology: Conversations with Yves Congar*. Edited and introduced by Bernard Lauret. Translated by John Bowden. Philadelphia, PA: Fortress, 1988.
Congregation for the Doctrine of the Faith. *Declaration Dominus Iesus: On the Unicity and Salvific Universality of Jesus Christ and the Church*. Vatican City: Libreria Editrice Vaticana, 2000.
Edwards, Denis. "Receptive Ecumenism and the Charism of a Partner Church: The Example of Justification." *Australasian Catholic Record* 86 (2009) 457–67.
Francis. *Evangelii Gaudium*. Strathfield: St Pauls, 2013.
Gamberini, Paolo. "A Leap Forward in Understanding *Subsistit in*." *Irish Theological Quarterly* 81 (2016) 362–84.
John Paul II. *Ut Unum Sint*. Strathfield: St Pauls, 1995.
Kasper, Cardinal Walter. "The Decree on Ecumenism—Read Anew after Forty Years." In *Searching for Christian Unity*, by John Paul II, et al., 18–36. Hyde Park, NY: New City, 2007.
———. *Harvesting the Fruits*. London: Continuum, 2009.

Kolb, Robert, and Timothy J. Wengert, eds. *The Book of Concord: The Confessions of the Evangelical Lutheran Church*. Minneapolis, MN: Fortress, 2000.

Lutheran-Roman Catholic Dialogue in Australia. *The Petrine Ministry in a New Situation: A Joint Statement on the Papacy by the Lutheran-Roman Catholic Dialogue in Australia 2011–2016*. Adelaide: Lutheran-Roman Catholic Dialogue in Australia, 2016.

The Lutheran World Federation (LWF) and the Roman Catholic Church (RCC). *Joint Declaration on the Doctrine of Justification*. Grand Rapids: Eerdmans, 2000.

Murray, Paul D. "Introducing Receptive Ecumenism." *The Ecumenist* 51 (2004) 1–8.

———. "Receptive Ecumenism and Catholic Learning: Establishing the Agenda." In *Receptive Ecumenism and the Call to Catholic Learning: Exploring a Way for Contemporary Ecumenism*, edited by Paul D. Murray, 5–25. Oxford: Oxford University Press, 2008.

Pope, Stephen J., and Charles Hefeling, eds. *Sic et non: Encountering Dominus Iesus*. Maryknoll, NY: Orbis, 2002.

Sullivan, Francis A. "Further Thoughts on the Meaning of *Subsisit in*." *Theological Studies* 71 (2010) 133–47.

———. "The Impact of *Dominus Iesus* on Ecumenism." *America* 183 (2000) 8–11.

———. "The Meaning of *Subsistit in* as Explained by the Congregation for the Doctrine of the Faith." *Theological Studies* 69 (2008) 116–24.

Tanner, Norman P., ed. *The Decrees of the Ecumenical Councils*. Washington, DC: Georgetown University Press, 1990.

Tillard, Jean-Marie R. "Conférences épiscopales et catholicité de l'Église." *Cristianesimo nella Storia* 9 (1988) 523–39.

———. *L'Eglise locale: Ecclésologie de communion et catholicité*. Paris: Cerf, 1995.

van Wijnbergen, Christine. "Reactions to *Dominus Iesus* in the German-Speaking World." In *The Ecumenical Constitution of Churches*, edited by José Oscar Beozzo and Giuseppe Ruggieri, 147–52. Concilium. London: SCM, 2001.

Visser 't Hooft, W. A., ed. *The New Delhi Report: The Third Assembly of the World Council of Churches, 1961*. London: SCM, 1962.

Watine Christory, Pascale. *Dialogue et communion: l'itinéraire oecuménique de Jean-Marie R. Tillard*. Leuven: Peeters, 2015.

Willebrands, Cardinal Johannes. "Vatican II's Ecclesiology of Communion." *One in Christ* 28 (1987) 179–91.

Wood, Susan K. *Sacramental Orders*. Lex Orandi Series. Collegeville, MN: Liturgical, 2000.

World Council of Churches. *The Church: Towards a Common Vision*. Faith and Order Paper 214. Geneva: WCC, 2013.

———. "The Unity of the Church as Koinonia: Gift and Calling." In *Signs of the Spirit: Official Report of the Seventh Assembly*, edited by Michael Kinnamon, 172–74. Geneva: WCC; Grand Rapids: Eerdmans, 1991.

10

Reading *Deus Caritas Est* Missiologically

—Peter John McGregor

In his encyclical Deus Caritas Est *Pope Benedict XVI examines the theological virtue of charity and how it is to be lived out by Christians in the life of the Church. Much of the analysis of and commentary upon the encyclical has focused on the relationship between agape and eros which is expounded upon in sections three to eight. However, section 25 of the encyclical identifies "two essential facts which have emerged from our reflections." Both of these facts are missiological. The first is that, "The Church's deepest nature is expressed in her three-fold responsibility" for kerygma-martyria, leitourgia, and diakonia, and that charity is meant to embrace not only the members of Christ's body, but to extend "beyond the frontiers of the Church." This chapter proposes to read the encyclical in light of these facts. What is revealed from such a reading is that Benedict's understanding of the nature of divine and human love grounds how he understands the three-fold mission of the Church. In the encyclical he addresses the nature of kerygma-martyria, leitourgia, and diakonia in the mission of the Church, and shows how they can be lived out in the Church. In order to live out this three-fold mission, our participation in the heart of Jesus through the gift of the Holy Spirit is essential. It is Mary who is the ultimate model of participation in this mission.*

After *Deus Caritas Est: On Christian Love* was promulgated on Christmas Day 2005 it generated a great deal of analysis and commentary. The reasons for this were twofold. It was the first encyclical of Benedict XVI, and it took an unexpected approach to the subject of Christian love by beginning with an analysis of the relationship between *eros* and *agape*. This intriguing opening captured the attention of many commentators, such that this relationship became the main focus of a substantial proportion of the commentary.[1] However, according to Benedict, our understanding of Christian love must have a ecclesiological matrix which gives birth to mission.[2] A little past the midpoint of the encyclical he makes this clear when he writes:

> Thus far, two essential facts have emerged from our reflections: (a) The Church's deepest nature is expressed in her three-fold responsibility: of proclaiming the word of God (*kerygma-martyria*), celebrating the sacraments (*leitourgia*), and exercising the ministry of charity (*diakonia*). These duties presuppose each other and are inseparable. For the Church, charity is not a kind of welfare activity which could equally well be left to others, but is a part of her nature, an indispensable expression of her very being. (b) The Church is God's family in the world. In this family no one ought to go without the necessities of life. Yet at the same time *caritas-agape* extends beyond the frontiers of the Church. The parable of the Good Samaritan remains as a standard which imposes universal love towards the needy whom we encounter "by chance" (cf. Luke 10:31), whoever they may be. Without in any way detracting from this commandment of universal love, the Church also has a specific responsibility: within the ecclesial family no member should suffer through being in need. The teaching of the Letter to the Galatians is emphatic: "So then,

---

1. As examples of this focus, see Böhnke, "Purificatio?" 225–42; Bonnewijn, "Commandment and Love," 152–68; Botero, "El Amor Conyugal," 343–62; Dulles, "Love, the Pope, and C. S. Lewis," 20–24; Egan, "Eros, Friendship, and Love," 131–50; Howsare, "Why Begin With Love?" 423–48; Ide, "La Distinction," 353–69; Mattison, "Movements of Love," 31–60; Merecki, "Has Christianity Poisoned Érōs?" 56–65; Prieto, "Érōs and Agápē," 212–26; Salmeri, "Érōs," 80–90; Schindler, "Redemption of 'Eros,'" 375–99; Schu, "Benedict Saves Érōs,'" 10–19; Wainwright, "Reflections on Pope Benedict XVI," 263–66; Weinandy, "Deus Caritas Est," 259–62; Wiker, "Benedict Contra Nietzsche," 18–23.

2. This missiological dimension has not gone entirely unnoticed. For commentary on the missiological significance of the encyclical, see Cordes, "Presentation," 9–10; "Reflections," 9–10; Murphy, "Charity, not Justice," 274–86; Schindler, "Way of Love," 29–45.

as we have opportunity, let us do good to all, and especially to those who are of the household of faith" (Gal 6:10).[3]

The Church's ministry of charity, her *diakonia*, is a part, not the whole, of her ministry. The mission of the Church is three-fold, what the Second Vatican Council and St John Paul II called its priestly, prophetic, and royal mission.[4] Furthermore, Benedict reminds us of the Pauline teaching that as members of Christ's body, we have a special responsibility to meet the needs of our brothers and sisters in Christ. Charity begins at home. In light of these two essential facts, I propose to read the encyclical from a missiological perspective in order to elucidate its missiological teaching. This should enable us to see how Benedict sees the ministry of charity in relation to the whole mission of the Church, as well as seeing that, while there is a *diakonia*, a ministry of charity, there is also charity in ministry. After explaining the genesis of the encyclical, I shall endeavour first to examine how Benedict understands the nature of divine and human love. This will be a necessary prerequisite for grasping how he then, in turn, understands the three-fold mission of the Church. Second, I shall seek to demonstrate that, from section 7 to 18 in Part I, Benedict addresses the nature of *leitourgia*, *diakonia*, and *kerygma-martyria* in the mission of the Church. Third, I shall show how he sees these being lived out in the Church. Fourth, I shall briefly address his exposition of the role of bishops in carrying out this three-fold mission. Fifth, I shall present the role played by the heart of Jesus in Benedict's understanding of this mission. Finally, I shall try to reveal how he presents Mary as the ultimate model of this mission. Hopefully, we shall see these three missiological responsibilities of the Church running like three golden threads through a tapestry.

Background to the Encyclical

In a 2007 presentation on *Deus Caritas Est* given by Archbishop Paul Cordes, the then president of *Cor Unum* revealed that since that Dicastery "deals with the praxis of love of neighbour as part of the Church's mission, John Paul II asked that I prepare for him a preliminary draft of a magisterial

---

3. Benedict XVI, *Deus Caritas Est* no. 25.

4. See Second Vatican Council, "Lumen Gentium" nos. 10–12, 31, 34–36; "Ad Gentes" no. 15. Some key texts for beginning to investigate St John Paul's understanding of the three-fold mission are Wojtyła, *Sources of Renewal*, 219–71; John Paul II, *Redemptor Hominis* nos. 16, 18–21; *Redemptoris Missio* no. 71; *Evangelium Vitae* no. 78; *Familiaris Consortio* nos. 47–48, 50–51, 55, 59–60, 63, 73; *Christifideles Laici* nos. 9, 14, 23, 33–34, 51–52, 62, 64; *Tertio Millennio Adveniente* no. 21.

writing regarding this theme."[5] In drafting a document on this initial theme, Cordes took what he calls an inductive approach, beginning with the humanism universally accepted in Western culture, followed by the initiatives of both State and Church in caring for the "neighbor," and concluding with the foundation of love of neighbor in God. This initial draft was read and corrected by Cardinal Ratzinger. Upon becoming pope, Benedict informed Cordes that he intended to write an encyclical on the theme of *Caritas*. According to Cordes, Benedict radically changed his first draft, such that the entire text is "Ratzinger." Therein, the pope takes a deductive approach, beginning with the theological formulation that "God is love." As Cordes explains, "In this way, he shows both in the temporal order as well as the order of values, the absolute primacy of the One 'who loved us first.'"[6] This change in emphasis was more than methodological. Rather, Benedict's fundamental perspective is theocentric, or perhaps one could say, Trinitarian. His basic impulse is to urge his audience to constantly search for the triune God. As Cordes says, "He never tires of speaking about the Heavenly Father, his Son Jesus Christ and the creative force of the Holy Spirit."[7] Since he was intimately involved in the preparation of the encyclical, and given his own abiding interest in evangelization, Cordes is sensitive to its evangelical dimension.[8] However, in his commentary on the encyclical, although he is aware of the three-fold "ecclesial vision"[9] of Benedict, he focuses upon the relationship between "evangelization and social service," "charity and the proclamation of the truth."[10] He does not address the element of *leitourgia*.

The Nature of Divine and Human Love

Part I of the encyclical speaks of the nature of the love of God, and what this means for human love. To begin with, Benedict states that the encounter

---

5. Cordes, "Presentation," 10. Cordes delivered this address to the Fifth General Conference of the Bishops of Latin America and the Caribbean in Aparecida, Brazil, on May 12, 2007.

6. Cordes, "Presentation," 10.

7. Cordes, "Presentation," 10.

8. As testimony to Cordes's concern for Catholic evangelization, one can point to not only his ministry in Cor Unum but also his work in the Pontifical Council for the Laity, the Congregation for the Evangelization of the Peoples, and the Pontifical Council for Justice and Peace. He is also the author of *Call to Holiness: Reflections on the Catholic Charismatic Renewal* and *Born of the Spirit: Renewal Movements in the Life of the Church*.

9. Cordes, "Presentation," 9.

10. Cordes, "Reflections," 9–10.

with Christ, the incarnate love of God, gives the life of a Christian "a new horizon and a decisive direction."[11] This encounter with Christ does not just give a new experience, but calls for a response, to love God and neighbor as God loves us. We must share this love of God with others.

Next, Benedict addresses the contemporary misuse and confusion surrounding the term "love." Why is this important to deal with? Because if we do not grasp the true meaning of love, we will not understand what the love of God is, or how we are to love God, or how we are to love our neighbor. Furthermore, if we do not understand these things we will not understand our mission as Christians. It is in this context that Benedict addresses the true nature of *eros* and its relationship to *agape*. True *eros* does involve an "ascent in 'ecstasy' towards the Divine."[12] However, true *eros* can only be achieved when human beings recognize their psycho-somatic unity, their anthropological reality. As Benedict writes, "it is man, the person, a unified creature composed of body and soul, who loves. Only when both dimensions are truly united, does man attain his full stature. Only thus is love—*eros*—able to mature and attain its authentic grandeur."[13]

Moving from the pagan, specifically Greek, understanding of love to the Hebrew understanding, Benedict shows how, in the *Song of Songs*, there is also a movement from one kind of love to another, from *dodim*, a term "suggesting a love which is still insecure, indeterminate and searching," to *ahabà*, which "expresses the experience of love which involves a real discovery of the other . . . [a love which] becomes concern and care for the other . . . [and] seeks the good of the beloved."[14]

Benedict affirms that this kind of love is an ecstasy, not in the sense of a moment of intoxication, "but rather as a journey, an ongoing exodus out of the closed inward-looking self towards its liberation through self-giving, and thus towards authentic self-discovery and indeed the discovery of God."[15] This is the path both proclaimed and lived by Jesus through his Cross and Resurrection, a path which starts "from the depth of his own sacrifice and reaches fulfilment therein."[16]

---

11. Benedict XVI, *Deus Caritas Est* no. 1.
12. Benedict XVI, *Deus Caritas Est* nos. 4, 5.
13. Benedict XVI, *Deus Caritas Est* no. 5.
14. Benedict XVI, *Deus Caritas Est* no. 6.
15. Benedict XVI, *Deus Caritas Est* no. 6.
16. Benedict XVI, *Deus Caritas Est* no. 6.

Benedict goes on to argue that an antithesis between *eros* as non-Christian "ascending, possessive or covetous love" and *agape* as Christian "descending, oblative love" is false.[17] Rather, even if *eros* begins as a

> [covetous] fascination for the great promise of happiness, in drawing near to the other, [it becomes] less and less concerned with itself, increasingly [seeking] the happiness of the other . . . concerned more and more with the beloved, bestows itself and wants to 'be there for' the other. The element of *agape* thus enters into this love, for otherwise *eros* is impoverished and even loses its own nature.[18]

In other words, *eros* needs to be *agaped*. Moreover:

> Man cannot live by oblative, descending love alone. He cannot always give, he must also receive. Certainly, as the Lord tells us, one can become a source from which rivers of living water flow (cf. John 7:37–38). Yet to become such a source, one must constantly drink anew from the original source, which is Jesus Christ, from whose pierced heart flows the love of God (cf. John 19:34).[19]

According to Benedict, there is an "inseparable connection between an ascending and descending love, between *eros* which seeks God and *agape* which passes on the gift received."[20]

Enter *Leitourgia*

Thus far, nothing which has been said would explicitly establish the missiological essence of *Deus Caritas Est*. This is because it is first essential to establish exactly how Benedict understands the nature of divine love and human love, since this grounds his understanding of mission. At this point in the encyclical, Benedict introduces the interpretation of Jacob's Ladder found in the *Pastoral Rule* of Gregory the Great. In this dream, Jacob sees

---

17. Benedict XVI, *Deus Caritas Est* no. 7. For Ratzinger's understanding of 'ascending' and 'descending,' *exitus* and *reditus*, see Ratzinger, *God of Jesus Christ*, 59–68; *Spirit of the Liturgy*, 24–34. It should be noted that the original context for his understanding is Christological, the descent and ascent of the Word through the Incarnation and the Cross, and our subsequent *theosis* through our participation in this *exitus* and *reditus*, a participation which is facilitated through liturgical prayer.

18. Benedict XVI, *Deus Caritas Est* no. 7.
19. Benedict XVI, *Deus Caritas Est* no. 7.
20. Benedict XVI, *Deus Caritas Est* no. 7.

the angels of God ascending to and descending from heaven. This Gregory interprets as an analogy of how "the good pastor must be rooted in contemplation. Only in this way will he be able to take upon himself the needs of others and make them his own."[21] Just as St Paul ascended to the mysteries of God so that he could descend to be all things to all men, just as Moses entered the tabernacle to converse with God so that he could emerge to help the people who were suffering, so the Christian must "ascend" to drink from the stream which issues from the heart of Christ in order to "descend" and became a source of living water for others.[22]

The burden of the next four sections (8–11) is that "God's *eros* for man is also totally *agape*."[23] God loves us with a personal, gratuitous, and forgiving love, a love which invites us into a personal relationship with him wherein we shall find our joy. Our union with God is a personal union wherein we remain ourselves yet become truly one with God.

At this point, Benedict returns to Christ as the love of God incarnate. Although he does not explicitly state it, this love is erotic, in the sense that, in Jesus, God comes in search of the stray sheep, lost and suffering human beings. In Christ, God desires us. Christ's death on the Cross, which raises us up and saves us, is God's love for us in its most radical form. If we are to grasp what this love truly is, and respond to it in loving God and neighbor, we must contemplate it in Christ. As Benedict says:

> By contemplating the pierced side of Christ (cf. John 19:37), we can understand the starting-point of this Encyclical: "God is love" (1 John 4:8). It is there that the truth can be contemplated. It is from there that our definition of love must begin. In this contemplation the Christian discovers the path along which his life and love must move.[24]

We now come to what might be called the Eucharistic heart of the encyclical, and of Benedict's missiology. Jesus's act of oblation, which we can gaze upon in Sacred Scripture, endures in the Eucharist. Not only may we gaze upon it, we can be drawn into it. As Benedict writes, "More than just statically receiving the incarnate *Logos*, we enter into the very dynamic of his self-giving."[25]

21. Benedict XVI, *Deus Caritas Est* no. 7.
22. Benedict XVI, *Deus Caritas Est* no. 7.
23. Benedict XVI, *Deus Caritas Est* no. 10.
24. Benedict XVI, *Deus Caritas Est* no. 12; cf. Ratzinger, *Introduction to Christianity*, 236, 241–42; *God is Near Us*, 42–43, 55; *Behold the Pierced One*, 47–69.
25. Benedict XVI, *Deus Caritas Est* no. 13; cf. 18: "The saints—consider the example of Blessed Teresa of Calcutta—constantly renewed their capacity for love of neighbour

Enter *Diakonia*

Our union in love with God is total. It is a psycho-somatic union. However, it is also a social union that is a sacramental union. All the communicants are one with each other because they are one in Christ. Communion is not just union with Christ, but union with all the members of his Body in him. In this communion, "Love of God and love of neighbour are now truly united: God incarnate draws us all into himself."[26]

Benedict sees that this unites worship and morality.

> Faith, worship and *ethos* are interwoven as a single reality which takes shape in our encounter with God's *agape*. Here the usual contraposition between worship and ethics simply falls apart. "Worship" itself, Eucharistic communion, includes the reality both of being loved and loving others in return. A Eucharist which does not pass over into the concrete practice of love is intrinsically fragmented.[27]

Here Benedict unites *leitourgia* and *diakonia* in the Eucharist. A celebration of the Eucharist that does not end beyond itself in love of neighbor is "intrinsically fragmented." Since the Eucharist is the sacrament of communion, if it does not end in true communion, it is to some degree an anti-Eucharist.

Moreover, in a way, this communion must extend beyond the communion of the members of the Body of Christ. This is how we should read the parable of the Good Samaritan, which universalizes the concept of neighbor.[28] This is how we should understand the Last Judgement (cf. Matt 25:31–46), which reveals that all are brethren of the Lord, and "in the least of the brethren we find Jesus, and in Jesus we find God."[29]

We cannot love God if we do not love our neighbor. Indeed, love of neighbor is "a path that leads to the encounter with God."[30] We encounter God in the incarnate Lord who remains present with us "in the men and women who reflect his presence, in his word, in the sacraments, and especially in the Eucharist. In the Church's Liturgy, in her prayer, in the living

---

from their encounter with the Eucharistic Lord." See also Ratzinger, *Jesus of Nazareth*, 226; Benedict XVI, *Sacramentum Caritatis* no. 14. For more on the relationship between the Eucharist and mission, see Ratzinger, *Pilgrim Fellowship of Faith*, 60–122.

26. Benedict XVI, *Deus Caritas Est* no. 14.

27. Benedict XVI, *Deus Caritas Est* no. 14; cf. Ratzinger, *Behold the Pierced One*, 76–81. This is found also in Ratzinger, *Pilgrim Fellowship of Faith*, 65–70.

28. Benedict XVI, *Deus Caritas Est* no. 15.

29. Benedict XVI, *Deus Caritas Est* no. 15.

30. Benedict XVI, *Deus Caritas Est* no. 16.

community of believers, we experience the love of God, we perceive his presence and thus we learn to recognize that presence in our daily lives."[31]

The love of God, and our love for God and neighbor is not just a sentiment, although it is important not to deny that it is emotional. However, it is also born of an encounter which "engages our will and our intellect . . . the 'yes' of our will to his will unites our intellect, will and sentiments in the all-embracing act of love."[32] To want what God wants is the fulfilment of loving God. As Benedict writes:

> The love-story between God and man consists in the very fact that this communion of will increases in a communion of thought and sentiment, and thus our will and God's will increasingly coincide: God's will is no longer for me an alien will, something imposed on me from without by the commandments, but it is now my will based on the realization that God is in fact more deeply present to me than I am to myself.[33]

What this means with regard to one's neighbor is that God's love and our love for them coincide so that:

> in God and with God, I love even the person whom I do not like or even know. This can only take place on the basis of an intimate encounter with God, and encounter which has become a communion of will, even affecting my feelings. Then I learn to look on this other person not simply with my eyes and my feelings, but from the perspective of Jesus Christ. His friend is my friend. Going beyond exterior appearances, I perceive in others an interior desire for a sign of love. . . . Seeing with the eyes of Christ, I can give to others much more than their outward necessities; I can give them the look of love which they crave.[34]

As Benedict ends the first part of the encyclical, he once more reminds us of the unity of worship and *ethos* by returning to the Eucharist. We cannot self-generate this love of neighbor. He reminds us that the saints "constantly renewed their capacity for love of neighbour from their encounter with the Eucharistic Lord, and conversely this encounter acquired its realism and depth in their service to others."[35]

---

31. Benedict XVI, *Deus Caritas Est* no. 17.
32. Benedict XVI, *Deus Caritas Est* no. 17.
33. Benedict XVI, *Deus Caritas Est* no. 17.
34. Benedict XVI, *Deus Caritas Est* no. 18.
35. Benedict XVI, *Deus Caritas Est* no. 18.

Enter *Kerygma-Martyria*

Yet what of *kerygma-martyria*, the proclamation of and witness to the gospel? At the end of Part I, Benedict states that there is a need to give to others something more than the relief of their outward necessities.[36] As he says, we need to give others "the look of love which they crave."[37] In the second part of the encyclical Benedict takes up the original theme contemplated by John Paul II, the praxis of love of neighbor as part of the Church's mission. In the beginning of Part II, Benedict emphasizes that it is through the gift of the Holy Spirt that the hearts of believers are transformed into the heart of Jesus.

> The Spirit, in fact, is that interior power which harmonizes their hearts with Christ's heart and moves them to love their brethren as Christ loved them, when he bent down to wash the feet of the disciples (cf. John 13:1–13) and above all when he gave his life for us (cf. John 13:1; 15:13).[38]

Not only do we need to participate in Jesus's love in his *diakonia* and *leitourgia*, we must also, through the Spirit, participate in his love in his *kerygma-martyria*. So Benedict writes:

> The Spirit is also the energy which transforms the heart of the ecclesial community, so that it becomes a witness before the world to the love of the Father, who wishes to make humanity a single family in his Son. The entire activity of the Church is an expression of a love which seeks the integral good of man: it sees his evangelization through Word and Sacrament, an undertaking that is often heroic in the way it is acted out in history, and it seeks to promote man in the various arenas of life and human activity. Love is therefore the service that the Church carries out in order to attend constantly to man's sufferings and his needs, including material needs. And this is the aspect, this *service of charity*, on which I want to focus in the second part of the Encyclical.[39]

---

36. Benedict XVI, *Deus Caritas Est* no. 18.

37. How can we incarnate Jesus's look of love (cf. Mark 10:12)? When Jesus looked at the young man and loved him, he invited him into a relationship of discipleship with himself!

38. Benedict XVI, *Deus Caritas Est* no. 19.

39. Benedict XVI, *Deus Caritas Est* no. 19.

Thus, this *kerygmatic* and *martyriatic* love is expressed through the Word, but also through *leitourgia* (Sacrament), and "it seeks to promote man in the various arenas of life and human activity," that is, though *diakonia*.

Diakonia in the Praxis of Love

In section 20, Benedict refers to this three-fold responsibility of *leitourgia*, *kerygma-martyria*, and *diakonia* in recounting the establishment of the diaconal office (cf. Acts 6:5–6), where he writes that the Apostles established this office so that they could be free of "serving tables" in order to devote themselves to "prayer (the Eucharist and the liturgy) and the ministry of the word" (*kerygma-martyria*).[40] In this section, and the subsequent four (nos. 20–24), Benedict treats of how the early Church, as God's family in the world, lived out its *diakonia* of love.

The rest of the encyclical after section 25 lays out how the Church of today is to live out its praxis of love in the world today. Regarding this, Benedict first raises the issue of the relationship between justice and charity. Within this issue, he deals with the subsidiary question of the relationship of the Church and the State in the just ordering of society. In this relationship, the role of the Church is to "purify and illuminate reason, making its own contribution to the formation of consciences, so that the true requirements of justice may be perceived, recognized and subsequently practiced."[41] Overall, Benedict's conclusion is that justice is necessary but not sufficient. Human beings need more than justice. They need to be loved. The State can provide justice, but not love. "There will always be suffering which cries out for consolation and help. There will always be loneliness. There will always be situations of material need where help in the form of concrete love of neighbour is indispensable."[42] People need "loving personal concern."[43] Moreover, this personal loving concern cannot be limited to meeting material needs. Rather, the Church, "alive with the love enkindled by the Spirit of Christ . . . does not simply offer people material help, but refreshment and care for their souls, something which often is even more necessary than material support."[44]

---

40. Benedict XVI, *Deus Caritas Est* no. 20.
41. Benedict XVI, *Deus Caritas Est* no. 28.
42. Benedict XVI, *Deus Caritas Est* no. 28.
43. Benedict XVI, *Deus Caritas Est* no. 28.
44. Benedict XVI, *Deus Caritas Est* no. 28; cf. Francis, *Evangelii Gaudium* no. 200: "I want to say, with regret, that the worst discrimination which the poor suffer is the lack of spiritual care. The great majority of the poor have a special openness to the faith; they

Kerygma-Martyria in the Praxis of Love

Love of neighbor is to be practiced in the form of *diakonia*. Yet it is to be practiced also in the form of *kerygma-martyria*. Benedict begins with an ecumenical perspective on this praxis.

> In the Catholic Church, and also in the other Churches and Ecclesial Communities, new forms of charitable activity have arisen, while other, older ones have taken on new life and energy. In these new forms, it is often possible to establish a fruitful link between evangelization and works of charity.[45]

This does not mean engaging in proselytism, that is, by using love as a means to the end of bringing people into the Church. On the other hand, God and Christ must not be excluded from the praxis of love. This is because love

> is always concerned with the whole man. Often the deepest cause of suffering is the very absence of God. Those who practise charity in the Church's name will never seek to impose the Church's faith upon others. They realize that a pure and generous love is the best witness to the God in whom we believe and by whom we are driven to love. A Christian knows when it is time to speak of God and when it is better to say nothing and to let love alone speak. He knows that God is love (cf. 1 John 4:8) and that God's presence is felt at the very time when the only thing we do is to love. He knows—to return to the questions raised earlier—that disdain for love is disdain for God and man alike; it is an attempt to do without God. Consequently, the best defence of God and man consists precisely in love. It is the responsibility of the Church's charitable organizations to reinforce this awareness in their members, so that by their activity—as well as their words, their silence, their example—they may be credible witnesses to Christ.[46]

---

need God and we must not fail to offer them his friendship, his blessing, his word, the celebration of the sacraments and a journey of growth and maturity in the faith. Our preferential option for the poor must mainly translate into a privileged and preferential religious care."

45. Benedict XVI, *Deus Caritas Est* no. 30.

46. Benedict XVI, *Deus Caritas Est* no. 31; cf. Francis, *Evangelii Gaudium* nos. 127–28, 200. For Francis's understanding of proselytism versus genuine evangelization, see McGregor, "*Leitourgia*," 59–60.

Leitourgia in the Praxis of Love

In order that we not be overwhelmed by immensity of human need, be driven towards the search for an ideological utopia, or think that nothing can be done, it is essential that we have "a living relationship with Christ" in order to be "guided by love in the service of others."[47] Prayer is not a waste of time which could be better spent in *diakonia*. Rather, it is "a means of drawing ever new strength from Christ."[48] The one who prays does not neglect effective and loving service of their neighbor, but finds in prayer "the inexhaustible source of that service."[49] In prayer, the Christian "seeks an encounter with the Father of Jesus Christ, asking God to be present with the consolation of the Spirit to him and his work."[50] In this "face to face" encounter "with the God who is Love" one can sense "the impelling need to transform [one's] whole life into service of neighbour, in addition to service of God."[51]

Bishops and the Three-fold Mission of the Church

In addressing the role of bishops in carrying out the Church's charitable activity, Benedict states that: "In conformity with the episcopal structure of the Church, the Bishops, as successors of the Apostles, are charged with primary responsibility for carrying out in the particular Churches the programme set forth in the Acts of the Apostles (cf. Acts 2:42–44)," and "the exercise of charity is an action of the Church as such, and that, like the ministry of Word and Sacrament, it too has been an essential part of her mission from the very beginning."[52] When we read this, it is most important that we turn to the actual scriptural verses referred to for elucidation of what Benedict thinks this program is "And they devoted themselves to the apostles' teaching and fellowship, to the breaking of bread and the prayers. And fear came upon every soul; and many wonders and signs were done through the apostles. And all who believed were together and had all things in common" (Acts 2:42–44). It is significant that Benedict does not just limit himself to verse 44: "And all who believed were together and had all things in common." The program is not just one of the *diakonia* of charity. The program

---

47. Benedict XVI. *Deus Caritas Est* no. 36.
48. Benedict XVI. *Deus Caritas Est* no. 36.
49. Benedict XVI. *Deus Caritas Est* no. 36.
50. Benedict XVI. *Deus Caritas Est* no. 37.
51. Benedict XVI. *Deus Caritas Est* no. 40.
52. Benedict XVI. *Deus Caritas Est* no. 32.

of the first believers was made up of the *kerygma* (the apostles' teaching), the *martyria* (the witness of wonders and signs), the *leitourgia* (the breaking of bread and the prayers, and filial fear), and the *diakonia* of charity (had all things in common). The matrix for this charity was *koinonia*—all who believed were together.[53]

Having the Heart of Christ through the Gift of the Holy Spirit

Benedict holds that people need a love which goes beyond the satisfaction of material needs, or the need for justice. They need more than "professional competence" or "technically proper care" or "the needs of the moment." They also need "heartfelt concern" which will enable them "to experience the richness of their humanity."[54] This means that:

> in addition to their necessary professional training . . . charity workers need a "formation of the heart": they need to be led to that encounter with God in Christ which awakens their love and opens their spirits to others. As a result, love of neighbour will no longer be for them a commandment imposed, so to speak, from without, but a consequence deriving from their faith, a faith which becomes active through love (cf. Gal 5:6). . . . The Christian's programme—the programme of the Good Samaritan, the programme of Jesus—is "a heart which sees." This heart sees where love is needed and acts accordingly.[55]

In this passage, Benedict is saying that our love for people must be affective as well as practical. Earlier in the encyclical, he had spoken of the need for love to be volitional and intellectual, as well as affective.

> Contact with the visible manifestations of God's love can awaken within us a feeling of joy born of the experience of being loved. But this encounter also engages our will and our intellect. Acknowledgment of the living God is one path towards love, and the "yes" of our will to his will unites our intellect, will and sentiments in the all-embracing act of love.[56]

---

53. Benedict XVI, *Deus Caritas Est* no. 32. For a fuller exposition of Benedict/Ratzinger's understanding of mission centered around Acts 2:42, see Ratzinger, *Behold the Pierced One*, 71–87; *Pilgrim Fellowship of Faith*, 60–77.

54. Benedict XVI, *Deus Caritas Est* no. 31.

55. Benedict XVI, *Deus Caritas Est* no. 31. The place of the heart in *Deus Caritas Est* has not gone unnoticed. Cf. Tremblay, "Open Heart of the Son," 8–9; Pietro, "Charity," 352–64;

56. Benedict XVI, *Deus Caritas Est* no. 17.

It is the totality of the human person which must be formed to love. If we are to understand what Benedict means by "formation of the heart" we must first grasp what he means by the term "heart." In *Mary: The Church at the Source*, he defines the heart of Mary as "that interior dimension where sense and spirit, reason and feeling, interior and exterior perception interpenetrate circumincessively."[57] Behind this understanding lies a biblical and theological Christology and anthropology, one which focuses on the human person as embodied spirit whose ultimate meaning and *telos* is to be found in the Word made flesh. Briefly, his understanding can be summed up in a passage from *Jesus of Nazareth*.

> "Blessed are the pure in heart, for they shall see God" (Matt 5:8). The organ for seeing God is the heart. The intellect alone is not enough. In order for man to become capable of perceiving God, the energies of his existence have to work in harmony. His will must be pure and so too must the underlying affective dimension of his soul, which gives intelligence and will their direction. Speaking of the *heart* in this way means precisely that man's perceptive powers play in concert, which also requires the proper interplay of body and soul, since this is essential for the totality of the creature we call "man." Man's fundamental affective disposition actually depends on just this unity of body and soul and on man's acceptance of being both body and spirit. This means he places the body under the discipline of the spirit, yet does not isolate intellect or will. Rather, he accepts himself as coming from God, and thereby also acknowledges and lives out the bodiliness of his existence as an enrichment for the spirit. The heart—the wholeness of man—must be pure, interiorly open and free, in order for man to be able to see God.[58]

For Benedict, the heart is not to be identified simply with the response of the passions to sensual perception. Nor can it be identified simply with the intellect, or the will, or the soul. Nor can it to be identified simply with the *ego*. Rather, for Benedict, it is the "place" of the integration of the intellect, will, passions, and senses of the body and the soul. One could say that, for him, the human heart *is* the personal integration, the integration by the person, of all the facets of their humanity. It is also the place wherein God dwells, and where one, as a person, encounters and relates to God.[59] Al-

---

57. Balthasar and Ratzinger, *Mary*, 71.
58. Ratzinger, *Jesus of Nazareth*, 92–93.
59. See McGregor, *Heart to Heart*, 279–80, 306–310.

though Benedict does not explicitly say it, if Jesus has a human heart, then this is the kind of heart which he has.

How does this formation of the heart take place? It takes place through an "encounter with God in Christ." This encounter activates the faith of the believer. It becomes a "faith which works through love (cf. Gal 5:6)."[60] The genesis and 'locomotive' of this love is the love of Christ. This love is active in the "hearts Christ has conquered with his love, awakening within them a love of neighbour."[61] This love is actually "the love of Christ [which] urges us on" (Gal 5:14).[62] For Benedict, the Christian can say that: "It is no longer I that live, but Christ that lives in me" (Gal 2:20). This love is also the believer's love for Christ, because that believer knows that, "in Christ, God has given himself for us, even unto death." This "must inspire us to live no longer for ourselves but for him, and, with him, for others."[63]

The encounter with God in Christ leads to loving with the love of Christ. It also leads to love of Christ. One who loves Christ "loves the Church, and desires the Church to be increasingly the image and instrument of the love which flows from Christ . . . so that the love of God can spread throughout the world."[64] Only if one loves the Church can one share "in the Church's practice of love." Those who share in this praxis of love wish "to be witnesses of God and of Christ, and they wish for this very reason freely to do good to all."[65] In the formation of heart which comes through an encounter with Christ, the believer becomes Christ to others. Hence, it results in a "deep personal sharing in the needs and sufferings of others . . . a sharing of my very self with them: if my gift is not to prove a source of humiliation, I must give to others not only something that is my own, but my very self; I must be personally present in my gift."[66] If we love in this way, we will become humble, because we will realise that our love, which is a participation in the love of Christ, is entirely a grace.

Benedict concludes the second part of his encyclical with the reminder that, for a Christian, love is not expressed in a vacuum. All three theological virtues must be exercised. We cannot love without hope in God, which is practised through patience and humility. Nor can we love without faith, since that would mean not knowing that God is love. We cannot love unless

60. Benedict XVI, *Deus Caritas Est* no. 33.
61. Benedict XVI, *Deus Caritas Est* no. 33.
62. Benedict XVI, *Deus Caritas Est* no. 33.
63. Benedict XVI, *Deus Caritas Est* no. 33.
64. Benedict XVI, *Deus Caritas Est* no. 33.
65. Benedict XVI, *Deus Caritas Est* no. 33.
66. Benedict XVI, *Deus Caritas Est* no. 34.

we can see "the love of God revealed in the pierced heart of Jesus on the Cross."[67] We have seen how Benedict emphasizes that it is through the gift of the Holy Spirit that the hearts of believers are transformed into the heart of Jesus.[68] The source of this transformation is the pierced heart of Jesus himself. This is why Benedict explains the starting point of his encyclical, that "God is love' by referring the reader to this pierced heart.[69] As he says later, "It is from there [the pierced heart of Jesus] that the Christian discovers the path along which his life and love must move."[70] Paradoxically, it is in this truly human heart, the "place" of the integration of the intellect, will, passions, and senses, of the body and the soul of Jesus, that the love of the Trinitarian God for us is revealed. As Benedict says:

> "If you see charity, you see the Trinity," wrote St Augustine. In the foregoing reflections, we have been able to focus our attention on the Pieced One (cf. John 19:37; Zech 12:10), recognizing the plan of the Father who, moved by love (cf. John 3:16), sent his Only-Begotten Son unto the world to redeem man. By dying on the Cross—as St John tells us—Jesus 'gave up his Spirit' (John 19:30), anticipating the gift of the Holy Spirit that he would make after his Resurrection (cf. John 20:22).[71]

The gift of the Spirit from the heart of Jesus becomes the Spirit who enables believers to love their brothers and sisters in Christ as Christ loves them. The Spirit fulfils the promise of:

> "rivers of living water" that would flow out of the hearts of believers, through the outpouring of the Spirit (cf John 7:38–39). The Spirit, in fact, is that interior power which harmonizes their hearts with Christ's heart and moves them to love their brethren as Christ loved them, when he bent down to wash the feet of the disciples (cf. John 13:1–13) and above all when he gave his life for us (cf. John 13:1; 15:13).[72]

The Spirit not only harmonizes the hearts of believers with the heart of Christ, but also harmonizes the hearts of believers together, so that the

---

67. Benedict XVI, *Deus Caritas Est* no. 39.
68. Benedict XVI, *Deus Caritas Est* no. 19.
69. Benedict XVI, *Deus Caritas Est* no. 1.
70. Benedict XVI, *Deus Caritas Est* no. 12.
71. Benedict XVI, *Deus Caritas Est* no. 19; cf. 10. See also Larrú, "Original Source of Love," 199–211.
72. Benedict XVI, *Deus Caritas Est* no. 19.

Church has an ecclesial heart.[73] Here Benedict intimates that which he says elsewhere explicitly: This heart is the Eucharistic Christ himself, into whose self-oblation our hearts are drawn, with the Eucharistic Prayer being the Church's heart of hearts.[74]

Conclusion—Mary and the Three-fold Praxis of Love

In papal encyclicals and apostolic exhortations, we have come to expect a final appeal to the intercession of the Blessed Virgin Mary. Certainly, Benedict follows this pattern in *Spe Salvi*, *Caritas in Veritate*, *Sacramentum Caritatis*, *Verbum Domini*, *Africae Munus*, and *Ecclesia in Medio Oriente*. However, in *Deus Caritas Est* he uses the saints and Mary to recapitulate the major points of the encyclical. Besides giving an obvious example of charity towards one's neighbor in St Martin of Tours, he also makes a surprising reference to St Anthony of Egypt. Rather than someone who has somewhat withdrawn from his neighbor, it is in the monk's "face to face" encounter "with the God who is Love" that he "senses the impelling need to transform his whole life into service of neighbour, in addition to service of God."[75]

Finally, Benedict presents Mary as the one who, even amongst the saints, stands out as the epitome of charity. He begins in an obvious way, by pointing to her "service of charity to her cousin Elizabeth, with whom she remained for 'about three months' (1:56) so as to assist her in the final phase of her pregnancy."[76] Yet he goes on to outline how Mary's humble faith, hope, and charity enable her *leitourgia*, *kerygma-martyria*, and *diakonia*.

Mary's one humble desire is to be the handmaid of the Lord, placing "herself completely at the disposal of God's initiatives."[77] Because she is a woman of hope, believing in God's promises and awaiting the salvation of Israel, she can receive the angelic visitation and place herself at the service of these promises.[78] Because she is a woman of faith, she prophetically responds with prayer to her encounter with the Word of God. As Benedict explains:

> [In the Magnificat] we see how completely at home Mary is with the Word of God, with ease she moves in and out of it.

---

73. Benedict XVI, *Deus Caritas Est* nos.13–14; cf. Ratzinger, *God is Near Us*, 42–55.
74. Ratzinger, *God is Near Us*, 49.
75. Benedict XVI, *Deus Caritas Est* no. 40.
76. Benedict XVI, *Deus Caritas Est* no. 41.
77. Benedict XVI, *Deus Caritas Est* no. 41.
78. Benedict XVI, *Deus Caritas Est* no. 41.

> She speaks and thinks with the Word of God; the Word of God becomes her word, and her word issues from the Word of God. Here we see how her thoughts are attuned to the thoughts of God, how her will is one with the will of God. Since Mary is completely imbued with the Word of God, she is able to become the Mother of the Word Incarnate.[79]

Because she is a woman of charity, who "thinks with God's thoughts and wills with God's will, she cannot fail to be a woman who loves."[80] Not only in her service to Elizabeth, but to the newly-weds at Cana, at the foot of the Cross, and in the Cenacle, Mary loves both God and neighbor.[81]

Benedict presents Mary, the Mother of all believers, as the formator of the heart *par excellence*. "Men and women of every time and place have recourse to her motherly kindness and her virginal purity and grace, in all their needs and aspirations, their joys and sorrows, their moments of loneliness and their common endeavours."[82] Indeed, Mary is likened to Christ, and her love to the gift of the Holy Spirit. Believers, "constantly experience the gift of her goodness and the unfailing love which she pours out from the depths of her heart."[83] She shows us what it is like to have a:

> most intimate union with God, through which the soul is totally pervaded by him—a condition which enables those who have drunk from the fountain of God's love to become in their turn a fountain from which "flow rivers of living water" (John 7:38). Mary, Virgin and Mother, shows us what love is and whence it draws its origin and its constantly renewed power[84]

In Benedict's writing of her that she "abandoned [herself] completely to God's call and thus became a wellspring of the goodness which flows forth from him,"[85] he even compares her with the Eucharist, which he elsewhere compares to a wellspring, showing us Jesus, and leading us to him, "so that we too can become capable of true love and be fountains of living water in the midst of a thirsting world."[86]

---

79. Benedict XVI, *Deus Caritas Est* no. 41; cf. Balthasar and Ratzinger, *Mary*, 67–75.
80. Benedict XVI, *Deus Caritas Est* no. 41.
81. Benedict XVI, *Deus Caritas Est* no. 41.
82. Benedict XVI, *Deus Caritas Est* no. 42.
83. Benedict XVI, *Deus Caritas Est* no. 42.
84. Benedict XVI, *Deus Caritas Est* no. 42; cf. Ratzinger, *Jesus of Nazareth*, 244; "Holy Spirit as Communio," 331.
85. Benedict XVI, *Deus Caritas Est* no. 42.
86. Benedict XVI, *Deus Caritas Est* no. 42; cf. Ratzinger, *God is Near Us*, 42–55.

Bibliography

Aldana, Ricardo. "'The Word of God Is not Chained' (2 Tim 2:9): The Encyclical *Deus caritas est* as an Exercise in Biblical Thinking." *Communio* 33 (2006) 491–504.
Balthasar, Hans Urs von, and Joseph Ratzinger. *Mary: The Church at the Source.* Translated by Adrian Walker. San Francisco: Ignatius, 2005.
Benedict XVI. *Deus Caritas Est: On Christian Love.* Strathfield: St Pauls, 2006.
———. *Sacramentum Caritatis: On the Eucharist as the Source and Summit of the Church's Life and Mission.* Strathfield: St Pauls, 2007.
Böhnke, Michael. "Purificatio?: Vernuft und Glaube sowie Eros und Agape bei Papst Benedikt XVI." *Theologie Und Philosophie* 83 (2008) 225–42.
Bonnewijn, Olivier. "Commandment and Love: From Friedrich Nietzsche to Benedict XVI." In *The Way of Love: Reflections on Pope Benedict XVI's Encyclical Deus Caritas Est*, edited by Livio Melina and Carl A. Anderson, 152–68. San Francisco: Ignatius, 2006.
Botero, Silvio. "El Amor Conyugal: Integración de 'Eros' y 'Agape' (Deus Caritas Est, nn. 2–11)." *Cauriensia* 2 (2007) 343–62.
Cordes, Paul. "Presentation on the Encyclical *Deus Caritas Est*: A Prophetic Message That Needs to Be Heard." English ed. *L'Osservatore Romano* 27 (2007) 9–10.
———. "Reflections on the Holy Father's Encyclical Letter '*Deus Cartias Est*': Charity, Evangelization, and the 'Signs' of the Saviour." English ed. *L'Osservatore Romano* 31 (2006) 9–10.
Dulles, Avery. "Love, the Pope, and C. S. Lewis." *First Things* 169 (2007) 20–24.
Egan, Keith J. "Eros, Friendship, and Love: The Future of Bridal Mysticism." *Studies in Spirituality* 16 (2006) 131–50.
Francis. *Evangelii Gaudium: On the Proclamation of the Gospel in Today's World.* Homebush: St Pauls, 2013.
Howsare, Rodney. "Why begin with Love? 'Eros, Agape' and the Problem of Secularism." *Communio* 33 (2006) 423–48
Ide, Pascal. "La Distinction entre 'Éros' et 'Agapè' dans 'Deus caritas est' de Benoît XVI." *Nouvelle Revue Théologique* 128 (2006) 353–69.
John Paul II. *Christifideles Laici: On the Vocation and the Mission of the Lay Faithful in the Church and the World.* Homebush: St Pauls, 1989.
———. *Evangelium Vitae: On the Value and Inviolability of Human Life.* Homebush: St Pauls, 1995.
———. *Familiaris Consortio: Regarding the Role of the Christian Family in the Modern World.* Homebush: St Pauls, 1982.
———. *Redemptor Hominis.* Homebush: St Pauls, 1979.
———. *Redemptoris Missio: On the Permanent Validity of the Church's Missionary Mandate.* Homebush: St Pauls, 1991.
———. *Tertio Millennio Adveniente: On Preparation for the Jubilee of the Year 2000.* Homebush: St Pauls, 1994.
Larrú, Juan de Dios. "The Original Source of Love: The Pierced Heart." In *Pope Benedict XVI's Encyclical Deus Caritas Est*, edited by Livio Melina and Carl A. Anderson, 199–211. San Francisco: Ignatius, 2006.
Mattison, William C., III. "Movements of Love: A Thomistic Perspective on Agape and Eros." *Journal of Moral Theology* 1 (2012) 31–60.

McGregor, Peter John. *Heart to Heart: The Spiritual Christology of Joseph Ratzinger.* Eugene, OR: Pickwick, 2017.

———. "Leitourgia: The Missing Link in *Evangelii Gaudium.*" *Irish Theological Quarterly* 84 (2019) 57–76.

Merecki, Jarosław. "Has Christianity Poisoned Érōs?" In *The Way of Love: Reflections on Pope Benedict XVI's Encyclical Deus Caritas Est*, edited by Livio Melina and Carl A. Anderson, 56–65. San Francisco: Ignatius, 2006.

Murphy, Charles M. "Charity, not Justice, as Constitutive of the Church's Mission." *Theological Studies* 68 (2007) 274–86.

Pietro, Maria Luisa di. "Charity and the Formation of the Heart." In *Pope Benedict XVI's Encyclical Deus Caritas Est*, edited by Livio Melina and Carl A. Anderson, 352–64. San Francisco: Ignatius, 2006.

Prieto, Antonio. "Érōs and Agápē: The Unique Dynamics of Love." In *Pope Benedict XVI's Encyclical Deus Caritas Est*, edited by Livio Melina and Carl A. Anderson, 212–26. San Francisco: Ignatius, 2006.

Ratzinger, Joseph. *Behold the Pierced One: An Approach to a Spiritual Christology.* Translated by Graham Harrison. San Francisco: Ignatius, 1986.

———. *God is Near Us: The Eucharist, Heart of Life.* Edited by Stephan Otto Horn and Vinzenz Pfnür. Translated by Henry Taylor. San Francisco: Ignatius, 2003.

———. *The God of Jesus Christ: Meditations on the Triune God.* Translated by Brian McNeil. San Francisco: Ignatius, 2008.

———. "The Holy Spirit as *Communio*: Concerning the Relationship of Pneumatology and Spirituality in Augustine." Translated by Peter Casarella. *International Catholic Review: Communio* 25 (1998) 324–39.

———. *Introduction to Christianity.* Translated by J. R. Foster. San Francisco: Ignatius, 2004.

———. *Jesus of Nazareth: From the Baptism in the Jordan to the Transfiguration.* Translated by Adrian J. Walker. New York: Doubleday, 2007.

———. *Jesus of Nazareth: Holy Week: From the Entrance into Jerusalem to the Resurrection.* Translated by Philip J. Whitmore. San Francisco: Ignatius, 2011.

———. *Pilgrim Fellowship of Faith: The Church as Communion.* Edited by Stephan Otto Horn and Vinzenz Pfnür. Translated by Henry Taylor. San Francisco: Ignatius, 2005.

———. *The Spirit of the Liturgy.* Translated by John Saward. San Francisco: Ignatius, 2000.

Salmeri, Giovanni. "Érōs: Ambiguity and the Drama of Love." In *Pope Benedict XVI's Encyclical Deus Caritas Est*, edited by Livio Melina and Carl A. Anderson, 80–90. San Francisco: Ignatius, 2006.

Schindler, D. C. "The Redemption of 'Eros': Philosophical Reflections on Benedict XVI's First Encyclical." *Communio* 33 (2006) 375–99.

Schindler, David L. "The Way of Love in the Church's Mission to the World." In *Pope Benedict XVI's Encyclical Deus Caritas Est*, edited by Livio Melina and Carl A. Anderson, 29–45. San Francisco: Ignatius, 2006.

Schu, Walter J. "Benedict Saves 'Eros.'" *The Homiletic and Pastoral Review* 107 (2007) 10–19.

Second Vatican Council. "Ad Gentes." In *The Documents of Vatican II with Notes and Index: Vatican Translation*, edited by Austin Flannery, 339–73. Strathfield: St Pauls, 2009.

———. "Lumen Gentium." In *The Documents of Vatican II with Notes and Index: Vatican Translation*, edited by Austin Flannery, 17–73. Strathfield: St Pauls, 2009.

Tremblay, Réal. "Reflections on the Holy Father's Encyclical Letter '*Deus Cartias Est*: Open Heart of the Son: Place of Trinity, Source of Church." English ed. *L'Osservatore Romano* 30 (2006) 8–9.

Wainwright, Geoffrey. "Reflections on Pope Benedict XVI's First Encyclical, *Deus Caritas Est*." *Pro Ecclesia* 15 (2006) 263–66.

Weinandy, Thomas G. "Deus Caritas Est: Defining the Christian understanding of Love." *Pro Ecclesia* 15 (2006) 259–62.

Wiker, Benjamin. "Benedict contra Nietzsche: A Reflection on 'Deus caritas est.'" *Crisis* 24 (2006) 18–23.

Wojtyła, Karol. *Sources of Renewal: The Implementation of the Second Vatican Council*. Translated by P. S. Falla. London: Collins, 1980.

11

The Festal Letter in the Life of the Church

A Study of the Festal Letters of St Cyril of Alexandria

—Kevin Wagner

> *The Festal or Easter Letter was a third-century innovation of the Alexandrian episcopacy. The first Festal Letters seem to have come from the stylus of Demetrius of Alexandria (188–230 AD). While Athanasius's collection of these letters is well-known, it is actually Cyril who provides us with the earliest quasi-complete corpus of Festal Letters; a body of literature dating from 414–442 AD. Incorporating rich examples of scriptural exegesis in the Alexandrian tradition, these letters conveyed far more than the date for the upcoming Pasch. This chapter will examine this set of epistles written by Cyril—which were written in times no more or less uncertain than our own—in order to extrapolate key elements of the Festal Letter. In doing so, we will show how the Festal Letter helped to build up the Church in Alexandria and how it may do likewise today.*

Alexandria—the home of such ecclesiastical luminaries as Clement, Origen, Athanasius, Theophilus, and Cyril—is said to have been founded by Mark the Evangelist.[1] Little is known of its Christian history

---

1. The Marcan foundation of the Alexandrian Church is traditional, but ultimately

before the end of the second century, but from the time of the episcopacy of Demetrius I (188–231 AD) documentary evidence is far more extensive.[2] It was Demetrius who first began the tradition of the festal letter.[3] The transmission of this document was useful for uniting the multifarious local churches of Egypt under their patriarch.

In this chapter I begin with a brief explanation of the form of the festal letter, noting that comprehension of the form of a text can provide insight into the function of the text, and *vice versa*. Next, in the middle section of the chapter, I discuss the purpose of Cyril's festal letters. These letters were written and promulgated to achieve particular pastoral objectives. Here I will argue that these objectives are still relevant today. Finally then, drawing on these reflections on Cyril's pastoral objectives, I put forward reasons why and how a twenty-first-century equivalent of the festal letter could serve the mission of the Church today.

The Festal Letter

A few words on the structure and context of the early Alexandrian Church are in order to clarify somewhat the purpose of the festal letter. The first point concerns the fact that, in the early Christian era, Alexandria was the only metropolitan city in Egypt.[4] This put the patriarch of the city in a powerful position as he assumed responsibility for the entire Egyptian Church. Practically this meant that other Egyptian bishops were suffragans, relying on the Patriarch for ordination and patronage.[5] Occasionally this led to conflict as heretical or apparently heretical views amongst the suffragan bishops resulted in corrections and reprisals from the Patriarch; the Meletian schism which began during the episcopacy of Alexander (312–326 AD) is a prime example of this.[6] On the positive side, the presence of a strong and orthodox patriarch went some way to ensuring the Church in Egypt

---

unverifiable. For a solid account of the difficulties in establishing the veracity of the tradition, see Davis, *Early Coptic Papacy*, 1–14.

2. Orlandi et al., "Alexandria."

3. Allen and Neil identify two distinct types of festal letters (*epistulae festales*): "The magisterial Paschal letters of the patriarchs of Alexandria, which announced authoritatively and well in advance the dates of the following Lenten Fast, Easter and Pentecost, and the short letters, more like greeting cards, that were exchanged on important feast days between bishops" (Allen and Neil, *Crisis Management*, 17). In this chapter we restrict our attention to the first of these types of letter.

4. McGuckin, "Cyril of Alexandria."

5. McGuckin, "Cyril of Alexandria."

6. Sheridan, "Coptic Christianity," 38; cf. Orlandi et al., "Alexandria."

remained orthodox; for proof of this one need only consider Athanasius, Theophilus, and Cyril.

A second critical historical matter lies in the prominence of Alexandria as a center for the sciences during the early years of Christendom. From the time of the Council of Nicaea, the expertise of Alexandrian astronomers eventually led to the city being given the responsibility for determining the date of the Pasch for the wider Church.[7] The original and primary function of the festal letter was therefore to promulgate the results of the Alexandrian astronomers work first to the Alexandrian Church, and then to Rome which took responsibility for sending them on to other churches.[8] Over the course of time the letter sent to the Egyptian Christian communities came to function as a tool for allowing the patriarch to communicate other pressing matters to his flock.

Eventually the genre of the festal letter established itself as a somewhat unique form of letter. In ancient times letter writing was an art in itself.[9] Writers took great pride in adhering to classic set forms and structures, knowing that the form of the letter could often communicate as much as the content itself. One thinks, for instance, of the Pauline letters, the classical persuasive letters sent between Roman politicians, the polemical letters of Ambrose, the friendship letters of Synesius, and so on. In each instance, the rules and etiquette of letter writing were to be kept if the message was to be communicated convincingly and coherently. It was within this tradition of letter-writing as rhetoric that the festal letter came to birth and developed.

In its mature form, the festal letter was a small message or discourse (*logidon*) composed of five principal parts.[10] It began with an introduction which called to mind the Pasch and recalled the Old Testament prophecies which pointed to Christ's Passion, death and resurrection.[11] The second and longest section dealt with various points of doctrine and catechesis. The third section exhorted the listeners to purity and charity. Section four announced the dates of Lent, Easter, and Pentecost. And finally, a postscript detailed episcopal nominations.[12] Let us now consider Cyril and his corpus of twenty-nine festal letters.

7. McGuckin, "Cyril of Alexandria," 223; cf. O'Keefe, "Introduction," 6.

8. O'Keefe, "Introduction," 6.

9. For a short summary of how boys were formed in the art of letter writing in ancient Greco-Roman cultures, see Stowers, *Letter Writing*, 32–35.

10. *Festal Letter* 22; 23 in Cyril, *Festal Letters 13–30*, 115, 126. Russell prefers to describe the *logidon* as a "small treatise" or "mini-oration" (Russell, "Church in the Commentaries," 83n5).

11. Camplani, "Festal Letters."

12. Camplani, "Festal Letters."

The Cyrillian Festal Letters

Cyril (c. 375/380–444 AD) succeeded his uncle Theophilus on the patriarchal throne of Alexandria in 412 AD.[13] A polarizing character, Cyril has been accused of all sorts of maleficence.[14] Elevated to the episcopacy in the interim between the Councils of Constantinople and Ephesus, Cyril was at the forefront of major battles for orthodoxy. It would not be a stretch to say that Cyril's episcopacy was shaped by his main opponents: the Eunomians (latter-day Arians), the Jews, the pagans (supremely embodied in the philosopher Hypatia), and later, Nestorius and his followers. These battles are played out in the festal letters as he attacks the heresy of the day sometimes more, sometimes less, aggressively.[15]

Cyril adopted the standard form of the festal letter and used it to convey the messages he believed his flock most needed to hear. Here—aside from the task of proclaiming the Pasch—I will identify three major

---

13. O'Keefe, "Introduction," 3.

14. One of the more recent slurs on the character of Cyril comes from Hans van Loon who describes Cyril as "a dual character." According to van Loon, Cyril is remembered "on the one hand, as the 'seal of the Fathers,' the 'Pillar of Faith' (in the Coptic Orthodox Church), a Doctor of the Church, as the one who dug the bed through which the stream of dogmatic developments has subsequently passed, so deeply that, generally speaking, it has never left it since (Hans von Campenhausen). On the other hand, as a church leader whose episcopate started with 3 years of violence, who expelled the Jews from Alexandria, who was associated with the murder of the neo-Platonic philosopher Hypatia, and who did not shun intimidation and bribery. A Saint who sinned" (van Loon, "Cyril of Alexandria," 181). Daniel A. Keating offers a far more balanced and considered assessment of Cyril's character: "It is difficult to settle the issue of Cyril's responsibility decisively. No one denies that Cyril was politically astute and able to wield his influence effectively in favour of his positions. He was a man of strong opinions, sure of himself and not given to remorse, and he made enemies. I am not persuaded, however, by the common portrait of Cyril as the cunning 'political animal' whose only aim in life was to advance his own power—and that of the Church of Alexandria—by whatever means available. He appears throughout his writings, rather, as a leader dedicated to the truth of the Christian gospel and the advance of the Christian church in the world. His zeal and sense of uprightness are, I believe, real and not feigned. This assessment does not absolve him from whatever responsibility he may bear for his actions against the Novationists, the Jews, the pagans, and even Nestorius, but it does run counter to the image of Cyril as the amoral, Machiavellian plotter. The sheer effort he expended over many years in the production of biblical commentary also belies the common caricature of Cyril. A man who is interested only in furthering his own political influence does not spend his entire career commenting on nearly the whole of the Bible for the training of his clergy and the welfare of his church" (Keating, *Appropriation of Divine Life*, 3–4).

15. For Cyril, the Jews and pagans are often lumped together as heretics.

functions of the Cyrillian festal letter. I do not claim this is an exhaustive list of functions.[16]

1) To Preach a Two-Fold Message

In the first instance, Cyril used the letters to preach a twofold message; orthodoxy and virtuous living. This message is clearly proclaimed in the first of his letters (dated 414 AD) and is repeated regularly throughout his corpus. Early in this first letter Cyril quotes Num 10:2, "Make for yourself two trumpets; you will make them of silver, and you will use them to summon and to dismiss the assembly."[17] While obscure perhaps to our modern ears, Cyril interprets this passage to mean that God orders the construction of two trumpets as

> the Church has two messages: one of them summons the ignorant to the right understanding of the sacred teachings, while the other warns against the defilement of wicked deeds.[18]

He continues, explaining the significance of the material of the trumpets:

> [God] commands the trumpets to be silver, since in both instances the message is bright and spotless, both when it keeps clear of error in teaching and when it presents what is to be chosen in one's actions.[19]

His purpose then was to preach on matters of doctrine and the moral life. This, he correctly interpreted, was his priestly duty.[20]

For the Jews, the trumpet was intimately associated with the priestly office and Temple worship.[21] In *Festal Letter* 9, drawing again from Num 10

---

16. Morgan, for example, posits that Cyril uses the festal letters to emphasize "asceticism's role in bringing about deification and engendering virtue in those who take up its practice" (Morgan, "Role of Asceticism," 145).

17. *Festal Letter* 1 in Cyril, *Festal Letters 1–12*, 40.

18. *Festal Letter* 1 in Cyril, *Festal Letters 1–12*, 40.

19. *Festal Letter* 1 in Cyril, *Festal Letters 1–12*, 40–41.

20. *Festal Letter* 11 in Cyril *Festal Letters 1–12*, 196.

21. For example, Sirach records that the sons of Aaron played as a part of the duties of their priestly office (Sir 50:16–19). We see too that trumpets accompanied David when he brought the Ark to Kiriath-jeriam (1 Chr 13:8) and then again as he brought the Ark into Jerusalem after it was captured by the Philistines (1 Chr 16:42). This theme is repeated later as a cohort of 120 priests praised God with trumpets as Solomon transported the Ark into the Temple (2 Chr 5:12) and then again one finds in the time of Hezekiah's restoration of Temple worship that priest-trumpeters played as the burnt offering took place (2 Chr 29:25). It is interesting to note that Cyril never directly

(now verses 9–10), Cyril notes that the Jewish priests used the trumpet to call people to war and to provide glad music during the sacrifices.[22] Cyril, inspired by Heb 10:1—"The Law, having but a shadow of the good things to come instead of the very image of these realities"—saw a deeper meaning to the plain sense of this text from Numbers.[23] First, according to Cyril, the Christian priest sounded the trumpet call to stir his flock to be courageous and prudently bold as they fought against the passions of the flesh. Second, the sonorous words of the priest filled the hearer with joy as they gave thanks for the salvific actions of the Lord performed during His Passion.

For Cyril then, the festal letter acted like the priestly trumpet of the Old Covenant. It was a means for proclaiming pure doctrine, for exhorting the faithful to courage in the face of worldly material temptations, and for rousing his flock to give joyful thanks for Christ's Passion. This brings us to consider a second major function of Cyril's festal letters.

2) To Teach the Skill of Reading the Scriptures

We have seen already that Cyril interprets Scripture in a way that is quite foreign to modern sensibilities. His exegesis deserves far deeper treatment than we can give it here. I would like simply to identify two features of his exegesis that stand out in his festal letters.

First, his method is the fruit of a youth spent reading and studying the Scriptures. It has been suggested that Cyril had a "profound" and "encyclopedic knowledge of the biblical text," and an examination of his festal letters suggests that this is probably true.[24] In these letters he often moves from passage to passage, adopting a method of free association whereby one text reminds him of another, each text adding a complexity of meaning to the other.[25] This method of interpretation can only be valid if one believes that the Scriptures are a unity; that they are inspired by the Spirit; and that God reveals His plan for salvation through them.[26]

---

quotes 1–2 Chr in his festal letters. This is a lacuna that deserves further investigation elsewhere.

22. *Festal Letter* 9.1 in Cyril, *Festal Letters 1–12*, 156–57.
23. *Festal Letter* 9.2 in Cyril, *Festal Letters 1–12*, 157.
24. McGuckin, "Introduction," 11; O'Keefe, "Introduction," 4.
25. The use of allusions and quotations from respected sources was expected of classically trained rhetoricians like Cyril. It served to demonstrate the expertise of the rhetorician and thus it added rhetorical force to the writing. See Young's masterly analysis of literary allusion in Young, *Biblical Exegesis*, 99–103.
26. Maxwell, "Introduction," 2:xxii–xxiii.

A second feature is Cyril's attention to the literal and spiritual senses. Cyril recognizes two senses of meaning in the Scriptures; the literal or historical sense (ἱστορία) and the spiritual sense (θεωρία πνευματική).[27] In the festal letters it is standard for Cyril to set out first the historical facts of an Old Testament passage and then move from this to interpret the text in the light of Christ. For Cyril, the Old Testament contained figures, shadows and types which pointed to the truth revealed in the New Testament.[28] In *Festal Letter* 13 (425 AD) while discussing the redemption, Cyril states this explicitly: "This has been recorded for us as well in the older Scriptures, as it were in shadows and figures still. For the law is a shadow, and is pregnant with the shape of truth."[29] We see that this understanding of the relationship between the Old Law and the New showed itself powerfully and jarringly in the rhetoric Cyril used in the festal letters (and elsewhere) when speaking of Judaism and the Jews.[30] For instance, the worship according to the Old Law was merely "figurative and corporeal" in form,[31] while the worship offered by Christians was true worship "in the Spirit."[32] The Ark of the Covenant was "bright with gold outside, and holding Moses's books within," while "each believer in Christ . . . is made a temple of the Spirit, receiving the source of sanctification."[33] And elsewhere we find that circumcision of the flesh was deemed by Cyril to be ridiculous as it called into question the skill of God, the Creator of the body;[34] literal circumcision was a mere shadow of the true circumcision required under the New Law, the circumcision of the heart.[35]

---

27. Keating explains that this spiritual sense "pertains to the things perceived through and in the Spirit (τὰ πνευματικά), and points in some sense to the mystery of Christ" (Keating, *Appropriation of Divine Life*, 15).

28. Examples of this are legion. For example: "I believe that Christ appears of necessity in Isaac's birth, expressed there as in figure" (*Festal Letter* 5.4 in Cyril, *Festal Letters 1–12*, 91).

29. *Festal Letter* 13.2 in Cyril, *Festal Letters 13–30*, 7.

30. O'Keefe notes that "dealing with the Jews and offering instruction in how to read the Bible correctly were two of Cyril's major concerns as he set out each year to compose a new festal letter" (O'Keefe, "Introduction," 26).

31. *Festal Letter* 1.1 in Cyril, *Festal Letters 1–12*, 36.

32. *Festal Letter* 1.1 in Cyril, *Festal Letters 1–12*, 36.

33. *Festal Letter* 4.5 in Cyril, *Festal Letters 1–12*, 77. The individual Christian's sanctification by the Holy Spirit is possible through the work of Christ who "sanctified his own temple by the Holy Spirit along with all creation, which came to be through him and to which sanctification applies" (Cyril, *John* 11.11 [Maxwell, 304]).

34. *Festal Letter* 6.7 in Cyril, *Festal Letters 1–12*, 112–13.

35. *Festal Letter* 6.8 in Cyril, *Festal Letters 1–12*, 115.

Cyril's reading of the Old Testament was thus christocentric as he—like many of the Fathers—held the Scriptures to be a unified text which is principally concerned with the redemptive work of God through Christ.[36] I would contend that this concern to apply a christological hermeneutic to the reading of Scripture was consistent with Cyril's overriding desire to defend the unity of the Godhead and the unity of the human and divine natures of Christ, and the ensure the unity of his flock.

3) To Preach and Bring about Unity

A third function of the festal letter was to preach both the unity of the Godhead and the unity of the human and divine natures of Christ, and also to call Christians to unity with one another as members of the Body of Christ. Here we will offer a summary account of Cyril's teaching on unity by drawing primarily from his *Commentary on John* 17:20–21. In the process we will show how this teaching is expounded in the more pastorally oriented festal letters.

Unity of the Godhead

Cyril describes the unity between the Persons of the Godhead as "natural," "essential," and "true."[37] These are the features of the unity inherent in God who is the archetype. We shall see that the unity which exists between us stands in contrast to that between the Divine Persons as archetype does to antitype. The Alexandrian Patriarch's concern to assert the unity of the Divine Persons is a response to opposing arguments put forward by Eunomius and others of his ilk. These heretical views threatened the consubstantiality of the Persons of the Trinity. *Festal Letter* 12 offers a standard patristic response to the Eunomians stressing that the Begotten is "of the same nature and substance as the begetter."[38] Here Cyril argues that if the Begotten is not of the same nature and substance as the Begetter, then this would be unique, as human beget humans, dogs beget dogs, and horses beget horses. Surely then, he contends, the divine must beget the divine![39] A little later in this twelfth letter, Cyril takes on the accusation that "ingenerate" and "generate" are indicative of a difference in substance. At this point Cyril launches

---

36. O'Keefe, "Introduction," 10.
37. Cyril, *John* 11.11 (Maxwell, 302).
38. *Festal Letter* 12.4 in Cyril, *Festal Letters 1–12*, 229.
39. *Festal Letter* 12.4 in Cyril, *Festal Letters 1–12*, 229.

into a refutation based on a (perhaps) Aristotelian account of genus and difference.[40] What is striking about this discussion is that Cyril seems to presume his hearers or readers are capable of following his argument. On the one hand, this suggests that Gregory of Nyssa's account of disputation on Trinitarian doctrine in the marketplace a generation or two earlier has some truth to it.[41] On the other hand, it is interesting to consider how one might promote such discussion amongst Christians today.

Unity of Christ

Cyril is perhaps most famous for his fight against Nestorius, the Patriarch of Constantinople, and Nestorius's teaching that denied the full unity of the human and divine natures of Jesus. This was a complex and crucial confrontation which profoundly influenced the course of the history of Christological doctrine. Here we will focus first on Cyril's explanation as to how the human and divine natures can be united and then his thoughts on the purpose of the Incarnation.

In his *Commentary on John* Cyril states,

> There is only one way union with God can take place, even in the case of Christ (insofar as he appeared as and bears the name of a human being). That way is this: the flesh is sanctified by union with the Spirit in an ineffable manner of concurrence [συνόδου][42] and thus ascends to an unconfused union [ἕνωσιν ἀσυγχύτως] with God the Word and through him to a union with the Father—a union by disposition [σχετικῶς],[43] that is, not by nature.[44]

---

40. *Festal Letter* 12.6 in Cyril, *Festal Letters 1–12*, 233.

41. "Si tu demandes de la monnaie, il te fait de la philosophie sur engendré et inengendré; si tu t'enquiers du prix du pain, 'le Père est plus grand,' répond-il, 'et le Fils inférieur'; si tu dis 'le bain est-il prêt?' il définit que le Fils existe à partir de ce qui n'est pas" (Cassin, "Grégoire de Nysse," 591).

42. Or alternatively, "union [of natures]," "coming together," or "conjunction."

43. The term σχετικῶς—"by relationship"—is used here to illustrate that the union between Christ, who is God made man, or any human person and the Father is a union of unlike natures.

44. Cyril, *John* 12.2 (Maxwell, 306). ὁ γὰρ τῆς πρὸς Θεὸν ἑνώσεως τρόπος οὐχ ἑτέραν ἔχει τὴν ὁδὸν καὶ εἰ νοοῖτο τυχὸν ἐπὶ Χριστοῦ, καθὸ πέφηνέ τε καὶ κεχρημάτικεν ἄνθρωπος· ἑνώσει τῇ πρὸς τὸ Πνεῦμα, κατὰ τὸν ἄρρητον τῆς συνόδου τρόπον, ἁγιαζομένης δῆλον ὅτι τῆς σαρκὸς, οὕτω τε πρὸς ἕνωσιν ἀσυγχύτως ἀναβαινούσης αὐτῆς πρὸς τὸν Θεὸν Λόγον, καὶ δι' αὐτοῦ πρὸς τὸν Πατέρα, σχετικῶς δῆλον ὅτι καὶ οὐ φυσικῶς. Pusey, *Sancti Patris Nostri Cyrilli*, 2.

The union between the divine and human natures in Christ is thus a union that occurs, not through nature, but by the will of the Father through the Son and in the Spirit.[45] Furthermore, it is only through this graced union of the flesh and the Spirit that the human person—be it Christ or not—can attain union with the Father, who is, of course, pure spirit.[46]

This leads us to consider why God willed the Incarnation. Cyril, McGuckin points out, "insisted that the incarnation is not for the sake of God, but for the redemption of the human race."[47] The Incarnation, Cyril maintains, willfully brings together disparate natures in Christ in order that through this true union we might "share and participate in the divine nature"; that is, so that we might become like God.[48] Cyril continues, declaring explicitly that sharing (μεταλαχεῖν) in the Holy Spirit and union with God (ἑνώσεως)[49] is possible due to the "mystery of Christ."[50] This point highlights why Cyril personally invested so much effort into defending the true unity of natures in Christ. If the divine Son did not truly become true man then the whole possibility of union with God (*henosis*) or deification (*theosis*) must be called into question.[51] Likewise, if God did not become true man then one must question what redemption could possibly mean; for if Jesus was not fully human and fully divine what effect could His suffering have for his creatures?

---

45. Cyril, *John* 12.2 (Maxwell, 306). "The Only Begotten says that what was given to his flesh was given to him—given, of course, by the Father through him and in the Spirit."

46. We see that this schema laid out by Cyril addresses the concerns held by Neoplatonists and others who believed it absurd that a purely spiritual God could take on corrupt flesh. Ultimately, for Cyril, it is the will of the Father that enables a true union of spiritual and corporal natures in the person of Christ; a union that is shrouded in mystery.

47. McGuckin, "Introduction," 34.

48. "He is God and a human being in the same [person] so that by uniting in himself, as it were, things that are very different by nature and essentially distinct from each other he may make humanity share and participate in the divine nature" (Cyril, *John* 11.11 [Maxwell, 304]). Maxwell notes in a footnote here that the Greek does not include "person," but rather, Cyril writes literally "in the same" (ἐν ταὐτῷ). See Cyril, *John* 11.11 (Maxwell, 304n193).

49. McGuckin points out that "Cyril consistently opposed the keyword of "Union" (*Henosis*) to that of the Antiochenes who used "Association" to refer to the relationship between the divine and the human in Christ" (McGuckin, "Introduction," 34).

50. Cyril, *John* 11.11 (Maxwell, 304).

51. Cyril's teaching may be summarized as such, "Jesus is the *person* of the Son *existing* as a man . . . it is truly the person of the divine Son who truly exists as a true man" (Weinandy, "Cyril and the Mystery," 43).

Ecclesial Unity

We may consider now Cyril's teaching on the unity of the Church; a unity which builds upon and depends on the unity of the Godhead and the unity of Christ. As we have seen, Cyril describes the unity between the Father, Son and Spirit as a "natural," "essential," and "true." The unity between human persons and God, and amongst human persons individually, Cyril posits, is an imitation of the archetypical unity which binds the Persons of the Godhead.[52] And the achievement and maintenance of this unity is attained through the reception of the Sacraments of Baptism and the Eucharist. Baptism unites the person to the Godhead and fellow Christians and the reception of the *corpus* of the Savior through Eucharistic Communion nourishes and sustains this union. Cyril contends then, that our unity with others and our unity with God has both corporeal and spiritual dimensions; that is, it is a "double participation in the divine life, a corporeal one maintained through the Eucharist and a spiritual one brought about by the reception of the Holy Spirit at Baptism."[53]

Spiritual unity is also achieved through Christ, who "sanctified his own temple by the Holy Spirit" in order to share this Spirit with all individual members of His Body.[54] Union in the Spirit occurs, then, as

> the Spirit is one and indivisible. He gathers together the spirits of others, who are cut off from unity (I mean in terms of their essence), into unity in his own personal subsistence, making them all one in himself. Just as the power of his[55] holy flesh makes those in whom it dwells one body, in the same way I think that the one Spirit of God, who dwells indivisibly in all, gathers everyone into spiritual unity.[56]

Human beings, then—being essentially different to God—are drawn into and united in the Body of Christ through the gratuitous reception of the

---

52. Cyril, *John* 11.11 (Maxwell, 302). "Their union is natural and true and may be seen in the definition of their being, but our unity imitates the form of their true unity. After all, how could the antitype be completely equal to the archetype?" Union created through Christ in the Spirit between human beings is a moral union (in contrast to the essential union inherent in the Godhead) which binds pagans and Jews together as one. See Cyril, *John* 11.11 (Maxwell, 303).

53. Cyril, *John* 11.11 (Maxwell, 303); Russell, *Cyril of Alexandria*, 19.

54. Cyril, *John* 11.11 (Maxwell, 304).

55. That is, Christ's flesh.

56. Cyril, *John* 11.11 (Maxwell, 305).

Holy Spirit in Baptism.[57] Such a union transforms participants into "'children of God' and 'gods'"[58]

The corporal dimension of unity is sustained by reception of the Eucharist. Drawing on the writings of Paul, Cyril notes that Christ, as Head of the Body, unites all those who "partake of the one bread" into His holy and mystical Body, the Church.[59] Subsequently, "when we come into participation with his holy body, we obtain a bodily union" with Christ.[60] Indeed, reception of the Eucharist brings life as the one who receives is "united (*synenoumenoi*) with the flesh of the Saviour in the same way that the flesh is united with the Word that dwells within it."[61] Christ is able to achieve this as "he is God and a human being in the same [person]."[62] What is clear from Cyril's Eucharistic theology, is that it is based solidly on his understanding of the hypostatic union. Furthermore, the unitive aspect of the Eucharist in the ecclesiology of Cyril explains to some extent the voracity of his attacks on Nestorian Christology.

This short discussion of unity highlights the fact that Cyril bases his teaching on unity among believers, first on the archetypical union found between the Persons of the Godhead, and second on the union of the divine and human natures of Christ. Unity amongst believers and the union between believers and God, in both their spiritual and corporeal dimensions, are thus images of these archetypical unions. In short, we see that Cyril's trinitarian theology flows on to his Christology, which filters down to his ecclesiology and theology of Eucharist. This schema in itself is perhaps radical to the modern ear.

Having examined the chief priorities of Cyril's pastoral ministry, which are reflected in his festal letters, we are invited to reconsider the polemical nature of these festal letters. In the first instance, Cyril's polemic against Jews and pagans—who deny the Trinity entirely—and the Eunomians—who had a heretical view of the Trinity—is in part a defense of Nicene trinitarian theology. As any student of the history of fourth-century Arianism and the life of Athanasius knows, the battle between the pro- and anti-Nicene factions was not always fought on theological grounds.[63] Cyril was not neces-

---

57. Russell, *Cyril of Alexandria*, 19.

58. Cyril, *John* 11.9 (Maxwell, 285).

59. Cyril, *John* 11.11 (Maxwell, 304).

60. Cyril, *John* 11.11 (Maxwell, 304).

61. Cyril, *John* 4.2; Russell, *Cyril of Alexandria*, 20, 115.

62. Cyril, *John* 11.11 (Maxwell, 305). Note again that the translator supplies "person" here.

63. Examples of this are legion. We consider, for instance, the allegations levied at Athanasius which lead to his many exiles. One is reminded too of the machinations

sarily innocent in this regard.[64] What seems more important, however, is the fact that Cyril is deeply aware that a deficient Trinitarian theology makes a sound Christology impossible, and thus faith in Christ's Church, sacraments, and pastors would be diminished. The fight over Nicene orthodoxy was thus one that had serious consequences for his flock. Indeed, Cyril's running battle against Nestorius—who denied the true union of the divine and human natures of Christ—was a fight on both Christological, and thus, soteriological grounds. With this in mind, it is unsurprising perhaps to see the Alexandrian bishop brought his considerable rhetorical abilities to bear on those who fought against the Nicene Symbol.[65]

A few points deserve mention with regards to the function of the final three parts of the festal letter. The third section calls the people to practice of the corporal and spiritual works of mercy. These works not only conform the individual to Christ, but they also bring the members of Christ's Body into union. While the formulaic nature of these exhortations may seem contrived at times, there is no good reason in my estimation to treat them as mere rhetoric. Following these exhortations, we find Cyril promulgating the dates for the Pasch. This announcement ensures unity of liturgical worship. Unity in the offering of worship to God the Father through Christ his Son— the Head of the Body—in the Holy Spirit is a powerful witness of ecclesial unity. While this view may sound unnecessarily provocative, I would suggest that the matter of dating the Pasch is still an unfortunate sacramental sign of disunity which we would do well to seek to resolve if we truly wish Christ's Body to breathe with both lungs.[66] Finally, the postscripts—which are found only in a Coptic copy of Cyril's first *Festal Letter*—give details of episcopal nominations.[67] Ensuring promulgation of episcopal succession was one way to ensure that believers knew which bishops were approved by the Alexandrian patriarch. As such, this would have helped the flock to know which shepherd they were to gather around.[68]

---

which occurred in the lead up to and at the Council of Constantinople which resulted in the deposing of Gregory Nazianzus as Patriarch of Constantinople.

64. Of particular note is Cyril's *Letter* 96 (dated 431 AD) detailing a long list of gifts to be given to persons of influence within the Constantinopolitan Court in order to achieve the required doctrinal ends at the Council of Ephesus. See *Letter* 96 in Cyril, *Letters 51–110*, 151–53. For the context of this letter, see Brown, *Power and Persuasion*, 15–17.

65. Wessel notes that Cyril never received advanced training in rhetoric. Rather, she states, he "absorbed aspects of sophistic rhetoric" by his exposure to Christian rhetoricians like the Cappadocians and John Chrysostom. See Wessel, *Cyril of Alexandria*, 199.

66. John Paul II, "Ut Unum Sint" no. 54.

67. Camplani, "Festal Letters."

68. It had been understood from at least as early as the time of Ignatius of Antioch

The Relevance of the Festal Letter Today

I would like to finish this chapter offering some reasons why the *raison d'etre* of the festal letter is still relevant today and why we would do well to find alternative ways to achieve some of the key functions of the festal letter.

The Effective Proclamation of Faith and Morals

First, the teaching of the Church on faith and morals, which has been handed down throughout the ages, has developed and been expressed in new ways in order to make it accessible to the people of God. Today, however, it seems there are significant, and perhaps unprecedented, challenges in communicating and translating this teaching in order that it can be accessible to the masses.

One challenge faced when trying to communicate Church teaching is rooted in the institutional nature of the Church. Institutions tend to develop structures and processes in order to serve the mission of the institution and its stakeholders. These features of institutional life can bring assurance and certainty for members of the institution. However, as anyone who has dealt with an institution knows, it can take considerable time for institutions to change their structures and processes. It is no slight to say that this is true for the Catholic Church. This, I would like to state emphatically, is not intended to be an attack on the Church. Indeed, slowness to adapt to the whims and wishes of the 'present day' has helped the Church to hold on to the core truths of the Faith throughout the ages. I would add too that the tardiness of the Church to change its structures and processes is entirely understandable given its universal reach. Sustainable and fruitful change must involve prayerful and reflective dialogue with particular churches. This takes time and cannot be rushed to suit the exigencies of the day.

Be that as it may, the problem remains that the institutional Church has struggled to adapt quickly to the fact that traditional means of communication are not as effective as they once were. We see, for instance, that as many societies have become more overtly secular, as scandals have plagued the Church, and as Mass attendance has fallen, that it has become increasingly difficult for the Church to reach both her own members and those outside her. Many of the traditional ways of promulgating Church teaching are no longer available or effective.[69] For instance, if members of

---

that the bishop is the center and guardian of unity for the local church. See, for example, Ignatius, "To the Smyrneans" 8–9.

69. Weddell points out that the traditional retention strategies for the Church were:

the Church are no longer attending Mass, then the homily is no longer the most effective didactic tool in the priest's toolbox. We note too, that Mass attendance is no guarantee that those in the pews are ready for catechesis. Indeed research suggests that one cannot assume that Mass-goers believe it is possible to have a personal relationship with God, let alone that they actually have a healthy and vibrant relationship with Jesus.[70] Without this relationship catechetical homilies become exercises in throwing seed on rock. In sum, it is not unreasonable to suggest that the institutional nature of the Church makes it more difficult to adapt to these new situations.

The solution to this problem is not, of course, to de-institutionalize the Church. Rather, it would seem that there is a need to return constantly to the famous words of Pope Paul VI in *Evangelii Nuntiandi*:

> "We wish to confirm once more that the task of evangelizing all people constitutes the essential mission of the Church." It is a task and mission which the vast and profound changes of present-day society make all the more urgent. Evangelizing is in fact the grace and vocation proper to the Church, her deepest identity. She exists in order to evangelize, that is to say, in order to preach and teach, to be the channel of the gift of grace, to reconcile sinners with God, and to perpetuate Christ's sacrifice in the Mass, which is the memorial of His death and glorious resurrection.[71]

Evangelization, which is a fruit of an encounter with the Person of Jesus, needs to be prioritized in order to bring people into a relationship with Christ and His Church so that they may then receive the teaching of the Church with open hearts and minds. This may mean that some traditional strategies are de-prioritized. New ways of facilitating encounters between God and His people need to be put into place and more effective modes of communicating the Word need to be found.[72]

Once people come to know and love Jesus, a second challenge arises; the Word needs to be translated into accessible language that remains faithful to the original. Unfortunately, the teachings of the Church on faith and the moral life are often inaccessible to many people today who are not

---

childhood catechesis, the sacraments, top-down interventions from the Confraternity of Christian Doctrine, and Catholic schools. Her statistical analysis shows that these strategies are no longer effective for maintaining and building up the Church. See Weddell, *Forming Intentional Disciples*, 34–39.

70. Weddell, *Forming Intentional Disciples*, 43–46.

71. Paul VI, "Evangelii Nuntiandi" no. 14.

72. Benedict XVI details numerous positives and negatives with the use of digital methods of communication in Benedict XVI, "Truth, Proclamation, and Authenticity."

cognizant of the cultures, history, and philosophies of the communities that formulated these doctrines. It is clear that this is a difficult problem to solve. The translation of texts is only a small part of the solution. What is more vital, it would seem, is a renewal in catechesis; a renewal that seeks to develop effective and sound tools for building the foundation required for Christians to know and love their faith.[73] This requires the development of materials and a reconsideration of the ways in which this material is delivered. It demands too that people be trained to deliver this material in accessible ways. I would argue that this is essential, as methods which seek to limit or remove interaction between persons threaten to turn catechesis into a process of information sharing. Catechesis is not simply a process of sharing of information about a Trinity of Persons, but rather, a step on the way into a deeper relationship with a Trinity of Persons.

A third challenge the Church faces as she seeks to share her teaching on faith and morals is overcoming her ignorance of those who oppose her teaching. While Cyril's tone is often harsh-sounding to the modern ear, one can't deny that Cyril made every effort to know his opponents and address their arguments head on. I don't suggest that we adopt Cyril's rhetoric or that we choose the same targets. Rather, it seems to me that we would do well to know better what we are opposing both within and outside the Church. This requires genuine dialogue with those who oppose orthodoxy and it demands courage to stand firm on the non-negotiables of the faith.

Teaching the Skill of Reading Scripture

In his festal letters Cyril demonstrates and explains how one ought to interpret the scriptures. The Alexandrian patriarch assumed the unity of the scriptures and utilized the best methods of interpretation available to him. Both these assumptions are now under attack.

There is a crisis in Biblical scholarship that won't be resolved any time soon.[74] The widespread utilization of historical-critical methods by Catholic exegetes in the post-Vatican II era has certainly brought some fruit. There

---

73. We note that the publication of the *Compendium of the Catechism of the Catholic Church* (2005), the youth catechism *YouCat* (2011), and the *Compendium of the Social Doctrine of Catholic Church* (2004) are important first steps in achieving this end. Winters gives a detailed account of post-Vatican II efforts to find new ways to proclaim the gospel in her thesis, Winters, "Communion Ecclesiology and Communication," 126–51.

74. A magisterial study on the crisis is provided in Carbajosa, *Faith, the Fount of Exegesis*, 13–24. See also Johnson, "What's Catholic about Catholic Biblical Scholarship?" 14–19.

is, however, a growing rebellion against the use of these methods of interpretation for sucking the life out of the Scriptures.[75] A key reason for this fightback is the recognition of the limits of these methods. One notes, for instance, that exegetes using historical-critical methods must restrict their study to individual textual units if they wish to remain true to the method. This stands in contrast to the official view of the Roman Church that interpretation is lacking if a more holistic approach is not adopted.[76]

One of the most forthright and renowned scholars in this regard is former President of the Pontifical Biblical Commission and Pope Emeritus, Benedict XVI. Both before and during his papacy, Benedict warned of the dangers of failing to consider the limits of historical methods. At the beginning of his three volume work *Jesus of Nazareth*, Benedict points out that these limits are due precisely to the historical character of the method. He states:

> We have to keep in mind the limit of all efforts to know the past: We can never go beyond the domain of hypothesis, because we simply cannot bring the past into the present. To be sure, some hypotheses enjoy a high degree of certainty, but overall we need to remain conscious of the limit of our certainties—indeed, the history of modern exegesis makes this limit perfectly evident.[77]

In essence, the problem with historical approaches to the Scriptures that extend beyond the limits of the method is that the Scriptures become a word from the past that are divorced from the dogma which has been founded on it.[78] Furthermore Jesus becomes a historical fact to know about, rather than a person who wishes to speak his Word to his people today.

The solution to this crisis is by no means obvious. For instance, there is no coherent, universally accepted method to put in place of existing historical-critical methods. As Ratzinger has indicated, a simple return to patristic exegetical methods is insufficient; for while the christocentrism of patristic exegesis needs to be reclaimed, this exegesis fails to give adequate attention

---

75. In the first paragraph of his famous essay, "Biblical Interpretation in Conflict," Ratzinger declared: "Today, to speak of the crisis of the historical-critical method has become almost a truism." He goes on to detail the growing unrest about historical methods. See Ratzinger, "Biblical Interpretation in Conflict," 91–94.

76. Drawing on *Dei Verbum*, the *Catechism of the Catholic Church* gives three criteria for interpretation: "Be especially attentive 'to the content and unity of the whole Scripture'; Read the Scripture within 'the living Tradition of the whole Church'; and Be attentive to the analogy of faith." (*CCC*, 112–14).

77. Pope Benedict XVI, *Jesus of Nazareth*, xvii.

78. Ratzinger, "Biblical Interpretation in Conflict," 99.

to historical considerations.[79] Ultimately, criticism of the criticism is necessary and this cannot exclude criticism of patristic methods.[80] In the midst of these challenges we are faced with the pastoral necessity of helping our laity and priests to navigate these complexities of this battle over hermeneutics. Like Cyril, who wrote his letters to teach his flock how to interpret correctly the Scriptures, we need to find means for achieving this same end.

Preaching and Bringing about Unity

We have already indicated that Cyril's teaching on unity was not restricted to preaching social or religious unity. Rather, his teaching was multifaceted, addressing the unity of the Godhead, the unity of natures in the person of Christ, and the importance of ecclesial unity. Certain manifestations of post-Vatican II communion ecclesiology would no doubt sit well with the Alexandrian patriarch, with their emphasis on both the horizontal and vertical dimensions of the ecclesial communion. One may consider this a definitive step forward as this opens the way to an ecclesiology which is founded on divine, rather than human, footings. Unfortunately, this refocusing on communion has led to the inevitable consequence that some theologians emphasize the horizontal aspect over the vertical.[81] Unsurprisingly, such bottom-up approaches lend themselves to proponents deeming traditional dogmas on the natures of Christ and the Trinity inconvenient or downright irrelevant.[82] While I have no comprehensive solution to correcting this tendency to downplay the vertical dimension of the Church, it is perhaps the time to revisit efforts like that of John Paul II in *Ecclesia de Eucharistia* in order to integrate eucharistic theology more firmly into a

---

79. Ratzinger points out that the exegesis of the Patristic era (and that of the Middle Ages) "was largely lacking" in terms of its attention to historical concerns; that is, it failed to consider that "texts have to be referred back to their historical setting and interpreted in their historical context." On the other hand, Ratzinger seems to give a positive assessment of the christocentrism of this earlier exegesis. See Ratzinger, "Biblical Interpretation in Conflict," 121.

80. Drawing from Ratzinger's essay "Biblical Interpretation in Conflict," Carbajosa provides a useful short summary of Ratzinger's method of critiquing criticism in Carbajosa, *Faith, the Fount of Exegesis*, 20–21.

81. If the 1992 statement by the Congregation for the Doctrine of the Faith (CDF) is any indication, it is clear that some models of the Church as communion are inadequate. See CDF, "Letter to the Bishops."

82. This is concerning for many reasons, not the least of which is that it is nigh on impossible to come to a correct understanding of the Church as the Body of Christ if one cannot comprehend how the divine and human natures are related in the Person of Christ.

theology of ecclesial communion.[83] Such a solution would no doubt please Cyril!

On another note, I would suggest that there are too few bishops and theologians today who adequately preach and teach the unity of the Divine Persons, Christ's natures, and the Church. The reality of the situation, I would argue, is that there is a fracture between dogmatic theology and so-called 'pastoral' theology. How wide this fracture is, I dare not say, but what seems sure is that there is a want for bishops and theologians who can successfully explain, teach, and preach dogmatic truths in pastorally accessible ways such that unity is built, not destroyed. This dearth has serious implications for the future of ecumenism and interreligious dialogue. In sum, efforts to achieve real and lasting unity between Christians, and between Christians and non-Christians, need to be founded on the sure basis of the unity of the Persons of the Godhead, and the unity of the natures of Christ, not on the unity of created types. So a sound Trinitarian theology and christology must form the cornerstone of a robust and truthful ecclesiology. Indeed, unity is fictive if it is not founded on the love of the Persons of the Trinity and on the correct understanding of the natures of Christ.

In this chapter we have shown how Cyril used the festal letter to preach orthodoxy and virtue, to demonstrate and teach his flock how to interpret the scriptures, and to help them to understand the unity of the Persons of the Trinity, the natures of Christ, and the importance of ecclesial unity. Having done this, we have argued that there is a need to find new ways today to achieve these same objectives. By way of conclusion, we may recall that Cyril's letters reinforce the fact that the spiritual and corporal works of mercy bind us together in unity. They are no mere 'obligation,' but rather, they are works which help us to conform to Christ who is the Head of the Body, the Church. Our theology then, if it is to be truly ecclesial theology in continuity with that of Cyril, must be the fruit of a union established at Baptism, nourished by the Eucharist, and demonstrated in acts of love.

Bibliography

Benedict XVI. *Jesus of Nazareth*. Translated by Adrian J. Walker. New York: Doubleday, 2007.

———. "Truth, Proclamation, and Authenticity of Life in the Digital Age." World Communications Day Message 2011. January 24, 2011. Online. http://w2.vatican.va/content/benedict-xvi/en/messages/communications/documents/hf_ben-xvi_mes_20110124_45th-world-communications-day.html.

---

83. John Paul II, "Ecclesia de Eucharistia."

Brown, Peter. *Power and Persuasion in Late Antiquity: Towards a Christian Empire.* Madison, WI: University of Wisconsin Press, 1992.

Camplani, A. "Festal Letters." In *Encyclopedia of Ancient Christianity [EAC]*, edited by A. Di Berardino. Westmont, IL: InterVarsity, 2014. Online. https://search-credoreference-com.ipacez.nd.edu.au/content/entry/ivpacaac/festal_letters/0.

Catechism of the Catholic Church (CCC). 2nd ed. Washington, DC: USCCB, 1997. Online. http://www.scborromeo.org/ccc.htm.

Carbajosa, Ignacio. *Faith, the Fount of Exegesis: The Interpretation of Scripture in the Light of the History of Research on the Old Testament.* Translated by Paul Stevenson. San Francisco: Ignatius, 2013.

Cassin, Matthieu. "Grégoire de Nysse, Sur La Divinité Du Fils et De L'esprit et Sur Abraham." *Conference* 29 (2009) 581–611.

Congregation for the Doctrine of the Faith (CDF). "Letter to the Bishops of the Catholic Church on some Aspects of the Church Understood as Communion." May 28, 1992. Online. http://www.vatican.va/roman_curia/congregations/cfaith/documents/rc_con_cfaith_doc_28051992_communionis-notio_en.html.

Cyril of Alexandria. *Commentary on John.* Edited by J. C. Elowsky. Translated by D. R. Maxwell. Vols. 1–2. Downers Grove, IL: IVP Academic, 2013–15.

———. *Festal Letters 1–12.* Edited by J. J. O'Keefe. Translated by P. R. Amidon. FOTC 118. Washington, DC: Catholic University of America Press, 2009.

———. *Festal Letters 13–30.* Edited by J. J. O'Keefe. Translated by P. R. Amidon. FOTC 127. Washington, DC: Catholic University of America Press, 2013.

———. *Letters 51–110.* Translated by John I. McEnerney. FOTC 77. Baltimore, MD: Catholic University of America Press, 2007.

———. *On the Unity of Christ.* Translated by John A. McGuckin. Crestwood, NY: St Vladimir's Seminary, 1995.

Davis, Stephen. *The Early Coptic Papacy: The Egyptian Church and its Leadership in Late Antiquity.* New York: American University in Cairo Press, 2004.

Ignatius of Antioch. "To the Smyrneans." In *The Apostolic Fathers: I Clement, II Clement, Ignatius, Polycarp, Didache*, edited and translated by Bart D. Ehrman, 248–61. Cambridge, MA: Harvard University Press, 2003.

John Paul II. "Ecclesia de Eucharistia." Encyclical Letter. April 17, 2003. Online. http://www.vatican.va/holy_father/special_features/encyclicals/documents/hf_jp-ii_enc_20030417_ecclesia_eucharistia_en.html.

———. "Ut Unum Sint." Encyclical letter. May 25, 1995. Online. http://w2.vatican.va/content/john-paul-ii/en/encyclicals/documents/hf_jp-ii_enc_25051995_ut-unum-sint.html.

Johnson, Luke T. "What's Catholic about Catholic Biblical Scholarship? An Opening Statement." In *The Future of Catholic Biblical Scholarship: A Constructive Conversation.* edited by Luke T. Johnson and William S. Kurz, 14–19. Grand Rapids: Eerdmans, 2002.

Johnson, Luke T., and William S. Kurz. *The Future of Catholic Biblical Scholarship: A Constructive Conversation.* Grand Rapids: Eerdmans, 2002.

Keating, Daniel A. *The Appropriation of Divine Life in Cyril of Alexandria.* Oxford: Oxford University Press, 2004.

Maxwell, D. R. "Introduction." In *Commentary on John,* edited by J. C. Elowsky, xv–xxv. Translated by D. R. Maxwell. Vols. 1–2. Downers Grove, IL: IVP Academic, 2013–15.

McGuckin, John A. "Cyril of Alexandria: Bishop and Pastor." In *The Theology of St Cyril of Alexandria: A Critical Appreciation,* edited by Thomas Weinandy and Daniel A. Keating, 205–236. London: T&T Clark, 2003.

———. "Introduction." In *On the Unity of Christ,* edited by John A. McGuckin, 9–47. Crestwood, NY: St Vladimir's Seminary, 1995.

———. *The Westminster Handbook to Patristic Theology* [WHPT]. Louisville: Westminster John Knox, 2004.

Morgan, Jonathan. "The Role of Asceticism in Cyril of Alexandria's Festal Letters." *The Downside Review* 135 (2017) 144–53.

O'Keefe, J. J. "Introduction." In *Festal Letters 1–12,* edited by J. J. O'Keefe, 1–32. Translated by P. R. Amidon. FOTC 118. Washington, DC: Catholic University of America Press, 2009.

Orlandi, T., et al. "Alexandria." In *Encyclopedia of Ancient Christianity* [EAC], edited by A. Di Berardino. Westmont, IL: InterVarsity, 2014. Online. http://ipacez.nd.edu.au/login?url=https://search.credoreference.com/content/entry/ivpacaac/alexandria/0?institutionId=1939.

Paul VI. "Evangelii Nuntiandi." Apostolic Exhortation. December 8, 1975. Online. http://w2.vatican.va/content/paul-vi/en/apost_exhortations/documents/hf_p-vi_exh_19751208_evangelii-nuntiandi.html.

Pusey, P. E. *Sancti Patris Nostri Cyrilli Archiepiscopi Alexandrini in D. Joannis Evangelium.* Vol. 3. Oxford: Clarendon, 1872. Online. http://stephanus.tlg.uci.edu/Iris/Cite?4090:002:2718353.

Ratzinger, Joseph. "Biblical Interpretation in Conflict." In *God's Word: Scripture, Tradition, Office,* edited by Peter Hünermann and Thomas Söding, 91–126. Translated by Henry Taylor. San Francisco: Ignatius, 2008

Russell, Norman. "The Church in the Commentaries of St Cyril of Alexandria." *International Journal for the Study of the Christian Church* 7.2 (2007) 70–85.

———. *Cyril of Alexandria.* London: Routledge, 2000.

Sheridan, Mark. "Coptic Christianity." In *From the Nile to the Rhone and Beyond Studies in Early Monastic Literature and Scriptural Interpretation,* by Mark Sheridan, 37–45. Roma: Pontificio Ateneo Sant'Anselmo, 2012.

Stowers, Stanley K. *Letter Writing in Greco-Roman Antiquity.* Philadelphia, PA: Westminster, 1989.

van Loon, Hans. "Cyril of Alexandria." In *The Wiley Blackwell Companion to Patristics,* edited by Ken Parry, 170–83. Hoboken, NJ: Wiley and Sons, 2015.

Weddell, Sherry A. *Forming Intentional Disciples: The Path to Knowing and Following Jesus.* Huntington, IN: Our Sunday Visitor, 2012.

Weinandy, Thomas. "Cyril and the Mystery of the Incarnation." In *The Theology of St Cyril of Alexandria: A Critical Appreciation,* edited by Thomas Weinandy and Daniel A. Keating, 205–236. London: T&T Clark, 2003.

Wessel, Susan. *Cyril of Alexandria and the Nestorian Controversy: The Making of a Saint and of a Heretic.* New York: Oxford University Press, 2004.

Wilken, Robert L. "Cyril of Alexandria." In *Handbook of Patristic Exegesis: The Bible in Ancient Christianity,* edited by Charles Kannengiesser, 840–69. 2 vols. Leiden: Brill Academic, 2004.

Winters, Marita. "Communion Ecclesiology and Communication in the Post-Vatican II Church." MA thesis, University of Notre Dame, Australia, 2017. https://researchonline.nd.edu.au/cgi/viewcontent.cgi?article=1177&context=theses.

Young, Frances M. *Biblical Exegesis and the Formation of Christian Culture*. Grand Rapids: Baker Academic, 2016.

12

In the Heart of the Church

The Church, the Catholic University,
and the State in Australia

—Michael Quinlan

> *The church is called to be the leaven and a light to the nations. Whilst the proportion has been falling, since written records have been kept, most Australians have identified as Christians. Today Catholics are the largest religious denomination in Australia. Since the arrival of the First Fleet, the Judeo-Christian influence has been embedded in the laws and customs of Australian society. Whilst Australian society has been moving away from those roots a huge majority of Australians consider that Australia has a responsibility to be a moral leader in the world. This chapter considers the role of the Catholic university in the Church and its relationship to the state in contemporary Australia. The chapter argues that a Catholic university must be different to other universities and takes Catholic law schools as an example. It argues that Catholic universities should be places of moral purpose, in which moral character and the virtues are developed, in which debate and critical thinking are encouraged and in which history and tradition are taught rather than ignored. The chapter concludes that Catholic universities have a critical role to play for the Church in contemporary Australian society. They have a key role in ensuring that universities continue to search for the truth even where that may challenge prevailing moral*

> trends. With their focus on ethics and on morality Catholic universities can be the leaven and by their light help Australia to be a moral leader in the world.

I shall make you a light to the nations so that my salvation
may reach the remotest parts of the earth (Isa 49:6).[1]

The church is called to be the leaven and a light to the nations (cf. Matt 13:33; Gal 5:9–10; Isa 49:6; Acts 13:47).[2] In Australia it is called to do so in what is now "one of the most religiously diverse countries in the world."[3] Whilst most Australians have identified as Christians since records have been kept, the proportion has been steadily falling.[4] In contrast there has been a significant increase in those who identify as having "No Religion."[5] Church attendance in Australia is also in decline.[6] Catholicism is the largest single religious denomination in Australia.[7] Since the arrival of the First Fleet, the Judeo-Christian influence has been embedded in the laws and customs of Australian society.[8] However, at the same time as the proportion of Australians who identify as Christians has been falling, Australian society has been moving away from its Judeo-Christian roots.[9] In this changing environment a huge majority of Australians continue

---

1. Unless expressly stated, references to the Bible in this chapter are from the New Jerusalem Bible. See also Luke 2:30–32; Acts 13:47.

2. See also *CCC* no. 2105. Except where the context indicates otherwise, church, when used in this chapter, refers to the Catholic Church.

3. Possamai et al., "'Muslim Students,'" 312. In particular, there has been a significant increase in those identifying with non-Christian faiths. See Australian Bureau of Statistics, "Reflecting a Nation." From around 7.2 percent of the total population in 2011 (up from 4.9 percent in 2001) to 8.2 percent of the total population in 2016 (Australian Bureau of Statistics, "2016 Census").

4. The proportion of the Australian population identifying with a Christian faith tradition has fallen from 68 percent (2001) to 52 percent (2016). See Australian Bureau of Statistics, "Reflecting a Nation"; "2016 Census."

5. Growing from 15 percent of the population in 2001 to 30.1 percent in 2016. See Australian Bureau of Statistics, "2016 Census."

6. Evans and Kelly, *Australian Economy and Society*, 35–36.

7. Catholics as a percentage of the Australian population declined from 25.3 percent in 2011 to 22.6 percent in 2016. See Australian Bureau of Statistics, "Census of Population and Housing."

8. Pasley, "Position of the Law School," 50–51.

9. Newton, "Speech on Retirement."

to consider that Australia has a responsibility to be a moral leader in the world and to set an example for other countries to follow.[10] In that context this chapter considers the role of the Catholic university in the Church and its relationship with the State in contemporary Australia.[11] Part One discusses the Australian university and includes a brief description of Catholic universities in Australia. Part Two examines the importance of diversity and identity within the Australian university sector. It supports Davis's view that there are benefits to Australian society in a university sector which is diverse.[12] It also identifies the risks where one world view, particularly on moral questions (or what ought to be recognized as moral questions) on which rational persons may disagree on rational grounds, dominates the academy and the State. Part Three considers the role of the Catholic university within the Church and argues that a Catholic university, because it is "Catholic," must be noticeably different to other universities. In order to demonstrate this argument Catholic law schools are considered as an example. In this Part the argument that universities, and most particularly Catholic universities and Catholic law schools within Catholic universities, should be places of moral purpose, is developed. It is argued that Catholic universities should be places where moral character and the virtues are developed, in which debate and critical thinking are encouraged and in which history and tradition are taught rather than ignored. The chapter concludes that Catholic universities have a critical role to play in contemporary Australian society. It argues that they have a key role to play in maintaining the diversity of Australian society and ensuring that universities continue to search for the truth even where that may challenge prevailing moral trends. With their focus on ethics and on morality Catholic universities can be the leaven and by their light can form an important element of the professed desire of the majority of Australians for Australia to be a moral leader in the world.

10. 83 percent. See Bricker, "World Affairs," 47.

11. This chapter does not consider the special position of ecclesiastical universities and faculties. For these, see Francis, "Veritatis Gaudium." Similarly, this chapter does not consider the particular position of Catholic theologians who demonstrate their fidelity to the Church by a formal *mandatum*. See USCCB, "Guidelines."

12. Davis, *Australian Idea of a University*.

Part One: The Australian University

Universities in Australia

Unlike the university sector in the United Kingdom and the United States of America, universities were not originally established in Australia by religious organizations and they did not have religious tests for admission to study. In Australia, until recent times, no universities were affiliated with any religious denomination.[13] This does not mean, however that from their foundation, Australian universities were opposed to or in conflict with religion. The absence of a particular religious affiliation in the foundation of Australian universities was a means of accommodating the various religious traditions of the population rather than evidencing an antipathy to religious belief.[14] This is demonstrated by the fact that, from the beginning, Australian universities allowed for religiously affiliated residential colleges.[15] Whilst not necessarily evident in their foundation, the absence of a religious driver or tether has, over time, had a very significant influence on the outlooks and approaches of Australia's public universities. It has at least contributed to what Davis considers to be a singular lack of diversity in Australian public universities today. Speaking of Australia's first public university, the University of Sydney, in observations which might similarly be made about Australia's other public and non-religious universities, Davis has observed that:

> In time, the absence of religion shaped acceptable language about the purpose of the new institution. This would be a utilitarian institution befitting a pragmatic society. It was devoid of a chapel; its workaday discourse was not mantled in appeals to God; there was no evocation of campus life as resonant with moral purpose. Likewise missing were American campus tropes about university forming moral character and instilling the virtues necessary for democracy. In its origin, the Australian university was determinedly prosaic.[16]

Given the fact that a huge majority of Australians continue to consider that Australia has a responsibility to be a moral leader in the world and to set an example for other countries to follow, this absence of a recognized moral purpose in public university education in Australia is noteworthy.

13. Davis, *Australian Idea of a University*, 45–46; Williams, *Post God Nation?* 202.
14. Davis, *Australian Idea of a University*, 45–46.
15. Davis, *Australian Idea of a University*, 46–47.
16. Davis, *Australian Idea of a University*, 45–46.

If Australia's public universities are indeed "fundamentally similar" in this and in other regards, it raises for consideration how Australia's leaders are to become equipped to perform the role of moral leadership which a great majority of the population expect of them if they are educated in public universities which disavow that purpose.

Catholic Universities in Australia

The first Catholic university was not established in Australia until 1989. In this year the University of Notre Dame Australia (Notre Dame) was created by an Act of the Western Australian Parliament The initial campus in Fremantle was supplemented by a campus in Broome in 1994 and a campus in Sydney in 2006.[17] Notre Dame is a private university although Davis opines that it embraces "the Australian idea of a university."[18] It has schools of Medicine, Law, Business, Philosophy and Theology, Arts and Sciences, Nursing, Education and Health Sciences and about 14,000 students across the country. About 7,000 students study in Fremantle and Sydney respectively. The Australian Catholic University (ACU) opened on January 1, 1991. ACU was created by the amalgamation of four Catholic tertiary institutions in eastern Australia. It has nearly 26,000 students.[19] ACU has campuses in Adelaide, Ballarat, Brisbane, Canberra, Melbourne, North Sydney, and Strathfield.[20] Whilst the numbers overall are large its campuses are comparatively small compared to Australian public universities.[21] ACU has faculties of Education and Arts, Health Sciences, Law and Business, and Theology and Philosophy.[22] There is a definitional debate as to whether ACU, which is a company, ought properly be characterized as a public or a private university.[23] Without seeking to resolve that debate when the term "public university" is used in this chapter it is used to refer to all Australian universities other than ACU and the three clearly private universities Notre Dame, Bond University and Torrens University Australia. As noted above, Davis describes Australia's public universities as "fundamentally similar."[24]

   17. University of Notre Dame Australia, "History of the University."
   18. Davis, *Australian Idea of a University*, 109.
   19. Australian Education Network, "Student Numbers."
   20. University of Notre Dame Australia, "History of the University."
   21. For example, the Melbourne campus of ACU has less than 9,000 students and the Brisbane campus of ACU about 5,000 students. See ACU, "Melbourne"; "Brisbane."
   22. ACU, "Faculties, Institutes, and Centers."
   23. Davis, *Australian Idea of a University*, 117.
   24. Davis, *Australian Idea of a University*, 59, 101–2.

As one of Australia's two Catholic universities is private and the other arguably so Davis may not intend his comments on Australia's public universities to extend to Notre Dame and ACU. If he does he ignores what ought to be the distinguishing characteristics of Catholic universities.

Part Two: The Importance of Diversity and Identity

Diversity and Identity

Australia's public universities are very large intuitions. They range in size from the 70,000 effective full-time students at Monash to the 10,350 students at Charles Darwin.[25] Davis describes Australia's public universities as "large, highly regulated, largely non-residential institutions offering standard degrees, linking research with teaching, stressing familiar pathways to professional standing."[26] In his view, they are "fundamentally similar."[27] Davis shares the view of the West Review in 1998 which reported on the sameness of Australian public universities:

> Apart from differences in emphasis, Australian public universities are all comprehensive institutions of higher education. The current system of centralized resource allocation and controls over tuition fees encourages "a one size fits all" system. While there is some diversity in mission, clientele, mode of delivery and style within the system, far greater differentiation is possible and indeed, desirable.[28]

Diversity is an important characteristic of a multicultural, pluralist and multi-faith society like Australia. It is valued in workplaces and professions alike.[29] It enables a society, workplace and profession not only to respect the motivations and characteristics of individuals and groups within society but also to learn from them. Different ways of thinking contribute more than the richness of diversity to society. They assist societies to learn and to develop and to accommodate difference rather than becoming monochromatic and dictatorial. As Benson has opined:

---

25. Davis, *Australian Idea of a University*, 118.
26. Davis, *Australian Idea of a University*, 16, 30–31.
27. Davis, *Australian Idea of a University*, 59, 101–2.
28. Department of Employment, Education, Training & Youth Affairs quoted in Davis, *Australian Idea of a University*, 124–25.
29. Bond and Haynes, "Workplace Diversity," 167; LSNSW, *FLIP*, 89.

> We need to be wary of claims that a particular position represents "the state interest" More often than not when what is at issue is a contestable viewpoint the state interest is multiple not singular. The state simply put should not have only "one" view on controversial matters. These are questions that the state should keep as open as far as possible.³⁰

This approach, which surely must be the objective of universities even were the State to adopt a "state interest," is to be contrasted with an approach described by Ahdar, which some in the Australian community would prefer and embrace:

> We have finally triumphed when it comes to gay rights, reproductive rights and so on but the conflict is stubbornly kept alive when the state is willing to grant exemption to recalcitrant citizens who refuse to move with the times.³¹

For diversity to exist in educational institutions, whether they be schools or universities, it is necessary for those institutions to have a clear identity. This is not a concept unique to universities. Sackville has written of the benefits of a Jewish school as follows:

> I want my children to understand. I want them to be familiar with their culture, background and history.... And so I enrolled them in a Jewish school. It is inclusive—all religions are welcome—but it incorporates Jewish Studies, Jewish History and Hebrew (the language of prayer) into the weekly lessons.³²

> Ultimately, the role of a religious school is to help minority groups maintain their sense of community, their understanding of their religion and their cultural heritage. After all, culture survives when it is passed down from generation to generation. Whether you are Jewish, Muslim, Indigenous, Roman Catholic, Greek Orthodox, Chinese, Irish or otherwise, your values and customs come not from your genetic load but from the lessons you learned from your parents and your teachers. Religious schools pass on knowledge, ideals and beliefs to the next generation in a formal structure and create a sense of community and belonging within the wider secular society.³³

---

30. Benson, "Politics of Drift," 45.
31. Ahdar, "Exemptions for Religion or Conscience," 209.
32. Sackville, "Calls to Ban Islamic Schools," 32.
33. Sackville, "Calls to Ban Islamic Schools," 32.

This sort of diversity is what some students want not just at school but also at university. Some students do not want to study at a large, comprehensive, metropolitan, public university.[34] As Davis has observed, "Some students want vocationally orientated courses, more flexible delivery, access to faith-based qualifications rather than the liberal education promoted by public institutions. They look to private offerings."[35] Like the West Report, Davis decries the lack of diversity he observes in contemporary public universities in Australia and argues for what he terms "a fifth wave of public institutions."[36] He suggests that this diversity might include differing sizes of institution, of mission, student mix, course offerings, language of instruction, and specialization.[37] For this diversity to be real universities which do have differences in identity need to be clear about what those differences are in order to build a sense of community and belonging. If they fail to do so they cease to really contribute to diversity. For such institutions this leads ultimately to the magnification rather than the reduction of problems as staff and students alike lose touch with the mission or objectives of the institution and the reasons for it being in any sense different. If these differences become vague, unclear, or forgotten they are unlikely to be maintained and calls for their removal are likely to be made. As, for reasons developed below, Catholic universities should be different, as there are two Catholic universities in Australia, at least if those institutions are really "Catholic" universities, there is already more diversity in the contemporary Australian university landscape than Davis allows for.

An essential step towards understanding what ought to be different about a Catholic university is recognizing that there are differing contemporary worldviews in Australia and in particular that there is a current conflict between the Catholic Worldview and, what this chapter terms, the Revisionist Worldview.

The Catholic Worldview

The world view represented by the Catholic intellectual tradition (the Catholic Worldview) is a comprehensive understanding of the person. It is beyond the scope of this chapter to explain the Catholic Worldview in detail and it is dangerous to attempt to summarize it in short compass as it has many interconnected parts. Nevertheless, accepting those caveats, some

---

34. Davis, *Australian Idea of a University*, 106.
35. Davis, *Australian Idea of a University*, 110.
36. Davis, *Australian Idea of a University*, 120.
37. Davis, *Australian Idea of a University*, 120.

observations about the Catholic Worldview are essential to understanding the differences that at least ought to exist between public universities and Catholic universities.

Critically the Catholic Worldview is motivated by love—of God and of neighbor (cf. Mark 12:28–34). The Catholic Worldview has a very particular focus on the value of every person because all are created in the image of God and deserve love and respect for that reason alone (cf. Gen 1:27). The Catholic Worldview speaks of the value of work and the need for its just reward (cf. Lev 19:13). It also calls on everyone to care for the homeless and the sick and the poor (cf. Matt 25:31–46). It draws a clear distinction between persons and actions as it does not consider any person but it does see some actions as "intrinsically evil." These include:

> Whatever is hostile to life itself, such as any kind of homicide, genocide, abortion, euthanasia and voluntary suicide; whatever violates the integrity of the human person, such as mutilation, physical and mental torture and attempts to coerce the spirit; whatever is offensive to human dignity, such as subhuman living conditions, arbitrary imprisonment, deportation, slavery, prostitution and trafficking in women and children; degrading conditions of work which treat laborers as mere instruments of profit, and not as free responsible persons.[38]

The fact that some acts are "intrinsically evil" in the Catholic Worldview does not mean that persons who commit an intrinsically evil act or who are tempted to do so are themselves "intrinsically evil" or that forgiveness is unattainable to all who genuinely ask for it, or that Catholics are generally called upon to judge individuals (cf. Matt 7:1–5). In the Catholic Worldview human beings are called to love one another—hating sin and identifying some acts as evil does not mean ceasing to love one's neighbor.

Importantly for a university context, Christ called on his followers to love God not just with the heart and the soul but "with all your mind" (Matt 22:37). The Catholic Worldview reflects this by respecting reason and the intellect. The Catholic Worldview considers that there is such a thing as objective truth and that ultimately that truth has a name and is a person: Jesus Christ (cf. John 14:6). The Catholic Worldview is not the relativism of Pontius Pilate questioning the whole idea of truth (cf. John 18:38). The Catholic Worldwide believes in the concept of truth and rejects the view that everything is relative. As such Sargent has argued that

---

38. Second Vatican Council, "Gaudium et Spes" no. 27

> a good Catholic must be committed to truth (including the Truth) and to justice. This assumes that truth and justice in fact exist and are knowable, and that one must live one's life (including one's professional life) ethically.[39]

Critical to the Catholic Worldview is an understanding not of conflict but rather of harmony between faith and reason.[40] The Catholic Worldview values conscience and religious freedom. Pope John XXIII's explanation of the natural rights of persons similarly forms part of that tradition. As he explained in *Mater et Magistra*:

> Man has a natural right to be respected. He has a right to his good name. He has a right to freedom in investigating the truth and . . . to freedom of speech and publication, and to freedom to pursue whatever profession he may choose. He has the right, also, to be accurately informed about public events. . . . Also among man's rights is that of being able to worship in accordance with the right dictates of his own conscience, and to profess his religion both in private and in public. . . . As a human being he is entitled to the legal protection of his rights, and such protection must be effective, unbiased and strictly just.[41]

The Catholic Worldview also recognizes the difference (body, mind and spirit) between men and women, the complementarity of one man and one woman and its significance to sex, sexuality and marriage (cf. Gen 2:18–24; Matt 19:1–12). As the Church is called to be the leaven and a light to the nations it does not intend that the Catholic Worldview is a way of thinking and of ordering a person's life which Catholics should keep to themselves and as something that is valuable only to guide the actions and behavior of Catholics. The church seeks to share the love of Christ and the truth with the broader society and seeks to encourage States to "measure their judgements and decisions against this inspired truth about God and men."[42] Part of the mission of the Church is:

> to pass moral judgements even in matters related to politics, whenever the fundamental rights of man or the salvation of souls requires it. The means, the only means, she may use are

---

39. Sargent, "We Hold These Truths."
40. See, for instance, John Paul II, "Fides et Ratio."
41. John XXIII quoted in Silecchia, "Doing Justice," 1169–70.
42. *CCC* no. 2244.

those which are in accord with the Gospel and the welfare of all men according to the diversity of times and circumstances.[43]

Particularly in relation to matters of sexual morality, the Catholic Worldview is not universally shared or supported in the contemporary Western world. As Hempton has observed:

> We live in a world, indeed in a nation [here speaking of the US but his observations are equally valid in relation to Australia] where religious ideas have been taken up by out-of-tune instruments, and many in the West, especially under the age of thirty, now believe the melody itself is detestable.[44]

Most importantly this antipathy to religion is particularly to be found in universities as "many cognitive scientists and behavioral and social psychologists from the Western academy see religion itself as a, or even *the*, primary threat to human flourishing."[45] Australia's public universities and contemporary Australia are no exception to that.[46] A detailed explanation of this phenomenon is beyond the scope of this chapter but its acceleration in recent times has been contributed to and reflected in the changing nature of Australia's population, the failure of the Churches to adequately address historical child sexual assault, the findings of the Royal Commission into Institutional Responses to Child Sexual Assault (the Commission), the reaction of the media to those findings and the growth of the Revisionist Worldview.[47]

The Changing Face of Australia and the Revisionist Worldview

Although the majority of Australians continue to identify as Christians the percentage of the population who do so has fallen rapidly and is now not much more than half of the population.[48] The downward trend away from Christianity is matched by a rapid growth in those who self-identify as being

---

43. CCC no. 2246.
44. Hempton, "Christianity and Human Flourishing," 58.
45. Hempton, "Christianity and Human Flourishing," 53–54.
46. Kelly, "New Secularism," 18.
47. Royal Commission, "Final Report." See Hodge, "Anti-Catholic Prejudice"; Henderson, "Anti-Catholicism."
48. The percentage of Australians who self-identified in the census has fallen from 88.2 percent in 1966 to 52.1 percent in 2016. See Australian Bureau of Statistics, "2016 Census."

of "no religion."⁴⁹ This category includes having secular beliefs, other spiritual beliefs or having no religion. This makes it hard to be sure what these Australians believe. What we do know is that there is a great deal of ignorance and misunderstanding about religion, and Christianity in particular, in Australia. For example, almost 18 percent of Australians know nothing about the Church in Australia and 8 percent know no Christians.⁵⁰ This is consistent with Hempton's observation of "the growing religious illiteracy of the West, especially the well documented case of the United States, [as] itself a dangerous reality."⁵¹ This issue is, if anything, more acute in Australia. As Brugger has observed:

> Australia is a more secularized country than the United States. Faith and religion, Christianity and its doctrines are further from the minds of the ordinary person here. In the US, everyone is conscious of religion and religious questions. Some are bitterly opposed to Christianity, others are devoted to it, and still others try to tiptoe gently around institutional religion to avoid being soiled by it. But there is no really religiously oblivious part of the United States. Here in Australia, there is an astonishing level of religious ignorance and oblivion. Religion is simply not in the daily categories of thinking, and Catholicism, in general, has a negative connotation on the streets here.⁵²

As Brugger notes the issue in Australia is more than ignorance. More than a quarter of Australians have a negative view of Christianity.⁵³ 6 percent have strong reservations about Christianity and 7 percent are passionately opposed to it.⁵⁴ An analysis of the findings of the Commission and the reaction of the media to those findings is beyond the scope of this chapter but they have clearly impacted on the place of religion, particularly Catholicism, which was a focus of the Commission.⁵⁵ It is sufficient to note that for 73 percent of Australians child sexual abuse and the involvement of church leaders in scandals cause the largest negative perception of Christianity.⁵⁶

---

49. "No Religion" has grown from 0.8 percent in 1966 to 30.1 percent in 2016. See Australian Bureau of Statistics, "2016 Census."

50. Renton et al., *Faith and Belief in Australia*, 10.

51. Hempton, "Christianity and Human Flourishing," 54.

52. Professor Christian Brugger as quoted in O'Neill, "Lifting Up the Faith Down Under."

53. 26 percent. See Renton et al., *Faith and Belief in Australia*, 9.

54. Renton et al., *Faith and Belief in Australia*, 31.

55. Henderson, "Journalistic Bias," 22.

56. Renton et al., *Faith and Belief in Australia*, 32–33.

Many Australians associate Christians with very negative stereotypes such as being judgmental, greedy, having outdated beliefs which they impose and with being opinionated, hypocritical, intolerant, insensitive and rude.[57] Generation X speaks of Christianity as "unaccepting of people who don't follow the rules" and of "a lot of bad things [having] been done [in the name of Christianity]."[58] Generation Y speaks of Christianity having rigid and outdated beliefs which demonize "normal human emotions and acts such as sexuality."[59] Rather than associating Christianity with reason and intellect 18 percent of Australians think that religion is a crutch for the weak to lean on.[60]

Whilst the broader Australian community may share a commitment to social justice and opposition to slavery with the Catholic Worldview, some aspects of the Catholic Worldview conflict with a different way of looking at the world which is here referred to as the "Revisionist Worldview." The Revisionist Worldview emphasizes personal autonomy in relation to sex, sexuality, marriage and life in what Somerville describes as "an era of intense individualism."[61] This approach results in very different views on matters such as sex, sexual identity, gender dysphoria, marriage, euthanasia, and abortion to the Catholic Worldview. In the Revisionist Worldview each individual has to work out for themselves, irrespective of their biological sex, whether they identify as a man or a woman or in some other way and whether they are attracted to men, women or both. The Revisionist Worldview does not recognize the complementarity of one man and one woman and argues that State recognition of marriage must be extended to two persons of any sex. It is an ideological approach which seeks to inform children of this view of sex, sexuality, and marriage and encourages children to identify themselves within one of an expanding group of sexual identities before adulthood.[62] In Australia, the Revisionist Worldview in relation to sex and sexuality is most closely associated with the Latrobe University Australian Research Center in Sex, Health and Society (the Center) and the Safe Schools Coalition Australia (SSCA). The SSCA was "a national network of organisations working with school communities to create safer and more inclusive environments for same sex attracted, intersex and gender diverse

---

57. Renton et al., *Faith and Belief in Australia*, 30, 35.
58. Renton et al., *Faith and Belief in Australia*, 30.
59. Renton et al., *Faith and Belief in Australia*, 30.
60. Renton et al., *Faith and Belief in Australia*, 14.
61. Somerville, *Death Talk*, 4.
62. Skowronska, "Fighting the Pronoun Police," 7–8.

students, staff and families."[63] The Center was heavily involved in the Safe Schools program and wrote the much criticized *Writing Themselves in 3* report.[64] The SSCA produced materials intended for use in schools including the *All of Us* teaching manual.[65] Whilst ostensibly intended to combat bullying, the SSCA materials attracted much controversy over their teachings on gender, sexual diversity, their sexual content and over the absence of parental engagement in their implementation in schools across Australia.[66] The recommendations on the SSCA website for students to access websites with pornographic content, sex shops and clubs and adult online communities also attracted criticism.[67] There is an irreconcilable conflict between the Catholic Worldview and the Revisionist Worldview.

Some proponents of some or all of the Revisionist Worldview are demonstrating increasing intolerance towards those who hold to some or all of the Catholic Worldview. This intolerance has been demonstrated by the reporting of the Archbishop of Hobart in 2013 for alleged discrimination.[68] The Archbishop's alleged misconduct was the publication of a booklet to parishioners and parents of children attending Catholic schools in his archdiocese explaining the Catholic understanding of marriage (Traditional Marriage). This understanding was consistent with the then definition of marriage contained in the 1961 "Marriage Act." In Australia under this legislation marriage was then defined as "the union of a man and a woman to the exclusion of all others, voluntarily entered into for life."[69]

Other examples of such intolerance include the abuse of hotel employees leading to the cancellation of a meeting of supporters of Traditional Marriage, attacks on a brewer because two politicians drank their beer whilst discussing marriage and calls for an academic and a businessman to be dismissed because of their support for Traditional Marriage.[70] This phenomenon is what some have described as the intolerance of tolerance.[71]

---

63. SSCA, "Safe Schools Coalition Australia."
64. Urban, "No Hard Evidence," 11.
65. French, "Respecting Difference," 111.
66. French, "Respecting Difference," 111.
67. French, "Respecting Difference," 116.
68. Shanahan, "Anti-Discrimination Test Looms," 3.
69. Shanahan, "Anti-Discrimination Test Looms," 3. See *Marriage Act, 1961* (Cth) (Austl).
70. Olding, "Pubs Boycott Coopers Beer"; Porteous, "Corporate Bullying," 18; Livingstone, "Catholic Archbishop"; Fisher, "Rogue Business,"8–9, 25; Dawes, "Loud Crowd's Gift for Intolerance."
71. Cf. Carson, *Intolerance of Tolerance*, 1–17.

Part Three: The Role of the Catholic University in the Church

The creation of Australia's Catholic universities coincided with John Paul II's Apostolic Constitution on Catholic universities *Ex Corde Ecclesiae* in 1990. This is a very rich document and it should govern the approach that Catholic universities take. By describing Catholic universities as being "in the heart of the Church" John Paul II made quite clear how important these institutions are for the Church. *Ex Corde Ecclesiae* calls on Catholic universities, among other things to engage in sincere dialogue, assisting staff and students "to achieve wholeness as human persons" and to promote unity in the community.[72] Consistent with this call *Ex Corde Ecclesiae* emphasizes the requirements placed on the university and its staff to integrate the Catholic faith and reason into everything that takes place.[73] The Catholic context should be "vitally present and operative" in all learning, teaching and research activities that occur because "Catholic ideals, attitudes and principles penetrate and inform university activities."[74] Catholic academics working in a Catholic university are called to be faithful to the Catholic Worldview in their research and their teaching.[75]

As the truth is an integrated whole, in a Catholic university, the Catholic dimension ought to be considered, not only in the study of theology but in other areas of study taught within the university's various schools and disciplines "for their mutual enhancement."[76] The promotion of this integration of knowledge means promoting dialogue between faith and reason and between Christian thought and modern science.[77] As Pope Francis has explained:

---

72. John Paul II, "Ex Corde Ecclesiae" no. 21.

73. John Paul II, "Ex Corde Ecclesiae" no. 22.

74. *L'Universite Catholique* as quoted in John Paul II, "Ex Corde Ecclesiae" no. 14. See also John Paul II, "Ex Corde Ecclesiae" art. 2.2, 4.

75. John Paul II, "Ex Corde Ecclesiae" art. 4.3.

76. John Paul II, "Ex Corde Ecclesiae" no. 16. Here John Paul II argues that truth is an integrated whole in relation to catechesis. There is good reason for this point equally to apply to the approach to learning and teaching of a Catholic university generally. As Christoph Cardinal Schönborn has said, we can "ensure that each individual truth, or doctrine, is seen in its fullness and richness by showing how it is connected to the whole of the Faith." See his "Introduction" in Willey et al., *Catechism*, xxxiii. The need for the Catholic dimension to be considered in all disciplines is made in relation to Catholic schools in Pell et al., *Catholic Schools at a Crossroads*, 10. It is equally true in relation to Catholic universities. See John Paul II, "Ex Corde Ecclesiae" art. 2.2, 4. The quotation is from John Paul II, "Ex Corde Ecclesiae" no.15.

77. John Paul II, "Ex Corde Ecclesiae" no. 17, 46. See Miscamble, *For Notre Dame*, 222.

> Catholic universities . . . by their very nature are committed to demonstrating the harmony of faith and reason and the relevance of the Christian message for a full and authentically human life. . . . [For this reason] essential in this regard is the uncompromising witness of Catholic universities to the Church's moral teaching, and the defence of her freedom, precisely in and through her institutions, to uphold that teaching as authoritatively proclaimed by the magisterium of her pastors.[78]

Resonating with these comments from *Ex Corde Ecclesiae*, Pope Francis confirms that the Catholic Worldview must be the institutional view of a Catholic university. This does not mean that a Catholic university ought only to expose its students to the Catholic Worldview, or provide, in effect, the opposite bias to what may be experienced by students studying elsewhere. In his final work Oliver Sacks bemoaned the fact that neglecting or forgetting history is common in science.[79] This phenomenon is also evident in many other disciplines today including ethics, philosophy and the law. An essential element of a Catholic university is that it recognizes that in seeking to find and understand the truth there is much to be learned by examining the past. In an Australian context this means recognizing that contemporary Australia did not emerge in a vacuum and that in order to understand contemporary Australia it is necessary to begin with an understanding of the influence of the Judeo-Christian tradition in modern Australia's foundations.[80] As Pasley has observed the Western legal tradition, the tradition around which Australia was founded, is saturated with the Judeo-Christian worldview. As he notes:

> We can and do find our Catholic tradition embedded in the common law. The fundamental conceptions of equality before the law, of the accountability of the ruler to God and the law, of civil rights and liberties, of the individual's responsibility for his own acts, of mens rea [intention as an essential element of a crime], of the sanctity of promises, in fact the whole structure and content of our constitutional, civil and criminal law are all received from the Judeo-Christian tradition and can only be fully understood by one who has studied and mastered that tradition.[81]

---

78. "Pope Praises."
79. Sacks, *River of Consciousness*, 186–87.
80. See Williams, *Post God Nation?*.
81. Pasley, "Position of the Law School," 50–51.

Whilst the historical place of the Catholic tradition is undeniable, Hempton has observed the continuing impact of the Enlightenment on the West and on the Western academy in particular. As he puts it:

> Scientific rationalism, functional utilitarianism, technological innovation, and the decline of the humanities has resulted in a separation of head and heart and a diminution of empathy, emotional intelligence and vigorous educational debates about questions of meaning or the well-lived life.[82]

In his view, "It is not at all clear . . . that the curriculum of the modern university is well placed to deal with issues relating to ethics, meaning and purpose."[83] The curricula of a Catholic university cannot suffer from the uncertainties identified by Hempton. Vigorous educational debates and discussion of truth, justice, ethics, meaning, purpose and what it means to live well must all be a focus and form an integrated part of teaching in a Catholic university. A Catholic university should seek to form graduates "capable of rational and critical judgment and conscious of the transcendent dignity of the human person."[84] In a Catholic university professional training in particular discipline areas must incorporate "ethical values and a sense of service to individuals and to society."[85]

The Catholic university must challenge students and encourage them to seek the truth. If a Catholic university is to be the leaven and a light for the broader community, its graduates must have an understanding not only of the Catholic Worldview but of the challenges made to it and of the arguments against it put within the Revisionist Worldview. The moral implications of actions, decisions and behaviors must be integral to the way each area is taught and this should involve a consideration of "the predominant values and norms of modern society" which should be examined from a Christian perspective as and when they arise in each discipline.[86] The Catholic university must seek to understand and critique the Revisionist Worldview and seek to encourage a greater understanding of the Catholic Worldview among its students and the broader society.[87] In a Catholic university "scholars must engage in research which analyses and critiques contemporary political, economic and social developments from a Catholic

---

82. Hempton, "Christianity and Human Flourishing," 53–54.
83. Hempton, "Christianity and Human Flourishing," 54.
84. John Paul II, "Ex Corde Ecclesiae" no. 49.
85. John Paul II, "Ex Corde Ecclesiae" no. 49.
86. John Paul II, "Ex Corde Ecclesiae" nos. 20, 23, 33.
87. John Paul II, "Ex Corde Ecclesiae" no.33.

perspective. Such scholars must be unafraid to undertake thoughtful social criticism in an effort to forge a more just and moral order."[88] As *Ex Corde Ecclesiae* explains, "If need be, a Catholic University must have the courage to speak uncomfortable truths which do not please public opinion, but which are necessary to safeguard the authentic good of society."[89] A Catholic university must also show special care for its staff and students. As *Ex Corde Ecclesiae* explains:

> A Catholic University is to promote the pastoral care of all members of the university community, and to be especially attentive to the spiritual development of those who are Catholics. Priority is to be given to those means which will facilitate the integration of human and professional education with religious values in the light of Catholic doctrine, in order to unite intellectual learning with the religious dimension of life.[90]

As is evident from this discussion, *Ex Corde Ecclesiae* envisages a Catholic university as quite different to its non-Catholic counterparts. Accordingly, any school within a Catholic university which was a "carbon copy" of its counterpart in a non-Catholic university simply could not be acting consistently with the blue print laid down in *Ex Corde Ecclesiae*. As Father Wilson Miscamble has expressed it:

> Surely genuine Catholic universities should manifest a distinct model of teaching and learning where both intellectual and moral virtues are witnessed and valued, where questions of ethics and character are not ignored. They will dare to be scholarly institutions unafraid to form consciences. Those who graduate from such schools will have an informed view of what is good and will have been encouraged and challenged to live a good life, a life in which faith is not sequestered in some private domain. It is through such graduates that the Catholic university should expect to influence the culture and society around it.[91]

The Catholic nature of a Catholic University ought to be clearly displayed everywhere on its campus, on its website and in its publications to students. A Catholic university need not be proselytizing and to the extent to which proselytizing invokes any element of anti-intellectualism a Catholic

---

88. Miscamble, *For Notre Dame*, 88.
89. John Paul II, "Ex Corde Ecclesiae" no. 32.
90. John Paul II, "Ex Corde Ecclesiae" art. 6.1.
91. Miscamble, *For Notre Dame*, 81.

university ought not engage in that practice.[92] A Catholic university need not be sectarian and both Catholic universities in Australia welcome Catholics and non-Catholics alike. However, in doing so it should be transparently clear that students are coming to a Catholic university.

This discussion demonstrates the significant task and challenge that *Ex Corde Ecclesiae* demands of a Catholic university. It involves a careful consideration within all course and programs as to whether and where a "Catholic dimension" can and should be introduced and explored. It also raises the need for academic staff to be sufficiently skilled and trained to not only identify issues which would warrant this approach but to be willing to and be comfortable about talking about them with confidence and in harmony with the Magisterium of the Catholic Church, but without preaching or proselytizing. The fact that students may join a Catholic university having been educated in or subscribing to the Catholic Worldview or the Revisionist Worldview or some other worldview presents a challenge to Australia's Catholic universities. A further challenge is that some members of the academic or student body may have personal experience of one or more of the actions which the Catholic Worldview considers to be intrinsically evil and that some may consider that even discussing the Catholic Worldview on, for example, sexual morality, abortion, euthanasia or Traditional Marriage is hateful and offensive. It is not just students who may join a Catholic university with this viewpoint. It must be recognized that not everyone in contemporary Australia is willing to consider the possibility that there is more than one reasonable and rational argument on issues such as these. The reaction by some corporations and journalists to Christian (but not Catholic) rugby player Israel Folau's answer to a theological question about homosexuality and the successful campaign to boycott Coopers's Lager in 2017 because it featured in a video of a respectful debate on marriage between two politicians demonstrates this fact.[93] A Catholic university must engage in full and open dialogue on contemporary social issues, sensitively and carefully, even though this may cause some students to react in this way. This does not mean forcing anything on to students but it does mean

---

92. The word "proselytize" here is used in the same pejorative sense in which the term is used in *Ad Totam Ecclesiam*: "The word 'proselytism' is here used to mean a manner of behaving, contrary to the spirit of the Gospel, which makes use of dishonest methods to attract men to a community—for example, by exploiting their ignorance or poverty" (SPCU, *Ad Totam Ecclesiam* no. 28n4; cf. Paul VI, "Dignitatis Humanae"). To put it another way "proselytising" in this sense is "forcing beliefs down students' throats" (see Pell et al., *Catholic Schools at a Crossroads*).

93. Fitzsimons, "Folaus's Thoughtless Comments," 51; Cullen, "Why Folau," 40; Mc-Cauley, "Rugby Boss," 5; Smith, "Izzy Can't Mix," 33; Olding, "Pubs Boycott Coopers Beer."

facilitating rational and coherent examination of issues and exposing students to the Catholic Worldview which students otherwise may never have heard, let alone had explained. In essence this is what a university should always be about, particularly a Catholic university, the search for knowledge and truth. A Catholic University, in particular, should encourage its students and staff to search for the truth.

The Catholic Law School

Having discussed Catholic universities in a general way, it is valuable to consider how particular schools within such a university might be called to be Catholic. This question will now be considered in the context of the Catholic law school. The law school has been selected as an example not only because the author is currently the Dean of an Australian Catholic law school, but because both Australian Catholic universities have law schools and because lawyers, particularly given the relatively small percentage that they comprise of the Australian population, are a very powerful group in Australia. Lawyers in Australia are not only advocates before the Courts, negotiators, arbitrators, mediators, and draftspersons, but they are the judges who interpret the Australian Constitution, the State Constitutions and the legislation which is passed by Acts of the relevant Parliament. Lawyers are heavily over-represented in Australia's parliaments. For example, although lawyers account for approximately one-fifth of 1 percent of the Australian population, in the last Parliament over 26.5 percent of Federal Parliamentarians were lawyers.[94] Many of Australia's Prime Ministers have completed law degrees or been practicing lawyers.[95] This means that lawyers are a disproportionally powerful group in Australia with a great ability to influence the law both in voting for changes to the law in Australia's Parliaments and in interpreting the law in Australia's Courts. Recognition of this fact should have real implications for all Schools of Law but most particularly in a law school within a Catholic university. It means that just learning what the law is at any particular time is not enough because this will not provide law graduates with any equipment by which to judge the appropriateness of the laws to be passed or guidance as to the standards by which legislation is to be interpreted and the common law developed.

---

94. Whitton, "Parliament of Australia(n Lawyers)."

95. Including Sir Edmund Barton, Alfred Deakin, John Watson, William Hughes, Stanley Bruce, Sir William McMahon, Harold Holt, Sir Robert Menzies, Gough Whitlam, John Howard, Bob Hawke, Tony Abbott, Julia Gillard, and Malcom Turnbull.

The Chief Justice of New South Wales, Tom Bathurst QC, has argued that law schools should do more than teach students legal doctrine. In his view law schools ought to also develop the ability to critique laws and contribute to reform.[96] Catholic law schools must do even more. As Tinnelly and Cahill have argued a Catholic law school should press for "fuller discovery, analysis and recognition of the lawyer's duties to God, to his fellowmen and to society under divine and natural law."[97] In Pasley's view, "It seems to me that there is really no good reason for the existence of a Catholic law school, as such, if it is only going to be a carbon copy of the nearest secular law school."[98]

Sargent has suggested that a Catholic law school:

i. should clearly and unapologetically be Catholic.
ii. should "facilitate discussion about religion and the law";
iii. must teach law in an ethical context and assist students "not just to recognize ethical dilemmas, but to resolve them in a principled way";
iv. must provide clinical legal education and pro-bono services to serve the poor; and
v. must enrol "a critical mass of Catholics."[99]

He argues that, "A Catholic law school can serve God by instilling in a variety of people, especially those who do not conceive of themselves as "confessional" Catholics, values that reflect the institution's Catholic and, more broadly, theistic traditions."[100]

Sargent's list well reflects the demands of *Ex Corde Ecclesiae* when translated to a law school. Whilst his views as to the centrality of service to the poor are well made, his view that this must be demonstrated by pro bono clinical legal service may be challenged. Whether this is the most appropriate avenue for any specific Catholic law school to serve the poor will depend on the extent to which such services are provided by others, the extent to which there are opportunities for students to obtain such placements and the resources which would be required for a given school to establish its own such venture. Alternatives to Sargent's proposal may include, for example, encouraging student volunteering, engaging in other social justice

---

96. Bathurst, "Legal Education," 11.
97. Pasley, "Position of the Law School," 50.
98. Pasley, "Position of the Law School," 50.
99. Sargent, "Alternative to the Sectarian Vision"; "We Hold These Truths." See Miscamble, *For Notre Dame*, 102.
100. Sargent, "We Hold These Truths."

initiatives and fund raising for the poor. Sargent argues that a Catholic law school should be animated by "a profound respect for the dignity of the individual" which in his view necessitates:

i. considering the legal issues that arise due to poverty, inequality and discrimination in a principled way; and

ii. educating all students about the error of considering material wealth, personal ambition and perfection of legal skills as the prime motivations for practice without regard to the impact on others, the consequences, justice or truth.[101]

In a contemporary Australian context a Catholic law school ought to be willing to engage with issues of relevance to Catholic faith and particularly those in which the Catholic Worldview is under challenge. These include areas such as religious freedom, freedom of conscience, marriage, religious confession privilege and life issues (in particular abortion and euthanasia). A Catholic law school ought to also discuss natural law and the actual and ideal relationship between law and morality and consider appropriate opportunities for service to the poor and of promoting them to students.

Conclusion

Notwithstanding the historical influence of the Catholic Worldview on Australian society, many within this society, public universities and the State itself are turning away from the Catholic Worldview in favor of the Revisionist Worldview. This in itself ought to be a matter of concern for all Australians who recognize the value of diversity. As Newton has observed:

> At no greater time in our history is Catholic education more important in Australia. Society is turning against the very fabric of our faith—society's moves to control or redefine birth, marriage and death are before us every day in the form of abortion, marriage equality and euthanasia legislation. Catholic education is and will be so important in the future to help establish and maintain the voice and values of our church and our beliefs, to defend and give expression to the cornerstones of our faith and to help balance the shifting sands of society on these fundamental moral issues.[102]

---

101. Sargent, "We Hold These Truths."
102. Newton, "Speech on Retirement," 5.

Catholic universities have a critical role to play in contemporary Australian society. They have a key role in maintaining the diversity of this society and ensuring that universities continue to search for the truth. This is so even where this may cause them to challenge the Revisionist Worldview and prevailing moral trends. If the Catholic Worldview is not kept alive within Catholic universities there is a risk that it will be lost from our society and that there will be no intellectual challenge to moves to continue to change society in favor of the Revisionist Worldview. Intellectual rigor and careful, critical analysis are key requirements for sound decision making both at an individual and State level. With their focus on ethics and on morality and by operating in the heart of the Church, Catholic universities can be the leaven and by their light can form an important element of the professed desire of the majority of Australians for Australia to be a moral leader in the world.[103]

Bibliography

Ahdar, Rex. "Exemptions for Religion or Conscience Under the Canopy of the Rule of Law." *Journal of Law, Religion, and State* 5 (2017) 185–213.

Australian Bureau of Statistics. "2016 Census Data Reveals 'No Religion' Is Rising Fast." *Australian Bureau of Statistics*, June 27, 2017. http://www.abs.gov.au/AUSSTATS/abs@.nsf/mediareleasesbyReleaseDate/7E65A144540551D7CA258148000E2E85?OpenDocument.

———. "Census of Population and Housing: Reflecting Australia—Stories from the Census, 2016." *Australian Bureau of Statistics*, June 28, 2017. http://www.abs.gov.au/ausstats/abs@.nsf/Lookup/by%20Subject/2071.0~2016~Main%20Features~Religion%20Data%20Summary~70.

———. "Reflecting a Nation: Stories from the 2011 Census." *Australian Bureau of Statistics*, April 16, 2013. http://www.abs.gov.au/ausstats/abs@.nsf/lookup/2071.0main+features902012-2013.

Australian Catholic University (ACU). "Brisbane." http://www.acu.edu.au/about_acu/campuses/brisbane.

———. "Faculties, Institutes, and Centers." https://www.acu.edu.au/about_acu/faculties,_institutes_and_centres.

———. "Melbourne." http://www.acu.edu.au/about_acu/campuses/melbourne.

———. "Our History." http://www.acu.edu.au/about_acu/our_university/mission_and_profile/our_history.

Australian Education Network. "Student Numbers at Australian Universities." 2017. http://www.australianuniversities.com.au/directory/student-numbers.

Bathurst, T. F. "Legal Education—Does It Make Good Lawyers?" Speech delivered at the 40th Anniversary of the Foundation of Macquarie Law School, Macquarie University, November 15, 2012. http://www.supremecourt.justice.nsw.gov.au/Documents/Publications/Speeches/Pre-2015%20Speeches/Bathurst/bathurst151112.pdf.

Benson, Iain. "The Politics of Drift." *Policy* 33 (2017) 45–53.

---

103. Bricker, "World Affairs."

Bond, Meg A., and Michelle C Haynes. "Workplace Diversity: A Social-Ecological Framework and Policy Implications." *Social Issues and Policy Review* 8 (2014) 167–201.

Bricker, Darrell. "World Affairs." Presentation delivered at the 2017 Halifax International Security Forum, Haifax, Nova Scotia, November 17, 2017. https://www.ipsos.com/sites/default/files/ct/news/documents/2017-11/Halifax-Security-Forum-Presentation-11-17-2017.pdf.

Carson, D. A. *The Intolerance of Tolerance*. Grand Rapids: Eerdmans, 2012.

Catechism of the Catholic Church (CCC). Homebush: St Pauls, 1994.

Cullen, Paul. "Why Folau—and His Apologists—Are Wrong." *Sydney Morning Herald*, April 8, 2018. 40.

Davis, Glyn. *The Australian Idea of a University*. Melbourne: Melbourne University Press, 2017.

Dawes, William. "The Loud Crowd's Gift for Intolerance: Who Will Protect the Christian Worker?" *Catholic Weekly*, April 6, 2017. Online. https://www.catholicweekly.com.au/loud-crowds-gift-intolerance-will-protect-christian-worker/.

Evans, D. R., and J. Kelly. *Australian Economy and Society 2002: Religion, Morality, and Public Policy in Perspective 1984–2002*. Leichhardt: Federation, 2004.

Fisher, Anthony. "Rogue Business." *Catholic Weekly*, April 16, 2017. 8–9, 25.

Fitzsimons, Peter. "Folaus's Thoughtless Comments are an Anathema to the Greatest of Rugby's Values." *Sydney Morning Herald*, April 8, 2018. 51.

Francis. "Veritatis Gaudium." Apostolic Constitution. January 29, 2018. Online. https://press.vatican.va/content/salastampa/en/bollettino/pubblico/2018/01/29/180129c.html.

French, Matthew J. "Respecting Difference: An Analysis of the Australian Safe Schools Program and Parental Rights in Education." *The Western Australian Jurist* 9 (2018) 102–129.

Hempton, David N. "Christianity and Human Flourishing: The Roles of Law and Politics." *Journal of Law & Religion* 12 (2017) 53–58.

Henderson, Gerard. "Anti-Catholicism in the Coverage of Child Sexual Abuse." *Quadrant*, November 21, 2018. Online. https://quadrant.org.au/magazine/2018/11/anti-catholic-media-coverage-child-sexual-abuse.

———. "Journalistic Bias Means No Religious News Is Good." *Weekend Australian*, April 8, 2018. 22.

———. "Wilson Case Offers a Study in Contrasting Coverage." *Weekend Australian*, December 16, 2018. 20.

Hodge, Joel. "Anti-Catholic Prejudice and Misdirected Blame Won't Further the Cause of Justice." *ABC Religion & Ethics*, March 6, 2018. Online. https://www.abc.net.au/religion/anti-catholic-prejudice-and-misdirected-blame-wont-further-the-c/10094934.

John Paul II. "Ex Corde Ecclesiae." August 15, 1990. Online. http://w2.vatican.va/content/john-paul-ii/en/apost_constitutions/documents/hf_jp-ii_apc_15081990_ex-corde-ecclesiae.html.

———. "Fides et Ratio." September 14, 1998. Online. http://w2.vatican.va/content/john-paul-ii/en/encyclicals/documents/hf_jp-ii_enc_14091998_fides-et-ratio.html.

———. "Veritatis Splendour." August 6, 1993. Online. http://w2.vatican.va/content/john-paul-ii/en/encyclicals/documents/hf_jp-ii-enc_06081993_veritatis-splendor.html.

Kelly, Paul. "A New Secularism Thrashes Tradition." *Weekend Australian*, April 16, 2017. 15, 18.

Law Society of New South Wales (LSNSW). *FLIP: The Future of Law and Innovation in the Profession*. Sydney: Law Society of New South Wales, 2017. https://www.lawsociety.com.au/sites/default/files/2018-03/1272952.pdf.

Livingstone, Tess. "Catholic Archbishop Fisher to CEOs: 'Butt out of Same-Sex Marriage Debate.'" *Australian*, April 1, 2017.

McCauley, Dana. "Rugby Boss Issues a 'Please Explain' after Folau Crosses the Line." *Weekend Australian*, April 8, 2018. 5.

Miscamble, Wilson D. *For Notre Dame*. South Bend, IN: Augustine's, 2013.

Newton, Stephen. "Speech Given on the Occasion of the Retirement from the Board of the University of Notre Dame Australia." Pioneer House, Broadway, November 23, 2017.

Olding, Rachel. "Pubs Boycott Coopers Beer Following Bible Society Marriage Equality Marketing Campaign." *Sydney Morning Herald*, March 14, 2017.

O'Neill, Eddie. "Lifting Up the Faith Down Under." *National Catholic Register*, July 29, 2017. Online. http://www.ncregister.com/daily-news/lifting-up-the-faith-down-under.

Oriel, Jennifer. "Harassment of Christians Is a Blind Spot for Ruddock." *The Australian*, December 17, 2018. 10.

Paul VI. "Dignitatis Humanae." Declaration. December 7, 1965. Online. http://www.vatican.va/archive/hist_councils/ii_vatican_council/documents/vat-ii_decl_19651207_dignitatis-humanae_en.html.

Pasley, Robert S. "The Position of the Law School in the University." *Catholic University Law Review* 52 (1966) 34–52. https://press.vatican.va/content/salastampa/en/bollettino/pubblico/2013/01/29/180129c.html.

Pell, George, et al. *Catholic Schools at a Crossroads: Pastoral Letter of the Bishops of NSW and the ACT*. Sydney: Catholic Education Office, 2007.

"The Pope Praises the Work of Notre Dame University." *Catholic News Singapore*, January 30, 2014. Online. https://catholicnews.sg/the-pope-praises-the-work-of-the-notre-dame-university.

Porteous, Julian. "Corporate Bullying Threatens Our Freedoms." *The Weekend Australian*, April 16, 2017. 18.

Possamai, Adam, et al. "'Muslim Students' Religious and Cultural Experiences in the Micro-Publics of University Campuses in NSW, Australia." *Australian Geographer* 47 (2016) 311–24.

Renton, Sophie, et al. *Faith and Belief in Australia: A National Study on Religion, Spirituality, and Worldview Trends*. New South Wales, Australia: McCrindle Research Pty Ltd., 2017. https://2qean3b1jjd1s878l2ool5ji-wpengine.netdna-ssl.com/wp-content/uploads/2018/04/Faith-and-Belief-in-Australia-Report_McCrindle_2017.pdf.

Royal Commission into Institutional Responses to Child Sexual Assault. "Final Report." December 15, 2017. Online. https://www.childabuseroyalcommission.gov.au/final-report.

Sacks, Oliver. *The River of Consciousness*. New York: Knopf, 2017.

Sackville, Kerri. "As a Parent, the Calls to Ban Islamic Schools Horrify." *Sydney Morning Herald*, April 9, 2017. 32.
Safe Schools Coalition Australia (SSCA). "The Safe Schools Coalition Australia." http://www.safeschoolscoalition.org.au/who-we-are.
Sargent, Mark A. "An Alternative to the Sectarian Vision: The Role of the Dean in an Inclusive Catholic Law School." *University of Toledo Law Review* 33 (2001) 171–89.
———. "We Hold These Truths: The Mission of a Catholic Law School." *Commonweal*, April 23, 2003. Online. https://www.commonwealmagazine.org/we-hold-these-truths.
Schonbörn, Christoph. "Introduction." In *The Catechism of the Catholic Church and the Craft of Catechesis*, edited by Willey Petrov, et al., xxi–xxxiv. San Francisco: Ignatius, 2008.
Secretariat for Promoting Christian Unity (SPCU). *Ad Totam Ecclesiam*. Ecumenical Directory. May 14, 1967.
Shenahan, Dennis. "Anti-Discrimination Test Looms over Church's Marriage Booklet." *Australian*, September 30, 2013. 3.
Silecchia, Lucia Ann. "On Doing Justice and Walking Humbly with God: Catholic Social Thought on Law as a Tool for Building Justice." *Catholic University Law Review* 46 (1997) 1163–87.
Skowronska, Wanda. "Fighting the Pronoun Police." *Annals Australasia*, March 8, 2017. 78.
Smith, Wayne. "Izzy Can't Mix Preaching with Playing." *Australian*, May 11, 2018. 33.
Somerville, Margaret. *Death Talk*. Montreal: McGill-Queen's University Press, 2001.
United States Conference of Catholic Bishops (USCCB). "Guidelines Concerning the Academic Mandatum (Canon 812)." June 15, 2001. Online. http://www.usccb.org/beliefs-and-teachings/how-we-teach/catholic-education/higher-education/guidelines-concerning-the-academic-mandatum.cfm.
University of Notre Dame Australia. "The History of the University." In *Strategic Plan 2013–2016*, 5. Fremantle, Australia: University of Notre Dame Australia, 2013. https://www.notredame.edu.au/__data/assets/pdf_file/0016/2176/StategicPlan20132016.pdf.
Urban, Rebecca. "'No Hard Evidence' for Safe Schools Rollout." *Weekend Australian*, April 9, 2017. 11.
Whitton, Evan. "The Parliament of Australia(n lawyers)." *Independent Australia*, August 23, 2013. Online. http://www.independentaustralia.net/2013/politics/the-parliament-of-australian-lawyers.
Williams, Roy. *Post God Nation?* Sydney: ABC, 2015.

13

Type and Antitype
Aspects of the Mary-Church Relationship in Pre-Conciliar Works

—M. Isabell Naumann, ISSM

> The notion of the inner reality of the Church was given a strong impetus by Pope Pius XII's encyclical *Mystici Corporis Christi*, in which he brought together the Body of Christ and the People of God united to Christ, and *Mediator Dei*. The different streams of this newly-inspired reflection upon the Church's inner reality, its mystery, flowed into the discussions of Vatican II, and placed the Church at the center of attention. The awareness of returning the image of the Church to patristic notions also brought into the ecclesiological foreground the patristic image of Mary and the Church intertwined. The task of Mary is also the task of the Church: "As it is the mother role of Mary to give to the world the God-man, so it is the mother role of the Church, culminating in the celebration of the Eucharist, to give us also Christ as the head, sacrifice and nourishment for the members of his mystical body."[1] Finally, the eschatological significance of the close association of Mary and the Church finds expression in the dogmatic definition of Mary's Assumption. During Vatican II the historical verification of the interrelatedness between Mary and the Church became an objective as a

1. De Lubac, *Méditation sur l'Eglise*, 251.

theme and was given specific magisterial consideration in chapter 8 of Lumen Gentium.

The First Vatican Council, compelled through exterior circumstances, could deal only with the position and task of the pope and could not go into the question of the Church's self-concept; a concept that should have found expression as the *corpus Christi mysticum* and as the true, perfect, spiritual and supernatural community.[2]

At the beginning of the twentieth century, a new understanding of the Church emerged—a move away from the scholastic, institutional concept to a biblical and patristic image, so relevantly expressed in Guardini's well-known words: "The Church is awakening in souls."[3] His writings and those of Congar and De Lubac address this new awakening.[4] Of this necessary corrective shift, De Lubac writes:

> The only real Church, the Church which is the Body of Christ, is not merely that strongly hierarchical and disciplined society whose divine origin has to be maintained, whose organization has to be upheld against all denial and revolt. That is an incomplete notion and but a partial cure for the separatist, individualist tendency of the notion to which it is opposed; a partial cure because it works only from without by way of authority, instead of effective union. If Christ is the sacrament of God, the Church is for us the sacrament of Christ; she represents him, in the full and ancient meaning of the term; she really makes him present.[5]

This notion of the inner reality of the Church received a strong impetus in Pope Pius XII's encyclicals *Mystici Corporis Christi*[6] and *Mediator Dei*.[7] In both encyclicals but particularly in *Mystici Corporis Christi*, the pope brings

---

2. Denzinger, *Enchiridion Symbolorum*, 3050, 3074; Schatz, *Vaticanum I, 1869–1870*, vol 3. For further study of this period, see Fries, "Wandel des Kirchenbildes," 269–72; Frisque, "Die Ekklesiologie," 3:192–243; Bosch, *Transforming Mission*, 262–345; Malmberg, *Ein Leib-Ein Geist*, 16–54.

3. Guardini, "Vom Erwachen der Kirche," 257–67.

4. E.g., De Lubac, *Corpus Mysticum*; *Splendor of the Church*; Congar, *Divided Christendom*.

5. J. A. Möhler cited in De Lubac, *Catholicism*, 76.

6. Pius XII, "Mystici Corporis," 193–248. For a study of the concept 'mystical' at that time, see Malmberg, *Ein Leib-Ein Geist*, 38–54. For a comprehensive reference work of the encyclical, see Pius XII, "De Mustico Iesu Christi Corpore," 73–154.

7. Pius XII, "Mediator Dei," 521–95.

together the two concepts of Body of Christ and the People of God united to Christ.

The different currents of this newly inspired reflection upon the Church's inner reality, its mystery, flowed into the discussions of Vatican II, and placed the Church at the center of attention.[8] The awareness of returning the self-concept of the Church to patristic notions also brought into the ecclesiological foreground the patristic image of *Mary and the Church* intertwined.

The task of Mary is the task of the Church: "As it is the mother role of Mary to give to the world the God-man, so it is the mother role of the Church, culminating in the celebration of the Eucharist, to give us also Christ as the head, sacrifice and nourishment for the members of his mystical body."[9] Finally, the eschatological significance of the close association of Mary and the Church finds expression in the dogmatic definition of Mary's Assumption.[10]

What follows here is a brief critique of the Mary-Church relationship in representative theological works during the decades prior to Vatican II, with special attention given to Semmelroth's concept of Mary as *archetype* of the Church.

Chiefly representative of Scheeben's ecclesial-mariological thinking is Feckes,[11] who follows him in his understanding of the basic Marian principle: the divine-bridal motherhood; Mary is mother because she is bride and helpmate of Christ.[12] By employing the "heart-head" reciprocal relationship, Feckes attempts to present the Church as the Christ-founded institution of salvation in which the ministerial priesthood, by sharing in the headship of Christ plays an important role in the mystical body of Christ.[13] Analogous to Augustine,[14] Feckes speaks of the Holy Spirit as the *soul* of the Church, as its animating and unifying power.[15]

In unison with Scheeben he refers to the relatedness between Mary's motherhood and that of the Church as a *perichoresis*.[16] Above all, Mary's

---

8. McPartlan, *Sacrament of Salvation*, 41–42; Koster, *Ekklesiologie im Werden*; Klinger, *Ekklesiologie der Neuzeit*; Congar, *Die Lehre von der Kirche*.

9. De Lubac, *Die Kirche*, 296. See also Köster, *Die Magd des Herrn*; Semmelroth, *Mary*, 26.

10. Pius XII, "Munificentissimus Deus," 753–73.

11. He is known as the interpreter of Scheeben's Mariology. For a comprehensive overview of Feckes Mariology, see Radkiewicz, *Auf der Suche*, 50–61.

12. Feckes, "Das Fundamentalprinzip der Mariologie," 266, 268.

13. Feckes, *Das Mysterium der heiligen Kirche*, 121–91.

14. See Augustine in *Patrologiae Latinae Completes*, 38:1229–31.

15. Feckes, *Das Mysterium der heiligen Kirche*, 180.

16. Scheeben, *Die Bräutliche Gottesmutter*, 189; Holböck, "Der Heilige Geist,"

place in the Church is characterized as that of the *heart*[17] and of *typos* of the Church.[18] Under the Cross she "becomes the mother of all the redeemed"[19] and the mediatrix of graces.[20] The most perfect and original way in which the idea of the Church is realized is in Mary,[21] for she is "the first of the redeemed, she is the ideal image of all the redeemed,"[22] and as the *pre*-redeemed she is Model and Archetype of the Church as the sum of *all* the *after*-redeemed.[23] The latter statement closely resembles the Marian teaching of Vatican II: Mary's model character for *all* the people of God.

Otto Cohausz too is strongly influenced by Scheeben,[24] and his reasoning is highly inspired by the Mary-Eve parallel by which Mary "restores the image of the woman."[25] Mary is the model and the representative of creation in the salvific event of Christ's Incarnation.[26] She is mother and

---

297–311.

17. Feckes quotes Scheeben: "So findet . . . insbesondere das Verhältnis Marias als der mütterlichen Braut des Logos seine vollkommene Analogie in dem organischen Wechselverhältnisse. . . . Hier wird nämlich das Haupt vom Herzen durch das von ihm ausgehende Blut gespeist und verdankt daher diesem seinen materiellen Bestand, während das Haupt seinerseits vermittelst der von ihm ausgehenden Nerven seinen Lebensgeist dem Herzen mitteilt und dadurch insbsondere auch das ihm von diesem geleistete ministerium moglich macht," Scheeben, *Handbuch*, 3:87n765, in Feckes, *Das Mysterium der heiligen Kirche*, 190–201.

18. Feckes, *Das Mysterium der heiligen Kirche*, 184.

19. Mary is co-sacrificing under the cross: "Ihr Mittun ist nichts anderes als ein Nicht—zurückstehen—Wollen der Braut; kein wesentlicher Beitrag, aber eine Verschönerung des großen Versöhnungsopfers. Sie steht da als die durch ihre bräutliche Gottesmutterschaft geweihte Stellvertreterin der zu erlösenden Menschheit, die im Namen des Geschlechtes mittut . . . [Sie ist] . . . wahrhaft Mutter aller Erlösten, die sie in Schmerzen gebiert," Feckes, *Das Mysterium der heiligen Kirche*, 187.

20. "Dem Mitwirken und Mitverdienen entspricht ein Mitausteilen-Dürfen, die letzte Möglichkeit zur Heranziehung der Zweitursachen. Maria als die wahre Braut des Erlösers verwaltet mit ihm die Gnadenschätze, um sie zur Bildung der Gotteskinder flussig zu machen," Feckes, *Das Mysterium der heiligen Kirche*, 187–88.

21. Scheeben, *Handbuch*, 3:504n1612; Feckes, *Das Mysterium der heiligen Kirche*, 188.

22. Feckes, *Das Mysterium der heiligen Kirche*, 188.

23. Feckes, *Das Mysterium der heiligen Kirche*, 188–89.

24. For example Cohausz, *Maria*, 102–13.

25. "Daß in der Erlösungsordnung dem zweiten Adam eine zweite Eva zugegeben wurde . . . ist vor allem die Ehrenrettung der Frau," Cohausz, *Maria*, 64–67.

26. Cohausz, *Maria*, 68. "Was also von uns zur Erlösung und Begnadigung zu leisten ist, das hat Maria geleistet und uns vorgelebt im Namen der ganzen Schöpfung"; and in reference to Gertrud von Le Fort, he continues: "Das Marianische Dogma bedeutet, auf eine kurze Formel gebracht, die Lehre von der Mitwirkung der Kreatur bei der Erlösung. (Le Fort, April 1, 1934)" Cohausz, *Maria*, 69.

bride of Christ,[27] and consequently our mother because she gave birth to us by giving birth to Christ.[28] Her motherhood toward the members of the Church continues in her task as mediatrix of graces.[29]

Less influenced by Scheeben were Karl Adam and Erich Przywara, who with a strong patristic bent, speak of Mary as "the inner form of the Church."[30] Alois Müller, after investigating patristic sources, concludes that "Mary is the perfect realization of the Church: the essential mystery of the Church is the mystery of Mary."[31]

Among the French theologians from the "Nouvelle Théologie" who took up this topic are in particular Henri de Lubac and Clement Dillenschneider. Lubac refers to the patristic tradition in which "the same biblical symbols are applied, either in turn or simultaneously, with one and the same ever-increasing profusion, to the Church and Our Lady."[32] All the sources of the Church's tradition point to the fact that everywhere the Church finds in Mary "its type and model, its point of origin and perfection: 'The form of *our mother* the Church is according to the form of *his* [Christ's] *mother*.'"[33]

Dillenschneider depicts Mary in her role as the mother of the Messiah; he shows her place next to Christ and deeply within the Church[34] as

---

27. Cohausz, *Maria*, 90–95. Mary "sollte nicht nur als Mutter ihrem Sohne die menschliche Natur schenken, die er dann selbständig, ohne sie, zu seinem Heilswerke benutzte; sie sollte vielmehr mit ihm eine *dauernde Gemeinschaft* bilden und sich dauernd an seinem *ganzen Werk beteiligen* und an seiner ganzen *Stellung teilnehmen*. Diese Lebens—und Wirkgemeinschaft gipfelt in der Mutterschaft, aber sie greift weiter als diese... Sollte Maria Evas Platz in der neuen Ordnung einnehmen, so folgt, daß ihr eigentlichster Beruf darin besteht, dem zweiten Adam, der Christus ist [Rom 5:14, 18], ebenfalls eine zur innigsten Lebens—und Werkgemeinschaft verbundene Gefährtin, Gehilfin und Schicksals-genossin, eine zweite Eva, zu sein. Das ist ihr letzter Sinn, das die grundlegende Stellung, die sie im Plane Gottes einnimmt, das der tiefste und umfassende Zweck, die die Mutterschaft nicht ausschließen, sie vielmehr als ihre höchste Entfaltung enthalten" Cohausz, *Maria*, 45.

28. Cohausz, *Maria*, 83, 128, 129–35.

29. Cohausz, *Maria*, 135–49.

30. Adam, *Das Wesen des Katholizismus*, 32, 153; Przywara, "Mutter aller Lebenden," 112–20.

31. Müller, *Ecclesia*, 239.

32. De Lubac, *Splendor of the Church*, 240.

33. Ps.-Ildephonsus quoted in De Lubac, *Splendor of the Church*, 242, 257.

34. The unity between Christ, Mary and the Church is indicated in Dillenschneider's introduction to *Maria im Heilsplan der Neuschöpfung*: "Keine Neuschöpfung ohne Christus, den neuen Adam, dessen Mutter und Gehilfin Maria ist. Keine Neuschöpfung ohne die Kirche, die neubegründete Menschheit, die in Maria, der Ersterlösten, in mehrfacher Hinsicht ihr Urbild und ihren Inbegriff findet," Dillenschneider, *Maria im Heilsplan der Neuschöpfung*, xv. For a detailed study of Dillenschneider's mariology see Radkiewicz, *Auf der Suche*, 76–91.

the *archetype* [*Urbild*] and inner portrait [*Inbild*][35] of the Church.[36] Mary stands with Christ, the Messiah, at the center of salvation history,[37] and as his helpmate she also cooperates as the representative of humanity and the Church in the Incarnation,[38] as well as on Golgotha in the Redemption.[39] Dillenschneider perceives Mary's mediating role to be a consequence of her *yes* at the Incarnation as well as her *yes* under the Cross. Her *yes* has an ecclesiological perspective since "her general intercession in heaven is nothing else but the highest form of the 'interceding' community of saints."[40]

The German Jesuit, Hugo Rahner, as well, emphazises of the unity between Mary and the Church in his extensive studies of the Church Fathers: "The early Church saw Mary and the Church as a single figure: type and antitype form one print as seal and wax."[41]

---

35. Dillenschneider takes as the beginning of Mary's representation as *Inbild* the scriptural text of Revelation 12. See Dillenschneider, *Maria im Heilsplan der Neuschöpfung*, 193; *Le principe premier*, 135–44.

36. Dillenschneider, *Maria im Heilsplan der Neuschöpfung*, 191–203. "Wenn wir Maria Urbild der Kirche nennen, so verstehen wir damit, daß beide, Maria und Kirche, koordinierte Zeichen des Heilswillens Gottes sind, mit dem Unterschied, daß das Ähnlichkeitsverhältnis Marias zur Kirche das einer überragenden Vollkommenheit einer minderen Vollkommenheit gegenüber ist. Maria ist in dem Sinne Typ der Kirche, daß der Typ den Antityp and Vollkommenheit übertrifft. In Maria ist das Gnadengeheimnis eine höhere Vorbildung des Kirchengeheimnisses," Dillenschneider, *Maria im Heilsplan der Neuschöpfung*, 191.

37. "Mary stands in the Church, she belongs to the People of God," and citing Gerhoh of Reichersberg, Dillenschneider continues: Mary is "Gipfelpunkt der Synagoge und nach ihrem Sohne der neue Anfang der heiligen Kirche," Gerhoh von Reichersberg quoted in Dillenschneider, *Maria im Heilsplan der Neuschöpfung*, 176.

38. "Auf dynamischer Ebene ist es somit durchaus einleuchtend, daß Maria ihre Zustimmung zum Kommen des Messias-Erlösers nicht bloß als Privatperson abzugeben hatte, sondern als befähigte Repräsentantin dieser ganzen Menschheit," Dillenschneider, *Maria im Heilsplan der Neuschöpfung*, 257.

39. "Maria, neue Eva, Gehilfin des Erlösers Christus, war in Kraft ihrer ekklesiologischen Mutterschaft und ihrer besonderen Vorerlösung als Immakulata befähigt, im Namen der ganzen Kirche, der ganzen erlösungsbedürftigen Menschheit, rechtsgültig in das Geheimnis unserer objektiven, durch ihren Sohn auf Kalvaria vollzogenen Erlösung einzugehen," Dillenschneider, *Maria im Heilsplan der Neuschöpfung*, 241.

40. Dillenschneider, *Maria im Heilsplan der Neuschöpfung*, 256, 257. "Maria [ist] nicht nur zur Kirche gehörend, der Kirche hervorragendstes Glied, sie ist die Kirche, Christi Braut, sie gleichsam personifi-zierend. Dementsprechend ist ihre Rolle in der Gemeinschaft der Heiligen allumfassend in ihrer Rangordnung, gleichwie in seiner Rangordnung die Rolle des Hauptes Christus allumfassend ist. Die gesamte streitende und triumphierende Kirche vereinigt sich somit in Maria mit Christus, dem höchsten Fürbitter beim Vater. Maria ist die betende Kirche in Höchstform," Dillenschneider, *Maria im Heilsplan der Neuschöpfung*, 258.

41. Rahner, *Our Lady and the Church*, 7.

Prior to Vatican II, the French Mariological Society made its particular contribution to the Mary-Church theme through its three year series of *Marian Studies*,[42] whereby special mention needs to be made of Canon Philips, one of its eminent members, who repeatedly wrote on this theme and who later became one of the main draftsman of chapter 8 of *Lumen Gentium*.[43]

The Church-Mary relatedness received a further impetus in 1958, when the International Mariological Congress in Lourdes took as its working theme *Maria et Ecclesia*.[44]

Among the German-speaking theologians, it was in particular the Jesuit Otto Semmelroth, who discussed mariology in its relatedness to ecclesiology under the aspect of archetype [*Urbild*]. For this reason we will consider his concept here in more detail.

As mentioned, Semmelroth's mariological thinking is ecclesiologically and salvation-historically centered and focuses on the integration of the mystery of Mary within the whole of salvation. He sees in Ambrose's expression—"Mary is the type of the Church"[45]—the sum of the Church's tradition "from the time when Mary was first compared to Eve. It sums up the entire tradition of the Fathers and theologians concerning the Church's knowledge of its own nature."[46] Hence, Mary's place in God's plan of salvation should be viewed ecclesiologically.[47] Semmelroth sees an essential element in the

---

42. "Marie et l Eglise," *Études Mariales* 9–11 (1951–53), 3 vols. See further the themes of the French Mariological Society of the following years: French Mariological Society, "La Nouvelle Eve"; "La maternié spirituelle de Marie"; "Mariologie et Oecuménisme." Indeed, the work of this Society is a good example of how the Marian chapter of Vatican II was prepared by various theologians. .

43. Philips, "L'orientation de la mariologie contemporaine," 209–53; "Marie et l'Eglise," 363–419. Philips acknowledged that many years of research prepared chapter 8 of *Lumen Gentium*. Particularly influential for Philips was the article by Henri Barré, "Du vénérable Bède," 56–143. See also Neumann, "Mary and the Church," 96–142.

44. Academia Mariana Internationalis, *Maria et Ecclesia*.

45. Ambrose in *Patrologiae Latinae Completes*, 15:1635–36: "Bene desponsata sed virgo quia est *ecclesiae typus* quae est immaculata sed nupta. Concepit nos virgo de spiritu parit nos virgo sine gemitu." For a detailed exposition of Saint Ambrose's concept of Mary as type of the Church, see Huhn, "Das Mariengeheimnis beim Kirchenvater Ambrosius," 101–128; Delahaye, "Maria Typus Ecclesiae," 25–86. See also Söll, "Maria als Urbild," 17–37. For a Protestant perspective of Mary as archetype or type of the Church over or against the Petrine archetype, see Richardson, "Mother of the Church," 48–61.

46. Semmelroth, *Archetype*, 26.

47. Semmelroth, *Archetype*, 26–27; "Die Stellvertretungsrolle," 360–67. For a concise summary of Semmelroth mariological-ecclesiological orientation, see Radkiewicz, *Auf der Suche*, 120–31.

relationship of Mary to the Church in the primitive etymological meaning of *type*,[48] which in the fullest sense is three-fold.

The three areas of significance are: (1) It can signify a personification or representation of a spiritual entity through some sort of image;[49] (2) it attests to "the similarity between Mary and the Church as the consequence of a very real, inner connection. The features that make the archetype similar to the image have somehow grown from the archetype into the image";[50] and (3) it can be a moral example as a result of this relationship.[51]

"When it has been established that Mary's relation to the Church and her members is factual and ontological," then there will be moral consequences, resulting in "a new relationship in the moral and exemplary order." Our lives will have to be ordered "according to the life led by the *Archetype* before us."[52] Subsequently, in search of a basic mariological principle, he claims:

48. Although the original meaning of *tuptein* [a hitting or a blow] was already lost in NT times, various semantic derived meanings in the NT are pointed out by Semmelroth, in reference to Thomas [τον τυπον των ηλων] [John 20:25], also in the discourse of Stephen [του' τυπου'] [Acts 7:43]. The transfer of the original idea in the spiritual sense of content is for example in Paul's use of τυπον διδαχή' [Rom 6:17]. He also mentions the NT use of the word in the sense of archetype, "both in the ontological as well as in the moral order [e.g., Rom 5:14]," Semmelroth, *Archetype*, 28. Semmelroth applies the German *Urbild* [meaning: very old or original picture] for *type* according to its meaning as implied in early Christian tradition. He mentions Neoplatonism exerting an influence on the Fathers as it "can be seen in their free use of the archetype-image relationship when they reflected on supernatural, grace-imbued reality. They did so rightly because the Neoplatonic concept of the image anticipated philosophically what was fully realized in the realm of grace, namely the existence of a very real contact and some sort of causal relationship between archetype and the image. One finds type in this sense frequently referred to by the Early Fathers . . . τυπο', συμβολον, and μυστηριον were almost synonyms in the early tradition," Semmelroth, *Archetype*, 28–31.

49. "The reality of the Church needs a typical representative figure . . . in her visible form we cannot touch her inmost reality," Semmelroth, *Archetype*, 30.

50. Semmelroth, *Archetype*, 30.

51. "The *archetype* is a living person. The *image* is a complete entity, which yet has no individual personality of its own because it is composed of various personalities who do not lose their identity in spite of the great reality of their oneness in the Mystical Body of Christ. Thus, the archetype has to be the moral example in personal attitude and subsequent actions for the members of the image. . . . Mary as type . . . does imply a program for the moral attitude of the Church's members. As the type of the Church, she represents its innermost essence and her personal figuration brings the Church closer to man. The united multiplicity of the Church is contained within her, as in a seed that unfolds in the breadth of time and space," Semmelroth, *Archetype*, 31–32.

52. "It is Mary's attitude that establishes her as an example for the Christians, and her attitude flows from her being rooted in God, a fact she expressed to the Angel at the Annunciation: 'Behold the handmaid of the Lord.' By these words a fact was both established and recognized. From this she drew the conclusion that was to mark

Because Mary was to be the type of the Church, she was given existence as the virginal Mother of God. There is no other Marian mystery which, as the intentional principle, could precede and give root to the position that Mary holds as type of the Church . . . all other Marian mysteries draw their inner meaning and connection from this basic mystery."[53]

At the center of the economy of salvation and its very essence is the *total* Christ, that is, Christ with the members of his mystical body. The Church is so intimately bound to Christ that she becomes his mystical body, united to him as to her head without any lessening of her bridal attitude toward him.[54] It follows that "the basic mystery of mariology will be that which brings Mary closer to the center of the economy of salvation, which is the Church. This coming together takes place through the bridal aspect of the divine motherhood, because here Mary shows herself as the completed bridal fiat for the advent and work of the Saviour."[55]

In this context, Semmelroth addresses also the question of co-redemption[56] and speaks of Mary as "the type of the truly coredeeming Church which gives salvation."[57] The task of the Church as the community of the redeemed in Christ[58] in God's salvific plan casts light on Mary's role within the history of salvation.

---

her entire life: 'be it done unto me according to Thy Word' [Luke 1:38]," Semmelroth, *Archetype*, 32.

53. Semmelroth, *Archetype*, 52.

54. Semmelroth, *Archetype*, 54. In reference to the encyclical *Mystici Corporis* 12, he sees the Church as the community of men united in a mystical-realistic and supernatural way, joined to the Mystical Christ for and through the reception of the fruits of salvation. See Semmelroth, *Archetype*, 81–82.

55. Semmelroth, *Archetype*, 54.

56. Semmelroth, *Archetype*, 72–91, 78.

57. Semmelroth, *Archetype*, 79. "The Church cooperates with Redemption, but not in a productive way, for Christ alone does this. The Church's cooperation is receptive which does not imply passivity alone: a point that should never be forgotten. This is the inner substance of the covenant. Revelation shows this quite clearly when it calls the Church the Bride of Christ. The fact that the characteristics of the Church as the bride of Christ and as Christ's Mystical Body are so closely united shows that humanity must exercise its self-determination and grace-inspired free cooperation in Redemption," Semmelroth, *Archetype*, 83–84

58. "The innermost essence of the Church means participation in Christ's Redemption. . . . To the extent that they [men] are the Church, men participate in Christ's Redemption. In its truest sense, this redemption can only be fulfilled where the inner grace of a life in Christ [a vital participation in the life of the Triune God] is present and simultaneously finds visible expression in visible membership in the organized Church, actually its sacramental sign," Semmelroth, *Archetype*, 153–54.

> Mary co-operated directly, not with *redemptio objectiva*, if by this term we mean the work of Christ alone; and not with *redemptio subjectiva*, if by this term we mean the work of Christ alone; and not with *redemptio subjectiva*, as long as this term is taken to mean only the application of the fruits of redemption to individual men. Rather, Mary co-operated with her own *redemptio objectiva*, which redemption, however, *simultaneously signifies* the reception of the fruits of salvation for the entire Church and which is therefore objective with regard to the individual. If we want to formulate this into a thesis we can say: Mary is the Type of the Church which imparts salvation, insofar as by assuming the work of Christ she receives the fruits of that work both for herself and for the whole Church.[59]

Thus, Semmelroth concludes that Mary, like the Church whose archetype she is, also mediates all graces[60] and affirms as type and pinnacle of the Church "Christ's work and thereby disposed both herself and the Church within her for the pleroma of salvation."[61] "In the divine motherhood, Mary was given the most perfect opportunity to prefigure the Church in a coredemptive way,"[62] and in her Immaculate Conception "the Church emerges as the one essentially redeemed, the one that could never exist tainted with original sin and therefore, in the womb of humanity."[63]

Mary "personifies the Church as a *symbol* . . . personifies the Church as the *primordial cell* from which the Church extends in time and space . . . and is gathered into a juridically representative oneness."[64]

---

59. Semmelroth, *Archetype*, 89. See also Semmelroth's references to Aquinas, *ST* III.30.ad1; Leo XIII, "Supremi Apostolatus Officio," 113–18; Pius X, "Ad Diem Illum Laetissimum," 449–62 Semmelroth, *Archetype*, 85, 89. In view of the *redemptio objectiva*, see Kelly, "Our Lady and Objective Redemption," 242–53.

60. Mary does so (1) as co-redeemer, she received the fruits of Christ's salvation and assumed them for herself and the Church; (2) through her 'intercession' she permits these fruits to flow into the Church; (3) and mediates by exemplifying that man must cooperate with his own redemption the way Mary cooperated with the redemption of the entire Church. See Semmelroth, *Archetype*, 102–3.

61. Semmelroth, *Archetype*, 103.

62. Semmelroth, *Archetype*, 117. "No other mystery could more accurately prefigure the receptive, coredemptive Church than that of Mary, the Mother of God, who opened a gateway for the Logos to enter humanity and gather men around him in the Church. And the Church, in turn, roots Christ's sacrifice into her heart and thereby becomes the maternal beginning of the Church's life," Semmelroth, *Archetype*, 135.

63. Semmelroth, *Archetype*, 148.

64. Semmelroth, *Archetype*, 99–100. Balthasar points in the same direction, when he speaks of the "parallels between Mary and the Church, which are increasingly elaborated in the Fathers," Balthasar, "Retrieving the Tradition," 127.

Eschatologically significant is also that the redeemed state of the physical cosmos at the end of time shines forth in her body in which she partook in Christ's death. As archetype, Mary's body shows in her Assumption the Church's fully redeemed body; and it lights the way for the body of the Church and shows that the transfiguration dwells like a seed within her corporeality.[65]

Mary, the archetype, represents also the ideal type, the model and moral example

> against whom the Church as a whole and all her members can examine their own attitude toward their redemption and fullness of grace as they work out their own lives. The individual Church-member's awareness of being the Church [a task to be accomplished by his own moral decision] must be seen as ontologically and morally perfected by Mary's ideal image and example. The Church living in her individual members needs Mary for her growth toward what she is and toward her hidden potential. Mary causes the essence of the Church to shine before individual human beings to appeal to their own moral efforts.[66]

Although Semmelroth emphasizes in the above exposition of Mary's relationship with the Church her archetypal function in the Church, that she is the "Archetype of the Church insofar as she is the bride of Christ and mother of the individual faithful,"[57] in actual terms *it refers only to the community of the lay faithful*. Christ as the bridegroom is, so to speak, the archetype of the ministerial priesthood, while Mary is archetype of the Church in so far as she is *laos*, as the community of the lay faithful, receiving and cosacrificing, encounters Christ, who through the office of the ministerial priesthood stands before the lay faithful.[68]

---

65. Mary "must completely represent and signify in every respect the hidden fundamental reason of the Church as the redeemed Bride of Christ. This is why the Church believes that her archetype dwells body and soul in perfection," Semmelroth, *Archetype*, 169.

66. Semmelroth, *Archetype*, 157–58.

67. Semmelroth, *Maria oder Christus?* 129.

68. "Die Erlösung bestand darin, daß Christus als Gesandter des Vaters zu den Menschen kam und von Maria glaubend aufgenommen wurde; daß er dann von den Menschen im Opfer zum Vater heimging und von Maria als dem Menschen, der sich sein Opfer zu eigen macht, begleitet wurde. Diese erlösende Begegnung wird in der Kirche dadurch dargestellt, daß ihre geweihten Amtsträger kraft des unauslöschlichen Weihemerkmals Christus vertreten, und daß die Gemeinde Mariens Empfangen und Mitopfern nachvollzieht, indem sie das Wort des Lehr-und Hirtenamtes hört und das Opfer des Priesteramtes mitfeiert. So ist denn Maria, genau genommen, nicht Urbild der Kirche einfachhin Amt und Gemeinde in ihrem Zusammenleben ist der ganze

Another influential representative of the Mary-Church relationship is the Belgian Dominican Edward Schillebeeckx, who in his early works presents a more (in contrast to his later writings) integral thinking when referring to Mary's position in the Church: Mary lives in communion

> with her Son's redemptive activity, joined to him in motherly love. Even though she is certainly outside the hierarchical Church and is fully a member of the community of the Church, she is nonetheless in the Church, the mother both of the ordinary believer and of the hierarchy. She is the mother in the Church both in the Church's teaching authority and in her governing authority and pastoral office, because she occupies an eminent position in the work of redemption which the hierarchical Church must draw on.[69]

In conclusion, the Second Vatican Council brought about a shift in emphasis in the self-concept of the Church, and correspondingly, in the Church's understanding of Mary's person and role. It was the task of the Council [*Lumen Gentium* as well as the proclamation *Mary, Mother of the Church*] to balance the somewhat prevailing perspective of contemplating Mary's relationship with the Church and her place in the Church in vertical/horizontal categories, in terms of being placed "against"—from one point of view, she is presented as being above the Church at the side of Christ, then, from another perspective she is regarded as the representative of the laity.

However, in the conciliar document *Lumen Gentium*, Mary, in her uniqueness as mother, helpmate, and associate of Christ in the entire work of redemption[70] transcends such categories: as the *pre*-redeemed person and as the immaculate original personification of the Church, she is the most excellent member and model of the Church, and at the same time the Mother of the Church, who is active as the educator of *all* the members.[71]

---

mystische Christus, Haupt und Glieder, Bräutigam und Braut, die eins geworden sind als 'zwei in einem Leibe,' eben dem mystischen Leibe Christi. Maria ist auch nicht eigentlich Urbild des geweihten Amtes: Das ist ja gerade Christus, der Bräutigam. Maria ist vielmehr eigentlichst das Urbild der Kirche, insofern sie als 'Laós,' als Laiengemeinde empfangend und mitopfernd Christus begegnet, der duch das Amt vor sie hintritt," Semmelroth, *Archetype*, 131; "Die Stellvertretungsrolle," 360–67. Köster expresses it similarly: It would not be a correct theological idea "das sakramentale Priestertum als Funktion der Mutterschaft der [in Maria kulminierenden] Brautkirche zu denken. Es scheint allein entsprechend, das sakramentale Priestertum als gnadenbewirkende Vaterschaft zu verstehen, der die Gesamtheit der Gläubigen mit einer Marianischmütterlichen Funktion gegenübersteht," Köster, *Die Frau*, 2:68.

69. Schillebeeckx, *Mary*, 164.

70. Kentenich, *Oktoberwoche*, 278.

71. See, in this context, Beinert, who writes: When in Mary's yes "der Mensch selbst

All the abovementioned pre-conciliar works contributed to the fact that the salvation-historical verification of the interrelatedness between Mary and the Church became an *objective* as a theme at the Council and was given specific magisterial consideration and confirmation in chapter 8 of *Lumen Gentium*.

Bibliography

Academia Mariana Internationalis. *Maria et Ecclesia: Acta Congressus Mariologici-Mariani in Civitate Lourdes Anno 1958 Celebrati*. 16 vols. Rome: Academia Mariana Internationalis, 1959–68.

Adam, Karl. *Das Wesen des Katholizismus*. Düsseldorf: Patmos, 1924.

Barré, Henri. "Du vénérable Bède à saint Albert le Grand." *Études Mariales* 9 (1951) 56–143.

Beinert, Wolfgang. "Maria im Geheimnis Christi und der Kirche." In *Communio Sanctorum. Einheit der Christen-Einheit der Kirche. Festschrift für Bischof Paul-Werner Scheele*, edited by J. Schreiner and K. Wittstadt, 284–309. Würzburg: Echter, 1988.

Bosch, David. *Transforming Mission: Paradigm Shifts in Theology of Mission*. Maryknoll, NY: Orbis, 1993.

Cohausz, Otto. *Maria in ihrer Uridee und Wirklichkeit*. Limburg: Steffen, 1938.

Congar, Yves. *Die Lehre von der Kirche: Vom Abendländischen Schisma bis zur Gegenwart*. Freiburg: Herder, 1971.

———. *Divided Christendom: A Catholic Study of the Problem of Reunion*. London: G. Bles/Centenary, 1939.

De Lubac, Henri. *Catholicism Christ and the Common Destiny of Man*. San Francisco: Ignatius, 1988.

———. *Corpus Mysticum*. Paris: Aubier, 1949.

———. *Die Kirche: Eine Betrachtung*. Einsiedeln: Johannes, 1968.

———. *Méditation sur l'Eglise*. Paris: Cerf, 1953.

———. *The Splendor of the Church*. San Francisco: Ignatius, 1986.

Delahaye, Karl. "Maria Typus Ecclesiae: Um das theologische Verständnis der Gestalt Mariens in den ersten beiden Jahrhunderten der Kirche." In vol. 5 of *Alma Socia Christi: Acta Congressus Mariologici-Mariani Romae Anno Sancto 1950 Celebrati*, edited by Academia Mariana Internationalis, 25–86. Rome: Academia Mariana, 1952.

---

auf vollendete Weise geheiligt ist, wenn Maria die einzigartige Gnade der Unbefleckten Empfängnis, der Sündenlosigkeit und der Aufnahme mit Leib und Seele in die Herrlichkeit des Himmels erfährt, dann ist alles dies Gnade für Maria persönlich *als* Gnade für den ganzen Christus, für seinen ganzen Leib, für die Communio. In der Communio mit Christus und in der durch diese Communio gewirkten Gemeinschaft mit Maria steht unser eigenes Glauben und Leben in einem neuen, veränderten Kontext. Menschsein ist anders, weil es einen Menschen gibt, der so ist wie Maria" (Beinert, "Maria im Geheimnis Christi," 308). See further, Kirwin, who writes: "Mary is more than a model, however; she exercises a direct action upon the Church," Kirwin, "Mary's Salvific Role," 42.

Denzinger, Heinrich. *Enchiridion Symbolorum: A Compendium of Creeds, Definitions, and Declarations of the Catholic Church*. Edited by Peter Huenermann. 43rd ed. San Francisco: Ignatius, 2012.

Dillenschneider, Clement. *Le principe premier d'une théologie mariale organique*. Paris: Alsatis, 1955.

———. *Maria im Heilsplan der Neuschöpfung*. Translated by E. Kretz. Colmar-Freiburg: Alsatia, 1960.

Feckes, Carl. "Das Fundamentalprinzip der Mariologie: Ein Beitrag zu ihrem Aufbau." In *Scientia Sacra, Theologische Festgabe an Kardinal Schulte, Erzbischof von Köln zum 25. Jahrestag der Bischofweihe, 19. März 1935*, by Carl Feckes, 252–76. Köln-Düsseldorf: Bachem/Schwann, 1935.

———. *Das Mysterium der heiligen Kirche: Dogmatische Untersuchungen zum Wesen der Kirche*. Paderborn: Ferdinand Schöningh, 1934.

French Mariological Society. "La Maternié Spirituelle de Marie." *Études Mariales* 15–17 (1959–61).

———. "La Nouvelle Eve." *Études Mariales* 12–15 (1954–57).

———. "Mariologie et Oecuménisme." *Études Mariales* 18–20 (1962–64).

Fries, Heinrich. "Wandel des Kirchenbildes und dogmengeschichtliche Entfaltung." In vol. 4/1 of *Mysterium Salutis: Grundriß heilsgeschichtlicher Dogmatik*, edited by J. Feiner and M. Löhrer, 223–79. Einsiedeln-Zürich-Köln: Benziger, 1965–76.

Frisque, Jean. "Die Ekklesiologie des 20. Jahrhundert." In vol. 3 of *Bilanz der Theologie im 20. Jahrhundert*, by Jean Frisque, 262–345. Freiburg: Herder, 1970.

Guardini, Romano. "Vom Erwachen der Kirche in den Seelen." *Hochland* 19 (1922) 257–67.

Holböck, Ferdinand. "Der Heilige Geist als Seele des Mystischen Leibes Christi bei Mathias Joseph Scheeben." *Divinitas* 32 (1988) 297–311.

Huhn, Josef. *Das Mariengeheimnis beim Kirchenvater Ambrosius*. Würzburg: Echter, 1954.

Kelly, Brian. "Our Lady and Objective Redemption." *Irish Theological Quarterly* 33 (1966) 242–53.

Kentenich, Joseph. *Oktoberwoche*. Unpublished manuscript, 1950.

Kirwin, George F. "Mary's Salvific Role Compared with That of the Church." *Marian Studies* 25 (1974) 29–43.

Klinger, Elmar. *Ekklesiologie der Neuzeit*. Würzburg: Echter, 1978.

Köster, Heinrich Maria. *Die Frau, die Christi Mutter war*. 2 vols. Aschaffenburg: Paul Pattloch, 1961.

———. *Die Magd des Herrn: Theologische Versuche und Überlegungen*. Limburg: Lahn, 1947.

Koster, Mannes Dominikus. *Ekklesiologie im Werden*. Paderborn: Ferdinand Schöningh, 1941.

Leo XIII. "Supremi Apostolatus Officio." Encyclical Letter. September 1, 1883. *Acta Apostolicae Sedis* 16 (1883) 113–18.

Malmberg, Felix. *Ein Leib-Ein Geist: Vom Mysterium der Kirche*. Freiburg: Herder, 1960.

McPartlan, Paul. *Sacrament of Salvation: An Introduction to Eucharistic Ecclesiology*. Edinburgh: T&T Clark, 1995.

Müller, Alois. *Ecclesia-Maria: Die Einheit Marias und der Kirche*. Freiburg, Schwitzerland: Universitätsverlag, 1953.

Neumann, Charles W. "Mary and the Church: *Lumen Gentium*, Arts. 60 to 65." *Marian Studies* 37 (1986) 96–142.
Patrologiae Latinae Completes. Series Latina. 217 vols. Paris: Migne, 1841–64.
Philips, Gerard. "La Nouvelle Eve dans la théologie contemporaine." *Études Mariales* 14 (1956) 101–8.
———. "L'Orientation de la mariologie contemporaine: Essai bibliographique 1955–1959." *Marianum* 23 (1960) 209–253.
———. "Marie et l'Eglise: Un thème théologique renouvelé." In vol. 7 of *Maria*, edited by H. du Manoir, 363–419. Paris: Beauchesne, 1964.
Pius X. "Ad Diem Illum Laetissimum." Encyclical Letter. February 2, 1904. *Acta Apostolicae Sedis* 36 (1904) 449–62.
Pius XII. "De Mustico Iesu Christi Corpore deque nostra in eo cum Christo coniunctione 'Mystici Corporis Christi' 29 iun. 1943. Textus et documenta in usum exercitationum et praelectionum academicarum." In *Litterae Encyclicae* N.2, edited by Sebastian Tromp, 73–154. Series Theologica 26. Rome: Gregoriana, 1963.
———. "Mediator Dei." Encyclical Letter. November 20, 1947. *Acta Apostolicae Sedis* 39 (1947) 521–95.
———. "Munificentissimus Deus." Apostolic Constitution. November 4, 1950. *Acta Apostolicae Sedis* 42 (1950) 753–73.
———. "Mystici Corporis." Encyclical Letter. June 29, 1943. *Acta Apostolicae Sedis* 35 (1943) 193–248.
Przywara, Erich. "Mutter aller Lebenden." In vol. 2 of *Religionsphilosophische Schriften*, by Erich Przywara, 112–20. Einsiedeln: Johannes, 1962.
Radkiewicz, Jan. *Auf der Suche nach einem Mariologischen Grundprinzip: Eine historisch-systematische Untersuchung über die letzten hundert Jahre*. Konstanz: Hartung-Gorre, 1989.
Rahner, Hugo. *Our Lady and the Church*. London: Darton, Longman, and Todd: 1961.
Richardson, Henry. "Mother of the Church." *The Current* 1.3–4 (1965) 48–61.
Schatz, Klaus. *Vaticanum I: 1869–1870*. 3 vols. Paderborn: Ferdinand Schöningh, 1994.
Scheeben, Matthias Joseph. *Die Bräutliche Gottesmutter*. Edited by C. Feckes. Freiburg: Herder, 1936.
———. *Handbuch der katholischen Dogmatik*. 6 vols. Freiburg: Herder, 1948–61.
———. *Mariology*. Translated by T. L. M. J. Geukers. 2 vols. St Louis: Herder, 1947.
Schillebeeckx, Edward. *Mary, Mother of the Redemption*. Translated by N. D. Smith. London; New York: Sheed and Ward, 1964.
Semmelroth, Otto. "Die Stellvertretungsrolle Mariens im Lichte der Ekklesiologie." In *Die Heilsgeschichtliche Stellvertretung der Menschheit durch Maria, Ehrengabe an die Unbefleckt Empfangene v. d. Mariologischen Arbeitsgemeinschaft deutscher Theologen*, edited by C. Feckes, 360–67. Paderborn: Ferdinand Schöningh, 1954.
———. *Maria oder Christus? Christus als Ziel der Marienverehrung, Meditationen*. Frankfurt: Josef Knecht, 1954.
———. *Mary, Archetype of the Church*. New York: Sheed and Ward, 1963.
Söll, Georg. "Maria als Urbild und Mutter der Kirche." In *Die Mutter Christi, Beiträge zur Marienlehre*, by Georg Söll, 17–37. Benediktbeurer Studien. München: Don Bosco, 1993.

www.ingramcontent.com/pod-product-compliance
Lightning Source LLC
Chambersburg PA
CBHW051518230426
43668CB00012B/1651